The Bloomsbury Introduction to Postcolonial Writing

The Bloomsbury Introduction to Postcolonial Writing

New Contexts, New Narratives, New Debates

**Edited by
Jenni Ramone**

Bloomsbury Academic
An imprint of Bloomsbury Publishing Plc

B L O O M S B U R Y
LONDON • OXFORD • NEW YORK • NEW DELHI • SYDNEY

Bloomsbury Academic
An imprint of Bloomsbury Publishing Plc

50 Bedford Square	1385 Broadway
London	New York
WC1B 3DP	NY 10018
UK	USA

www.bloomsbury.com

BLOOMSBURY and the Diana logo are trademarks of Bloomsbury Publishing Plc

First published 2018

© Jenni Ramone, 2018

Jenni Ramone has asserted her right under the Copyright, Designs and Patents Act, 1988, to be identified as Author of this work.

All rights reserved. No part of this publication may be reproduced or transmitted in any form or by any means, electronic or mechanical, including photocopying, recording, or any information storage or retrieval system, without prior permission in writing from the publishers.

No responsibility for loss caused to any individual or organization acting on or refraining from action as a result of the material in this publication can be accepted by Bloomsbury or the editor.

British Library Cataloguing-in-Publication Data
A catalogue record for this book is available from the British Library.

ISBN: HB: 978-1-4742-4008-6
PB: 978-1-4742-4007-9
ePDF: 978-1-4742-4010-9
eBook: 978-1-4742-4009-3

Library of Congress Cataloging-in-Publication Data
Names: Ramone, Jenni editor.
Title: The Bloomsbury introduction to postcolonial writing : new contexts, new narratives, new debates / [edited by] Jenni Ramone,
Nottingham Trent University.
Description: London ; New York : Bloomsbury Academic, 2017. |
Includes bibliographical references.
Identifiers: LCCN 2017003736 | ISBN 9781474240086 (hb) | ISBN 9781474240079 (pb)
Subjects: LCSH: Postcolonialism in literature. |
Decolonization in literature. | Postcolonialism.
Classification: LCC PN56.P555 B55 2017 | DDC 809/.93358–dc23
LC record available at https://lccn.loc.gov/2017003736

Cover design: Eleanor Rose
Cover image © Alice Marwick

Typeset by Integra Software Services Pvt. Ltd.

To find out more about our authors and books visit www.bloomsbury.com.
Here you will find extracts, author interviews, details of forthcoming events and the option to sign up for our newsletters.

For Scotty and Seren

From the moment that power is deemed culpable in any way, each family unit should… make a ritual of throwing their breakfast slop at a pinned-up photograph of the symbol of power before going out to earn a living under an insupportable system.

Wole Soyinka, *The Man Died*

Contents

Notes on Contributors xii
Acknowledgements xv

1 **Introduction: Postcolonial Studies Now**
   Jenni Ramone 1

Part I New Contexts

2 **'Another World Is Possible': Radicalizing World Literature via the Postcolonial**
   Wendy Knepper 11

3 **The Global and the Neoliberal: Indra Sinha's *Animal's People*, from Human Community to Zones of Indistinction** Philip Leonard 33

4 **Postcolonial Economics: Literary Critiques of Inequality** Melissa Kennedy 53

5 **The Postcolonial Book Market: Reading and the Local Literary Marketplace**
   Jenni Ramone 71

6 **Disaster, Governance and (Post)colonial Literatures** Upamanyu Pablo Mukherjee 89

7 **Postcolonial Studies in the Digital Age: An Introduction** Roopika Risam 105

Part II New Narratives

8 **Postcolonial Poetry** Emma Bird 125

9 **Postcolonial Noncitizenship in Australian Theatre and Performance: Twenty-First-Century Paradigms** Emma Cox 141

10 **Graphic History: Postcolonial Texts and Contexts** Binita Mehta and Pia Mukherji 159

11 **Postcolonial Life-Writing** Jocelyn Stitt 177

12 **Decolonization and Postcolonial Cinema in Canada, Brazil, Australia and Nigeria** Kerstin Knopf 191

13 **Postcolonial Gaming: An Interview with Seth Alter, creator of *Neocolonialism: Ruin Everything* (Subaltern Games)** Seth Alter and Jenni Ramone 205

Part III New Debates

14 **Postcolonial Refugees, Displacement, Dispossession and Economies of Abandonment in the Capitalist World System** Stephen Morton 215

15 **Postcolonial Sexualities and the Intelligibility of Dissidence** *Humaira Saeed* 237

16 **Contemporary Migration and Diaspora Studies: Current Debates and the Role of Literature** *Subha Xavier* 255

17 **Postcolonialism and African American Literature** *John Cullen Gruesser* 273

18 **Faith, Secularism and Community in Womanist Literature from the Neocolonial Caribbean** *Dawn Miranda Sherratt-Bado* 291

19 **Secularism in India: Principles and Policies** *Manav Ratti* 307

Glossary of Key Terms and Concepts Dawn Miranda Sherratt-Bado 323
Bibliography Compiled by Conna Ray 330
Index 354

Notes on Contributors

Emma Bird is a postdoctoral researcher at the University of Warwick undertaking research into Bombay's poetry scene. In February 2013, Emma defended her doctoral research entitled 'Re-imagining Bombay: Poetic Representations of Urban Space'. She is currently working on a project on Bombay's publishing communities.

Emma Cox is Senior Lecturer in Drama and Theatre at Royal Holloway, University of London. Emma Cox's research and teaching is concerned with the representation and participation of asylum seekers, refugees and migrants in theatre, film, activism and writing. She edited *Staging Asylum: Contemporary Australian Plays about Refugees* (Currency Press, 2013).

John Cullen Gruesser is Professor of English at Kean University. He is author of *Confluences: Postcolonialism, African American Literary Studies and the Black Atlantic* (2005), *The Empire Abroad and the Empire at Home: African American Literature and the Era of Overseas Expansion* (2012) and *Race, Gender, and Empire in American Detective Fiction* (2013).

Melissa Kennedy lectures in English Literature, Culture and Media Studies at the University of Vienna. She has published widely on Maori, Francophone and indigenous Japanese postcolonial literature and cultural studies, including a monograph on Maori writer Witi Ihimaera (Rodopi, 2011) and a monograph on postcolonial economics, forthcoming with Cambridge University Press.

Wendy Knepper teaches and researches in globalizing literary studies at Brunel University. She is the author of *Patrick Chamoiseau: A Critical Introduction* (2012) and the *York Notes Companion to Postcolonial Literature* (2011). She has published widely in world literature and postcolonial studies with particular focus on Caribbean and black British fiction and contemporary women's writing.

Kerstin Knopf is Professor of Postcolonial Literary and Cultural Studies at the University of Bremen. She is author of *Decolonizing the Lens of Power:*

Indigenous Films in North America (2008), is editor of *North America in the 21st Century: Tribal, Local, and Global* (2011) and *Aboriginal Canada Revisited* (2008), and is writing a monograph on nineteenth-century American and Canadian female gothic literature.

Philip Leonard is Professor at Nottingham Trent University. He is the co-editor of *Writing Technologies*, and author of *Literature after Globalization: Text, Technology and the Nation-State* (Bloomsbury, 2013) and *Nationality between Poststructuralism and Postcolonial Theory: A New Cosmopolitanism* (Palgrave, 2005).

Binita Mehta holds a doctorate from the Graduate School and University Centre of the City University of New York. She is Chairperson of the French Department and Director of International Studies at Manhattanville College, Purchase, New York, and teaches courses in French language, literature, culture and film, and literature and film of the South Asian diaspora.

Stephen Morton, Professor at Southampton University, has published books and co-edited collections of essays on Spivak, Foucault and Rushdie, and recently published *States of Emergency: Terrorism and Colonialism in Literature and Culture 1905–2005*. His research interests include colonial states of emergency, Anglophone literatures from Canada and South Asia, postcolonial theory, critical theory, poetics, politics and visual culture.

Upamanyu Pablo Mukherjee, Professor at the University of Warwick, is the author of *Crime and Empire: Representing India in the Nineteenth-Century* (OUP, 2003), *Postcolonial Environments: Nature, Culture and Contemporary Indian Novel in English* (Palgrave, 2010) and *Natural Disasters and Victorian Imperial Culture: Fevers and Famines* (Palgrave, 2013).

Pia Mukherji holds a doctorate from the Graduate School and University Centre of the City University of New York. Her published work is on British modernism and gender and postcolonial area studies. Recently, she has taught at Tufts University, Medford, and Lesley University, Cambridge.

Jenni Ramone is Senior Lecturer in Postcolonial Studies and co-director of the Centre for Colonial and Postcolonial Studies at Nottingham Trent University. She is the author of *Postcolonial Theories* (Palgrave, 2011) and *Salman Rushdie and Translation* (Bloomsbury, 2013). Her book on Cuban, Nigerian, South Asian and Black British writing, *Postcolonial Literature* and the Local Literary Marketplace: Locating the Reader* is contracted with Palgrave.

Manav Ratti is Associate Professor of English at Salisbury University and author of *The Postsecular Imagination: Postcolonialism, Religion, and Literature* (Routledge, 2013).

Roopika Risam is Assistant Professor of English at Salem State University. Her co-authored monograph *Postcolonial Digital Humanities* is under contract with Northwestern UP. Her digital scholarship includes 'Postcolonial Digital Humanities', dedicated to global explorations of race, class, gender, sexuality and disability within cultures of technology.

Humaira Saeed holds a doctoral research from the University of Manchester. Her interdisciplinary research is concerned with how cultural texts navigate the ongoing effects of imperial occupations, through a discussion of the gendered experience, performance and imposition of nationhood.

Dawn Miranda Sherratt-Bado is Lecturer in English at Maynooth University. Her book *Connective Caribbean Readings: Decolonial Womanism in the Fiction of Jamaica Kincaid and Gisèle Pineau* will be published by Palgrave as part of their 'New Caribbean Studies' research monograph series in 2016.

Jocelyn Fenton Stitt is Program Director for Faculty Research Development at the Institute for Research on Women and Gender, University of Michigan. Stitt has published essays on postcolonial literature in *Ariel*, *Michigan Feminist Studies* and *Small Axe*, and co-edited *Mothers Who Deliver: Feminist Interventions in Public and Interpersonal Discourse* and *Before Windrush: Recovering a Black and Asian Literary Heritage within Britain*.

Subha Xavier is Assistant Professor of French at Emory University. She is the author of *The Migrant Text: Theory and Practice of a Global French Literature* (McGill-Queen's University Press) and teaches in the Institute of African Studies and the Postcolonial and Minority Studies Program.

Acknowledgements

I would like to acknowledge the SPUR (Scholarship Projects for Undergraduate Researchers) scheme at Nottingham Trent University and Helen Puntha who runs the scheme for valuable support. Conna Ray and Connor Murphy were some of the research students working with Jenni Ramone and Humaira Saeed, enabling us to undertake larger scale research projects than would have been possible otherwise. Their research supports our ongoing projects, and they have contributed brief, related sections to our chapters in this book.

1

Introduction: Postcolonial Studies Now

Jenni Ramone

How, precisely, might we categorize postcolonial studies, or postcolonial literature, 'now'? In an essay on postcolonial studies and globalization theory, Timothy Brennan rightly identifies the tendency of postcolonial studies to engage with the immediate present and the future in enthusiastic ways. Brennan suggests that postcolonial studies and globalization theories ignore the earliest writers (from the sixteenth century to the Second World War) who bring together theories of 'globalizing features of world history and human societies' and 'colonial practices and anticolonial challenges'. He asks, in sum, whether globalization is really a new phenomenon at all, suggesting it is the same process that has existed for centuries, and that only now is it being 'accompanied by ... heraldic futuristic utterances'.[1] Brennan notes that the term 'globalization' is at once hopeful – 'it holds out hope for the creation of new communities and unforeseen solidarities' – and fearful, as 'it appears ... to euphemize corporatization and imperial expansion'.[2] Postcolonial perspectives are, he suggests, 'presentist' – 'the "now" is the new, and the new is rapturously and exuberantly embraced'.[3] While this trait to focus on the 'now' can be a result of an exuberance or rapture he identifies, it is just as likely to originate from regular charges of irrelevance or inadequacy levelled against this most self-conscious and self-reflexive of academic fields. Postcolonial Studies has been accused of creating heroes of its dominant spokespersons, the founding thinkers in the field: Edward Said, Gayatri Spivak, Frantz Fanon, Homi Bhabha. Detractors ask what postcolonial studies will do as the period of decolonization following the

Second World War, the decades when most former colonies were declared independent, moves ever further away. This introduction is not ashamed to use the word 'now' in its title, but it does so with Brennan's warnings firmly in mind, and is alert to his analysis of the relationship between postcolonial studies and globalization, a concern that recurs throughout this collection.

This collection of essays identifies ways in which the postcolonial as a period is far from over, while acknowledging that debates and contexts characterizing the postcolonial as a commitment have shifted ground. As Graham Huggan suggests in relation to the spatiality of postcolonial analysis and its critical exploration of the territorial 'imperatives' of colonialism, postcolonial studies remains an adaptable and robust critic of global inequalities, resulting from the rampant colonialism of the nineteenth and early- to mid-twentieth centuries, or from more recent neocolonial systems. Postcolonial studies provides a 'frequently speculative consideration of alternatives to those imperatives ... in the shape of "open" and/or "rhizomatic" cultural cartographies, or more socially and ecologically responsible attitudes towards environment and place'.[4] This ability to redraw its boundaries and to reimagine those that persist can be extended beyond postcolonial studies' interrogation of geographies and spaces, and is evidenced in the variety of forms, locations and debates addressed in the chapters of this book. While this collection includes chapters on many of the texts and ideas shaping the field, there are inevitable omissions due to the constraints of space and time. Two of the important omissions, which this introduction will try to rectify in part, are the postcolonial medical humanities and Dalit literature.

Alice Hall notes that 'literary representations of disability open up discussions about some of the most pressing issues of our age: about austerity, empathy, minority status, social care, and citizenship'.[5] In the context of postcolonial studies, the postcolonial medical humanities is a field that continues to attract attention since Clare Barker's *Postcolonial Fiction and Disability: Exceptional Children, Metaphor and Materiality* (2011) which explores the ways in which disabled children symbolize the postcolonial state as both fragile and damaged, and at the same time resistant and demonstrating the potential for change. Barker's work examines important postcolonial literary texts including Salman Rushdie's *Midnight's Children* (1981), Patricia Grace's *Potiki* (1986), Tsitsi Dangarembga's novels *Nervous Conditions* (1988) and *The Book of Not* (2006), Bapsi Sidhwa's *Cracking India* (1991), and Ben Okri's *The Famished Road* (1991) to demonstrate the significance of the disabled child figure but also to analyse health and disability representation in postcolonial contexts. More recently, Alice Hall's work has examined the representation of disability in postcolonial and contemporary literature including Morrison, Faulkner, Coetzee and Allende. Hall also works on the representation of disability outside literary fiction, and has recently published an article on the representation of disability in visual culture, exploring how a photographic art collection and corresponding book project help to achieve Tobin Siebers' aim of moving disability 'out of the asylum, the sick house, and the hospital to take up residence in the art gallery, the museum, and the public square'.[6] Disability studies is notable for its practical attention to the academy, and to the experience of students with disabilities, and postcolonial disability studies is alert to 'complex intersectional identities'[7] and like many other branches of postcolonial studies, reaches widely for its contexts. This is evidenced by the two special issues of the *Journal of Literary and Cultural Disability Studies* edited by Clare Barker with Stuart Murray and with Siobhan Senier, which explore the representation and the functions of disability in literature and culture from New Zealand, Native America, Haiti, Zimbabwe, the Pacific region, Ghana and the postcolonial diaspora.

The field of Dalit literature is complex and controversial, and although there has been a recent upsurge in work in this important field, Dalit writers, writing and contexts remain relatively unknown outside India, as Judith Misrahi-Barak and Joshil Abraham note in their extensive introduction to the field, *Dalit Literatures in India* (2015). Dalits (formerly known as 'Untouchables' in India, and comprising approximately 20 per cent of the country's population) usually write in Indian languages, making their work less accessible to the Euro-American academy, and disturb some of the more settled assumptions of colonialism by asserting that 'oppression in societies such as India is derived not only from the conjunction of imperialism, capitalism and colonialism'.[8] Dalit literature represents and re-evaluates marginalized cultures, and is one of the most significant recent developments in Indian writing. Dalit literature is often highly innovative in its form, narrative perspectives, and use of language, and a large body of work by Dalit authors has been translated into English and other European languages, often in substantial anthologies including the recent Oxford India anthologies of Tamil, Telugu and Malayalam Dalit writing. North India remains unrepresented in anthologized works. In their edited collection of essays, Misrahi-Barak and Abrahams include chapters which resonate with prominent themes in postcolonial literary studies, but which require very different treatment in the context of Dalit Literatures: faith and secularism is explored through questions of caste and democracy, politics and representation; local religious cultural practices; and faith and Muslim-Dalit interactions. Literary and publishing contexts are dominated by the politics of translation, but also by the urgent need to be alert to intersections between oral history, testimonio and autobiography. Questions of gender, the body and subalternity are framed through readings of the female Dalit body as 'pollution', and comparative analyses of black slaves and Dalit women's experiences. Dalit literature has a history in resistance movements, and its origin as a distinct literary field is often traced to the intervention by the Dalit Panthers in Maharashtra in the 1970s, which was a revolutionary movement led by writer-activists. The Dalit Panthers were both a militant and a literary-intellectual political activist group, and their manifesto, issued in 1973, is available in *The Exercise of Freedom: An Introduction to Dalit Writing*, edited by K. Satyanarayana and Susie Tharu, who have also edited *No Alphabet in Sight*, an anthology of South Indian Dalit writing translated from Tamil and Malayalam, and *From Those Stubs, Steel Nibs are Sprouting*, which collects writing translated from Kannada and Telugu. Like many of the available anthologies, this substantial collection includes literary fiction and non-fiction, poetry and prose, as well as interviews. Nicole Thiara has recently led an AHRC-funded network with Judith Misrahi-Barak on writing, analysing, translating Dalit literatures.[9] As well as work on Dalit literature in translation, which dominates many of the available anthologies, scholars working on Dalit literature in Hindi include Laura Brueck, translator and academic, whose *Writing Resistance* was published in 2014, and Toral Jatin Gajarawala, who published *Untouchable Fictions* in 2013. As a developing field in postcolonial studies, there are many gaps in the coverage of published materials, in part because the development of Dalit literature in different regions of India had significant distinctions.

The essays in this volume combine accessibility for scholars new to postcolonial literary studies by foregrounding relevant contexts in which their textual and theoretical debates are situated, while representing original contributions to the field that are exemplary of the wealth of research being undertaken in postcolonial studies. Essays are both grounded in the origins of the field, and alert to the impact of new contexts, narratives and debates informing its ongoing development. These three categories – new contexts, new narratives and new debates – provide organizing sections for contributors' ideas.

Part I of the book includes six chapters collected under the heading 'New Contexts'. These chapters address the field of Postcolonial Studies in the context of recent debates on 'world' and 'global' literature, neoliberalism and other market forces. The 'spectre' of World Literature haunting postcolonial studies, as a neoliberal force that threatens to erase postcolonial commitment and specificity, was brought into sharp focus by James Graham, Michael Niblett and Sharae Deckard in their 2012 essay, 'Postcolonial studies and world literature'. The authors compare neoliberal celebrations of world literature with pronouncements of the impossibility of a singular world literature which collapses linguistic and other boundaries, and focus on Franco Moretti's proposition that if there is 'one' literature, this a literature that, like the rest of the capitalist world system, is 'one, yet unequal';[10] it is from this point that world literature should be approached. Wendy Knepper's chapter, on the radicalism of 'world' literature, addresses this debate in detail, focusing on Caribbean writers Edwidge Danticat and Dany Laferriere, as well as Amitav Ghosh and Ngugi wa Thiongo. Chapters by Philip Leonard and Melissa Kennedy engage with debates surrounding neoliberalism and the economics of postcolonial studies. While Philip Leonard presents Indra Sinha's *Animal's People* as 'a novel about the brutalizing effects of global production and commerce' through a close reading of effects of industrial poisoning on the body, Melissa Kennedy surveys a range of literary texts to demonstrate how fiction might enable narratives of resistance to assumptions of neoliberal inevitability, examining texts by Amitav Ghosh and Kiana Davenport. Also in Part I, Jenni Ramone surveys recent work on the postcolonial literary marketplace, arguing for a focus on the local – rather than global – literary marketplace in understanding the role played by moments of reading in postcolonial literature, considering reading moments in short stories by Nigerian writers Jide Adebayo-Begun and Chimamanda Ngozi Adichie. Remaining chapters in Part I consider further contexts underpinning contemporary postcolonial studies: Pablo Mukherjee considers how continuities and oppositions emerge in the comparison of two writers in India – Rudyard Kipling and Mahasweta Devi – both of whom, for different purposes, use the figures of the journalist and the administrator, the famine environment, governance and gender relations. Roopika Risam, in a survey of the history and debates surrounding the fields, describes rich connections between postcolonial studies and the digital humanities.

Part II of this book, on New Narratives, provides a space for the genres less studied by postcolonial scholars, where the postcolonial novel remains dominant. Chapters by Emma Bird, Emma Cox, Kerstin Knopf, Binita Mehta and Pia Mukherji, and Jocelyn Fenton Stitt address poetry, theatre, film, the graphic novel, and life-writing respectively. It is hoped that these rich discussions of the forms will encourage emerging postcolonial scholars to engage more fully with texts other than the novel, particularly as the essays presented here engage with fascinating and timely debates, including refugeeism (Cox), indigeneity (Knopf) and postcolonial guilt (Mehta and Mukherji). These chapters address texts from India, Australia, Canada, Algeria, Nigeria and the Caribbean, including coverage of both Francophone and Anglophone postcolonial studies, as is the case with chapters in the other sections of the book by Xavier and Knepper. In almost all cases, the chapters engage with both of these postcolonial traditions, often comparing texts and contexts without demonstrating the requirement to fully separate the two linguistic contexts. This is likely to be due, in part, to the ways in which Francophone postcolonial and anticolonial founding figures (Frantz Fanon, Albert Memmi, Aime Cesaire) have been embraced wholly by Anglophone postcolonial scholars. Though there are clear distinctions between the operation of these two colonial systems, in the context of neoliberalism there are also important ways in which the two traditions need to be compared and addressed in parallel, in the ways demonstrated by many of these chapters.

Some of the traditional debates that circulate around postcolonial studies, such as the traditional Marxist (or materialist) versus post-structuralist split in postcolonial studies, as represented by figures like Neil Lazarus and Benita Parry in the materialist camp, and Homi Bhabha as opposing post-structuralist, seem to have made way for discussions drawing from both positions, and focusing more explicitly on global economics and the embodied impact of materialism, which is often conveyed most effectively through close (perhaps, post-structuralist) analysis of literary texts. Other debates that have been important in shaping postcolonial studies continue to hold attention, and these are presented in Part III of this book, 'New Debates'. Humaira Saeed argues that, while explorations of postcolonial sexuality are not new, the significance of sexuality as a factor in postcolonial studies must be recognized as being 'as integral to discussions of postcolonialism as considerations of the nation state, the globalization of capital, and the rise of secularism'. Secularism, a concept gaining ground in the wake of mass media coverage of state regulation of faith, is addressed in South Asian contexts by Manav Ratti, and in Caribbean contexts by Dawn Sherratt-Bado. Three further chapters in Part III each consider migration, the cornerstone of postcolonial studies from different, and very timely, perspectives. Stephen Morton considers postcolonial refugees in the context of neoliberal economics, drawing attention to the false distinction drawn between legitimate asylum seekers and supposedly illegitimate economic migrants. John Cullen Gruesser considers ways in which African American Studies and postcolonial studies might be brought closer together, while offering scholars of African American literature a route towards those texts from the perspective of theories relevant to postcolonial studies. Subha Xavier surveys foundational theories of migration and diaspora before considering the ways in which two writers, Shan Sa and Dany Laferriere, deploy textual strategies to navigate multilingual and intercultural contexts within contemporary literatures of migration and diaspora.

Emerging from the essays is a narrative of resistance, of radicalism, activism and consciousness, demonstrating that postcolonial studies remains committed to resisting colonialism in all of its forms, and to addressing the impact of ongoing neocolonial relationships, especially where they make contact with discourses of globalization and neoliberalism, the digital, migration and refugeeism, disaster and ecocriticism, and sexuality.

Notes

1. Timothy Brennan, 'From Development to Globalization: Postcolonial Studies and Globalization Theory', in *Global Literary Theory: An Anthology*, ed. Richard J. Lane (London: Routledge, 2013), 876–887, 880.
2. Brennan, 'From Development to Globalization', 880.
3. Ibid.
4. Graham Huggan, *Interdisciplinary Measures: Literature and the Future of Postcolonial Studies* (Liverpool: Liverpool University Press, 2008), 15.
5. Alice Hall, *Literature and Disability* (London: Routledge, 2015), 1.
6. Tobin Siebers, *Disability Aesthetics. Corporealities: Discourses of Disability* (Ann Arbor: University of Michigan Press, 2010), 139.
7. Hall, *Literature and Disability*, 4.
8. Judith Misrahi-Barak and Joshil K. Abraham, eds., *Dalit Literatures in India* (Hoboken: Taylor and Francis, 2015), 2.
9. http://translatingcultures.org.uk/awards/related-awards/writing-analysing-translating-dalit-literature/ (accessed 1 November 2016).
10. Moretti in James Graham, Michael Niblett and Sharae Deckard, 'Postcolonial Studies and World Literature', *Journal of Postcolonial Writing* 48, no. 5 (2012): 465–71, 466.

Part I

New Contexts

2 'Another World Is Possible': Radicalizing World Literature via the Postcolonial
3 The Global and the Neoliberal: Indra Sinha's *Animal's People*, from Human Community to Zones of Indistinction
4 Postcolonial Economics: Literary Critiques of Inequality
5 The Postcolonial Book Market: Reading and the Local Literary Marketplace
6 Disaster, Governance and (Post)colonial Literatures
7 Postcolonial Studies in the Digital Age: An Introduction

2

'Another World Is Possible': Radicalizing World Literature via the Postcolonial

Wendy Knepper

In the twentieth century, postcolonial writing emerged as a radical strand of world literature, widely recognized for its struggles to overcome injustice through representations of history from below, challenges to underdevelopment and capacity to remediate the prevailing world imaginary. This incarnation of world literature could hardly be categorized as a timeless classic or masterpiece whose aesthetic excellence, circulation and influence were distanced from the global realities of inequality and unfreedom. Today the study of world literature has been decentred, extended and politicized in no small part thanks to the role and influence of postcolonial perspectives. Yet, with the emergence of global literary studies and world literature in recent years, the postcolonial perspective has been supplemented, arguably even supplanted, by new theorizations of world literary spaces, systems and scales of analysis. Theorists of world literature have revived and extended Goethe's concept of *Weltliteratur*, effectively repositioning it as 'a problem that asks for a new critical method'.[1] Influential and debated new critical approaches have included Franco Moretti's world-systemic analysis of inequalities,[2] Pascale Casanova's world republic of letters with its violence and rivalries,[3] and David Damrosch's circulatory reading of world literature with its emphasis on discrepant and proliferating significations.[4] Despite their differences, these theorists share a common interest in identifying and assessing the worldly contexts and conditions that give particular shape to creative expression, production, translation/circulation and reception.

In response to world literary theorizations and the globalization of literary studies, postcolonial studies has entered into what has arguably become a productive crisis[5] and regeneration of the field in the postmillennial era. Debates about the postcolonial eclipse,[6] world-systems/literary world systems and polysystems approaches,[7] planetary thinking,[8] cosmopolitanism,[9] and a renewed emphasis on the importance of knowledge production[10] and world literary knowledges,[11] interdisciplinarity,[12] and postcolonial literacies[13] have emerged. Meanwhile, advocates for global justice and alter-globalization have recognized that there are significant overlaps between these two approaches to justice on a planetary scale, particularly evident in the World Social Forum's motto that 'another world is possible' through forms of opposition to 'neoliberalism and to domination of the world by capital and any form of imperialism'.[14] As John C. Hawley observes, advocates of alter-globalization and postcolonial critique share a common commitment to acknowledging the claims of peripheral peoples, knowledges and perspectives on the dominant global imaginary.[15] In both instances, reconstituted forms of planetary thought and action inform resistance to predatory development and enable alternative articulations of development and transformation to emerge.

This chapter considers how postcolonial writing and theory might shed light on the contours of a radical world literature of development and transformation. It builds on Pheng Cheah's account of a world-making fiction that seeks to be 'disseminated, read, and received around the world so as to change that world and the life of a given people within it'.[16] Such a world literature acknowledges that culture may be complicit with unequal economic change or express malaise, even despair, in response to turbulent politics. But it also investigates the capacity of world culture to contribute to the expression of 'development as freedom', a concept that Amartya Sen defines as 'the expansion of the "capabilities" of persons to lead the kinds of lives they value – and have reason to value'.[17] Such a world literature has an important role to play in tracking and assessing development, most particularly through its narrative re-integration of peripheral cultural perspectives, disavowed global knowledge and repressed histories of developmental transformation. Bringing postcolonial theory and writing into dialogue with the cultural and materialist strands of Goethe's *Weltliteratur*, this chapter considers how a radical world literature might critique and remediate the prevailing global culture of development, especially through its ethically oriented capacity to reframe the prevailing frameworks for understanding intended and immanent change in the world.

World literature and the postcolonial

As framed by Goethe, the construct of 'World Literature' or *Weltliteratur* considers vital questions about writing in relation to transnational development and global transformation. Indeed, the radical potential of world literature could be said to begin with Goethe's recognition of the heterogeneity of literary creation as well as his speculations concerning an emergent world culture that exceeds its often violent origins and influences. Goethe positions world literature as part of a process of increasing interconnection, exchange and knowledge in and about the world, processes that we today recognize as part of globalization:

> General world literature can only develop when nations get to know all the relations among all the nations. The inevitable result will be that they find in each other something likeable and something repulsive, something to be imitated and something to be rejected.
>
> This too will contribute to the expanding economic relations, for the recognition of common convictions will further a prompter and deeper confidence.[18]

Goethe stresses the importance of global knowledge production through exchanges, building upon transculturation and cultural exchange to create new spaces and possibilities for dialogue.

This cosmopolitan orientation suggests world literature might emerge as a democratizing form of transaction and exchange among equals. Importantly, it grounds the normative (and perhaps utopian) understanding of world literature in world cultural interactions, recognizing that new ethically oriented forms of creativity might arise in response to a prevailing global culture of embattled exchanges, rivalries and unequal exchanges. In fact, his welcoming of world literature as a future of an increasingly transnational world of exchange can be seen as a recognition of the rise of globalization itself. Goethe is often thought to be forward-looking in his construction of world literature, but he also read laterally and historically, as evidenced by his comments on Chinese and Serbian literatures, for example, as well as readings of Shakespeare and Byron. His reading may be cosmopolitan, but he does not escape hierarchical thinking, when he claims: 'In our pursuit of models, we ought always to return to the Greeks of antiquity in whose works beautiful man is represented.'[19] The West retains a pre-eminent position in his mapping of world literature.

Responding to Goethe's normative conception of world literature in *The Location of Culture*, Homi Bhabha asks, 'What of the more complex cultural situation where "previously unrecognized and spiritual needs" emerge from the imposition of "foreign" ideas, cultural representations, and structures of power?'[20] His interactionist view of world culture acknowledges the impact of developmental action in the reconfiguration of subjects and communities, especially through forced migration and unequal processes of hybridization. Likewise, Mariano Siskind argues that 'it is impossible to embrace the normative side of cosmopolitan discourses such as world literature before accounting for the global hegemonic relations that shape them'.[21] For Bhabha 'there may be a sense in which world literature could be an emergent, prefigurative category that is concerned with a form of cultural dissensus and alterity, where non-consensual terms of affiliation may be established on the grounds of historical trauma'.[22] Consequently, he recognizes the transnational and transcultural sphere of 'migrants, the colonized, or political refugees – these border and frontier conditions' as 'the terrains of world literature'.[23] The resistant, contested and accommodating 'Third Space' of world cultural exchange and world literary inscription registers and remediates the prevailing relations, discourses and epistemologies of knowledge, identity and global co-existence. Ensuing work, such as Jahan Ramazani's *Transnational Poetics*, has focused on the ethical and political potential of uneven, often violent, transformations, while advocating for 'the poetic imagination as transnational, a nation-crossing force that exceeds the limits of the territorial and juridical norm'.[24] David Farrier's *Postcolonial Asylum: Seeking Sanctuary before the Law*, Stephen Morton's *States of Emergency: Colonialism, Literature and Law* and Stef Craps' *Postcolonial Witnessing: Trauma Out of Bounds* offer varied perspectives on (post)colonial resistance to a global culture of injustice that emerges through long histories of displacement, exclusion and exception. The exclusions of world culture and world literature are as much at stake as its inclusions.

Had Goethe been able to perceive the wider impact of the Napoleonic Wars on an emergent world culture, he might have remarked on how the histories of competing world empires impacted the formation of the global and creolized Caribbean experience. In particular, St Lucia was known as the Helen of the West Indies during the eighteenth century because it passed hand so frequently between the French and English; that her final colonial abduction was associated with the signing of the Treaty of Paris in 1814 seems ironically fitting. These shifting hegemonies affected the people's creolizing processes, such that the St Lucian-born author, Derek Walcott, writes in a worldly form of English that bears the imprint of various cultures and languages of development, most notably French. This work reflects his understanding of Antillean culture as a worldly culture: 'Deprived of their original language, the captured and indentured tribes create their own, accreting and secreting fragments of an old, an epic vocabulary, from Asia and Africa, but to an ancestral, an ecstatic rhythm in the blood that cannot be subdued by slavery or indenture.'[25] Walcott's *Omeros* renews the classical world epic tradition by calling upon cultural resources born of uneven social formation, conflict and imperial violence. His poetic quest to find a home in a world beyond dispossession reframes the present-day Caribbean experience – postcolonial, neocolonial and diasporic – within a more expansive planetary framework that extends through colonial history to the present.

Today world literature is no longer defined as a masterpiece, but Walcott has certainly set out to rework radically this tradition by blending canonical world literary traditions, multiple world languages, creolized forms, sacred traditions, diasporic folk cultural knowledge and indigenous history. Walcott's creolized Homeric epic reawakens the Dantean vernacular epic, told in 'terza rima' form, repositioning world literature through an act of Caribbean reincorporation, which shifts world literary frameworks, working to create another kind of world literary republic of letters through its engagements with Dante, Joyce and Shakespeare, among others. As a call-and-response narrative, Walcott's *Omeros* may invoke Homer, but it also elicits a radically other world: '"Omeros",/and O was the conch-shell's invocation, *mer* was both mother and sea in our Antillean patois, *os*, a grey bone, and the white surf as it crashes/and spreads its sibilant collar on a lace shore.'[26] Walcott's inclusive vision shows that the wounds of history have affected the colonizer and colonized subject, witness his account of the Middle Passage or the intertwined stories of the Ghost Dance and Catherine Weldon. Nonetheless, 'this epic of the dispossessed'[27] sharply thematizes the socio-economic and political forces that render some lives more precarious than others, particularly on account of enduring racisms, labour exploitation and strategic economic underdevelopment. Walcott's epic generates critical and creative global developmental literacies, working on behalf of communities and readers to generate new shared spaces of recognition and potential dialogue through the time and space of global culture, thus recognizing and rising to the radical challenge of awakening a more equitably integrated world culture.

Walcott seeks to understand the postcolonial experience as part of a non-totalizing totality through his errant epic, understood in the Glissantian that 'the thinking of errantry conceives of totality but willingly renounces any claims to sum it up or to possess it'.[28] Undertaking meridian crossings,[29] Walcott engages in a world mapping that encompasses tribal, colonial, postcolonial and contemporary global constructions of social transformation and worldly co-existence. As a figure in the poem, Walcott, an exiled world writer, stands as a kind of witness to the (dis)integrative logic of global capitalist development as well as longer scales of violent developmental transformation, but he also recognizes that 'another world is possible' through his anxiously creative re-articulation of the worldly experiences, knowledge and aspirations of individuals and collectives. For instance, the 'No Pain' Café, represents a creolized and ironic commentary on a land without bread ('pain' is the French for 'bread') that also dreams of a world beyond the pains of underdevelopment. Within the epic context of world history, his work insists on the planetary importance of small-scale struggles to survive and thrive, providing a world stage for postcolonial subjects in a globalizing world, such as Helen, Achille, Hector and Philoctete, among others, in *Omeros*. This intimate epic shares Edward Said's conception of world literature, which, according to Jonathan Arac, 'requires a vividly concrete sense of geography and an acknowledgement both of large-scale relationships of political power and also of human-scale circumstances of individual lives'.[30]

Recent fictions of migration and displacement interrogate globalized histories of violence from postcolonial vantage points, notably Khaled Hosseini's *The Kite Runner*, Kamila Shamsie's *Burnt Shadows*, Mohsin Hamid's *The Reluctant Fundamentalist*, Meena Alexander's *Raw Silk*, Edwidge Danticat's *Brother, I'm Dying*, Michelle de Kretser's *Questions of Travel* and Samar Yazbek's *The Crossing: My Journey to the Shattered Heart of Syria*. Many of these decolonizing narratives assess how laggard processes of decolonization and re-awakened forms of resistance to empire have played a role in the events of 9/11, wars in Iraq as well as Afghanistan (often in relation to longer histories of armed conflicts), policies and practices of asylum and detainment and asymmetric experience of mobility. This radical strand of world literature interrogates the failures of transnational governance by representing the claims of dispossessed peoples, disavowed knowledges and peripheralized cultures. To do so, this literature expands and shifts the reader's world mappings, global cognitive frameworks and developmental literacies in more ethically oriented, politicized directions, whether by bringing the tourist into contact with the refugee, documenting the lives of the displaced, tracking the intersectional influences of conflict or testifying to the precarious conditions of the migrant subject. Such a literature extends beyond Goethean cosmopolitanism to investigate and interrogate the role, status and labour of culture in a world fraught by inequality and violence.

This ethos lies at the heart of Edwidge Danticat's *Create Dangerously: The Immigrant Artist at Work*, which addresses the terror of colonialism, postcolonial dictatorship and environmental disaster on a people whose revolutionary actions have never been fulfilled due to imperialistic and world-systemic peripheralization. She argues that any writer has a 'creation myth' that propels his or her literary world-making activities.[31] Danticat reconfigures her resistance to acts of terror within Haiti by revisiting the Edenic myth of creation and exile as a creatively precarious condition of vitality: 'We, the storytellers of the world, ought to be more than grateful than most that banishment, rather than execution was chosen for Adam and Eve, for had they been executed, there would have never been another story told, no stories to pass on.'[32] *Create Dangerously* rethinks world literature as 'a revolt against silence, creating when both the creation and the reception, the writing and the reading, are dangerous undertakings, disobedience to a directive'.[33] Like Eve biting the apple, her pursuit of knowledge cannot be contained and her reflections on exile take her to an accounting with another sacred world literary tradition that predates the Christian and undergirds Haiti's own planetary consciousness, namely that of the dialogue with the dead: 'One of the many ways a sculptor of ancient Egypt was described was as "one who keeps things alive".'[34] If Goethe's world literature looks forward to cross-cultural and post-conflict cultures, Danticat's world literature shows that this worldly writing and storytelling is historically grounded in the past, requiring a deliberate effort to reawaken the vocation, knowledge and politics of creative expression to the world from which it has exiled itself.

Danticat's account of the resonance of Camus' play *Caligula* within Haiti highlights how a world literary text may gain new meaning as it is repoliticized within different yet comparable world contexts from which it originated. A kind of universal affiliation and solidarity comes into being through this idea of world republic of letters, one relinked to revolutionary values of liberty, equality and solidarity rather than determined by Paris as its 'Greenwich' standard. Danticat observes: 'Create dangerously, for people who read dangerously. [...] Writing knowing in part that no matter how trivial your words may seem, someday, somewhere, someone may risk his or her life to read them.'[35] Thus, her canon of world literary works allows for the joining of 'Albert Camus and Sophocles to Toni Morrison, Alice Walker, Osip Mandelstam, and Ralph Waldo Emerson to Ralph Waldo Ellison.'[36] Through their interventions, world writers 'have given us a passport, making us honorary citizens of their culture'.[37] At the same time, writers themselves at home in the world in new ways as they are read and received, such that Dany Laferrière is able to claim that he is a Japanese writer, find a correspondence with Oscar Wilde writing in exile in Paris, or see Basho as his double, a traveller who encounters the perilous beauty of his birthplace. He observes, 'I repatriated without giving it a second thought, all the writers I read as a young man, Flaubert, Goethe, Whitman, Shakespeare, Lope de Vega, Cervantes, Kipling, Senghor, Césaire, Roumain, Amado, Diderot, they all lived in the same village that I did. Otherwise, what were they doing in my room?'[38] Laferrière domesticates world literature and sees it as a localizing act of imagined community-building. These postcolonial accounts of world literature indicate that a poetics of relation, to borrow a concept from Edouard Glissant, also re-politicizes worldly relations through newly configured and imagined solidarities that bring the world home anew to its readers.

Postcoloniality and the world-system

Another perspective concerning postcolonial literature as world literature seeks to understand the impact of global capitalism on worldly cultures of development, a Marxist extension of Goethe's idea of world literature as a form of cultural commerce, but with an emphasis on the book as a commodity. As Mads Rosendahl Thomsen observes, 'Where Goethe's idea of world literature can be seen as leaning clearly to the idealistic side, Karl Marx and Friedrich Engels' more than rudimentary mention of world literature in *The Communist Manifesto* from 1848' takes a realistic or cynical standpoint, wherein world literature is seen as a consequent of the globalizing economy.'[39]

While the world itself has been drawn together through global capitalism, this appears to heighten inequalities rather than produce a world of even exchanges. Indeed, in an era characterized by world economic uncertainty and neoliberal globalization, the recognition of 'a prompter and deeper confidence' as described by Goethe is hardly likely. In a world of uneven development, how do we understand the status and role of world literature in terms of its capacity to register and resist the inequalities that have already structured and continue to influence its inscription, position and influence in the world? If world literature is a 'product' of combined and uneven development, how might it, if at all, inscribe and express development as freedom?

Marxist-oriented practices of postcolonial criticism, notably in the research carried out by Benita Parry and Neil Lazarus, have gone some way to problematizing the world-systemic inequalities of global capitalism as it structures world cultural relations, writing and literary production. Lazarus puts the matter as follows: 'The problem, put simply, is that scholars in the field have tended to pay insufficient attention to the fact that colonialism is part and parcel of a larger, enfolding historical dynamic, which is that of capitalism and its global trajectory.'[40] Along with the other members of the Warwick Research Collective, Parry and Lazarus have called for the use of world-systems analytic perspectives and called attention to the combined and uneven development associated with the global capitalist world-system: 'A single but radically uneven world-system; a singular modernity, combined and uneven; and a literature that variously registers this combined unevenness in both its form and content to reveal itself as, properly speaking, world literature – these propositions sum up the kernel of our argument.'[41] The notion of a world literature of combined and uneven development extends the work of Immanuel Wallerstein, Franco Moretti and earlier Marxists, such as Leon Trotsky, potentially realigning postcolonial studies with development studies.

Rethinking postcolonial writing as world literature, James Graham, Michael Niblett and Sharae Deckard argue that in such works 'the world-system is not a distant horizon only unconsciously registered in immanent form, but rather consciously or critically mapped – that is, to literature that is in some way world-systemic in its perspective.'[42] Such a form of criticism may draw on Wallerstein, but it is also open to literary sociological perspectives, such as those found in Pascale Casanova's *The World Republic of Letters* or Sarah Brouillette's *Postcolonial Writers and the Global Literary Marketplace*.[43] World-literary criticism does not insist on a particular theoretical framework, but it does focus on materialist and new comparative approaches to the unevenness of global literary production. In the 50th anniversary special issue of *Journal of Commonwealth Literature*, Elleke Boehmer and Alex Tickell observe:

> From the vantage point of 2015 it is interesting to speculate as to whether the postcolonial will eventually be seen less as a fixed and cumulative field of study, as it appeared towards the end of the 1990s, than as a transitional stage from the Commonwealth to world literary criticism, or from a focus on what Amitav Ghosh calls the Anglosphere, to Immanuel Wallerstein's far more broadly conceived 'world-systems'.[44]

Certainly, world-systems theory seems to afford a more encompassing view of change and transformation that a narrowly construed focus on colonialism, both through its latitudinal analysis of centre, semi-periphery and periphery interactions as well as his longitudinal analysis of the long historical interactions among mini-systems, world-empires and the global capitalist world-system.

A world literature of development, attentive to processes of capitalist incorporation, can track and account for the impoverishment and underdevelopment of world culture, even as it works to re-incorporate planetary knowledge and perspectives that have been deliberately or inadvertently lost, effaced or repressed. The prevailing world-culture of development, associated with capitalism, bears the residual traces of long historical scales of world-making activities, particularly through the partial incorporations of mini-systems (tribal societies) and world-empire; the influences of antecedent world trading networks, cosmopolitan social configuration and transnational/subnational/prenational formations; and the interactions of the Anthropocene and the environment. A world literature that seeks to tell the entire story of development (including both its accumulations and losses) can reopen and acknowledge the fullness of world culture and world literature, particularly through a capacity to track longer scales of change, renew the claims of the dispossessed, frame more inclusive social frameworks and alternative formations and incorporate knowledges that exceed global linear thinking. Such a world literature addresses the realities of hegemonic development, even as it explores alternatives from within the historical realities and cultures of world development.

To offer an example of this approach, postcolonial literature as world-literature can perform a decolonizing function by repositioning the (post)colonial moment in a more expansive framework. Ghosh's 'Ibis trilogy' addresses the globalized opium trade, inter-imperial conflict and the overlaps of colonialism and capitalism, but it also takes an epic turn through its inscription of alternative constructions of worldhood and cosmopolitan formation. In *Sea of Poppies*, the *Ibis* is described as a reconditioned slave ship,[45] which has now become a vehicle for the opium trade in the global capitalist world-system, but within that system competing empires and new globalized socio-economic groupings are also depicted, especially through the presence of the Lascars. Ghosh initiates his contemporary global reader into the world history of Asia through the postcolonial American perspective of Zachary, the son of a Maryland freedwoman (invoking a history familiar to many Americans through the life of Frederick Douglass): 'He had thought that the lascars were a tribe or a nation, like that of the Cherokee or Sioux: he discovered now that they came from places that were far apart, and had nothing in common, except the Indian Ocean; among them were Chinese and East Africans, Arabs and Malays, Bengalis and Goans, Tamils and Arakanese.'[46] In the process, the novel dramatizes how incorporation into the capitalist world-system produces new social arrangements: Zachary's ability to act as a mimic man, his 'power to undertake an impersonation',[47] makes him a useful representative for the Lascar interests. The history of the East India Trading Company, the rise of indenture[48] or 'girmits', and the sometimes precarious interdependencies of an emerging global economy are registered within this narrative of economic imperialism, tracking concerns about the long history of market-driven rationales for readers in a post-millennial world of neoliberal globalization and capitalist crisis. With its code-switches among standard English, various form of world English and incorporation of other languages, this world literary text inaugurates readers into a literary world that reawakens the politics of global development through its capability to render audible silenced voice and develop the global knowledge and literacies of its readers.

'Can "World Bank Literature" be a new name for postcolonial studies?', ask Amitava Kumar.[49] Kumar proposes '[t]he focus on the World Bank, as an agent [of underdevelopment and persistent inequality] and as a metaphor, helps us to concretize the "wider context" of global capitalism',[50] serving to 'recognize and contest the dominance of Bretton Woods institutions but also to rigorously oppose those regimes of knowledge that would keep literature and culture sealed from the issues of economism and activism'.[51] Arundhati Roy's *The God of Small Things* is cited as the exemplar of World

Bank Literature, as Kumar notes: 'one of the main characters is described as "walking along the banks of the river that smelled of shit and pesticides bought by World Bank Loans". The house of the Communist Leader has turned into a luxury tourist hotel. [...] Communism has given way to the dubious victory of market capitalism'.[52] Philip E. Wegner argues that the term 'World Bank Literature' 'reminds us of a fundamental absence of issues of political economy in many conceptualizations of both world literature and postcolonial literature'.[53] In his view, such texts ask readers to reflect more critically on the totality and relationality of global interchanges on various levels and among various locales.

Wizard of the Crow by Ngũgĩ wa Thiong'o exemplifies World Bank Literature's capacity to register and challenge neoliberal globalization through its global cognitive mapping and planetary aesthetics. This satirical novel examines an African dictator's efforts to secure a loan from the Global Bank in order to construct Heavenscrape or Marching to Heaven, a kind of modern-day Tower of Babel, depicts anti-global protests much along the lines as those seen at the World Economic Forum events in Seattle and elsewhere. The Global Bank is shortened to GB, an acronym which one character misinterprets as Great Britain, a creative misunderstanding that highlights the overlapping effects of colonialism and neoliberal globalization.[54] The loans to Free Republic of Aburĩria are withheld until the leader can demonstrate his efforts to address human rights concerns to which he responds by expanding size and giving birth to Baby D, an allegedly new form of democracy, which is encoded as little more than 'hot air' as the dictator's body begins to levitate beyond the earth. At its most cynical, the ascending dictator, Tajirika, observes that 'the Global Bank and Global Ministry of Finance are clearly looking to privatize countries, nations, and states',[55] leading him to predict that '[t]he world will become one corporate globe divided into the incorporated and incorporating'.[56] The African dictator of postcolonial transition falls prey to a newly bureaucratic figure in a globalized world, one who manipulates terror and neoliberal economic policies and practices to achieve his ends. Thus, the legacies of violence are passed down, both intact and expanded upon in both necropolitical[57] and necro-economic terms.[58]

This World Bank novel registers and resists the hegemonic development under neoliberal globalization. In fact, Ngũgĩ does not position his work in terms of the World Bank, but from the perspective of 'the riches of poor theory', a concept he outlines in *Globaletics*,[59] where he brings Marxist methods of historical materialism and dialectics to revisit history from multiple locations and positionings to create a new cognitive mapping of the world. In his politicized re-versioning of the cliché that 'necessity is the mother of invention', he argues that '*poor* means being extremely creative and experimental in order to survive'.[60] 'The homeless,' he observes, 'try to make a home anywhere, even in places that do not suggest a home'.[61] He argues that 'Fiction is the original poor theory'[62] in the sense that it takes the form of '*theoria*, meaning a view and contemplation'[63] that offers 'a framework for organizing what is seen and a thinking about the viewed'.[64] In *Wizard of the Crow*, Ngũgĩ remains committed to the idea of collective voice and action on the part of the people, which it finally renders visible at the end of this epic novel in the description of Eldares Mountains:

> They took him to their farms where they grew foods, millett, sorghums, yams, and arrowroots, as well as varieties of Aburĩrian berries. Elsewhere Aburĩrian soil was dying from being doused with pollutants, imported fertilizer. Here they were working with nature, not against it. The forest was a school to which they often came to hear what it had to tell them: You take, you give, for if you only take without giving back, you will leave the giver exhausted unto death [...] the healing of the land had to start somewhere.[65]

Ultimately, the novel grounds its global aesthetic and postcolonial perspective in local communal efforts to forge sustainable forms of development. But it nonetheless continues to rely on weapons in the service of political struggles for social justice, acts of insurgency against terror, the creation of a 'common store'[66] of knowledge housed in an underground library, new forms of healing spaces, initiatives for unity across race and ethnic lines and carvings of African deities that represent 'a global conversation'.[67] Nonetheless, the epic's itinerant narrative pathway entails so many blockages, detours and false appearances along the way that the novel also highlights the global and national challenges that hinder and marginalize social transformation.

Postcolonial literature as world literature participates in a wider accounting of history, with an agenda oriented towards overcoming the material precarities and disadvantages, a world literature that recognizes the calls of the impoverished, disadvantaged, terrorized and stateless in the one and unequal system of capitalism, a re-articulation of the capitalist violence that drove colonialism itself. *The Wizard of the Crow*'s creative effort to find a home in the world through the bonds of politics and of love,[68] an idea prefigured in the writing of Rabrindranath Tagore on world literature, involves an epic quest to reframe the prevailing *theoria* (or view) of knowledge, labour and co-existence. Ngũgĩ describes this condition of alterity as a dialectical one:

> Globalectics is derived from the shape of the globe. On its surface there is no one center; any point is equally a center. As for the international center of the globe, all points are equidistant to it – like the spokes of a wheel that meet at the hub. [...] The global is that which humans in spaceships or on the international space station see: the dialectical is the internal dynamics that they do not see. Globalectics embraces wholeness, interconnectedness, equality of potentiality of parts, tension, and motion. It is a way of thinking and relating to the world, particularly in the era of globalism and globalization.[69]

Consequently, Ngũgĩ's world literature bridges globalization and the postcolonial, seeing the peripheralization of peoples, knowledges, cultures and creativity as part of a rationalized global world, which has yet to accommodate the wholeness and interconnectedness of the world in its totality.

Ngũgĩ's work shows that another world literature is already present: one that reframes the horizons of global justice through a periphery whose planetary horizons exceed the imprint of colonial and capitalist oppression. In *Wizard of the Crow*, written in Gĩkũyũ and translated into English by the author himself, Ngũgĩ draws on thousands of years of African cultural history, including its proverbs, vernacular traditions and accounts of its longstanding trade networks, to rethink development beyond the immediacies of neoliberal globalization. The Wizard and his dream of flying in bird form, the tale of the girl sacrificed in a lake and traditions for Gĩkũyũ female protest appear in the fabric of the tale. As Simon Gikandi notes, 'the folktale floats in the novelistic universe as a part of the characters' way of making sense of the world'.[70] This folkloric and experimental epic indicates that another world literature and another world development have already been seeded within vernacular culture; its satirical quest to locate the Voice of the People crosses various strata of society, brings quests for economic opportunities in the present into dialogue with older world economic memories of the British East India company, African world-trading systems and the Indian Ocean as 'a cultural highway with constant migration and exchange'.[71] This world literary text elicits a new space of visibility/audibility for Africa's long historical developmental transformations, creating a sociopolitical forum for the re-articulation of development as freedom from multiple, contested perspectives, both for the community it represents and the global readership it addresses.

Exercising literature's radical world-making capabilities

What is the value of postcolonial literature as a radical world literature? One answer is that literature dares to dream of development as freedom, or as Ngũgĩ claims: 'For me, dreaming to change the conditions that confine human life is the mission of art [...]'.[72] It plays an active role in reconfiguring developmental history and transformation in all its plurality and diversity. In the process, this radical strand of fiction revitalizes world literary knowledges, renewing latent and emergent epistemologies in 'intellectually rigorous and ethical grounded'[73] ways, very much embodying the principle that 'there is no global social justice without global cognitive justice'.[74] Such a dissident world literature politicizes development and transformation, opening up new spaces of cognition, speech and action. It demonstrates that peripheralized peoples, knowledge and culture might more fully inform the world imaginary as opposed to being merely incorporated in the service of profit or power. The expansive and critical reclamation of knowledge should be seen as a necessary regrounding and accompaniment to the reconstruction of development as freedom as outlined by Amartya Sen. As Sen observes, the pursuit of freedoms entails a firm commitment to overcoming major sources of unfreedom, such as poverty, tyranny, state-based oppression, patriarchal violence and intolerance, among others.[75] This ethico-political understanding of development relies in part on worldly narrative processes and methods of evaluation, which world literature, particularly the postcolonial, seeks to fulfil through its expansive and participatory accounts of change.

As demonstrated, a radically agonistic mode of world literature tracks, maps and remediates development and transformation, seeking to uncover the long-term drivers of inequality, reconstitute the prevailing global culture of development and assess various claims about more ethical and emancipatory modes of transformation. Such a world literature plays an important role in the articulation of development as freedom by dramatizing the lives of subject and communities as well as conveying their aspirations, but it also provides a forum for readers to expand and sharpen their own global developmental literacies through an encounter with the literary world. This world literature reframes the global culture of development through its ability to track and account for change in the world. Such a world literature calls attention to the fusions, unpredictable affiliations and rearticulations of development from below, representing world development in its totality through efforts to reclaim and reintegrate the losses that have 'developed' along the way. Attending to the dispossessions and deprivations of culture, a world literature of development can enrich an impoverished global imaginary.

A radical world literature, particularly one that reconfigures global literacies through its representations of development, can intervene in the dominant global developmental culture, both for the communities it represents and the readers it addresses. The dissident postcolonial text intervenes to disrupt the hegemonic carving up of space and time,[76] especially as designated by the global Mercatorian model and forms of global linear thinking as theorized by Carl Schmitt in *The Nomos of the Earth*.[77] Through its more inclusive reckonings of development from below, this world literature renders perceptible what was formerly imperceptible, un-represses the repressed, generates new cognitive mappings and elicits newly configured relations among individuals and collectives. Through the language it employs, the egalitarian relationships among literatures it configures, the unfreedoms it exposes and the creative liberties it takes, this radical world literature exercises its world-making capabilities. The radical qualities of this literature do not so much lie in the 'solutions' it offers as the new perspectives it awakens for its world readership, concerning to the problematic of 'development as freedom'. Pheng Cheah has argued that world literature should be understood 'as a site of the processes of worlding and as an agent that participates and intervenes in these processes'.[78] Postcolonial writing does not just dream of another world: it shows the ways in which the dreams of freedom and hopes for equality have been trampled along the way, seeking to return to history and global consciousness the content and forms of its violent repressions. A radical world literature acknowledges the latent but as yet-unrealized potentiality of a global alterity that takes the conditions of its estrangement as grounds for dissent.

This agonistic understanding of development – rendering it open to recognition debate, and ethically oriented forms of collective articulation – characterizes a radical world literature of social transformation. Cheah argues for a more complex understanding of the world, seen as the effect of dynamic contestation among various scales of community, such that its development is 'not referred back to a teleological end of universal progress' but emerges 'as a limitless field of conflicting forces that are brought into relation and overlap and flow into each other without return, because each force, as part of a world, is necessarily opened up to what lies outside'.[79] A radical world literary aesthetic induces this experience of worlding, if only for a moment, such that the problem of development as freedom is perceived anew. This understanding of world literature complements Ngũgĩ's idea of globalectic reading practice as 'a way of approaching any text from whatever time and place to allow its content and themes to form a free conversation with other texts of one's time and place'.[80] By working to ethically re-integrate – rather than unevenly incorporate – the peoples, cultures, economies and knowledges of the world, postcolonial as a radical world literature fosters a more just and participatory culture of development on a planetary scale.

In summary, postcolonial literature as world literature can resist global linear thinking, supplementing and even supplanting the prevailing rationale of economic development with an interactionist and multi-scalar view of the processes of change and transformation. Such a radical world literature returns the world to the fullness of worldly existence and creation, seeing in and through literature the possibilities for more ethical forms of planetary co-existence. Postcolonial literature as world literature provides a forum and vehicle for analysing global challenges, particularly through its ability to reframe injustice by providing more expansive and nuanced reckonings of history. A radical world literature urges its readers to think comparatively and relationally across cultural moments of development to assess the universality of justice in planetary terms: to grapple with the totality of transformation in non-totalizing terms. The creative and critical literacies postcolonial literature fosters, the mappings it generates and the tensions it elucidates can be repositioned in the context of a universal world literature that is universal without becoming universalizing. Another world literature is not only possible but vitally necessary in our era of neoliberal globalization and capitalist crisis, a world very much in transition and therefore open to creative and critical intervention, partly through postcolonial literature's reawakening to its planetary position and world-making capabilities.

Acknowledgements

I would like to acknowledge Jenni Ramone and Lorna Burns for their comments on an early draft of this chapter. I would like to thank Brunel University for the research leave that made this work possible.

Notes

1. Franco Moretti, *Distant Reading* (London: Verso, 2013), 46.
2. Moretti, *Distant Reading*, 127.
3. Pascale Casanova, *The World Republic of Letters*, Trans. M. B. Debevoise (Cambridge: Harvard University Press, 2004), 11, 12.
4. David Damrosch, *What Is World Literature?* (Princeton: Princeton University Press, 2003), 6, 291.
5. See Yolanda Martinez-San Miguel, 'Postcolonialism', *Social Text* 27, no. 3 (2009): 188–93; Patricia Yeager, 'Editor's Column: The End of Postcolonial Theory', *PMLA* 122, no. 3 (2007): 633–51.
6. Ania Loomba, Suvir Kaul, Matti Bunzl, Antoinette Burton and Jed Esty, eds. *Postcolonial Studies and Beyond* (London: Duke University Press, 2005), 8.
7. Neil Lazarus, *The Postcolonial Unconscious* (Cambridge: Cambridge University Press, 2011). See the 'Forum of Literary World Systems', *The Cambridge Journal of Postcolonial Literary Inquiry* 2, no. 2 (2015): 253–86.
8. Gayatri Spivak, *Death of Discipline* (New York: Columbia University Press, 2003), 71–102.
9. Kwame Anthony Appiah, *Cosmopolitanism: Ethics in a World of Strangers* (London: Penguin, 2007); Robert Spencer, *Cosmopolitan Criticism and Postcolonial Literature* (London: Palgrave, 2011).
10. Dipesh Chakrabarty, *Provincializing Europe: Postcolonial Thought and Historical Difference* (Princeton: Princeton University Press, 2000).
11. Revathi Krishnaswamy, 'Toward World Literary Knowledges: Theory in the Age of Globalization', *Comparative Literature* 62, no. 4 (2010): 399–419.
12. *The Oxford Handbook of Postcolonial Studies,* ed. Graham Huggan (Oxford: Oxford University Press, 2013). See Part IV 'Across the Disciplines' for various examples.
13. Neil Ten Kortenaar, *Postcolonial Literature and the Impact of Literacy: Reading and Writing in African and Caribbean Writing* (Cambridge: Cambridge University Press, 2011). See Ezra Yoo-Hyeok Lee, 'Globalization, Pedagogical Imagination, and Transnational Literacy',

CLCWeb: Comparative Literature and Culture 13, no. 1 (2011): http://dx.doi.org/10.7771/1481-4374.1705 (accessed 10 January 2015).
14. World Social Forum: https://www.fsm2016.org/en (accessed 10 January 2015).
15. John C. Hawley, 'Agencies for Resistance, Prospect for Evolution', in *The Postcolonial and the Global*, eds. Revathi Krishnaswamy and John C. Hawley (Minneapolis: University of Minnesota Press, 2008), 28, 29.
16. Pheng Cheah, 'What Is a World? On World Literature as World-Making Activity', *Daedalus* 137, no. 3 Special Issue: 'On Cosmopolitanism' (2008): 36.
17. Amartya Sen, *Development as Freedom* (Oxford: Oxford University Press, 1999), 18.
18. Johann Wolfgang von Goethe, 'On World Literature', in *World Literature: A Reader*, eds. Theo d' Haen, César Domínguez and Mads Rosendahl Thomsen (London: Routledge, 2012), 14–15.
19. Goethe, 'On World Literature,' 11.
20. Homi Bhabha, *The Location of Culture* (London: Routledge, 1994), 12.
21. Mariano Siskind, *Cosmopolitan Desires: Global Modernity and World Literature in Latin America* (Evanston: Northwestern University Press, 2014), 58.
22. Bhabha, *The Location of Culture,* 12.
23. Ibid.
24. Jahan Ramazani, *A Transnational Poetics* (Chicago: University of Chicago Press, 2009), 2.
25. Derek Walcott, 'The Antilles: Fragments of Epic Memory', in *What the Twilight Says* (New York: Farrar, Strauss and Giroux, 1998), 70.
26. Derek Walcott, *Omeros* (New York: Farrar, Straus and Giroux, 1990), 14.
27. Robert D. Hamner, *Epic of the Dispossessed: Derek Walcott's* Omeros (Columbia: University of Missouri, 1997).
28. Edouard Glissant, 'Errantry, Exile', *Poetics*, 21.
29. Walcott, *Omeros*, 189, 191, 196.
30. Jonathan Arac, 'Edward W. Said: The Worldliness of World Literature', in *The Routledge Companion to World Literature*, eds. Theo D'haen, David Damrosch and Djelal Kadir (London: Routledge, 2011), 119.
31. Edwidge Danticat, *Create Dangerously: The Immigrant Artist at Work* (Princeton and Oxford: Princeton University Press, 2010), 5–7.
32. Danticat, *Create Dangerously*, 6.
33. Ibid., 11.
34. Ibid., 20.
35. Ibid., 10.
36. Ibid.
37. Ibid.

38 Dany Laferrière, *I Am a Japanese Writer*. Trans. David Homel (Vancouver: Douglas & McIntyre, 2008), 14.
39 Mads Rosendahl Thomsen, *Mapping World Literature: International Canonization and Transnational Literatures* (London: Continuum, 2008), 13, 14.
40 Neil Lazarus, 'What Postcolonial Theory Doesn't Say', *Race & Class* 53, no. 1 (2011): 7.
41 Warwick Research Collective, *Combined and Uneven Development: Towards a New Theory of World-Literature*. Postcolonialism across the Discipline 17 Series Editors Graham Huggan and Andrew Thompson (Liverpool: Liverpool University Press, 2015), 49.
42 James Graham, Michael Niblett and Sharae Deckard, 'Postcolonial Studies and World Literature', *Journal of Postcolonial Writing* 48, no. 5 (2012): 468.
43 Sarah Brouillette, *Postcolonial Writers in the Global Literary Marketplace* (New York: Palgrave, 2007).
44 Elleke Boehmer and Alex Tickell, 'The 1990s: An Increasingly Postcolonial Decade', *Journal of Commonwealth Literature* 50, no. 3 (2015): 326.
45 Amitav Ghosh, *Sea of Poppies* (London: John Murray, 2008), 12.
46 Ghosh, *Sea of Poppies*, 14.
47 Ibid., 52.
48 Ibid., 75.
49 Amitava Kumar, 'Introduction', in *World Bank Literature*, ed. Amitava Kumar (Minneapolis: University of Minnesota Press, 2003), xx.
50 Kumar, 'Introduction', xix.
51 Ibid.
52 Ibid., xxi.
53 Phillip E. Wegner, 'Soldierboys for Peace: Cognitive Mapping, Space, and Science Fiction as World Bank Literature', in *World Bank Literature*, 281.
54 Ngũgĩ wa Thiong'o, *Wizard of the Crow* (London: Vintage Books, 2007), 51.
55 Ibid., 746.
56 Ibid.
57 Achille Mbembe, 'Necropolitics', in *Biopolitics: A Reader*. Trans. Libby Meintjes, eds. Timothy Campbell and Adam Sitze (Durham: Duke University Press, 2013), 161–92.
58 Warren Montag, 'Necro-Economics, Adam Smith and Death in the Life of the Universal', *Radical Philosophy* 134 (2005): 7–17.
59 Ngũgĩ wa Thiong'o, *Globalectics Theory and the Politics of Knowing* (New York: Columbia University Press, 2012).
60 Ngũgĩ wa Thiong'o, *Globalectics*, 3.
61 Ibid., 3.
62 Ibid., 15.
63 Ibid.

64 Ibid.
65 Ngũgĩ wa Thiong'o, *Wizard*, 758.
66 Ibid., 759.
67 Ibid., 760.
68 Ibid., 763.
69 Ngũgĩ wa Thiong'o, *Globalectics*, 8.
70 Simon Gikandi, 'The Postcolonial Wizard: A Review of Ngũgĩ wa Thiong'o's *Wizard of the Crow* (2006)', *Transition* 98, no. 1 (2008): 163.
71 Ngũgĩ wa Thiong'o, *Wizard*, 84.
72 Ngũgĩ wa Thiong'o, *Penpoints, Gunpoints, and Dreams* (Oxford: Oxford University Press, 1998), 132.
73 Krishnaswamy, 'Toward World Literary Knowledges', 415–16.
74 Boaventura de Sousa Santos, João Arriscado Nunes and Maria Paula Meneses, 'Opening up the Canon of Knowledge and Recognition of Difference', in *Another Knowledge Is Possible: Beyond Northern Epistemologies*, ed. Boaventura de Sousa Santos (London: Verso, 2007), xix.
75 Sen, *Development*, 3.
76 Jacques Rancière, *The Politics of Literature*. Trans. Julie Rose (Cambridge: Polity, 2011), 4.
77 Walter Mignolo, 'I Am Where I Think: Remapping the Order of Knowing', in *The Creolization of Theory*, eds. Françoise Lionnet and Shu-mei Shi (Durham: Duke University Press, 2011), 159–92.
78 Pheng Cheah, 'World against Globe: Towards a Normative Conception of World Literature', *New Literary History* 45, no. 3 (2014): 303.
79 Cheah, 'What Is a World?', 36.
80 Ngũgĩ wa Thiong'o, *Globalectics*, 60.

3

The Global and the Neoliberal: Indra Sinha's *Animal's People*, from Human Community to Zones of Indistinction

Philip Leonard

I

In December 2005, during a ceremony at New York University in which he was awarded an honorary degree, Alan Greenspan delivered his final public address as Chairman of the US Federal Reserve. Over the course of this address, some of the principles that had defined his nineteen-year term in office, and had therefore underpinned US economic policy during this period, were reaffirmed: the virtue of free competition within open markets, the imperative for growth in international trade, integrity as a structural requirement of competitive exchange, economic prosperity as a measure of national and international significance, the primacy of individual opportunity and merit, and the need for democratic government to protect the free market.

During this address, Greenspan also restated two further – for him, axiomatic – ideas which remained central to the canon of rules that shaped his tenure, and which led to his description by Noam Chomsky as the 'most revered'¹ economist of recent years. First, the principle of competitive exchange was described as the source of social cohesion and the guarantor of national and international security; 'Open and free markets are the antithesis of violence',² Greenspan told his audience. Second, he situated these economic and social values in the context of an increasingly globalized system of exchange. 'World standards of living are rising', Greenspan asserted, 'in large because of the widening embrace of competitive free markets, especially by populous China and India'.

Much can be harnessed to this idea that a distinctive political economy has emerged in recent decades. First, as Henry Giroux observes: 'Consumption has become the authentic mark of citizenship, while individual competition and personal responsibility are elevated to the new gospel of wealth and material salvation'.³ As well as dismantling the state apparatus and promoting corporate autonomy, this value system can therefore also be seen as normatively attaching a greater significance to the individual as both intentional actor and entrepreneurial consumer – what Michel Foucault terms '*homo economicus*'⁴ – at the centre of political systems.

Second, alongside this heightened sense of personal accumulation and entrepreneurial citizenship, money has become firmly established as the pre-eminent signifier of value. Goods and objects, Marx observes in the first volume of *Capital*, have no relative value or utility without an independent instrument that can establish the foundations for exchange. Functioning as just such an instrument, money, he famously writes, is 'a crystal formed of necessity in the course of the exchanges, whereby different products of labour are practically equated to one another and thus by practice converted into commodities'.⁵ However, it is not simply the case that monetary value now extends beyond market exchange. Central to contemporary capitalism are the 'new kinds of financial markets based on securitization, derivatives, and all manner of futures trading',⁶ David Harvey writes. According to Ben Fine, this 'current era of financialization' represents 'the extension of finance into ever more areas of economic and social reproduction',⁷ and David M. Kotz points to 'the growing role and power of finance in the political economy of capitalism'.⁸ Trade in immaterial products – the commodification of money itself can therefore be understood as initiating not simply a shift in commerce and exchange, but also a new apparatus for determining social value.

Third, this value system needs to be understood as distinctively global. The increased mobility of capital and commodities across national and international markets, combined with the displacement of production to regions with cheaper labour and fewer employment protections, means that the contemporary moment, more so than at any point in the past, is not only marked by heightened levels of exchange across borders and between markets. It is also characterized by the perception that global society – a connection across nations and regions, and a sense of attachment to the universal community of the world – has resulted from this transborder trade. 'Increasingly freed from the regulatory constraints and barriers that had hitherto confined its field of action, financial activity could flourish as never before, eventually everywhere', Harvey observes, resulting in 'far more sophisticated global interconnections'.[9]

Finally, in addition to the idea that intensified transnational commerce has eroded spatial barriers and national borders, the liberalization of exchange has, it is argued, effected a contraction of time, and perhaps even the overcoming of history. Such an idea develops most famously in Francis Fukuyama's 1992 *The End of History and the Last Man*, a work that often echoes Greenspan's sense of where social value is to be found. At the centre of this book is the claim that our contemporary moment represents the culmination of History, which in Fukuyama's Hegelian formulation is conceived as an overcoming of the polarized divisions that previously characterized relations within and between nations. Spreading prosperity across the world's populations, the free market is, Fukuyama proposes, successfully conquering the ideological, national and religious antagonisms that have divided the world from itself, and is allowing the notion of political freedom to become a universally valued principle. 'Liberal democracy remains the only coherent political aspiration that spans different regions and cultures around the globe',[10] he writes, and it is this quality of universal aspiration that is allowing what he describes as 'the post-historical world' to emerge as the vanguard of global polity. No longer committed to the conflict that saturates 'the historical world's' sense of ethnic, regional and ideological differences – no longer invested in an authoritarian Cold War adversarialism – in the post-historical world: 'the chief axis of interaction between states would be economic, and the old rules of power politics would have decreasing relevance… Economic rationality… will erode many traditional features of sovereignty as it unifies markets and production'.[11]

It is as a signifier of this perceived erosion of sovereignty that the term 'neoliberal' has gained currency in recent decades. Since market deregulation is seen to act as an economic stimulant, intervention by governments or other regulatory agencies is understood as constituting interference in the internal mechanisms that would otherwise allow the market to operate as a self-ordering and functional system. The responsibility of national governments and regulatory agencies is thus reconfigured in this moment: increasingly reluctant to impose trade rules or to control commercial transactions, state and international bodies are instead becoming merely guardians of the conditions that make commerce possible. Voluntarily abdicating some of its power and authority and granting private corporations the right to self-governance, the neoliberal state's primary role in this moment is recalibrated as promoting free enterprise, protecting monetary value and extending the ethic of open and competitive exchange to areas – across a now globalized world – that will provide new opportunities for the market.

II

Such claims that free commerce provides the conditions for worldwide cohesion and universal connectedness need to be disputed, and not only because the celebration of an inclusive and self-ordering market obscures the many exclusions, marginalizations and asymmetries that have prevented exchange from functioning according to the ethic that is promoted by advocates of global trade. Certainly, the persistence of uneven exchange and discrepant access to the market points to the constancy of imbalances in a supposedly liberalized market, and Greenspan recognizes the persistence of these imbalances in a rare moment in which he vacillates over the capacity for the market to function correctly. During a Congressional Hearing convened in 2008, as the extent of the banking crisis was becoming evident, he registers his 'state of shocked disbelief'[12] at the failure of deregulated commerce to respect ethical considerations. This failure, he states, should be attributed to unscrupulous agents whose reckless behaviour transgresses the fundamental principles of trust and honesty which should, for him, inform market exchange.

However, whereas Greenspan views such transgressions as aberrations (merely 'a flaw'[13]) that would be overcome as a truly functional system of open commerce evolves, they can be more compellingly understood as structurally embedded in, and symptomatic of, what Giroux describes as a 'marauding market fundamentalism'.[14] For example, assertions of a newfound pluralism, and of unrestricted trade as the harbinger of social liberty and international peace, point to the installation of liberal democracy as the politics of the right and the true, with the notion of shared and participatory global belonging at its centre. For Chomsky, however, 'Just about every element of the neoliberal package is an attack on democracy',[15] since, for example, the threat of capital flight (the transfer of assets or investment to other regions in response to unfavourable economic conditions) provides financial organizations with the kind of leverage that interferes with governance by elected bodies. Similarly emphasizing the masquerade of openness that informs the idea of liberalized exchange, Arundhati Roy describes the World Bank and the International Monetary Fund as institutions that ensure an asymmetrical distribution of power across the regions of the world and operate against the principle of representative and open governance. They are, she writes, 'Two of the most opaque, unaccountable organisations in the world [which] go about demanding transparency and accountability from the governments of poorer countries'.[16]

For Jacques Derrida too, elementary questions need to be raised about liberal democracy as an equal and inclusive mode of social organization, though for him these questions relate both to a refusal to recognize the discriminatory practices that are intrinsic to a unified world market and a misplaced faith in the idea such a unification would constitute the culmination of human history. 'At a time when some have the audacity to neo-evangelize in the name of a liberal democracy that has finally realized itself as the ideal of human history', he writes in *Specters of Marx*, it is necessary to deliver the forceful reminder that:

> never have violence, inequality, exclusion, famine, and thus economic oppression affected as many human beings in the history of the earth and of humanity...instead of celebrating the 'end of ideologies' and the end of the great emancipatory discourses, let us never neglect this macroscopic fact...: never have so many men, women, and children been subjugated, starved, or exterminated on the earth.[17]

The sense of a post-adversarial and post-historical present, marked by the disappearance of discrepant populations and the collapse of global antagonisms, is therefore yet another feature of a liberal utopianism that refuses to acknowledge both the persistence of ongoing modes of oppression and the new forms of subjugation that it produces. 'There *was* history once, but now there is no longer any history',[18] Slavoj Žižek writes, ventriloquizing

Marx's parody (in *Poverty of Philosophy*) of the normative and idealized assertion of the present as the moment that has managed to extract itself from the contingencies of history.

III

Such a sense of the failed – for Derrida, 'monstrous'[19] – utopianism that has fuelled narratives of market liberalization also motivates Indra Sinha's novel *Animal's People*. Published in 2007, this novel offers a fictionalized narrative of the Bhopal disaster of 1984, documenting the many traumas that this event enacted upon the minds and bodies of those who experienced it, but also situating this disaster in a social and historical moment in which corporate crime became possible precisely because of how markets had been opened up to global commerce. 'Let us…turn to art and literature for forms of resistance to the precarity contrived by neoliberalism',[20] Maebh Long writes, and *Animal's People* answers such an appeal in its interrogation of the social and economic principles that have recently become attached to the concept of freedom: financial deregulation as a social virtue, the benefits of transnational commodity production, mobile capital as solution to regional underemployment, and open and competitive exchange as a pre-requisite for world society. And, in addition to exploring asymmetries of global power, this text demonstrates how the contemporary novel can provide a response to what Emily Johansen and Alissa G. Karl describe as 'the capacious mobility of neoliberalism itself'.[21]

The focal point of Sinha's novel is Animal, the otherwise anonymous principal character who is so-named because of the profound reshaping of his body following the chemical disaster that contaminated his town, Khaufpur (the novel's version of Bhopal). 'I used to be human once. So I'm told', he remarks in the novel's opening pages, 'I don't remember it myself, but people who knew me when I was small say I walked on two feet just like a human being'.[22] Moving around Khaufpur on his hands and feet, prone to biting when angry, and with an easily mottled skin ('Like a leopard!'[23]), he soon becomes cast as less than human. But the question of Animal's human character extends beyond his appearance and behaviour because he functions in Sinha's novel as a figure who embodies an India transfigured by the principle of transnational modernity. Animal's animality is attributed not to a cruel and unjust perception of deformed personhood, and neither is *Animal's People* a testament to courageous personal struggle. Rather, Sinha's novel places this character at the centre of a series of contextual shifts that cannot be overcome though acts of heroic will: Animal is rendered bestial because the system of commercial production that disfigures his body is also one that impairs his capacity to act.

As well as being a novel about the brutalizing effects of global production and commerce, this text also rejects the opportunity to work unambiguously in the mode of documentary history when navigating the imagined space of Khaufpur. This is a story about storytelling, and about the transformative act of recording that occurs in the act of transferring experience to narrative. A prefatory 'Editor's Note' describes what follows as a 'story recorded in Hindi on a series of tapes by a nineteen-year-old boy in the Indian city of Khaufpur. Apart from translating to English, nothing has been changed'.[24] Despite this declaration, Animal's testimony challenges the idea that committing words to tape, and their translation, could result in anything other than modification and distortion: 'You talk of *rights, law, justice*' he says to the journalist who commissions his recorded account, 'Those words sound the same in my mouth as in yours but they don't mean the same, Zafar says that such words are like shadows the moon makes in the Kampani's factory, always changing shape. On that night it was poison, now it's words that are choking us'.[25] And, rather than a spontaneous or authentic response to the depredations of global exchange, this narrative's origins are attributed to the financial incentive that the journalist offers to Animal; the literary equivalent of disaster tourism, the value of this narrative is measured in terms of monetary value. 'You know you're paying shit for something priceless', he tells the journalist, and he describes his associate who negotiates this arrangement as having 'no shame...he has taken a fortune for a thing he considers worthless'.[26]

Despite offering such reflexive moments, this novel makes little effort to disguise itself as a response to the leak from Union Carbide's Bhopal chemical plant in 1984, which resulted in thousands of deaths and hundreds of thousands of injuries. Its description of the 'Kampani's' pesticide plant in Khaufpur eighteen years after the leak matches in close detail the facility that was subsequently abandoned by Union Carbide: 'Here and there are holes in the wall as if a giant has banged his fist through, it's where people have dug out bricks for their houses...Look inside, you see something strange, a forest is growing, tall grasses, bushes, trees, creepers that shoot sprays of flowers of flowers like fireworks.'[27] Although apparently becoming reclaimed by nature, and although providing resources for those living in its vicinity, this building remains a contaminated and hostile place: 'Step through one of these holes, you're in another world.... Listen how quiet it's. No bird song. No hoppers in the grass. No bee hum. Insects can't survive here.... Once inside, it's careful hands, careful feet. Fucking place is full of cobras.'[28] The factory in Sinha's novel, as the one in Bhopal, both haunts the town as a reminder of the death that it delivered and remains a threat to those who remain in its shadow:

> See that thing rising above the trees, those rusty pipes and metal stairs going nowhere? That's the place where they made the poisons. It used to be bigger, but bits keep falling off. Each big wind pulls more iron sheets loose. We hear them falling like angry ghosts.... Its belly is a tangle of pipes like rotting guts. Huge tanks have split, stuff's fallen out that looks like brown rocks... if fire reached these brown lumps, poison gases would gush out and it'd be that night all over again.[29]

Confirming its thematic attachment to Bhopal, this novel's account of the socio-legal consequences of such a disaster also closely reflects events that occurred there. Largely because of Union Carbide's efforts to distance itself from accusations of procedural failings, Bhopal has become a case study in corporate malpractice, criminal negligence and the avoidance of ethical, social and economic responsibility. Accusations of such wrongdoing have cited workplace practices (in particular, a failure to maintain the Bhopal plant at a safe standard) as the cause for the leak, though corporate and governmental actions in the aftermath of the disaster have resulted in perceptions of a greater and more calculated deceit. The US-based Union Carbide Corporation persistently denied that low safety standards resulted in the leak (citing employee sabotage as the cause), and it devolved responsibility for compensation and site decontamination to its subsidiary, Union Carbide India. In what Rob Nixon terms an act of 'corporate necromancy', Union Carbide's purchase by Dow Chemicals in 2001 allowed it and its representatives to avoid any subsequent legal action: at this point, Union Carbide, 'the name indelibly associated with disaster evaporated, further confounding the quest in Bhopal for environmental justice, compensation, remediation, and redress.'[30] Bhopal is the primary event around which *Animal's People* is formed, shaping its sense of the need to resist destructive corporate practices. But, as Zafar's petition demonstrates, Sinha's novel situates these practices firmly in the context of a heightened transnationalism: here, the operations – and, indeed, the ethic – of the market are also self-evidently incompatible with the notion that social equity will result from inclusive transborder production and open competition.

IV

Animal's People makes this tension between the discourses and experiences of globalization visible on a number of levels. The idea that global production is an expression of the world's harmonious ecology, or of a socially responsible capitalism that is attentive to the environmental consequences of its actions, is seen to conflict with the many instances of degradation that are enacted upon Khaufpur. 'Our wells are full of poison', one of Sinha's characters is told, 'It's in the soil, in our blood, it's in our milk. Everything here is poisoned.'[31] Similarly, this novel considers the tension between the ethic of the open market and access to global society by refusing to endorse the images of an urbane cosmopolitanism that have become a familiar feature of everyday cultural discourses of global belonging. Certainly, the idea of connection across borders and cultures is seen to be seductive here, and characters find it difficult to distrust the promise that they too belong in the world. Thus, when imagining himself soaring above the earth, Animal dreams of an aerial perspective that would allow him to see the world as it truly is: 'Up high and early, my eye dreams of the start of this Khaufpuri day. I see the world and me in it. So high I'm, the earth curves away from me, the upper air's full of brilliance. I see the world spread out like a map, roads from all sides coming to the city.'[32] This sense of a planetary wholeness occurs again when Animal, finding it difficult to sleep, glimpses the moon and indulges in a fantasy of shared planetary connection: 'Above my head there are holes in the roof, through them I see the moon a silver ball and I think of all the people who are also looking at the moon and I wonder what they are thinking.'[33] Elsewhere, when sleep does come to him, Animal imagines those pursuing justice for Khaufpur as the bearers of a global responsibility: 'Last night I dreamed of Zafar.... On his head was his favorite red turban, his beard was untrimmed, on his back he carried a shining world, blue as a flycatcher's wing, criss-crossed by tiny lines.... Heavy the world must have been, Zafar was staggering.'[34]

However, throughout Sinha's novel such a vision of a compact and conveyable world is announced as a fantasy, and delusions of global connection and belonging are repeatedly counterposed by images of incomplete, imbalanced and uneven spaces that remain atomized and inscrutable. Animal's imagined aerial view of the world eventually comes to rest on Khaufpur, seen not as one of the world's many confederated places but as a space that is recognizable only as global modernity's vanishing-point: 'eye slides along a road lined with dirty buildings, snarling away in dust and truck smoke, till it reaches a place where the city's turned to jungle, railway tracks come running up and vanish, beyond its terrain harder to interpret, mottling of brown, which on looking closer resolves to the innumerable roofs of the very poor'.[35] Ultimately, Animal abandons his desire to rise above the contaminated soil of Khaufpur – to take flight in the air and to see the world as a consummate whole – when he later arrives at a more grounded perspective on the world: 'How well I know this city's ... ground, from an altitude of two feet, this is my home earth'.[36] And, when he laments that in Khaufpur, 'history finished without warning when no-one was expecting it',[37] this character is not invoking the notion of a post-historical world that Fukuyama imagines. Here, it is the passage of global time – of a modernity that moves progressively across the world's regions – that comes to an end in the moment that poison spills from the factory's walls.

Animal's People therefore conceives the idea of distributed and inclusive transnational polity as a fantasy that conceals the uneven experiences of liberalized commerce and world society. More than this, Sinha's novel actively resists any suggestion that the conditions experienced by those in Khaufpuri are to be attributed to a national failure to adapt to the opportunities that are provided by free exchange and borderless association. Certainly, the novel addresses the question of official complicity in the promotion of transnational production, attaching responsibility for the Kampani's arrival in Khaufpur in part to a system of governance which pursues growth – and which measures social progress – in terms of participation in open markets and transnational production. When, for example, the novel reflects on the possibility for action in the face of a political ethic that accommodates disaster and death as tolerable consequences of economic development, it suggests that a popular uprising is needed in order to shake the foundations of official order:

> *janata ké chalé paltaniya, hillélé jhakjor duniya*
> *the people's platoon's are on the march*
> *the earth trembles, mountains quake,*

the motion ripples rivers and lakes
huge waves rush across the ocean
the whole world shakes, when the people march[38]

However, as Sinha's novel unfolds, the transformative potential of populist insurgency is seen inevitably to evaporate. Just as it reaches a heady state of revolutionary hyperbole – 'now that the fury of the people has been let loose who knows where it'll stop, it's a storm battering everything in its path, it's an avalanche pouring down a mountain',[39] Animal remarks – the novel retreats to a more circumspect sense of what protest can achieve. 'Of course it can't last',[40] he observes.

The cause of this failure is not, ultimately, the agents of the Indian state who meet Khaufpuri protesters with force, but the townsfolk's inability to pursue those who would otherwise be held accountable for the disaster. Rather than promoting the idea that protest movements or popular struggles have the capacity to make the world tremble, the world (or, more specifically, the transnationalism that has resulted in discrepant access to global society) is seen in this novel to hamper efforts to resist political authority. As with Bhopal, the Kampani's ability to evade prosecution is attributed in the first instance to the legal power that its considerable wealth grants: 'Our people are so poor that thirty three thousand of them together could not afford one Amrikan lawyer, the Kampani can afford thirty three thousand lawyers.'[41] But the status of international law in the context of global production is also established as the source of the Kaufpuris' frustrations when pursuing justice: 'For the past eighteen years these Amrikan defendants have not shown up in this court... They sit in Amrika claiming this court has no jurisdiction over them, yet nothing can be achieved without them being here.'[42] This lack of effective transnational governance, it reveals, leaves regions and populations of the world, and especially the poor, unable effectively to confront the new forms of abuse, dispossession and insecurity that globalization brings to them.

V

Sinha's text therefore locates the people of Khaufpur in a domain in which legal rights do not exist, and where the sense of ethical responsibility – on the part of either the company that has reshaped this space or the regional or national bodies that have a duty of care over them – is refused. It might be tempting to treat this apparatus of subjugation – this denial and refusal of rights and responsibilities – as the result of system of global production that arrives from outside as a neocolonial force that would overcome a place like Khaufpur. However, any such treatment risks overlooking the fact that it is specifically the formation and maintenance of subjugated groups and places that enables and sustains global the asymmetries of global power. In addition to contesting the claims to an inclusive and equal participation that motivate recent discourses of transnational society, any critique of neoliberalism needs to also address the various ways in which subjugated groups and places are integral structural features of a supposedly open and prosperous world community.

Attending to the many ambivalences and tensions that shape the politics of modernity, Giorgio Agamben assembles a compelling model for theorizing precisely the ways in which contemporary modes of social organization sustain absolute – sovereign – power by preserving the precarity of minority populations. The maintenance of supreme authority is not, for him, merely an arbitrary feature of political rule; it is not a willed intention to safeguard elite privilege or an authoritarian practice that might, following the progressive refinement of representative politics, be overcome. It is, rather, *the* immanent structural principle – the 'inner hidden norm',[43] according to Ewa Plonowska Ziarek – that is fundamental to modernity, and two concepts at the centre of Agamben's thinking point to how sovereign rule is reasserted through the authoritarian suspension of legal rights and practices.

First, 'bare life'. In *Homo Sacer: Sovereign Power and Bare Life*, Agamben formulates this concept as an alternative to Aristotle's and Hannah Arendt's categories of *zoe* (the primary state of biological existence; being alive) and *bios* (the condition of social and political life; the sphere of human action). Bare life is the kind of life that fits neither category: this is life that can be taken up, silenced, subjected to assault, cruelty and brutality, and ended with impunity by those who claim supreme authority. Crucially, for Agamben, these actions do not separate bare life from the social and political space; rather, they maintain it as an entity that is both incorporated and externalized; it is 'consigned to the mercy of the one who abandons it', Agamben writes, 'at once excluded and included, removed and at the same time captured'.[44] Such life is forced to remain within the orbit of a political system and yet will never be fully integrated into, or be protected by, that system. It inhabits what he describes in *State of Exception* as 'a threshold, or a zone of indifference, where inside and outside do not exclude each other but rather blur with each other'.[45] This is the life that provides a justification for the law to be suspended and for sovereign authority to remain self-authorizing.

In order to ensure its own exceptional status – as both the maker of rules and an entity that guarantees its authority by claiming an affinity to a higher, extra-political, law – sovereign power thus requires an equally exceptional figure that is regulated not through disciplinary control, but through an unpredictable disregard for official norms and practices. This is what Agamben describes as the state of exception: power invokes its right to licence its own actions and certain groups and populations are rendered aberrant. This dual manifestation of supreme power serves both to justify the violence that minority groups are forced to endure and to strengthen the authority of rule. 'The most proper characteristic of the exception', he writes:

> is that what is excluded in it is not, on account of being excluded, absolutely without relation to the rule. On the contrary what is excluded in the exception maintains itself in relation to the rule in the form of the rule's suspension.... In this sense, the exception is truly, according to its etymological root, *taken outside* (*ex-capere*), and not simply excluded.[46]

In this context, Animal's reflexive 'I used to be human once' takes on a different resonance, referring not simply to his posture or quadrapedal movement, not only to how he has been disfigured by a toxic leak and not merely to a beastly or inhuman condition. Rather, his uncertain classification reveals how he exists precariously between the human and the non-human, between life and being alive. His repeated return to this uncertain self-image emphasizes this sense of a life rendered bare by transnational production. 'I'm not a human', he tells the American doctor who sets up a health clinic in Khaufpur; in response to her sympathetic platitudes ('There's simple humanity? Isn't there?'), he replies, 'No good asking me...I long ago gave up trying to be human'.[47] Similarly, when the narrative records the moment in which Animal learns how to write, it describes his name as one that seems only to signify a meagre existence: 'I learned to spell my own name... Jaanvar, meaning Animal. Nisha said that it was my name and I should be proud of it. Jaan means "life". Jaanvar means "one who lives"'.[48] Rather than able to inhabit the world of human community – political life, the realm of *bios* – Animal becomes resigned to a condition of solitary detachment, even as he feels the impulse to remain rooted and attached to being in the world:

> I am a small burning, freezing creature, naked and alone in a vast world, in a wilderness where is neither food nor water and not a single friendly soul.... If this self of mine doesn't belong in this world, I'll be my own world.

> I'll be a world complete in myself... what am I but a complete miniature universe stumbling around inside this larger one, little does this tree realise that the small thing bumbling at its roots, scraping at its bark, clawing a way into its branches, is a fully fledged cosmos.[49]

One who lives barely because of a generalized devastation of his natural and social environment, Animal himself comes to recognize this destitute existence. A disfigured outcast who cannot fully withdraw from the world he becomes a metonym of an aberration-producing transnationalism, rather than a vital life that can belong in the world.

Bearing witness to the fact that regions and populations will suffer as consequence of free commerce and open exchange, *Animal's People* therefore testifies to how global society's sovereign authority both requires the presence of marginalized groups and denies them the social recognition and legal representation that entry into transnational community should apparently guarantee. Moreover, Sinha's novel emphasizes how this bare life results in a form of unacknowledged death. *Homo Sacer*, the figure in Roman law that for Agamben embodies bare life, names just such a death. Designating the person who 'may be killed and yet not sacrificed',[50] *homo sacer* is set apart – taken outside, *ex-capere* – in the moment that it is put to death. Rather than accorded the usual ceremonial rituals associated with a religious sacrifice or granted the legal recognition that is the pre-requisite of a death sentence, this figure is 'subtracted' from the political order so that it can be killed without explanation or accountability.

Subtracted from global – human – community, from self-disclosure and counter-narrative; killed without being sacrificed: this is what *Animal's People* reveals to be the condition of the people of Khaufpur, even as they are drawn into the discourse of autonomy, flexibility and universal citizenship:

> The dead in their hundreds are sprawled in the roads, they are leaning half upright in doorways, their mouths are open and they are singing, out of their throats the death raga pours in green gusts, it swirls around them and flies in your face, in that green burning fog your world is lost.[51]

To attribute these deaths, as well as the suffering of those who continue to inhabit the contaminated space of Khaufpur, to corporate malpractice would be to recognize them as the casualties of what is otherwise proclaimed as a fundamentally liberating shift to an intensified transnationalism. As a result, these non-sacrificial deaths occur as though in a vacuum, and any response to this condition can be voiced only as a muted howl: 'This raga fills you with fear and despair. Your mouth opens and emits no sound'.[52]

Second, Agamben's concept of 'camp' allows Khaufpur and Bhopal to be understood as an exceptional site of subjection, not simply a place in which unusually cruel repression occurs but a space that is controlled by its separation from normal social practices. In *Homo Sacer* Agamben finds this managed separation exemplified by Nazi camps, as well as the football stadium used by the Italian police in 1991 to contain Albanian immigrants, *zones d'attente* in or near French airports (where those seeking refugee status are held), and gated housing estates in the United States; in *State of Exception* Agamben cites the US camp at Guantanamo as yet another site where this 'bare life reaches its maximum indeterminacy'.[53] However, functioning as a '*dislocating localization*' which operates as the exception to political order, Agamben notes that the camp needs to be understood not simply as the type of enclosed detention space that is suggested by these examples, but as somewhere that is carved out as a specific and extraordinary place, a regulated 'zone of indistinction'[54] rather than a more determinable site of incarceration and captivity.

When taken in the context of Agamben's comment that *Homo Sacer* was 'conceived as a response to the bloody mystification of a new planetary order',[55] along with his claim that 'The growing dissociation of birth (bare life) and the nation-state is the new fact of politics in our day',[56] the concept of 'camp' can be extended to those other populations and places where the suspension of law arises specifically as a consequence of global exchange and polity. 'The neoliberal exception allows for a measure of sovereign flexibility in ways that both fragment and extend the space of the nation-state', Aihwa Ong writes, and 'in Southeast and East Asia, zoning technologies have carved out special spaces in order to achieve strategic goals of regulating groups in relation to market forces'.[57] Certainly, Sinha's novel examines the opportunistic relocation of chemical production to a region of the world that becomes formed as such a carved-out space, and the ease with which the Kampani moves into and then away from Khaufpur provides a blunt contrast with both Animal's routine mobility problems and the inability for others to leave a space that is maintained in a state of contained isolation. Integral to the operations of global production, but excluded from perceptions of where human value is to be found, places like Khaufpur and Bhopal need to be viewed as further instances of the camp or zone of indistinction, yet another exceptional space in which law is suspended and where the sovereignty of global power is guaranteed.

VI

Sinha and Agamben therefore intervene in debates not only about the reach and effects of market liberalization, but also about what the term 'neoliberal' might contribute to the lexicon of socio-cultural theory. In respect of the social conditions that it diagnoses and the modes of critique that it enables, this term inevitably lacks precision. Its imprecision, Taylor C. Boas and Jordan Gans-Morse note, results not from an unencompassable multitude of definitions, but – uncharacteristically for social and political theory – from a reluctance on the part of critics to seek a definition of it:

> As scholars, we are accustomed to addressing the problems associated with essentially contested concepts like democracy, and we have learned to justify our preferred definitions from among a range of alternatives. But academic use of neoliberalism is problematic in an entirely different way: its meaning is not debated, and it is often not defined at all.[58]

As a result of this observation, Boas and Gans-Morse submit that the term 'neoliberalism' must be 'imbued with substantive meaning as to what is new or distinct about this form of liberalism';[59] for them this would refer to the specific features of free market capitalism, to the asymmetries that open commerce has effected between developing countries and industrialized nations, and to how all national markets have been reshaped in recent years. Against this appeal for conceptual and terminological exactitude, Jamie Peck questions the methodological contradiction upon which it rests, namely the idea that a term invested with absolute content can fully capture a fluid and adaptable configuration. 'Attempts to transcendentally "fix" neoliberalism are destined to be frustrated', he writes, because 'the neoliberal project is paradoxically defined by the very *unattainability* of its fundamental goal – frictionless market rule'.[60] Such elusively flexible and mobile aspirations lead Peck to conclude that 'pristine definitions of neoliberalization are therefore simply unavailable; instead, concretely grounded accounts of the process must be chiseled out of the interstices of state/market configurations'.[61]

Justifiable though Peck's comment is in respect of other efforts to define neoliberalism, the cautionary methodological note that he strikes must surely return to haunt his petition for an alternative, 'concretely grounded', approach. Sinha and Agamben draw attention to dimensions of neoliberalism that are not so easily understood in terms of state and market, or in terms of a coherently intelligible actuality. Just as Agamben allows global power to be regarded in terms of the mobile, variable and capricious enactment of authority and subjection, so Sinha reflects on how the putative principle of neoliberal political thinking – to provide a foundation for equal exchange and representation – is always unsettled by the indistinct and precarious zones that transnational exchange demands. With their writing and thinking, the critique of neoliberalism is extended and proliferates by confronting what Jeremy Gilbert terms the 'neoliberal technical assemblage',[62] an apparatus of expansive transnational rule which functions through the uneven and unstable, discrepant and dislocating, production of life in modernity.

Notes

1 Noam Chomsky, *Hopes and Prospects* (Chicago: Haymarket, 2010), 58.
2 Alan Greenspan, 'Remarks by Chairman Alan Greenspan: Acceptance of Honorary Degree, New York University, New York, New York December 14, 2005', http://www.federalreserve.gov/boarddocs/speeches/2005/20051214/default.htm (accessed 16 June 2015).
3 Henry Giroux, 'Beyond Neoliberal Common Sense: Cultural Politics and Public Pedagogy in Dark Times', *JAC: A Journal of Rhetoric, Culture, & Politics* 27, no. 1–2 (2007): 18.
4 Michel Foucault, *The Birth of Biopolitics: Lectures at the College de France 1978–79*. Trans. Graham Burchell (Basingstoke: Palgrave Macmillan, 2008), 226.
5 Karl Marx, *Capital* Volume 1, in *Collected Works*, Volume 35, eds. Karl Marx, Friedrich Engels (London: Lawrence & Wishart, 1996), 97.
6 David Harvey, *A Brief History of Neoliberalism* (Oxford: Oxford University Press, 2005), 33. Also see David Harvey, *The Condition of Postmodernity: An Enquiry into the Origins of Cultural Change* (Oxford: Blackwell, 1990), 285ff.
7 Ben Fine, 'Locating Financialisation', *Historical Materialism* 18, no. 2 (2010): 112.
8 David M. Kotz, 'Financialization and Neoliberalism', in *Relations of Global Power: Neoliberal Order and Disorder*, eds. Gary Teeple and Stephen McBride (Toronto: University of Toronto Press, 2011), 1.
9 Harvey, *A Brief History of Neoliberalism*, 33.
10 Francis Fukuyama, *The End of History and the Last Man* (London: Penguin, 1992), xiii.
11 Fukuyama, *End of History and the Last Man*, 276.
12 Edmund L. Andrews, 'Greenspan Concedes Error on Regulation', *New York Times*, 23 October 2008. http://www.nytimes.com/2008/10/24/business/economy/24panel.html?_r=1& (accessed 16 June 2015).

13 Andrews, 'Greenspan Concedes Error on Regulation'.
14 Giroux, 'Beyond Neoliberal Common Sense', 12.
15 Chomsky, *Hopes and Prospects*, 91.
16 Arundhati Roy, 'Capitalism: A Ghost Story', *Outlook* (26 March 2012). http://www.outlookindia.com/article/Capitalism-A-Ghost-Story/280234 (accessed 16 June 2015).
17 Jacques Derrida, *Specters of Marx: The State of the Debt, the Work of Mourning, and the New International*. Trans. Peggy Kamuf (London: Routledge, 1994), 85.
18 Slavoj Žižek, *First as Tragedy, Then as Farce* (London: Verso, 2009), 21.
19 Derrida, *Specters of Marx*, 85.
20 Maebh Long, 'Precarity, the Humanities and Slow Death', *Australian Humanities Review* 58 (2015): 99.
21 Emily Johansen and Alissa G. Karl, 'Introduction: Reading and Writing the Economic Present', *Textual Practice* 29, no. 2 (2015): 211.
22 Indra Sinha, *Animal's People* (London: Simon & Schuster, 2007), 1.
23 Sinha, *Animal's People*, 17.
24 Ibid., i.
25 Ibid., 3.
26 Ibid., 10.
27 Ibid., 29.
28 Ibid.
29 Ibid., 30.
30 Rob Nixon, 'Neoliberalism, Slow Violence, and the Environmental Picaresque', *MFS: Modern Fiction Studies* 55, no. 3 (2009): 459.
31 Sinha, *Animal's People*, 108.
32 Ibid., 133.
33 Ibid., 277.
34 Ibid., 83.
35 Ibid., 133.
36 Ibid., 272.
37 Ibid.
38 Ibid., 264.
39 Ibid., 310–11.
40 Ibid., 311.
41 Ibid., 228.
42 Ibid., 52.
43 Ewa Plonowska Ziarek, 'Bare Life', in *Impasses of the Post-Global: Theory in the Era of Climate Change*, Volume 2, ed. Henry Sussman (Ann Arbor: Open Humanities Press, 2012), 196.
44 Giorgio Agamben, *Homo Sacer: Sovereign Power and Bare Life*. Trans. Daniel Heller-Roazen (Palo Alto: Stanford University Press, 1998), 110.

45 Giorgio Agamben, *State of Exception*. Trans. Kevin Attell (Chicago: University of Chicago Press, 2005), 23.
46 Agamben, *Homo Sacer*, 17, 18.
47 Sinha, *Animal's People*, 186.
48 Ibid., 35.
49 Ibid., 350.
50 Agamben, *Homo Sacer*, 8.
51 Sinha, *Animal's People*, 274.
52 Ibid.
53 Agamben, *State of Exception*, 4.
54 Ibid., 26.
55 Agamben, *Homo Sacer*, 12.
56 Ibid., 175.
57 Aihwa Ong, *Neoliberalism as Exception: Mutations in Citizenship and Sovereignty* (Durham: Duke University Press, 2006), 7.
58 Taylor C. Boas and Jordan Gans-Morse, 'Neoliberalism: From New Liberal Philosophy to Anti-Liberal Slogan', *Studies in Comparative International Development* 44 (2009): 156.
59 Boas and Gans-Morse, 'Neoliberalism', 139.
60 Jamie Peck, *Constructions of Neoliberal Reason* (Oxford: Oxford University Press, 2010), 15, 16.
61 Peck, *Constructions of Neoliberal Reason*, 16.
62 Jeremy Gilbert, 'What Kind of Thing Is "Neoliberalism"', *New Formations* 80/81 (2013): 20.

4

Postcolonial Economics: Literary Critiques of Inequality

Melissa Kennedy

In nineteenth-century London and Manchester, Charles Dickens toured slums and factories, witnessing the miserable living and working conditions of the poor, which he distilled into his fiction. In his Preface to *Martin Chuzzlewit* (1849), he states, 'In all my writings, I hope I have taken every available opportunity to show the want of sanitary improvements in the neglected dwellings of the poor,'[1] and in regard to factory work conditions, particularly of child labour, he vowed to 'strike the heaviest blow in my power for these unfortunate creatures'.[2] In 1937, John Steinbeck travelled incognito to labour camps in California, to report on the humanitarian crisis of 70,000 unhoused, unemployed migrants from the Oklahoma dustbowl. He vowed 'I want to put a tag of shame on the greedy bastards who are responsible for this'.[3] Steinbeck first published his condemning report in journalism, before interpreting the migrant experience in *The Grapes of Wrath* (1939).

In these two anecdotes, the authors voice their drive to record in fiction the social injustice of inequality and poverty on behalf of those marginalized and left behind by the economic growth usually considered as progress and development. In 1840s industrializing Great Britain and 1930s Depression-era USA, Dickens and Steinbeck were writing at moments when the gap between rich and poor was at historical highs. In the first half of the nineteenth century, termed 'Engel's Pause', inequality rose drastically as wages stagnated while profit doubled,[4] creating the situation of great wealth alongside great poverty. Dickens captures the spatial proximity of grossly different material conditions and thus life experiences in his descriptions of London city and portrayals of Londoners. More than simply registering the presence of social inequities, however, Dickens overtly critiques several theories of political economy popular in his era. Examples include satire of Thomas Malthus's forecasts of a population explosion among the poor, in the antipathetic character of Ebenezer Scrooge, in his *A Christmas Carol* (1843),[5] critique of the moral repercussions of the anti-charity sentiment arising from the 1846 Corn Law repeal in the character of Oliver Twist,[6] and castigating the economic rationale that reduces human life to labour value, 'something to be worked so much and paid so much, and there it ended'.[7] Set in the wake of the 1929 Great Depression, Steinbeck's novel also records a decade in which the rich recuperated their losses while many poor were displaced and unemployed. By 1937 there were over 100,000 homeless and jobless migrants from the mid-West in California, living in squalor, suffering starvation and disease. Relief was not forthcoming, as the State and Congress dragged their feet under pressure from the strong agricultural owners' lobby,[8] which, furthermore, had the power to lower the wage rate even as production increased by 125 per cent from the previous year.[9]

While the atrocities portrayed in Dickens and Steinbeck might be assumed to have disappeared with the growth and progress achieved over the twentieth century in the developed world, the 2008 financial crisis and ensuing global recession marks the third spike in the history of economic inequality. With the gap in salaries between rich and poor in the United States reaching levels not seen since 1930,[10] and that in the UK touted in mainstream media as almost at Victorian levels,[11] Dickens and Steinbeck no longer read as outdated. The 2008 world financial crisis shifted public interest to renewed scrutiny of the economy. In particular, the Occupy Wall Street movement, with its slogan 'We Are the 99%' highlighted inequality by comparing the lives and lifestyles of the ultra-rich with the opportunities afforded to a shrinking middle class and a growing number of people living in housing and work precarity, such as on 'zero-hour' contracts or earning under the 'living wage' level. In a post-2008 repetition of the Okies dispossession from their failing farms by bank creditors who 'breathe profits; they eat the interest on money',[12] up to ten million Americans lost their homes to bank foreclosures while those same financial institutions were bailed out by the government. Since the crisis, the richest 1 per cent of the population in both the UK and the United States have recuperated their losses and their wealth is growing again,[13] while across Europe austerity policies have cut benefits and pruned public expenditure on housing, transport and education that affect a growing proportion of people at the bottom of the socio-economic scale.

The post-2008 focus on heightened inequality challenges the common perception of the developed world as free from the problems that plague underdeveloped nations. The ongoing – and increasing – presence of inequality and concomitant poverty even in the richest nations challenge economic tenets such as the 'free' market, meritocratic opportunity, the level playing field of open competition, trickle-down wealth and the idea that a growing economy benefits everybody. Post-crash, several new statistics support the intuition of world-level similarities and comparability of economic inequality. Thomas Piketty's longitudinal data in *Capital in the Twenty-first Century* (2014) shows 'the poorer half of the population [in the UK and US] are as poor today as they were in the past, with barely 5% of total wealth in 2010, just as in 1910'.[14] In a world-level comparison of income inequality, Serge Latouche states that in 1970 the richest 20 per cent of the world population earned thirty times the income of the poorest 20 per cent; in 2004 the gap has become seventy-four to one.[15] A 2014 Oxfam study calculates that the eighty-five richest people in the world hold a combined wealth equivalent to that of the world's poorest 3.5 billion people – half the world's population.[16] Such statistics compellingly argue against a linear trajectory of improvement and progress through development created by unregulated capitalism. Although these statistics are likely based on different data sets and forms of measurement, their circulation in mainstream media and public discourse attests to a growing interest in articulating inequality.

In Dickens's and Steinbeck's portrayals of stark inequality, the attitudes of the rich to the poor, and the social impacts of financial precarity that cause or exacerbate mental and physical illness, violence, crime, addiction, broken familial and social ties, and underachievement in education and employment, the contemporary reader is shocked to recognize patterns still common today.[17] This familiarity interrupts the discourse of modernity, progress and development, asking the reader to consider commonalities between past and present. For the postcolonial reader in particular, Dickens's portrayal of slums and Steinbeck's of displaced migrants chime with many fictional narratives from across the decolonized world. To claim similarities between historical and contemporary expressions of poverty in key literature of the American and English canon and its postcolonial margins challenges the conceptualization of the world as split in two incommensurate halves: the First and the Third world; the developed and the developing; the North and the Global South; the West and the rest; the capitalist core and its peripheries. A focus on fictional representations of economic inequality reveals the presence of third-world living conditions among the impoverished of the first world, the repetition of London's nineteenth-century slums in present-day Lagos, Mumbai, Manila and Rio de Janeiro, as well as disconcerting levels of wealth and conspicuous consumption among the elite minority in these developing-world metropoles. The shock of recognizing contemporaneity in Dickens and Steinbeck makes these texts, in Rita Felski's terms, 'newly timely:' 'texts from the past [which] can interrupt our stories of cultural progress, speak across centuries, spark moments of affinity across the gulf of temporal difference'.[18]

The periodicity of Dickens and Steinbeck, and the resonance of their fiction post-2008, affirms the cyclicity of the global capitalist economy, with recurring instances of labour abuse, human displacement, and issues of privation and poverty recurring alongside profit, growth, development and wealth. These themes, as well as the author's impassioned pledge to document immiseration and injustice as part of a broader commitment to social justice, are also common in postcolonial fiction. No longer in need of a Dickens or a Steinbeck to give voice to the marginalized and alienated, postcolonial writers have always been particularly attentive to inequalities between rich and poor, the failures of the promises of development and the unevenness of the distribution of wealth under colonial, neocolonial and latterly neoliberal globalization. Paulo Lins directly blames the 'white elite' for the racism and poverty existing in Brazil's favelas which motivated him to write *City of God* (2006 [1997]) as 'a gift to the middle class',[19] an attestation of lives rarely covered. Leila Aboulela, who has a M.Phil. from the London School of Economics, in *Minaret* (2005) sketches an economics lecture at the University of Khartoum which applies Rostow's Take-off theory of catch-up development to Sudan, followed by '"the Marxist criticism of Rostow's explanation for underdevelopment". So it wasn't true after all. We were not going to take off'.[20] In *Londonstani*, *Financial Times* journalist, Gautam Malkani, puts his theory of an alternative 'Bling-Bling Economics' Retail Price Index in the mouths of second-generation immigrant gang youths, whose financial savvy is as well-honed as their sensitivity to maintaining their street cred.[21] Mohsin Hamid, who graduated from Harvard Law school and worked as a management consultant, applies his financial advice in the medium of satire, writing *How to Get Filthy Rich in Rising Asia* in the second person as a self-help guide to wealth creation and management.[22] In distilling their professional knowledge of economics into fiction, these writers stake a claim for the relevance of literature to address and critique the political economy of *laissez-faire*, free-market global capital.

Although these and many other postcolonial writers offer fictional representations of how the political economy functions in their respective colonial nations, along with sustained critiques and imagined alternatives to capitalism, their interest in economics has been largely overlooked in postcolonial critical studies. The rise of minority rights discourse and subaltern studies in the 1980s, and of globalization discourse in the 1990s, has dominated postcolonial literary discourse. By coupling deconstruction with subaltern studies notions of the impossibility of the text's ability or the critic's right to representation, the discipline has embraced incommensurable difference of identity and culture while ignoring the financial and material living conditions on which many kinds of difference are based. Responding to global and historical economic inequality, however, challenges the current disciplinary boundaries and founding principles. In order to engage with, as Diana Brydon argues, 'the systemic violences promoted by neoliberal globalization',[23] the postcolonial emphasis on cultural difference and the exclusivity of experience requires balancing by its opposite. Attention to cross-cultural commensurability and repetition of common patterns and experiences of immiseration and inequality illuminates how the postcolonial peripheries are an integral part of the capitalist world-system: singular and pervasive – if not hegemonic – and everywhere marked by resistance.

The difficulty of naming economic inequality as key to analysis of marginalization, subjugation, discrimination and persecution is not restricted to postcolonial studies. A culturalist focus across the humanities and social science disciplines has similarly rendered unfashionable attention to the economic motivations of empire's exploration of new and distant markets, the settlement of trading posts, and the appropriation of 'free' lands and their resources. In regard to the importance of British colonial imperialism to the rise of global capitalism, historian Bernard Porter cites disciplinary pressures behind the reluctance to contextualize empire within an economic frame. In the Preface to the 2005 edition of his 1975 introductory text, *The Lion's Share: A Short History of British Imperialism*, he notes the shifting bias:

> A few years ago this materialist explanation of British imperialism used to be widely contested, because it was felt to be ignoble, and tarred with the neo-Marxist theory that used imperialism's 'capitalist' origins to condemn it ... Today ... Capitalism is respectable again. Its association with British imperialism seems obvious, and no longer a Marxist smear. [...] This needs to be reiterated today, I think, when the essential structure of British imperialism is in danger of being obscured by more 'cultural' approaches.[24]

More emphatically than Porter, Marxist geographer and critic of neoliberalism, David Harvey, denigrates the ineffectual intellectual Left, nurtured 'by thinkers such as Michel Foucault and all those who have reassembled postmodern fragmentations under the banner of a largely incomprehensible post-structuralism that favours identity politics and eschews class analysis'.[25] Harvey's sense of frustration echoes the postcolonial concern that its past emphases on culture, identity, and national imaginary no longer adequately capture the energies and foci of the contemporary postcolonial world, in which terrorism and economic and refugee migrancy are indicative of the shifting geopolitical power relations that challenge the West's centrality. In order to respond to the ever-changing issues portrayed in contemporary fiction from ex-colonized spaces, postcolonial literary studies must continually update its remit and expand its view. In the post-2008 era where economic inequality has largely supplanted cultural identity politics as the main arena of social contestation within and between nation states, postcolonial literary critique also needs to become (re)-acquainted[26] with economic theories, perspectives and vocabularies, particularly of labour, ownership, income, capital and, more broadly, the structures and mechanics of capitalism. Refocusing on the material substance of lives and livelihoods represented in the fiction enables critical inquiry to notice aspects of economic inequality that postcolonial writers have long been aware of.

This chapter offers two examples that demonstrate postcolonial writers' significant understanding of the history of capitalism in its colonial, neocolonial and neoliberal forms, with particular attention to how inequality is produced and maintained. Amitav Ghosh's *The Glass Palace* (2000) deploys the term 'imperialism' to span the history of Burma from the 1885 British annexation to 1996, during the communist military junta. In *Shark Dialogues* (1994), Hawaiian writer Kiana Davenport applies the language of contemporary free-market neoliberalism to the history of Hawaiian resistance, from the arrival of the first American and British traders to the 1990s sovereignty movement. These novels' focus on spaces often left out of the regular postcolonial remit usefully highlights some of the lacunae of postcolonial studies, which forget the nineteenth-century importance of South-East and East Asia in the European power struggle for maritime and commodity trading supremacy, and ignores US imperialism, which disturbs tidy colonizer-colonized categories of Eurocentric force and autochthone victimization, and problematizes the understanding of imperialism as ending with decolonization. Rather, to look for the economic motivations of empire reveals similarities between the 1824 first British military invasion of Burma, led by the East India Company, a private trading consortium with government-granted monopoly rights and its own army, and the 1893 US military overthrow of Hawaiian sovereignty, illegally enacted by the sugar barons who controlled the local government and militia. While both Britain and the United States nominally castigated the private actions of their unruly colonists, in practice Burma provided an important British presence in the lucrative East Indies commodities trade market (Britain annexed Burma in 1885, after two more wars against the Burmese monarchy), and the United States quickly annexed Hawaii as military base for its 1897 imperial war against Spain in the Philippines. Written in the contemporary postcolonial, neoliberal era, Ghosh and Davenport narrate and re-enact fine historical details to claim that such imperial history remains of contemporary importance for understanding modern-day Burma and Hawaii.

Historical novels have been a mainstay of postcolonial fiction since its inception, recording the irruption of Western modernity and the impact of colonization on traditional societies. In particular, epic novels which span several generations, such as Ghosh's and Davenport's, and clusters of novels that feature the same characters or communities, such as by Ngũgĩ wa Thiong'o, Chinua Achebe, and Tsitsi Dangarembga, enable a sustained study of how capitalist economic structures continue despite changing political regimes. Historical narratives argue for enduring structures of domination, from the first era of globalization under imperialism to the second era of globalization under the neoliberal free-market. In both the colonial past and the neoliberal present, a small elite hold the power over a relatively impoverished majority, whose marginalization and subjugation as the losers of capitalism is often split along gendered and ethnic lines. Historical fiction's *longue durée* frame is useful for noticing continuity and confluence, offering 'a prehistory of the present'[27] that renders difficult economic concepts into narrative forms that are easy to relate to and identify with. With its attention to and critique of economic inequality, much postcolonial fiction contains useful critiques of capitalism and suggests options and alternatives that can inform and contribute to the post-2008 disillusion with hegemonic neoliberal capitalism.

Ghosh's *The Glass Palace* begins in Mandalay with the 1885 third Anglo-Burmese War, a typical example of imperial British aggression that used a predominantly Indian colonial army to invade and annex Burma on behalf of the British Empire. 'A war over wood',[28] the British depose the Burmese King to gain control of the teak timber trade, the land and its resources, thereby securing for Britain a key trading hub in the South-East Asian mercantile market dominated by the French and Dutch. Ghosh's highly visual, roving eye narrates the events from multiple third-person perspectives, including from an Indian orphan, a royal maidservant, a middle-class merchant, the Malayan Queen and from several ranks in the imperial army. The effect is to build up a complex web of power relations that demonstrate multiple forms of exploitation and inequality that do not fit a simple colonizer-colonized binary. In the novel's portrayal of the monarchy's abusive treatment of commoners, the colonizer's subjection of the colonized, the Indian entrepreneurs' exploitation of indentured labours, and the Burmese military junta's suppression of civil rights, Ghosh argues that inequality and injustice are features not only of colonialism, but rather of rich over poor everywhere.

Although the Burmese Queen is certainly a victim of British colonial subjugation, she also exploits those in her service. She practices fratricide to eliminate competition to her husband's throne and is brutal to her servants, many of whom are sold into service by their impoverished families. When given a chance for upward mobility, the national army generals vie to turn over the family to the British,[29] the poor of Mandalay loot the palace and the servants quit the royal family's service once it is no longer profitable to be in their employ.[30] Similarly, exploitation within the British colonial infrastructure is also multi-layered. The British co-option of mercenary Indian sepoys into the imperial army, deployed not only in Burma but also in China, Malaya and Singapore, are 'used to fight other people's wars with so little profit for themselves'.[31] Even Britons in the colonial service do not escape the profit motive, either in the civil service or in the private companies under royal charter. For example, young overseers in the teak logging camps succumb quickly to malaria or dengue fever, a fact that is calculated into company management:

> The company know this very well; it knows that within a few years these men will be prematurely aged, old at twenty-one; and that they will have to be posted to city offices [...] the company must derive such profit from them

as it can. So they send them from camp to camp for months on end with scarcely a break in between.³²

The Western insertion of capitalism into Burma also creates niches for local compradors to join the new capitalist economy and ensure its further spread into existing societies. Rajkumar's rags-to-riches entrepreneurship from orphan Indian immigrant to owner of a Burmese timber mill and Malayan rubber plantation mimics British exploitative practices, in which human welfare is secondary to their labour function in the employers' efforts to maximize profit in predominantly extractive industries. Rajkumar raises the necessary start-up capital for his timber mill and secures a cheap labour source for his rubber plantation by indenturing Indian labourers for the coolie trade: 'There was no quicker money to be made anywhere. Many foreign companies were busy digging for oil and they were desperate for labour. They needed workers and were willing to pay handsomely'.³³ As an Indian himself, Rajkumar is not a colonialist; however, he is an aggressive capitalist, and this leads him to exploitative behaviour often associated with the British. As well as assiduous networking and corruption to garner favour from the colonial administrators, he is violent and racist towards his Indian and Burmese workers, and provides poor living conditions while demanding high work output. Rajkumar mimics not colonial *culture* but colonial *economics*, aiding and abetting the incrustation of global capitalism and ensuring its continuation long after independence.

The long epic novel ends in Yangon in 1996, amid the physical and intellectual privations of the military dictatorship, in power since 1962. This modern setting is contemporary enough for the reader to recognize Myanmar today: underdeveloped, riven by ethnic strife, corrupt, its failed attempt at socialism ridiculed by US and EU economic sanctions, the country occupies a very low position on the Human Development Index and is one of the world's poorest nations.³⁴ The novel's epic format enables Ghosh to connect historical colonial plunder to Myanmar's current underdevelopment, tracing from past to present the continuation of imperial structures of economic inequality. The rubber plantations established in the 1920s with colonial investment, are 'little empire[s]', taken from the jungle and 'moulded' and 'domesticated' into a 'vast machine, made of wood and flesh'.³⁵ The Indian minority in Burma is described as 'rich Indians live like colonialists, lording it over the Burmese',³⁶ an inequality that leads the Burmese nationalist movement to call for expulsion of the Indians as well as the British. Among the muddled layers of victimization and the injustice of historical wrongdoing, Uma Dey, a pro-independence agitator, sympathizes 'with the fears of the Indian minority and yet it troubled her that they believed their safety lay in [...] the pattern of imperial rule and its policy of ensuring its necessity through the division of its subjects'.[37] Post-independence, the military junta is also described as another form of imperialism, with its socialist claims masking a totalitarian power structure: 'It was because of the imperialists that Burma had to be shut off from the world; the country had to be defended against neocolonialism and foreign aggression'.[38] Ghosh's characters, however, see through the guise: 'in fact, it is they who invoke the old imperial laws and statutes to keep themselves in power',[39] the regime's censorship 'growing out of the foundations of the system that that had been left behind by the old Imperial Government'.[40] Ghosh untethers the term 'imperialism' from its colonial moorings, applying it to any group that derives power and wealth for the elite few, supported by the ruling political regime and enforced by its monopoly on violence in the form of military and police.

When Rajkumar embraces the opportunities to generate wealth that capitalism provides, he also internalizes the values that underpin and justify its rootedness in society. In response to Uma Dey's accusation that he is 'a slaver and a rapist', 'an animal, with your greed, your determination to take whatever you can – at whatever cost', Rajkumar retorts: 'Have you ever built anything? Given a single person a job? Improved anyone's life in any way?'[41] This response could be straight from a neoliberal handbook, portraying the labour market as a gift to workers with the benefits of investment in industry and wages construed as improvement and positively connoted development. Rajkumar rejects Uma's ethical slur, confident that his moral responsibility as an individual has been replaced by the external, neutral, self-regulating laws of Adam Smith's invisible hand of the market. By contrast, Uma embodies the priorities of the postcolonial nation: she is educated and liberal, denigrates the injustices of Empire, supports the Burmese independence movement and agitates for women's and ethnic minorities' rights. Indeed, it is through her perspective or in dialogue with her that Ghosh narrates many of the criticisms of imperialism, quoted above. Her ideals are anachronistic within the novel's timeline, betraying a wholly modern, postcolonial mentality most likely shared by the contemporary reader. Through Uma's constant interjections, Ghosh criticizes multiple forms of inequality and injustice, drawing the reader's attention to colonial and neocolonial practices driven by greed for profit and facilitated by abuses of power accepted at each historical moment. While his sustained critique is cutting, however, the author refrains from offering alternatives or models for more equitable distribution of Burma's considerable natural resources.

Ghosh's contemporary free market argument in 1920s Burma is given an even earlier starting date in Kiana Davenport's *Shark Dialogues*. The Hawaiian novel's historical timeline begins with the arrival in 1655 of a Dutch orphan sent by an alms-house to work for the Dutch West India Company in New York State, and ends in 1990s Hawaii with militant eco protest for land restitution. Whereas Ghosh applies the language of imperialism to postcolonial economic practices, Davenport applies the language of contemporary neoliberalism to the imperialist US settlement and annexation of Hawaii, comfortable with the language of trade tariffs, finance capital and the stock market. Through the fortunes and relationships of the novel's central family dynasty, Davenport portrays Hawaii as an important link in global capitalism. Copying European imperial techniques, such as gunboat diplomacy, unequal trading treaties and direct annexation, the United States forced open Hawaii as a Pacific hub for whaling, opium and other products from the Asian silk and spice trade, and plantation cash crops. These economic benefits were secured for the United States by its 1897 annexation of Hawaii under the pretext of national military security.

Like Ghosh, Davenport uses the epic timeline to emphasize ongoing and systemic inequality as inherent to the free market economy, forced on Hawaii by the Hudson Bay Company in 1834 to facilitate trade, as it was in India and South-East Asia by the British East India Company in 1600. She illuminates how the commodities boom was enabled by labour exploitation and illegal trading practices (including monopolies, embargoes and tariff manipulation) in nineteenth-century America, as it was across the Atlantic during the Industrial Revolution: 'In the early 1840s, wealth was being accumulated overnight in Honolulu – human cargo smuggled in from the Orient as cheap labour, opium packed in champagne bottles, rare jade and gold slipped past immigration authorities',[42] and a decade later, 'how rapidly Hawai'i was changing, how radically rich and poor classes were growing. In 1853, there was no middle class. White traders and merchants were becoming millionaires in Honolulu'.[43] By the 1920s, the city physically and spatially embodies the dire gap between the rich and poor, a segregation that predominantly follows ethnic lines, as Hawaiians are relegated to marginal land and ghettoized in slums growing on the outskirts of Honolulu. By contrast, 'white monopolies controlled every aspect of the sugar and pineapple business. Banking. Insurance. Utilities. Merchandising. Transportation. Shipping. Labor'.[44] In naming repeating patterns of economic inequality, Davenport highlights the disparity between the plantation or ranch owners' wealth and the workers' low incomes, poor living conditions, and lack of ownership. She sets these in tension through direct comparisons, often in the same sentence or paragraph. For example, 'Rich *haole* built huge plantation estates as the quality of life deteriorated for Hawaiians;'[45] and 'Over eight thousand Asian immigrants and Hawaiians were packed into less than forty acres near Honolulu's waterfront, charged outrageous rents by white landowners'.[46] In the 1990s, the same dynamic of American and foreign investment that dispossesses Hawaiians from the land has a different face, with a $900 million yacht resort displacing fishermen, who become 'no-job, no-land people:' throughout history, Davenport asserts, '[t]he pattern kept repeating itself'.[47]

Davenport employs recurring terms that span the historical time frame to suggest the corollary between historical and contemporary forms of capitalist inequality. Thus, 'slavery' is applied to different labour groups and across the economic sectors to denote any form of labour exploitation, from forced labour to lack of other employment options, low pay or harsh working conditions: in 1892, Asians are 'imported for "slave work" on plantations',[48] as are indigenous Hawaiians dispossessed of their lands which are converted to plantations in the 1920s, where they work 'twelve and fifteen hours of scorching stoop work, paid only forty cents a day [...] no sick leave, or rest, they were the reservoir of slaves'.[49] During the nationalist movement of the 1970s, issues of unemployment, demands for welfare for low-income families, unfair bank loans and the lack of scholarships for indigenous students are grouped together under the umbrella of 'economic slavery of [Hawaiian] people'.[50] By the 1990s, this generalized explanation of submission has become more focused, directly tied to land ownership: 'sell the land, you sell your souls, you will damn yourselves to slavery, and keep the whites in power'.[51] The similar term 'indentured' applies to the dangerous work and degrading pay of pineapple-plantation coolies in 1901[52] and to indigenous cowboy ranch hands in the 1970s: 'they owned you for three bucks an hour. [...] And if he left the job, all benefits would cease. He was indentured, like the rest of them'.[53] The example also serves to underline the material expression of that economic inequality between rich and poor: the ranch workers live 'in single men's dorms, fifteen to a one-room bunkhouse' while 'Hundred-thousand-acre ranches owned by rich *haole* in Palm Springs, men who showed up twice a year in cashmere breeches, English riding boots'.[54]

In using clusters of strongly connoted terms as leitmotifs for economic inequality, Davenport recounts step by step how Hawaiians were brought into a capitalist social, political and economic system that extracts or creates great riches through often physically brutal and psychologically damaging exploitation of the alienated workers, who are predominantly indigenous peoples, immigrants and women. Focalized through several Hawaiian and mixed-minority characters, the reader is encouraged to empathize with each narrator, a common technique in postcolonial fiction that castigates injustice against marginalized communities through an insider perspective. More overt criticism comes from exposing the hypocrisy of capitalist social values that mask its violent, illegal, unfair or exploitative mechanisms by couching it in the language of freedom and equality. Hawaiians first open the right for foreigners to buy land when King Kamehameha III 'let himself be persuaded by white merchants and ex-missionaries to "abolish feudalism and make land-rights equal"'.[55] An indigenous lawyer campaigning for plantation workers' rights is the target of a smear campaign from the powerful Sugar Planters Association, which labels him a 'labour agitator, constantly linked with subversives. [...] A *kanaka*, related to the degenerate Coenradstens, descendants of... a cannibal!'[56] Post-Second World War, a Filipino hotel porter attends night school and a Chinese-American returned serviceman uses the G.I. Bill in the hope of the upward mobility promised by the American Dream, 'To be someone, become someone, something more than stoop-work "coolie"',[57] but racism denies them respectable jobs; both remain in the Honolulu slum as the legacy of poverty passes through successive generations. By following the lives of these characters, Davenport illuminates how systemic economic inequality functions insidiously, hidden behind and within socio-cultural values that privilege and encourage individual gain, competitiveness, an ethic of work as the path to financial and thus social success, and an insatiable desire to earn more invest more and consume.

Hawaiians are not, however, simple victims of Western imposition, but complicit in their own subjugation. As one Hawaiian eco-activist puts it, 'We were lost when we were born because we're Polynesians, intelligent, competitive, vain. We coveted things *haole* owned. They gave us progress, we gave them land'.[58] Davenport is as harsh on the consumerist desires that lead Hawaiians to sell their land as she is on the trickery and theft of earlier dispossession policies. In each generation, strong female characters fight both insiders and outsiders, railing against the anaesthetizing effect of consumerism that makes people lose sight of non-commercial values, such as religion, community, language and traditional forms of honour, prestige and inter-generational obligation. Even so, the central indigenous matriarch, Pono, does not reject capitalism: 'No one in history has ever respected those who did not own their *own land*. [...] Hawaiians who are stupid and greedy, sell their honor with their land for easy money, then find whites laugh at them, think of them as low, lazy, without culture'.[59] On her coffee plantation, kept in the family with great difficulty, Pono models a more inclusive, fairer Hawaiian economy: workers from all minority ethnicities receive a job for life, good wages, health insurance and school for their children. While the concept is certainly attractive, Davenport resists a facile happy ending. As well as uncontrollable outside events and changes, including natural disasters, wars, policy changes, waves of migration and new trends in global finance that affect investment in Hawaii, there are deep conflicts and tensions within the family that threaten continuity in every generation. Davenport suggests that solidarity, the desire to fight injustice and the motivation to foster unique aspects of Hawaiian social practices that remain outside of capitalism are difficult to maintain in the face of relentless social, cultural, political and economic pressure to conform to mainstream norms. Like Ghosh's character Rajkumar, Davenport implicates her characters in motivations and mechanics of capital accumulation and its consumption, which complicates the colonial-neocolonial-postcolonial divide and thus calls for closer critical attention to the ways in which the colonized embrace and assimilate as well as contort and resist capitalism.

The Glass Palace and *Shark Dialogues* both record the specific histories of capitalism in distinctly different geographical areas and formed by different political and socio-cultural pressures, yet their specificities are everywhere shot through with similarities and recurring patterns, of both how capitalism generates inequality, and how these iniquities shape social relations across, between, and within nations, communities and families. To focus on postcolonial fiction's significant, often sustained engagement with economic issues argues for the importance of the imaginary in interpreting the range of human responses across time and space to the economic system that is today worldwide and quasi-hegemonic. Considerations of postcolonial economics reveal that fiction has a valuable role to play in the critique of capitalism, joining the literary voice to the neoliberal critique that has gathered steam across the disciplines and in public, popular discourse since the 2008 financial crisis and global recession. Both postcolonial studies and neoliberal critique are deconstructive methodologies that expose the man-made and self-interested underpinnings of the political economy, including of the socio-cultural norms that support it; both advocate for the under-represented and marginalized, motivated by a desire to name instances of injustice as the first step towards change. In a world where the 'there is no alternative' rhetoric of mainstream economics continues to dominate, the literary text's fictionality may be envisaged not as a limitation and liability but as a freedom and potentiality to explore alternatives, to which postcolonial fiction's recourse to unique social structures and cultural beliefs is valuable.

Notes

1   Charles Dickens, Preface to *Martin Chuzzlewit* (1849; repr. Marblehead: Trajectory, 2014), n.p.
2   Charles Dickens, letter to E.M. Fitzgerald, 29 December 1838, in John Butt and Kathleen Tillotson, *Dickens at Work* (London: Routledge, 2009), 177.
3   John Steinbeck, letter to Elizabeth Otis, 1937, in Jackson J. Benson, *John Steinbeck, Writer: A Biography* (New York: Penguin, 1984), 370–71.
4   Robert C. Allen, 'Engels' Pause: A Pessimist's Guide to the British Industrial Revolution', Oxford University, Department of Economics Discussion Papers (April 2007), 5.
5   Jerry Bowyer, 'Malthus and Scrooge: How Charles Dickens Put Holly Branch through the Heart of the Worst Economics Ever', *Forbes*, http://www.forbes.com/sites/jerrybowyer/2012/12/24/malthus-and-scrooge-how-charles-dickens-put-holly-branch-through-the-heart-of-the-worst-economics-ever/2/ (accessed 24 December 2012).
6   Paul Young, 'Political Economy', in *Charles Dickens in Context*, eds. Sally Ledger and Holly Furneaux (Cambridge: Cambridge University Press, 2011), 248.
7   Charles Dickens, *Hard Times*, Book 2, Chapter 6 (1854), quoted in Young, 'Political Economy', 247.
8   Benson, *John Steinbeck, Writer: A Biography*, 368–71.
9   Devra Weber, *Dark Sweat, White Gold: California Farm Workers, Cotton, and the New Deal* (Berkeley and Los Angeles: California University Press, 1994), 170.
10 Thomas Piketty, *Capital in the Twenty-First Century*, trans. Arthur Goldhammer (Cambridge, MA: Belknap, 2014), 291.
11 A 2012 High Pay Commission report projected at the current rate of growth pay inequality will reach Victorian levels by 2040. 'Cheques with Balances: Why Tackling High Pay Is in the National Interest', *The High Pay Commission* 16 (2012), http://highpaycentre.org/files/Cheques_with_Balances.pdf (accessed 23 August 2015).
12 John Steinbeck, *The Grapes of Wrath* (Harmondsworth: Penguin, 2002), 32. The citation has been used in several post-2008 popular economics books on economic crisis and neoliberal capitalism. See, for example, Gerard Hastings, *The Marketing Matrix: How the Corporation Gets Its Power – And*

How We Can Reclaim It (London: Routledge, 2013); David McNally, *Global Slump: The Economics and Politics of Crisis and Resistance* (Oakland: PM Press, 2011).

13 Immanuel Saez, 'Striking it Richer: The Evolution of Top Incomes in the United States', University of California, Berkeley (September 2013), http://eml.berkeley.edu/~saez/saez-UStopincomes-2012.pdf (accessed 23 August 2015). A 2014 Oxfam report finds, 'In the US, the wealthiest one percent captured 95% of post-financial crisis growth since 2009, while the bottom 90% became poorer' in 'Working for the Few: Political Capture and Economic Inequality', *Oxfam Briefing Paper 178*, 20 January 2014: 3, https://www.oxfam.org/sites/www.oxfam.org/files/bp-working-for-few-political-capture-economic-inequality-200114-en.pdf (accessed 23 August 2015).

14 Piketty, *Capital in the Twenty-first Century*, 261.

15 Serge Latouche, *La scommessa della descrescita* (Milano: Feltrinelli, 2007), 37. My thanks to Paola Della Valle for this information.

16 Oxfam, 'Working for the Few: Political Capture and Economic Inequality', 5.

17 See Richard Wilkinson and Kate Pickett, *The Spirit Level: Why Equality Is Better for Everyone* (London: Penguin, 2010).

18 Rita Felski, *Uses of Literature* (Oxford: Blackwell, 2008), 120.

19 Paulo Lins, *City of God*, trans. Alison Entrekin (London: Bloomsbury, 2006), 1.

20 Leila Aboulela, *Minaret* (London: Bloomsbury, 2006), 42, 43.

21 Gautam Malkani, *Londonstani* (London: Harper Perennial, 2007), 169–73.

22 Mohsin Hamid, *How to Get Filthy Rich in Rising Asia* (London: Hamish Hamilton, 2013).

23 Diana Brydon, 'Cracking Imaginaries: Studying the Global from Canadian Space', in *Rerouting the Postcolonial: New Directions for the New Millennium*, eds. Janet Wilson, Cristina Sandru and Sarah Lawson Welsh (Abingdon: Routledge, 2010), 108.

24 Bernard Porter, *The Lion's Share: A History of British Imperialism 1850 to the Present* (London: Routledge, 2005), 8.

25 David Harvey, *Seventeen Contradictions and the End of Capitalism* (London: Profile, 2015), xiii.

26 Part of this process of expanding the discipline's foundations include re-evaluating early theoretical engagement with these themes, predominantly from Marxist perspectives, from theorists considered foundational to postcolonial studies, including Rosa Luxemburg, Frantz Fanon, Edward Said, Jacques Derrida and Fredric Jameson.

27 John Marx, *Geopolitics and the Anglophone Novel, 1890–2011* (Cambridge: Cambridge University Press, 2012), 126.

28 Amitav Ghosh, *The Glass Palace* (London: Harper Collins, 2001), 15.

29 Ghosh, *The Glass Palace*, 25.
30 Ibid., 31, 41, 53.
31 Ibid., 29, 30.
32 Ibid., 74.
33 Ibid., 124.
34 The IMF ranked Myanmar in the poorest 10 per cent of nations in the *International Monetary Fund World Economic Outlook Database*, April 2013, https://www.gfmag.com/global-data/economic-data/worlds-richest-and-poorest-countries (accessed 31 August 2015).
35 Ghosh, *The Glass Palace*, 232, 233.
36 Ibid., 240.
37 Ibid., 243.
38 Ibid., 537.
39 Ibid., 543.
40 Ibid., 535.
41 Ibid., 248.
42 Kiana Davenport, *Shark Dialogues* (New York: Plume, 1995), 45.
43 Davenport, *Shark Dialogues*, 48, 49.
44 Ibid., 88.
45 Ibid., 51.
46 Ibid., 75.
47 Ibid., 225.
48 Ibid., 66.
49 Ibid., 120.
50 Ibid., 196.
51 Ibid., 338.
52 Ibid., 78.
53 Ibid., 225.
54 Ibid.
55 Ibid., 46.
56 Ibid., 78.
57 Ibid., 201.
58 Ibid., 385.
59 Ibid., 337, 338.

5

The Postcolonial Book Market: Reading and the Local Literary Marketplace

Jenni Ramone

In their editorial to a special issue of the *Journal of Commonwealth Literature*, Sarah Brouillette and David Finkelstein describe the emergence and development of the study of the postcolonial literary marketplace, or book market, as a research field. They endorse Graham Huggan's claim in his 2001 book, *The Postcolonial Exotic*, that scholars of postcolonial literature must consider the material forces that support and structure the production of books and other printed objects sold as postcolonial. Since that time, Brouillette and Finkelstein note, 'scholarship sharing Huggan's point-of-view – that the nature of the postcolonial text is illuminated by study of cultural markets and the economic and political forces that those markets mediate – has proliferated, to the extent that it is now possible to identify a substantive materialist turn within postcolonial literary studies'.[1] The marketplace is, as Brouillette and Finkelstein assert, 'never quite separable' from the text itself. In this chapter, I survey some of the major works that constitute the field of the postcolonial literary marketplace, before explaining the need for greater emphasis on the local literary marketplaces that perform such significant functions in the everyday lives of readers and communities in postcolonial locations. In the final part of this chapter, I will focus on my ongoing research project that analyses moments of reading in postcolonial literary texts, undertaking close analysis of moments of reading in short stories by Nigerian writers Chimamanda Ngozi Adichie and Jide Adebayo-Begun.[2]

The postcolonial literary marketplace

Research on the postcolonial literary marketplace and postcolonial readers and reading is a lively field, and a number of significant works have been produced in recent years. Graham Huggan's *The Postcolonial Exotic: Marketing the Margins* (2001) was among the first to consider the material conditions informing postcolonial writing, in terms of the impact of publishers' processes and academic influence on the production and consumption of postcolonial literature. *The Postcolonial Exotic* is concerned with the global reception of postcolonial literary texts in a manner that flattens and repackages cultural differences in particularly marketable ways. Huggan cites Aijaz Ahmad's claim that the imperialism of late capitalism constructs an ideal reader who can read without the constraints of 'stable identities of class, nation, gender'.[3] Huggan agrees with Ahmad's assessment to the extent that it cultivates a taste for the generalized 'exotic' in readers of postcolonial literature, which is encouraged by publishers who seek such texts that they consider to be eminently marketable. Sarah Brouillette offers a different take on the postcolonial literary marketplace, in response to Huggan's book.

In *Postcolonial Writers in the Global Literary Marketplace* (2007), Sarah Brouillette argues convincingly that the postcolonial literary text is dependent on its material conditions of production and consumption and questions how far this might be 'dehistoricizing and depoliticizing'[4] in the way that Huggan suggested, noting that, at the time of writing, relatively few studies of reading practices in postcolonial contexts had been carried out. James Procter and Bethan Benwell's *Reading Across Worlds: Transnational Book Groups and the Reception of Difference* (2014) is an important corrective to this omission, particularly because of its focus on comparing responses to postcolonial literature (*Things Fall Apart*, *White Teeth*, *Brick Lane* and *Small Island*) between reading groups from across a number of locations (including England, Scotland, Canada, the Caribbean, India and Nigeria). Procter and Benwell compare discreet reading communities – book groups – to analyse and compare the ways in which readers in different locations respond to bestselling postcolonial literary texts. My project explores, instead, larger reading communities by placing literary texts in their local literary marketplaces to consider how texts are circulated in the contexts of local publishing, bookselling and literary contexts including libraries, educational contexts, literary events, festivals and the digital presence of niche literary organizations in an effort to understand the place of reading in its location and enable an analysis of market forces that inform the form and function of literature and reading in each context.

Sarah Brouillette's work in *Postcolonial Writers in the Global Literary Marketplace* explores authorship and the author as global figure, concentrating on, as the title states, the global marketing and reception of those authors' works. In her chapter on Coetzee, though, she makes a compelling argument regarding the assumed – or, as she points out, strategically employed – demarcation between local and global readerships. Brouillette notes that as Coetzee's global readership grew, his local readership exerted more pressure on him to conform to their very real political needs, pushing for this globally successful South African writer to convey a clear anti-apartheid message, and, in service of this, to employ a documentary realist style and employ accessible language and structure. Brouillette argues that Coetzee's insistence on two reading publics exerting separate pressures on his work can be understood as 'a defensive commentary on the perceived constraints of South Africa's local cultural climate and the effect of those constraints on Coetzee's career as a whole'.[5] She suggests, too, that while the particular case of South Africa in the context of the anti-apartheid struggle may well have exerted such pressures on writers, it is not necessarily productive to 'give too much weight to any tendency to unduly polarize the local literary market and the global cultural sphere often constructed as situating the world's localities'.[6] Nevertheless, I suggest it remains important to analyse instances of reading in postcolonial literary texts by placing them in their local literary marketplaces in order to make some observations about the functions and value of reading and of literature in literary national or place-based marketplaces that operate outside or in a marginal relationship with mainstream publishing, global markets or the neoliberal economy. Brouillette has continued to explore postcolonial writing and global markets in her recent work, *Literature and the Creative Economy* (2014), which considers the creative economy as a whole, and the ways in which authors are expected to operate within national and global structures, paying particular attention to the British context under New Labour (1997–2010).

In *Literature and the Creative Economy*, Brouillette analyses New Labour's position, which they gleaned from their think tank, that 'it was only through culture that "a viable capitalist social order" would manage to "organize and sustain itself"' and considers New Labour's employment of this claim in order to 'monitor and foster the economic value of culture and the arts' to the extent that 'public and cultural diplomacy policies at times blurred into one another, as it trumpeted the use of culture, including literature, in nation-branding strategies that would encourage investment in the UK and sell British foreign policy decisions'.[7] Brouillette questions received knowledge about the work of the artist, and she observes that contrary to the popular depiction of the artist as free to work uninhibited by market or other restraints, their work is subject to the same restrictions as other workers in the capitalist economy:

> both artists and nonartists routinely face contradictory imperatives: critical of the institutions that employ them but devoted to the work they do within them; enjoined to make work an expression of who they really are but in circumstances that leave them with little time for thought about what that might mean and that ask us to package that expression into a readily tradable form.[8]

In her 2000 study *Bearing Witness*, Wendy Griswold uncovered the effect of this Western myth of Authorship for Nigerian writers who repeatedly indicate that they do not consider themselves to be 'writers' because writing cannot sustain them financially and is an activity that they must undertake alongside other, more lucrative, occupations.[9]

An example of important work exploring local readerships is a recent journal article by Ranka Primorac. In 'Reasons for Reading in Postcolonial Zambia' (2012), Primorac analyses the reading practices of book buyers in a Zambian bookshop, with the aim of outlining a conceptual framework within which a 'local literary-historical narrative'[10] can be perceived as operating alongside global literary networks interacting with Zambia through, for example, the African Writers Series. Her aim in the article is to locate a set of Zambian literary practices, considering reading, writing and bookselling, in a context that is often overshadowed by the more prominent South African and Zimbabwean literary cultures. It is inspired by her work with Zambian writers who she observed operated 'within a local node of [...] literary modernity that was separate and different from the globally sanctioned system' and that literary value is perceived in '*local*' ways, rather than based on 'global consecration conferred by a prestigious transnational publishing house such as Penguin'.[11] Interestingly, Primorac's project is presented as having been instigated, to an extent, by reading about a Lusaka bookshop in a literary text, Nadine Gordimer's *A Guest of Honour* (1970). Having read about a bookshop stocking only bestsellers and British popular fiction in Gordimer's novel, Primorac visited a Lusaka bookshop to survey the customers and analyse their reading habits and their reasons for reading. This fascinating example of an empirical study of reading practices uncovers a local literary marketplace. Primorac's approach is to focus on contemporary readers and their declared reasons for reading, and she argues forcefully that the work done by scholars of word literary systems, Franco Moretti, Pascale Casanova and others, has not paid sufficient attention to local literary marketplaces: a 'comparative study of [...] local systems is something that neither Moretti nor Casanova explicitly insist upon; they therefore remain spectral, only partly visible and understood'.[12] My work makes a contribution to a project to bring the local literary marketplaces to attention, focusing on Nigeria (as demonstrated briefly in this chapter), Cuba, South Asia and Black British writing.

Pascale Casanova's *The World Republic of Letters* (2004 English translation) draws attention to the ways in which the global literary canon is constructed, assuming that creativity exists separately from economic forces and as though it inhabits 'the best of all possible worlds where universality reigns through liberty and equality'.[13] Casanova's work explores the mechanisms by which national literatures are described and permitted into a global literary system. Casanova's work is important and ground breaking and, like many other recent works exploring the global networks and processes governing the literature that is published, read and written, offers significant insight into what operates beyond the book (to borrow a phrase from the important study of reading communities undertaken by Danielle Fuller and DeNel Rehberg Sedo[14]).

Readers and reading in postcolonial literature

My ongoing research project asks: why do so many novels and short stories by postcolonial writers include moments where characters encounter books? What meanings are associated with the acts of buying a book, reading a book or rejecting a book in those texts? My research suggests that we can access some of these meanings by contextualizing the postcolonial literary text within local, as opposed to global, literary marketplaces. Moments where characters encounter books in postcolonial literary texts are multiple and varied, as are the local literary marketplaces that I explore as contexts for these moments. I argue that the most productive way to interpret the functions performed by instances of reading in literary texts is to engage with the local literary marketplaces and reading contexts that are relevant to those texts: black consciousness bookshops, second-hand book markets, kerbside booksellers, private libraries. Important work has been done recently on global literary marketplaces, but their analogues are in the local literary marketplaces that perform such significant functions in the everyday lives of readers and communities in postcolonial locations. The prevalence, variety and significance of moments of reading in postcolonial literary texts uncovers the fundamental importance of literature to the postcolonial imaginary, to neocolonial intervention, to understanding the local and the global in each location, to identity and to wider society. This project has, so far, been supported by a number of funded undergraduate research assistants, each working on collating instances of reading, and one undertaking interviews with booksellers in Lagos, Nigeria. One of these researchers is Conna Ray, who discusses, in the section below, her findings on the functions of reading in novels by Caryl Phillips.

Interlude: Unfinished reading in the work of Caryl Phillips
Conna Ray

Caryl Phillips has been described by Maya Jaggi as a 'chronicler of displacement and precarious belonging'.[15] The multi-layered narratives, shifting perspectives and non-linear chronology of his novels depict characters who are troubled by 'the effort of trying to face (at least) two ways at once'.[16] In these ways, Phillips's work engages with the notion of the 'black Atlantic', the idea of a diasporic space of intercultural exchange and transformation that exists between 'Europe, America, Africa, and the Caribbean' since colonial times.[17] According to Paul Gilroy, this space is 'continually crisscrossed by the movements of black people', resulting in a 'political exchange and transformation' that destabilizes 'nationality, location, identity, and historical memory'.[18] Phillips's texts represent this idea through the depiction of individuals who forge links across this space, moving across the black Atlantic through migration, letter writing, storytelling and acts of remembering.

Phillips's work is also preoccupied with literature and ways in which literature can be of value to individuals. Phillips stated that during his childhood in Britain, his mother 'instilled in [him] the notion that [he] had to achieve, that the only way forward England had to offer was education'.[19] It is perhaps unsurprising, then, that books recur in Phillips's work. An example of this respect for the educational powers of literature is Cambridge, an educated slave in Phillips's novel of the same name, who learns to read in order to become 'civilized'.[20] In *Higher Ground,* the protagonist Rudi Williams spends his time in solitary confinement in an American prison reading. He states 'Just as I tone, trim and develop the muscles of my body, I need to do the same with my mind'.[21] Rudi writes letters to his family, urging them to read in order to develop their minds and educate themselves in the history of slavery and the oppression of black peoples. Amongst the authors Rudi encourages his family to read are Mao, Marx and Lenin, Frantz Fanon and W. E. B. Du Bois, Richard Wright and Nelson Mandela.[22] Rudi describes reading as his only form of comfort and salvation whilst he is in prison. In fact, Rudi sees reading as so integral that he calls it 'the arena of combat'[23] for black people in the fight against oppression. In this example, reading is portrayed as vital and necessary for resistance in a postcolonial world.

Texts are also shown to serve a practical function. For example, in *A Distant Shore,* when he first arrives in Britain from Africa, Gabriel sells magazines on the streets of London in order to make enough money to survive.[24] In *A State of Independence*, Bertram watches children walking home from school, 'their books balanced neatly on their heads to protect them from the sun'.[25] Here, texts physically and practically protect individuals from the elements and starvation. Practical salvation of this kind is implied throughout Phillips's texts, through the trope of likening literature and reading to food. For example, in *Higher Ground,* Irene's enjoyment of reading is described as a 'hunger for words'.[26] In *Cambridge*, it is said that the 'staple diet' of the colonies is 'unappetizing English novels'.[27] Leila in *The Final Passage* describes the room in which her and her mother 'cooked, ate, talked and read'.[28] This conflation of literature with vital human needs emphasizes the importance of reading in the novels.

However, the respect for literature constructed throughout the texts is continually undermined in subtle yet important ways. For example, Bertram, the protagonist of *A State of Independence,* wins a scholarship to England to study because he is educated and well-read as a young adult. His scholarship is looked upon as his ticket to a better life, yet he returns to the island of his birth twenty years later with nothing to show for his time away but alienation. Similarly, in *Higher Ground*, Rudi upholds literature as a powerful mode of change. However, 'excessive reading' actually causes Rudi's eyesight to deteriorate, leaving him physically weak and almost blind.[29] In both cases the potential for good to come from literature is not realized. This conflicting relationship to literature is alluded to within *Higher Ground* when Rudi says 'the European raped, pillaged and exploited our people with two instruments; the Bible and the gun'.[30]

This ambivalent relationship with reading is also seen in Phillips's novels through the recurrent image of an unopened or unfinished text. In *The Final Passage*, Leila reads to her mother every night. However, the night before her wedding day Leila notes: 'in front of her mother an uneasy pile of books rested on a small circular table. The present book lay on top, face down, leaves spread wide like a square butterfly come to rest'.[31] This image of a book poised halfway through reading represents not only the story of Leila herself as she prepares to leave the Caribbean for England, but also stands as a symbol for the unfinished story of the whole of the African diaspora. This image is one which resonates throughout Phillips's texts. As Phillips has stated, 'the narrative [of diaspora] didn't begin in Leeds or Brixton,[32] but in a more complex space that, to cite Paul Gilroy again, can be termed the 'black Atlantic'.[33] By portraying texts and reading in this way, Phillips emphasizes that the narrative of the black Atlantic is not an uncomplicated one with a clearly defined structure and plot, but is instead a multi-layered and complex entity which remains 'uneasy' and unfinished.

The local literary marketplace: Readers and Nigerian writing

My longer research project considers the functions of reading in literary texts from four separate locations: Cuba, South Asia, Nigeria and in Black British writing. My findings thus far indicate that the texts read and the reasons for reading those texts differ between these locations. In Cuban literature there is a preponderance of reading spaces: second-hand book markets, private bookshelves and libraries, public and university libraries, poetry readings and writing workshops. South Asian literature records instances of literature associated with esteem, while in Black British writing there is pressure on the reader to read something that is valuable, that will enable the individual's journey towards consciousness. In *Fix-Up* by Kwame Kwei-Armah, it is more important that the local community engages with black consciousness material than it is that the bookshop survives, and in *Romance* by Joan Riley, reading white romance novels is considered self-destructive. Locating a conscious black identity through reading, as Conna Ray suggested in the interlude above in relation to Caryl Phillips's work, is repeatedly reinforced by examples from black British writing.

In Nigeria, there is a more pronounced emphasis on education, both in the popular literature published and in reported findings from previous research on readerships. In her 2000 book, *Bearing Witness: Readers, Writers, and the Novel in Nigeria*, Wendy Griswold discussed what, and why, Nigerian readers read. The readers she interviewed routinely cite similar reasons for reading: 'for information – to see how people live and cope with their problems;' 'for knowledge and entertainment, "to know what's going on in the world;"' to find out 'about useful things;' and one of Griswold's readers notes that this is symptomatic of the way reading is presented to children: 'parents and teachers promote reading strictly as a tool for study and achievement'.[34]

In Nigerian literature, instances of reading almost always have something to do with education, which is invariably education of an independent kind, and which is found in numerous forms: from young men undertaking reading while at university, as in classic Nigerian novels by Chinua Achebe, journalists and political candidates reading to instruct their work and improve their careers as found in Cyprian Ekwesi's novels, to instances of reading self-help or teach-yourself guides in more contemporary novels and short stories including the story 'Bridge' by Jide Adebayo-Begun. This is supported by Wendy Griswold's work with Nigerian readers in *Bearing Witness*; her findings suggested that reading for pure pleasure or escapism was not recognized by any of the readers she interviewed and that instead, all readers identified self-improvement, often directly related to a perceived direct link with improved social, employment and financial circumstances, as their reason for reading (to borrow Ranka Primorac's 'reasons for reading' phrase). The Onitsha book market literature, too, had a strong educational function – in this case, the intention was the promotion of moral education, as is apparent from the titles of the popular texts, including *African bachelor's guide and lady's guide, The (to be read before marriage and after it); Bribery and* corruption: (bane of our society); *How to write and reply letters for marriage, engagement letters, love letters, and how to know a girl to marry*; and *Mabel the sweet honey that poured away*, which laments a young woman's loss of virginity before marriage.[35] The Onitsha book market was the sole selling outlet for high numbers of small and large publishing houses in the 1950s and 1960s, while today in Lagos the hundreds of city bookshops are joined by street hawkers selling books at roadsides, as fictionalized by Jide Adebayo-Begun in the Caine Prize finalist short story 'Bridge', where a woman buys an American self-help book in traffic on the vast Third Mainland Bridge on her way home from work, alongside plantain chips, meat and mobile phone credit. The motivation for self-improvement pervades the story and all familial relations it depicts: the protagonist is undertaking this hostile and uncomfortable commute in his aunt's car as a necessity in his effort to improve his socio-economic status; he is travelling to the home of his aunt who he last saw as a toddler and the encounter is painful because it is predicated only on the compulsion to advance.

Wendy Griswold notes that every Nigerian schoolchild reads the novel *Eze Goes to School* by Onuora Nzekwu (1963). The story follows Eze overcoming various obstacles and eventually gaining a scholarship for secondary education, upholding the value of formal education over ties to his community and its traditions, and the plot depends upon both good and bad luck culminating in, as Wendy Griswold explains, 'a parable showing how the mastery of books can change a child's destiny'.[36] The mass readership of this novel conveying the message that reading will enable social mobility, a readership extended through a televised series based on the book in 2012–13,[37] helps to explain why reading is so closely connected with education, self-improvement and employment opportunities for Nigerian readers.

The instance of reading in Adebayo-Begun's 'Bridge' (2009) engages with the theme of independent education for self-improvement. However, in Chimamanda Ngozi Adichie's collection of short stories, *The Thing Around Your Neck* (2009), though reading for education is a recurrent theme, it is a peripheral one: in 'On Monday of Last Week' books to educate residents of a Philadelphia suburb about Ethiopian Jews are donated to a Jewish temple, and children take part in a read-a-thon. In 'The Shivering', student Ukamaka's bookshelves are the focus of attention rather than her books, as her house guest Chinedu mentions pictures and shoes on those bookshelves, leans against them, stands by them, but any books that we might expect a student to use are never mentioned. By contrast his flat is full of books that do not belong to him – education is taken for granted as a context for their relationship as they live in student halls, but Ukamaka finds out that Chinedu is staying in a friend's room and posing as a student as a result of the lack of opportunity he has encountered as a result of his migration from Nigeria to the United States. 'The Headstrong Historian' is a response to Chinua Achebe's *Things Fall Apart*, frequently acknowledged as the classic postcolonial novel. Adichie's story is concerned with later female generations of Obierika's community, and it repositions 'The Pacification of the Primitive Tribes of Southern Nigeria', the text referred to by the colonial administrator at the end of Achebe's novel, as an unrealistic chapter in a school textbook, unsettling its position as the final statement on that community. As a result of her teacher's attempt to present the chapter as valid, schoolgirl Grace undertakes a lifelong project to correct the false assumptions about her community expounded in colonial writings and eventually rewrites the essay as a book, *Pacifying with Bullets: A Reclaimed History of Southern Nigeria*. This instance of reading and rewriting is typical of the postcolonial project to reclaim lost histories, but perhaps the most compelling story about reading, 'Jumping Monkey Hill', enables a more active context for resistance through the medium of collective writing and collaborative reading.

'Jumping Monkey Hill' focuses on the notion of an 'African' literary marketplace, in the European publisher's perception of the form and function of African writing. Ujunwa is one of eight African writers who are brought together as short story competition finalists for a residential workshop held in a tourist resort in Cape Town. Edward is an editor for the fictional literary journal *Oratory*, the name of which both implies privilege in its similarity to The Oratory boys' boarding schools in Reading, England, and is an ironic reference to Edward's 'art' in public speaking, or, making pronouncements in public contexts which ring false with his listeners. The writing workshop in 'Jumping Monkey Hill' is reminiscent of the Caine Prize for African Writing which is generally held to be a very positive and enabling variety of a literary prize, as it involves a workshop and a published collection of short stories for all shortlisted writers, and thus promotes the careers of numerous writers, while most literary prizes focus on one winner. Though the story refers to the fictional Lipton African Writers Prize, funded by the equally fictional Chamberlain Arts Foundation, the published writers, as well as the African Writers' Series, discussed by the workshop participants when they first meet, are real. They debate over the merits of Achebe's writing, express fury at the suggestion that they should be thankful to Conrad, and share the same impression of writers Alan Paton, a South African anti-apartheid writer who they agree was 'patronizing', the 'astonishing' Zimbabwean poet and novelist Dambudzo Marechera who died at the age of thirty-five, and 'unforgivable' Isak Dinesen, the pen-name for Danish writer Karen Blixen whose *Out of Africa* is a romance of white colonial life in Kenya. The literary landscape they discuss demonstrates their sensitivity to the perception of writing about Africa in the global literary marketplace, and to the expectations that precede their entry into such a marketplace.

In 'Jumping Monkey Hill', the process of collaborative reading and writing enacts a resistant response to this global literary marketplace, with partial success for the African writers whose stories are described. The eight workshop participants are introduced according to their nationality, and these labels (for instance, 'the Ugandan man', 'the Zimbabwean woman') are maintained as the only naming devices throughout the story for all apart from the protagonist Ujunwa, and the workshop organizers, white British Edward and his wife Isabel. The national identities serve to both counteract Edward's notion of an 'African' literature to which all their separate writings must adhere, and to recall the colonial project that constructed the territories that they are now required to represent. The workshop involves each participant reading their work to the group for critique, with workshop leader Edward's criticism carrying the most weight as he is 'connected and could find them a London agent'.[38] This warning prevents Ujunwa from challenging Edward when he insults her with a vulgar sexual remark (suggesting she should 'lie down for' him when she offers him her chair in the shade). Unable to resist the subordinate position that Edward's comment creates for her on her own, it is the process of collective writing and reading that enables Ujunwa to react. Edward responds to each story with an attempt to flatten meaning and expression so that it suits his impression of 'Africa' as conveyed by global mass media: the Zimbabwean's story is considered 'passé' and insignificant because it does not address 'all the other things happening in Zimbabwe under the horrible Mugabe;'[39] the Senegalese writer's story is rejected because 'homosexual stories of this sort weren't reflective of Africa;'[40] and Ujunwa's own story about pressure exerted on women to undertake a form of sexual service in order to maintain a 'professional' career is described as 'implausible', as 'agenda writing', even though it is a recollection of Ujunwa's experience immediately before arriving at the writing workshop.[41] Only the passive and complicit Tanzanian's story about a militiaman is commended by Edward because it conforms to his expectations of an Africa that Europe could recognize, because it was violent and 'brought news', and thus could be misread as ethnographic data to fill in gaps in news stories covering similar topics. Ujunwa's response differed entirely – for her, 'it read like piece from *The Economist* with cartoon characters painted in'.[42] Finally able to discuss both her experience of Edward's lechery and his responses to the writing with the other participants, Ujunwa asks, 'why do we always say nothing?', rejects the black South African's defence of harmless old Edward as the sort of response that enabled apartheid, and walks out of the workshop after rejecting Edward's analysis of her story.[43] Ujunwa's minor victory is her maintenance of authority over her own story while she exposes Edward's false representation of African literature – as well as the implication that a neocolonial agenda is his reason for maintaining that false representation. This victory is undercut by the question left open at the narrative closure: 'she wondered whether this ending, in a story, would be considered plausible'.[44] Leaving the workshop means that Ujunwa's story, or a version of it, will remain peripheral to the machine of African Literature that Edward's publishing world keeps in motion. Yet the acts of collective reading and writing enable resistance because they precipitate Ujunwa's response to Edward as well as her separate rejection of a startled Isabel: Isabel attempts to legitimize her presence in Africa by insistent claims to support animal rights, and by praising Ujunwa's beauty as denoting her 'royal' Nigerian lineage. Ujunwa's acquiescence to this designation at the beginning of the narrative, though playful (she lies that her royal ancestors captured and kept oiled in a cage a seventeenth-century Portuguese trader) signals her inability to challenge Isabel's secure perceptions about Africa and Africans, her inability to voice her question over whether 'Isabel ever needed royal blood to explain the good looks of friends back in London'.[45] At the end of the text, Ujunwa again tells a playful lie when she pretends that her fake ivory is real, but in this instance the objective is to derail Isabel's impression of Africa, Africans and her place there. Collective reading enables a new confidence among the other writers too, who, immediately before Edward's critique, openly praise Ujunwa's story as 'strong', 'believable', 'realistic', and suggest that it captures a recognizable Lagos and familiar women's experiences.[46]

The story both promotes local literature from all African countries and regions, and calls into question the notion of an 'African' literature, and consequently shows that to read and to write is essential in the process of resistance to the effects of colonialism that linger in the present, both in the representation of Africa outside its local control and in the interactions between people who have supposedly become reconciled to former brutal inequalities. It is also an invitation to the reader to seek encounters with literature from African writers operating outside mainstream publishing. Graham Huggan observes that the practice of flattening out cultural difference into recognizably marketable packages as portrayed in the story by Edward's publishing power is a process that has been in action for some decades. He explores the Heinemann African Writers Series as a keen example. Editors demonstrate what Huggan calls 'symptoms of a controlling imperial gaze'[47] leading to a series of books that claimed to be a representation of contemporary African writing but in fact reflected Euro-American preconceptions in terms of content and packaging, with book covers deliberately designed to appear primitive and 'authentic', and the texts themselves highly manipulated in terms of selection and editors' interventions.[48] Huggan notes, though, that a sizeable African reading public bought the African Writers Series books, a factor further complicating the literary marketplace in Africa.

In terms of the resources and distribution of literature, Huggan suggests that 'a workable structure for publishing in Africa [...] can still hardly be said to exist'.[49] Although this may be true in terms of Huggan's argument about the ways in which global readers can access African writing, this implies a necessarily cosmopolitan readership of the kind that Huggan critiques in his work. I argue that perceived limitations of African publishing structures in comparison with Euro-American ones should really not be considered as such, especially when considering the mass market for Onitsha literature in Nigeria, in a country of 178.6 million in population. Repeatedly, African writers insist that they do not require the patronage or attention of a Euro-American global publisher who does not represent their target audience.[50] Instead, it is necessary to consider texts within local literary marketplaces and their specific modes of operation. A reliance on analysis based on international publishing and reception inevitably divorces the texts from their local marketplaces; the value and function of literature can be best approached through re-placing the literary text into the operations of local contexts of reading, bookselling and book production. Adichie's 'Jumping Monkey Hill' neither conveys the writer's complicity in writing for a global reader's exotic taste nor a strategic exoticism in response to it, but instead portrays the distinction between a singular global and the multiple local literary marketplaces, as well as the pressure exerted on the individual writer to accommodate these market forces.

Conclusion: The local postcolonial literary marketplace and postcolonial studies

Homi Bhabha's discussion of the English book in his essay 'Signs Taken for Wonders' provokes questions about the relevance and meaning of English literature and of literature 'out of place' in postcolonial writing, and of the potential for undermining colonial power by strategic reading and misreading. The postcolonial writer might, as Bhabha has claimed with reference to the ambivalent status of English books uncovered by colonial writers, employ instances of reading in literary texts to undermine colonialism and to interrogate the assumed cultural value of colonial literature in postcolonial contexts. However, instances of reading are multiple and complex in postcolonial literature. While Bhabha's proposition offers one potential way to interpret the prevalence and the significance of these moments, questions remain about the many functions of instances of reading in postcolonial literature.

For Marlow, the English book sustains English cultural authority,[51] but Bhabha notes the accompanying ambivalence that the text produces: 'it is in-between the edict of Englishness and the assault of the dark unruly spaces of the earth, through an act of repetition, that the colonial text emerges uncertainly'.[52] The text is, ultimately, 'a sign of difference',[53] the text discovered in the wilderness itself only meaningful because of its displacement from its more usual housing in the English library.

Because it occurs out of place, the moment of encountering a book – which, in Bhabha's analysis is an English text in colonial-period writing – is a moment that 'disturbs the visibility of the colonial power and makes the recognition of its authority problematic'.[54] We might expect this pattern of questioning colonial authority due to the hybrid nature of colonial contact to be repeated in later postcolonial texts where canonical European literary texts are read or otherwise encountered. Indeed, there are examples where this, to an extent, plausibly accounts for the act of reading in the text. However, the undoing of colonial authority is only one of a multitude of functions performed by the instance of reading in postcolonial literature. The very multiplicity and variety of instances of reading within postcolonial literature – the fact that such instances are not concentrated in specific locations, periods, literary forms, genres or narrative themes – invites a materialist approach as fundamentally necessary to any developed understanding of why such instances appear so frequently, and how their functions might differ according to their relationships with literary marketplaces.

Notes

1. Sarah Brouillette and David Finkelstein, 'Postcolonial Print Cultures', *The Journal of Commonwealth Literature* 48, no. 1 (2013): 3–7, 3.
2. My monograph *Postcolonial Literature and the Local Literary Marketplace: Locating the Reader* is contracted for publication with Palgrave Macmillan in 2019.
3. Ahmad 1992, cited in Graham Huggan, *The Postcolonial Exotic: Marketing the Margins* (London: Routledge, 2001), 10.
4. Brouillette, *Postcolonial Writers in the Global Literary*, 24.
5. Brouillette, *Postcolonial Writers*, 124.
6. Ibid., 118.
7. Sarah Brouillette, *Literature and the Creative Economy* (Stanford: Stanford University Press, 2014), 4.
8. Brouillette, *Creative Economy*, 207.
9. Wendy Griswold, *Bearing Witness: Readers, Writers, and the Novel in Nigeria* (Princeton: Princeton University Press, 2000).
10. Ranka Primorac. 'Reasons for Reading in Postcolonial Zambia', *Journal of Postcolonial Writing* 48, no. 5 (2012): 497–511, 498.
11. Primorac, 'Reasons for Reading in Postcolonial Zambia', 502.
12. Ibid., 508.
13. Pascale Casanova, *The World Republic of Letters* (Cambridge: Harvard University Press, 2007), 12.
14. Reading Beyond the Book was a large AHRC project. Resulting publications include a book of the same title (Routledge, 2013).
15. Maya Jaggi, 'Rites of Passage', *The Guardian* (2001) http://www.theguardian.com/books/2001/nov/03/fiction.artsandhumanities (accessed 26 October 2015) (para. 4 of 47).
16. Paul Gilroy, *The Black Atlantic: Modernity and Double Consciousness* (London: Verso, 1993), 3.
17. Gilroy, *The Black Atlantic*, 4.
18. Ibid., 16.
19. Jaggi, 'Rites of Passage' (para. 13 of 47).
20. Caryl Phillips, *Cambridge* (London: Vintage, 2008), 143.
21. Caryl Phillips, *Higher Ground* (London: Vintage, 2006), 67–68.

22 Phillips, *Higher Ground*, 68.
23 Ibid., 82.
24 Caryl Phillips, *A Distant Shore* (London: Vintage, 2004), 172.
25 Caryl Phillips, *A State of Independence* (London: Faber and Faber, 1999), 20.
26 Phillips, *Higher Ground*, 177.
27 Phillips, *Cambridge*, 46, 47.
28 Caryl Phillips, *The Final Passage* (London: Vintage, 2004), p. 31.
29 Phillips, *Higher Ground*, 133.
30 Ibid., 76.
31 Phillips, *The Final Passage*, 31.
32 Jaggi, 'Rites of Passage' (para. 25 of 47).
33 Gilroy, *The Black Atlantic*.
34 Griswold, *Bearing Witness*, 89–92.
35 A digital archive project lists many titles of Onitsha Market literature, as well as offering contextual information and some digitized texts. Accessible via http://onitsha.diglib.ku.edu/index.htm (accessed 20 November 2015).
36 Ibid. 88. The novel is still taught in most primary schools.
37 'Eze Goes to School', 2012–13. Available via http://www.naijastories.com/tag/eze-goes-to-school/ (accessed 20 November 2015).
38 Chimamanda Ngozi Adichie, 'Jumping Monkey Hill', *The Thing Around Your Neck* (London: Fourth Estate, 2009), 95–114, 113.
39 Adichie, 'Jumping Monkey Hill', 107.
40 Ibid., 108.
41 Ibid., 114.
42 Ibid., 109.
43 Ibid., 112, 114.
44 Ibid., 114.
45 Ibid., 99.
46 Ibid., 113.
47 Huggan, *The Postcolonial Exotic*, 52.
48 Ibid., 52, 53
49 Ibid., 36.
50 Primorac, 'Reasons for Reading in Postcolonial Zambia', 502. Zambian novelist Malama Katulwende differentiates good writing from writing published by Penguin, in other contexts an automatic marker of literary 'quality'.
51 Homi Bhabha, *The Location of Culture* (London: Routledge, 1994), 150.
52 Bhabha, *The Location of Culture*, 153.
53 Ibid., 154.
54 Ibid., 159.

6

Disaster, Governance and (Post)colonial Literatures

Upamanyu Pablo Mukherjee

Much of the critical debate about and within the field of postcolonial studies has been, famously, about periodization implied by that 'post'. If it proposes a radical break from the historical era of modern Euro-American colonialism, does it not help to obscure the various political, economic and cultural *structures and processes* that are common to the periods before and after the moments of formal decolonization? On the other hand, in emphasizing the continuities between these eras, do we not run the risk of obscuring some of the very real differences between them – particularly regarding the political, economic and cultural *agency* gained by some sections of the formerly colonized peoples? But as numerous scholars such as Neil Lazarus, Benita Parry, Aijaz Ahmad and Fredric Jameson have long argued, these debates about the prefix may be misconceived to the extent that they do not really take into account the signal feature of the colonial and postcolonial eras – the four-century-long uneven and combined globalization of capitalism that knit the world together in a single but differentiated system.[1] That is, once we properly understand the colonial/postcolonial question as a part of a larger enquiry about what Jameson calls 'a singular modernity', we should be able to see continuity and breakage not as irreconcilable or baffling paradoxes of postcolonial theory but the logically necessary component of a dialectically related structure.[2]

In what follows, I will try to show that the colonial-postcolonial dialectic becomes even clearer not only when we admit to the vision of a capitalist *longue duree*, but also to, in the words of Jason Moore, of capitalism itself as a world-ecological system.³ If all historical processes are by definition eco-geographical, then we will of course need to integrate the 'environment' in any analyses of colonialism and its aftermaths. Our question as literary and cultural critics is how we do so – how do texts register and represent the historical environment of capitalism and (post) colonialism as form and content? As will be evident from my discussion below, part of the answer will perforce rely on a comparative method that probes the grounds of similarity and incommensurability between colonial and postcolonial literature without ever disavowing their relationality.

At first sight it seems wilfully perverse to compare two vastly different writers such as Rudyard Kipling, considered to be the pre-eminent bard of British empire, and Mahasweta Devi, one of the most powerful anti-imperial and anti-capitalist voices of our times. Yet in so doing, my aim here is not to propose some ideological equivalence between them. Rather, I argue that despite being separated by time, events and commitments, both the writers respond to some common problems – the disastrous 'world-ecological' conditions of colonialism and imperialism; the related problems of governance and sovereignty; and the search for adequate literary registration of these. Indeed, locating Kipling and Devi together within the same interpretative horizon allows us to discern and distinguish the lines of continuity and discontinuity between colonialism/imperialism and their 'post' conditions – particularly in relation to their literary, cultural and economic dimensions.

One cluster of events that allow us to trace these connections and ruptures in modern South Asian life is that relating to food scarcity usually bundled into term 'famine'. The Victorian debates and practices about famines showcased some fundamental ideas about modern governance. One was that states should not respond with any welfare measures to ease the distress of the famine-struck population since this would be an *unnatural* interference against the *natural* laws of the market. Faced with the demands of relief in the famine that struck the provinces of Bengal and Orissa in 1865, R. B. Chapman of the Indian Board of Revenue wrote:

> To mitigate this evil, the Board of Revenue have already arranged for the early and regular publication of the retail prices current in each district. This will ensure such remedy being applied to the case of each place as the ordinary laws of political economy can supply. The Board presumes that it is

quite unnecessary for them to discuss any suggestions or projects that are not entirely in accordance with those laws.⁴

Again, while giving evidence to the Indian Famine Commission in 1898, J. E. O'Connor, the Director General of the statistics department of the government of India, declared that official intervention in the grain market during the time of famine was a 'most colossal error' since by its very size and nature governments were incapable of limited and rational action.⁵ Between Chapman's note in 1865 and O'Connor's declaration in 1898, an estimated 11 million Indians starved to death – collateral damage of the policy of imperial rulers.⁶

A second Victorian idea was that by refining and improving its bureaucratic, managerial and technological capacities, the state would be able to bring effective relief to (some of) its famine-struck subjects. In a dispatch to the government of India in 1867 the British Secretary of State Stafford Northcote began by enumerating the factors that made ruling the country difficult – a tropical monsoonal climate, imperfect means of communication and an ignorant population – but identified the faulty command structure of the imperial government as *the* major culprit for famines.⁷ For the Victorians, one way of correcting this administrative glitch was to harness the powers of new technology such as railways.⁸

A third key element in the Victorian governmentality in South Asia was the idea of 'tropical backwardness' where indigenous historical and the climactic systems were seen as the agents of disaster. This understanding of 'tropicality' produced what might be called a realist strand of governance – since disaster cannot be avoided, energy should be directed towards limiting *some* its effects for *some* of the subjects. As Charles Blair put it – 'India has been, and still is, in a chronic state of famine, and ever will continue so. The nature of her climate and soil cannot be altered, but the disadvantages attached thereto can fortunately be mitigated.'⁹ And if climate was one component in the construction of this disastrous 'tropicality', history was another. C. E. R. Girdlestone imagined medieval Indian kings like Muhammad bin Tughlaq ordering his troops to chase and hunt down those famine-struck peasants who could not pay their taxes.¹⁰ The *Westminster Review* compared the Indian rulers of the nominally independent princely states to an 'animal [...] now fortunately as extinct in Western Europe as the comparatively innocent cave hyeana'.¹¹ No better than these obsolescent Indian rulers were the abject Indians, paradigmatic amongst whom were the Indian aboriginal tribes who attracted the hostility of both British bureaucracy and indigenous non-tribal populations:

> The efforts of Government to teach these people the elements of civilization have generally failed though their grosser habits of human sacrifice, and the like, have been suppressed [...] They are thriftless, improvident and careless of the future; they accumulate no wealth, and are possessed of no reserve of resources [...] They then wander in the forests and live on what they can pick up there, without the usual addition of a small portion of some cereal.[12]

Much of this kind of 'governmentality' has become common sense in today's postcolonial statecraft, theories of international development as well as in social relationships.

But we would do well remember that Victorian ideas and practices regarding famine disasters were not homogenous. Indeed, assumptions about 'backward' tropical empires were regularly challenged in British non-administrative accounts. Investigative journalists often employed the full range of melodramatic or gothic tropes in order to drive home their central argument – that what appeared to be the 'natural' disasters of famine was in reality produced by the political and economic imperatives of imperialism. In William Digby's sensational *expose* of the famine relief campaign in southern India in 1876–8 what scandalized his readers was the scrupulous attention he paid to the decaying bodies of the dying Indians – people following rice carts to nibble at the grain that fell from it; a family starving to death in sight of thousands of bags of grain that had been hoarded and priced beyond their reach; dogs fighting over the bloated corpse of a young child, and above all, the skeletal spectres of the famished – 'the gluteal muscles are replaced by a fold of loose skin, giving a deformed and repulsive aspect to the figure; the face has the look of a corpse, and the voice and strength are almost gone'.[13] By 1901, Digby could pronounce without hesitation – 'We are in India to make money, and all shadow of pretence at even making money honestly, was cast aside'.[14] It is this economic force that Digby saw as not only being the cause of the entrenchment of a permanent disaster environment, but also its *normalization*:

> So much has the fact of famine having come to stay grown into the warp and woof of our ordinary life in Britain, that we hear of tens of millions of our fellow-subjects actually perishing, and [...] we pass by on the other side of the way as if the fact concerned us not at all. Or, we say, 'A Good thing, surely.

There are too many people in India.' This – will it be believed? – is said to me by two out of every four Englishmen to whom I mention the fact of India's gruesome state[15]

For a writer such as Rudyard Kipling such forked debates and practices regarding the disastrous tropics provided productive resource for fiction. The figures of the administrator and journalist were not only to recur as key tropes in his writing but also turned out to be fundamental ideologemes of his world view. In a series of revealing letters to Margaret Burne-Jones, Kipling worked up a powerful vision of the imperial administrator's vocation being those of the scrupulous care and bodily relief of his stricken subjects. In effect, the youthful Kipling imagined British presence in India as a form of palliative imperialism:

> What else are we working in the country for? For what else do the best men of the Commission die from overwork, and disease, if not keep the people alive in the first place and healthy in the second? We spend our best men on the country like water and if ever a foreign country was made better through the 'blood of martyrs' India is that country.[16]

Disease was not the only discourse through which the heroes of Kipling's palliative imperialism were presented. They were also mythologized through a particular investment in expert labour – specifically infrastructural work whose purpose was to defeat the malign forces of tropical environment such as famines and floods. For example, two entries by Kipling in the *Civil and Military Gazette*, dated 2 March and 6 August 1887, offer us the spectacle of British administrator engaged in bridge building and repairing of railway lines damaged by sudden flooding – situations that would later find their way into short stories such as 'The Bridge Builders', 'In Flood Time' and 'The Head of the District'. Kipling's privileging of the imperial administrator as an expert labourer, has of course, been noted by commentators. In Benita Parry's judgement:

> More than any other single author, Kipling articulated the pride which a segment of the British people took in seeing themselves as a nation of law-givers, for it was he who gave a spurious grandeur to their posturing, and endowed the discomfort of the job of the imperial ruler with the glory of suffering and sacrifice.[17]

And in a shrewd essay, Noel Annan long ago pointed out the central role played by British experts – 'technicians, engineers, and public servants' – in the formation of what he calls Kipling's 'new conservatism'.[18]

This fiction of confronting tropical disasters with the nobility of labour elicited pleasure and discomfort in almost equal measures in Kipling's readers. The reviews of his early shorter fiction swung between praise for his realism and his alleged sensationalist excesses. In this respect, the *Edinburgh Review*'s discussion of *Plain Tales from the Hills* can be taken as paradigmatic. On the one hand, the reviewer judged Kipling to be a great innovator who had found a 'fortunate mean' between the increasingly tired schools of the 'scientific realism' of Zola and that of hackneyed imperial romance – 'the dominions of Prester John'.[19] This 'fortunate mean' combined the picturesque, the romantic and 'extreme realism' to produce a new kind of writing:

> He adopts a method of pictorial treatment, of which daring directness, sharpness of outline, and naked reality, are the characteristics [...] His scenes are painted with the minimum of space, and with the maximum of vividness. [...] The gift of telling a short story, which is complete in itself and does not appear to be a fragment of a larger whole, is a rare one, and Mr. Kipling possesses it to a very remarkable degree of perfection.[20]

But this new kind of fiction also comes burdened with a compulsive straying into what is euphemistically called a zone of 'unpleasantness:'

> In his stories of Anglo-Indian society, Mr. Kipling has either had bad luck, or is afflicted with a morbid taste [...] if it is some episode of social life which had better perhaps not be told, or which, if told at all, should be handled with delicacy, Mr. Kipling conspicuously fails. The professional instincts of the paragraphist of a society newspaper seem to overpower the natural instincts of refinement and good breeding.[21]

This tension between form and content of Kipling's fiction, I have been suggesting, is the manifestation of nothing less than a total artistic attempt to register the disastrous environment of Britain's south Asian empire. By looking at his short story 'William the Conqueror' in some details we can see how among other things gender emerged as a predominant category through which such a problem was worked through by Kipling.

The narrative begins with the news of a devastating famine animating the conversation between two imperial administrators – Martyn, the Acting Superintendent of Police of an unnamed district, and Scott, who works in the Irrigation Department. Martyn and Scott are, as all good Kipling heroes, energized by these disastrous events and look forward to implementing some tried and tested robust relief measures of the 'Punjab school'.[22] Into this scene of homosocial bonhomie enters, on horseback, the eponymous William – who turns out to be Martyn's sister. Not only do her name and her riding habits un-gender William, her unmarried status and single-minded devotion to her debt-ridden brother also problematize the heterosexual norms of the Victorian imperial family. What the story sets out to resolve in part then, is how to reintegrate William into the proper matrix of patriarchal desire that ends in marriage and not a quasi-incestuous arrangement. Unsurprisingly, it turns out again that this resolution can only be achieved through the 'outbreak narratives' of disaster, disease and care.

William appears to us for the first time irredeemably marked by the tropics – her forehead scarred by tropical boils because

> her brother was in debt and could not afford the expense of her keep at even a cheap hill-station.[23] (p. 175) We also hear of her other experiences of tropical life – surviving cholera, nearly drowning in a river in spate, typhoid, attack of thieves, administration of rough justice in the form of whipping and caning – in short, the standard accoutrements of an imperial disaster zone. She looks "more like a boy than ever", as she rolls cigarettes with her brother, and declares "I like men who do things".

This mimic masculinity not only valorizes the work of empire but also re-states the problem that lies at the heart of imperial romance – what is the proper degree to which femininity can be allowed to infiltrate the world of homo-social exchanges?

The answer, of course, lies in the nature of the work itself – the provision of care for stricken subjects that demands in equal measure physical hardships and courage as well as affective capacities and emotional energies. It is this kind work, Kipling suggests, that provides the real mating ground for his heroes and heroines, their union finally guaranteeing the continuing legitimacy of the empire. The afflicted subjects move as a swarm through the parched landscape and appear to the heroic triumvirate in nightmare montages:

> They clamoured for rice [...] and, when they found there was none, broke away weeping from the sides of the cart [...] The starving crept away to their bark and weeds, grubs, leaves, and clay, and left the open sacks untouched. But sometimes the women laid their phantoms of children at Scott's feet, looking back as they staggered away.[24]

The famine babies, abandoned by their dying mothers and adopted by the heroic British administrators now become the focal point not only to underscore the general affective care of the imperial state but also specifically of the feminization of Scott, who goes from the billiard-playing and horse-riding macho stereotype to a nurse who improvises the provision and administration of milk to the children:

> When you have to keep connection unbroken between a restless mother of kids and a baby who is at the point of death, you suffer in all your system. But the babies were fed. Morning, noon and evening Scott would solemnly lift them out one by one from their nest of gunny-bags under the cart-tilts [...] and the milk was dropped into their toothless mouths drop by drop, with due pauses when they choked.[25]

This nursing hero, of course, is the symmetrical counterpoint to the horse-riding heroine, in that doing the good work of empire has enabled them to be strategically flexible with Victorian gender stereotypes. And it is after this (strictly temporary) role-reversal that Scott and William prove their credentials as the proper heterosexual couple:

> 'Hai, you little rip,' said Scott, 'how the deuce do you expect to get your rations if you aren't quiet?'
> A cool white hand steadied the brat, who forthwith choked as the milk gurgled into his mouth.
> 'Mornin',' said the milker. 'You've no notion how these little fellows can wriggle.'
> 'Oh, yes, I have.' She whispered, because the world was asleep. 'Only I feed them with a spoon or a rag. Yours are fatter than mine.'[26]

Parental credentials sealed, the final part of the story lovingly details Scott's hard work through which his re-entry into the realm of the boy's-own-heroism (now tempered by the recognition and incorporation of its dialectical opposite – imperial femininity). The end of the famine coincides with that narrative moment in which the romance plot is also resolved. After contracting a bad case of fever and delirium, of which his loyal Indian servant Faiz Ullah cures him, Scott rides back to the camp and to William. This is the imperial tableaux that Kipling's disaster narratives often yearn towards – famine and disease have been thwarted by the actions of the civilian hero and heroine who are nevertheless marked by the sufferings they have endured. The loyal, but marginal, presence of the Indian subject pronounces a valediction on their union that is duly achieved after the imperial couple successfully recovers from their ordeal. If diseases and disasters mark the turbulence and obduracy of Britain's south Asian empire, they also provided the means through which imperialism could be re-written as romance.

Turning from Kipling to Mahasweta, it is difficult not to be immediately overwhelmed by the differences between their respective narrative styles – most dramatically revealed in the latter's use of sharply juxtaposed, multiple points of view and perspectives of the indigenous elites, subalterns and those of a narrative consciousness that spans a geo-historical *longue duree* and decisively historicizes the experience of modernization in postcolonial South Asia.[27] Yet, a second glance reveals with equal promptness the continuities between the two writers – above all in the use of the figures of the journalist and the administrator, the famine environment, governance and gender relations. Of course, Mahasweta uses these elements to craft fiction of a radically different kind to that of Kipling, and to an extent the logic of this difference follows that of those between the colonial and the postcolonial state's response to the disasters of famine.

Comparing famine relief measures between colonial and postcolonial India, Jean Dreze finds in the latter *both* the enshrinement of the recommendations by the landmark Victorian Famine Commission of 1880 *and* welfare steps that radically departed from such instances of colonial governmentality.[28] Of such new measures, Dreze highlights three in particular:

> the real resources allocated to relief have increased, and the range of measures they support has broadened; the Government has resolutely entered the previously sacrosanct domain of food supply management, and ensured a large measure of price stability; [...] the real but weak commitment of the British Administration to the prevention of famines has evolved into a political compulsion to respond.[29]

Others such as B. M. Bhatia have reminded us that if such interventions by the postcolonial state have been successful in staving off large-scale famine outbreaks, they have also often had the paradoxical effect of entrenching chronic food scarcity disproportionately suffered by the marginalized sections of the population, general rise in food prices and an unfavourable balance of trade due to import of essential food grains from abroad.[30] One of the signal achievements of Mahasweta's fiction has been to alert us to the tragic consequences of such structural paradoxes of postcolonial state and society.

'Pterodactyl, Puran Sahay and Pirtha' adapts the imperial tableaux that clinches the valedictory moments of Kipling's 'William the Conqueror' insofar that the imagined union between the administrator/bureaucrat and his subaltern subject (mediated by the romance of the heteronormative union – the marriage plot) is now radically reconfigured by the recognition of the agency of that subject that demands a new kind of love altogether. Puran, a maverick journalist who relishes exposing the devastating inequities of independent India is also a widower who fails to make 'room for a fleshly, hungry, thirsty, human relationship' with Saraswati, despite their mutual love and attraction to each other.[31] Thus rendered 'half-human', he accepts an invitation from Harisharan, an old friend who now works as an administrator in Pirtha, a tribal district in central India. His brief is to investigate an undeclared famine in the district, as well as the rumour of an airborne spirit that is reportedly haunting the area.

Unlike Kipling, Mahasweta does not use the famine environment to offer the consolation of affective governance. Indeed, the postcolonial elite's encounter with the tribal subaltern dramatically demonstrates the impossibility of *any* kind of governance whatsoever. As Shankar, one of Puran's interlocutors says: 'Oh, we had our ancestor's graves! They were ground underfoot to build roads, houses, schools, hospitals. […] you can't do anything for us. We have become unclean as soon as you entered our lives. No more roads, no more relief – what will you give to a people in exchange for the vanished land, home, field, burial-ground?'[32] Since 'development' that disproportionately benefits the ruling classes – roads, houses, schools, hospitals – remain the horizon of postcolonial statecraft it by definition excludes and is in fact compelled to exterminate those whose lives elude its span: 'You don't understand. The government doesn't want that we live. That's why they don't give us any help. The forefathers have been insulted, we could not protect their dignity. Now our life and death are not in our hands'.[33] Pirtha presents Puran with two enigmas that confounds the logic of postcolonial governmentality – first, a population that is dying of scarcity when official statistics and political expediency can admit to no famine; second, a flying 'ancestral spirit' that turns out to be a pre-historic pterodactyl whose presence cannot be explained by science. Puran thinks that his sympathy for their plight makes him the natural ally of the tribals. What he finds is that he does not have any language or cognitive tools to understand what to them is perfectly comprehensible as perpetual hunger and the supernatural.

The brilliance of Mahasweta's narrative tactic lies at least in part in the critically irrealist presentation of the encounter between Puran and the pterodactyl, both of whom seemingly cannot belong to the same world and yet do so:

And, when the rain symphony was at its peak, then into Puran's room came the soul of the ancestor of Shankar's people, half claw scratching, half floating.

[…] From the other side of millions of years the soul of the ancestors of Shankar's people looks at Puran, and the glance is so pre-historic that Puran's brain cells, spreading a hundred antennae, understand nothing of that glance.[34]

As Neil Lazarus puts it, the directness of this depiction allows Mahasweta to represent both the content of subaltern consciousness and 'reconstructed truth that subaltern consciousness only partially represents', that is to say, the truth of the historical experience of (post-) colonial, imperial and capitalist modernity.[35]

This point might be better understood by comparing Mahasweta's fiction to Michael Taussig's investigations into another apparently inexplicable phenomenon in the peripheries of the modern world-system – the devil lores in the tin mines of Bolivian highlands. Taussig asks why the miners – displaced peasants who are compelled to sell their labour to the giant Andean mineral extraction industry – understand those among them who succeed in securing a contract with relatively inflated wage as having made a deal with the devil to the detriment of the collective life of the community.[36] Taussig's fieldwork shows that far from being an instance of primitive superstition, the Bolivian devil lores are in fact perfect symbolic representation of 'a way of life losing its life […] what it means to lose control over the means of production and to be controlled by them'.[37] What is crucial to understand is that this kind of magical thinking is a powerful critical tool that understands historical transition between one mode of production (peasant) and another (industrial capitalist) where radical alienation is the ruling sign over collective structures of feeling. Thus, instead of magic as traditional ritual or superstitious backwardness it would be more accurate to see it as a creative response to a conflict between what Taussig calls use-value and exchange-value orientations.

The similarities between Andean peasants and central Indian tribals are clear enough – both communities find themselves at historical transition points where utter loss of control and agency over labour and modes of production are the predominant features of life; both communities are marginalized by a political dispensation (the postcolonial state) that supervises the mechanics of such a transition; both communities register their historical experience through complex magical thought (devil lores, ancestral spirit). Yet, it is equally instructive to consider the crucial difference that Mahasweta inserts in her representation of tribal sensibilities. The pterodactyl appears *first* as the artwork that registers the tribal's experience of (post-) colonial modernity in the child Bikhia's drawings of the ancestral spirit; *then* it appears as the material strata of that artwork, a pre-historic creature that has inexplicably survived and whose presence throws open for the self-consciously modern subject, Puran, the whole question of understanding the category of history itself.

This concretization of myth or magic does more than perform the dialectical deconstruction of the modern mind of Puran – alive though he acutely is to the perils of modernization itself. It signifies incommensuration and incomprehension as *positive* forces in the potential reforming of the whole fraught issue of (post-) colonial governance. For Kipling, the affective power of imperial governance rested in the final instance on his administrator-heroes' perfect comprehension of the trajectory of modernity itself. Mahasweta proposes that any break with this practice must begin with the surrender of the reactionary elite claim of comprehending the direction of history. For Puran, the 'final word' is that there can be no communication between the pterodactyl and the modern world – despite it being a 'myth and a message' at the same time.[38] The precise counterpart of this incomprehension is echoed in his realization that his world is incommensurable to that of Bikhia and his people, and he can never easily assume his alliance with them on the basis of the accidental sharing of an extraordinary experience.[39]

Mahasweta's symmetrical reversal of imperial sensibility manifest in Kipling's heroes can finally be registered in her treatment of the love theme. In Kipling, the romantic union between William and Scott was blessed by the presence of Scott's loyal Indian servant (the only subaltern who *can* speak) that in turn signalled the sanctification of the imperial social contract. In Mahasweta, the problem that the story started with – Puran's 'half-manhood' – is not resolved in this manner. Rather, a very different kind of love visits him:

> Love, excruciating love, let that be the first step. Now Puran's amazed heart discovers what love for Pirtha there is in his heart, perhaps he cannot remain a distant spectator anywhere in life.
> Pterodacyl's eyes.
> Bikhia's eyes.[40]

If Puran can no longer maintain a spectator's detachment 'anywhere in life' after his visit to the heart of India, perhaps there is hope yet for him and Saraswati. But they can only come together after he surrenders to the excruciating pain of loving fellow subjects of the postcolonial state he cannot represent or control.

What at first appeared to be a perverse comparison between Rudyard Kipling and Mahasweta Devi in fact then enables us to evaluate the cultural logic of South Asia's long and disastrous modernity by foregrounding the subcontinent's historical environment. The integral role played by governmentality and statecraft in both the perpetuation and modest containment of this disastrous environment is acknowledged in the works of both the writers. Spanning the periods of high imperialism and postcolonialism, they nonetheless attest to the continuous challenge posed by the uneven unfolding of capitalist modernization across time and space by finding appropriate literary registers for this process. In so doing, they achieve simultaneously their consecration as great artists and fulfil great art's obligation to the world it inhabits.

Notes

1   See Lazarus, *The Postcolonial Unconscious*; Benita Parry, *Postcolonial Studies: A Materialist Critique* (London: Routledge, 2004); Aijaz Ahmad, 'Postcolonial Theory and the "Post-" Condition', *Socialist Register* 33 (1997): 353–81; Fredric Jameson, 'Third-World Literature in the Era of Multinational Capitalism', *Social Text* 15 (1986): 65–88.
2   Fredric Jameson, *A Singular Modernity: Essay on the Ontology of the Present* (London: Verso, 2013).
3   I use 'world-ecology' following Jason Moore 'Capitalism as World-Ecology: Braudel and Marx on Environmental History', *Organization and Environment* 16, no. 4 (2003): 431–58. He understands the term as signifying ecogeographical processes that dialectically 'permeate the ever-shifting relations of region, state, and world-economy – even the bodies of workers and peasants!', 432.
4   East India (Bengal and Orissa Famine): Papers and Correspondence Relative to the Famine in Bengal and Orissa, Including the Report of the Famine Commission and the Minutes of the Lieutenant Governor of Bengal and Governor General of India. House of Commons Parliamentary Papers (335, 335-I, 335-ii) Ll.1 (1867), 12.
5   Report of the Indian Famine Commission, House of Commons Sessional Papers [C.9178] xxxi (1898), 6.

6   Brahma Nand, ed. *Famines in Colonial India: Some Unofficial Historical Narratives* (New Delhi: Kanishka, 2007), 1, 2; Mike Davis, *Late Victorian Holocausts* (London: Verso, 2001), 7.
7   Bengal and Orissa Famine (1867), 2.
8   See Indian Famine Commission's endorsement of railways as solution to food scarcity in India – 'It is to the future extension of railways that we look as the most complete justification of our belief that the trade of the country may be confidently left to provide for the supply of food in time of scarcity', Report of the Indian Famine Commission, House of Commons Sessional Papers [C.2591], Lll.387 (1880), 63.
9   Charles Blair, *Indian Famines: Their Historical, Financial and Other Aspects* (Edinburgh and London: William Blackwood, 1874), 6.
10 C. E. R. Girdlestone, *Report on the Past Famines in the North-Western Province* (Allahabad: Government Press North-Western Provinces, 1868), 5.
11 Anon., 'The Indian Famine: How Dealt with in Western India', *The Westminster Review* 53, no. 1 (1878): 141.
12 East India (Distress at Ganjam): Reports by Mr. J. H. Garstin, C. S. J. on Condition of Ganjam, Madras, House of Commons Parliamentary Papers 137, LVIII (1889), 316–17.
13 William Digby, *The Famine Campaign in Southern India*, vol. i (London: Longman, Green & Co, 1878), 109.
14 William Digby, *'Prosperous British India': A Revelation from Office Records* (London: T. Fisher Unwin, 1901), 24.
15 Digby, 'Prosperous British India', 120, 121.
16 Thomas Pinney ed., *The Letters of Rudyard Kipling*, vol. i. (London: Macmillan, 2004), 98.
17 Benita Parry, *Delusions and Discoveries: India in the British Imagination 1880–1930* (London: Allen Lane, 1972), 190.
18 Noel Annan, 'Kipling's Place in the History of Ideas,' *Victorian Studies* 3, no. 4 (1960): 336, 337.
19 Anon., 'Plain Tales from the Hills', *Edinburgh Review* 174, no. 355 (1891): 136.
20 Anon., 'Plain Tales from the Hills', 137.
21 Ibid., 140.
22 Rudyard Kipling, 'William the Conqueror', *The Day's Work* (London: Macmillan, 1898), 172, 173.
23 Kipling, 'William the Conqueror', 176.
24 Ibid., 189, 190.
25 Ibid., 191.
26 Ibid., 197.
27 Lazarus, *The Postcolonial Unconscious*, 155, 156.

28 Jean Dreze, *Famine Prevention in India* (London: London School of Economics, 1988), 38.
29 Dreze, *Famine Prevention in India*, 110, 111.
30 B. M. Bhatia, *Famines in India: A Study in Some Aspects of the Economic History of India* (London: Asia, 1967), 340–43.
31 Mahasweta Devi, 'Pterodactyl, Puran Sahay, and Pirtha', in *Imaginary Maps*, trans. Gayatri Chakravorty Spivak (New York and London: Routledge, 1995), 97.
32 Devi, 'Pterodactyl, Puran Sahay, and Pirtha', 120.
33 Ibid., 129.
34 Ibid., 141. I use 'critical irrealism' after Michael Lowy, who in 'The Current of Critical Irrealism: "A Moonlit Enchanted Night"' in Matthew Beaumont ed., *Adventures in Realism* (Oxford: Blackwell Publishing, 2007) argues that the term denotes art forms that do not *oppose* realism but signal its *absence*, yet retain the power to critically present social reality.
35 Lazarus, *The Postcolonial Unconscious*, 155, 156.
36 Michael T. Taussig, *The Devil and Commodity Fetishism in South America* (Chapel Hill: University of North Carolina Press, 1980), 13–38.
37 Taussing, *The Devil and Commodity*, 17.
38 Devi, 'Pterodactyl, Puran Sahay, and Pirtha', 195.
39 Ibid., 182.
40 Ibid., 196.

7
Postcolonial Studies in the Digital Age: An Introduction

Roopika Risam

Among recent debates within postcolonial studies, its intersections with the emerging field of the digital humanities have come to the fore as a rich area of study for the twenty-first century. Over the past decade, the digital humanities have gained currency within the academy as a new methodology for literary study. While the sub-field of humanities computing, which focuses on computer-assisted analyses of texts, is often narrowly described as the sole predecessor of the digital humanities, the practices of the digital humanities are vast and varied. As Kathleen Fitzpatrick defines:

> [I]t has to do with the work that gets done at the crossroads of digital media and traditional humanistic study.... On one hand, it's bringing the tools and techniques of digital media to bear on traditional humanistic questions. But it's also bringing humanistic modes of inquiry to bear on digital media. It's...thinking about what computation is, how it functions in our culture, and then using those computing technologies to think about the more traditional aspects of culture.[1]

Fitzpatrick's definition suggests that the digital humanities are broad in scope, derived not only from humanities computing but also new media studies, computers and writing, rhetoric and composition, communications, and science and technology studies, among others.

Critiques from within digital humanities offer a place for rich connections between postcolonial studies and the digital humanities. Postcolonial digital humanities has been central to rethinking the cultural dimensions of the digital humanities from the margins. Building a community of scholars invested in the utility of postcolonial critique for the digital humanities, postcolonial digital humanities promotes 'global explorations of race, class, gender, sexuality, and disability within cultures of technology'.[2] Grounded in this conversation, this chapter explores the landscape of postcolonial studies in the digital age. First, it outlines the history of postcolonial approaches to the digital humanities, situating them in mid-1990s internet-based postcolonial projects, postcolonial science and technology studies, and new media studies. Then, it offers a vision of postcolonial approaches to digital humanities practice, based on emerging conversations about critical digital humanities. Finally, it looks more closely at the postcolonial dimensions of digital archiving and computational textual analysis, considering exemplar projects that showcase both what the digital humanities offer postcolonial studies and what a postcolonial approach brings to the digital humanities.

Postcolonial digital humanities: A history of the present

Although they have been left out of the history of the digital humanities until recently, postcolonial scholars were some of the early adopters in the field. Websites like Deepika Bahri's *Postcolonial Studies at Emory* (1996), George P. Landow's *The Postcolonial Web: Contemporary Postcolonial and Postimperial Literature in English* (early 1990s), and Masood Raja's *Postcolonial Space* (2002)[3] are among early digital humanities projects. Recently, in her work recovering diverse histories of the digital humanities, Amy Earhart has drawn attention to the role of these types of projects in the emergence of the sub-field.[4] They demonstrate the utility of emerging internet culture as a space for producing and disseminating knowledge for the growing field of postcolonial studies. Embracing the affordances of Web 1.0 technologies – static websites primarily used to share information – these projects identify key stakes, theorists and terms for postcolonial studies. They publicized the work of postcolonial writers and critics, often for an audience of advanced undergraduate and early-career graduate students learning about postcolonial studies for the first time. Emphasizing their pedagogical nature, such sites include material written by graduate students taking classes in postcolonial literature and theory, whom Bahri describes as 'arguably the most voracious and critical readers in the academy today'.[5]

As a result, these early projects bear the hallmarks of the practices that shape the digital humanities today: the desire to develop a public face for the humanities; collaborations that challenge typical hierarchies between graduate student and professor or faculty and staff; the use of links and hypertext to visualize connected data; and pedagogically minded project development.

Alongside these websites, which comprise one genealogy of postcolonial digital humanities, theoretical engagements with postcolonial studies emerged within science and technology studies. However, because they came out of the history of science, a different discipline than postcolonial literary studies, these efforts have not traditionally been considered in relation to each other. Sandra Harding is arguably the most significant figure to put postcolonial thought and science and technology studies in conversation. Since the early 1990s, she has demonstrated the importance of reconsidering how technological development is often represented as the sole domain of the 'West.'[6] Making the case for the need of corrective narratives, Harding argues for revisiting scientific traditions from non-Western cultures to uncover the value of alternative epistemologies for science.[7] She has been a leading voice articulating the need for more attention to the influence of imperialism on scientific discourse, making the case for multicultural analyses of science and postcolonial critique of digital cultures and technologies. Harding's pioneering work has facilitated a range of analyses that centre indigenous methods and rewrite the historical narratives of science silenced by imperialism. For example, Warwick Anderson's work on 'postcolonial techno-science' emphasizes the need for a critical approach to science that traverses geopolitical boundaries to uncover flows of knowledges, technologies and scientists,[8] while Itty Abraham has refined Anderson's argument, making the case for attention to local specificity in a way that does not reduce the postcolonial to an underdeveloped world.[9] Similarly, Amit Prasad's exploration of 'imperial technoscience' positions scientific culture as the product of fluid transnational histories.[10]

Among the scholarship emerging from Harding's work is 'postcolonial computing', which focuses on applications of postcolonial thought to material computing. Developed by Lilly Irani, Janet Vertesi, Paul Dourish, Kavita Philip and Rebecca Grinter, postcolonial computing offers a critique of Human Computer Interaction for Development (HCI4D), which focuses on digital divides in the 'developing world'.[11] Irani et al. underscore the questions of legitimacy, power and authority implied in narratives of

HCI4D and 'development' in the Global South. Postcolonial computing argues for alternatives to technology design that begin with the particular, the local context for emerging technologies. They expose the ways that culture and power subtend notions of 'good' design practices, criticizing the universal 'good' presupposed in the creation of computer technologies, systems and design aesthetics. They reinforce the need for ongoing analysis of how cultural and colonial dynamics shape technology design, decentring 'global' (i.e. Global North) forms of knowledge in favour of a local approach that foregrounds the influence of uneven development on production.[12] For the digital humanities, this body of work in postcolonial science and technology studies offers an approach to computing that insists on the situatedness of the local in the creation and use of technologies, attention to labour practices, and the decentring of the Global North in the technological landscape.

Just as postcolonial studies has been expanded by interventions insisting on the significance of decoloniality, critical race theory, and renewed attention to Marxist and materialist analyses, so too have postcolonial approaches to the digital humanities. Accordingly, Syed Mustafa Ali has begun developing a theory of 'decolonial computing', positioning it as both a critique of and alternative to postcolonial computing. Decolonial computing emerges from Charles Mills' work on the racial contact, which argues that white supremacy subtends Enlightenment social contract theory,[13] and Walter Mignolo's decolonial theories of the Global South.[14] Ali argues for greater attention to the role of white supremacy, systematic racism and racial materiality within computing. Decolonial computing is an attempt to theorize computing from the peripheries, emphasizing delinking, South-to-South connections and border theories that resist dependence on Global North centres.[15] For example, Ali considers the role of race in creating humanoid robots, asking about the presumptions of race implied in design and the impact of artificial intelligence on deemphasizing the centrality of race to the human experience.[16]

These questions of race, technology and neocolonialism have appeared in the context of new media studies as well. While postcolonial science and technology studies, postcolonial computing and decolonial computing constitute one lineage for postcolonial digital humanities, new media studies is another. With the advent of Web 2.0, participatory forms of culture have emerged, enabled by low barriers to entry for both civic engagement and creative expression on the internet. This participatory culture positions users in the role of producers, rather than simply consumers of knowledge.

Through such participation, the question of identity on the internet has come to light as an important one. Theories of embodiment within new media studies have addressed questions of race, ethnicity, gender, power and imperialism that resonate with postcolonial scholarship. Scholars who work on these concerns explore how the seemingly disembodied internet is, in fact, a space in which axes of identity are reinscribed, amplified and circulated. Wendy Chun's work, for example, has argued that insufficient attention to difference has led to deceptive beliefs that the internet is disembodied and shielded from social inequalities,[17] and Lisa Nakamura has examined the operations of stereotypes in online and offline spaces.[18] Similarly, Anna Everett has argued that intersectional forms of difference influence African American women's experiences online, the digital public sphere and video games.[19] This scholarship has influenced the development of a specifically postcolonial dimension of new media studies. Radhika Gajjala's work draws on theories of globalization to explore South Asian technospaces and the way voice and silence are manipulated online.[20] Focusing on ethnic minority media, Isabel Rigoni has argued that there has been little attention to the ways that postcolonial migration, gender and race create unequal access to media power.[21] Responding to an absence of postcolonial theory in electronic media, María Fernández makes the case for interpretive frames for media that resist the utopian universalism of colonialism and neocolonial formations.[22] Pramod Nayar has further attended to the possibilities of cyberspace for India's Dalits (the modern term for 'untouchables'). He urges greater attention to digital engagement of Dalit communities to complicate narratives of India's connectivity and technological boom.[23] Such interventions have served to complicate the conversations surrounding participatory culture on the internet.

These genealogies come together through a relatively recent intervention in the digital humanities: the critical digital humanities. This approach is situated in earlier digital humanities scholarship that has made the case for cultural critique in the sub-field. They are centred around three questions: Alan Liu's 'where is cultural critique in the digital humanities?', Tara McPherson's 'why are the digital humanities so white?', and Amy Earhart's 'can information be unfettered?'[24] Liu makes a powerful case for the centrality of cultural criticism to digital humanities; McPherson provides a model of examining deeply embedded racial ideologies within technology; and Earhart calls for attention to early digital humanities recovery projects for African American literature that have been lost, reflecting dynamics that shape literary canons. Critical digital humanities further considers the presumptions and limits of tools employed in digital humanities methods. As Julia Flanders describes:

> Digital literary study must thus consider, as a central problem, the empowerments and disempowerments contingent on its use of tools, not because they are tools, but rather because of the questions they raise about how we are situated in relation to our objects and methods of study. The human scholar of literary studies must be present in the inquiry at its end points – as the initiator of questions and consumer of answers – and also *inside* the process, *inside* the tools, as they mediate between us and the field we are seeking to grasp.[25]

Though they are often seen as neutral, tools, code, standards and design aesthetics are not universal but are constructed and inflected by the contexts in which they are developed. Critical approaches to digital humanities also attend to the complex networks of power relations that enable the subfield. These include the grant machine that makes advancement of projects possible and creates jobs – but only for defined amounts of time. Analysis of such practices reveals the multiple types of labour needed to produce a project and raises issues of how credit is distributed among project directors, professors, librarians, alternative academic (or #alt-ac) staff and graduate students.

Growing out of this history of forking paths, postcolonial digital humanities emphasizes the significance of postcolonial theory for examining the seeming underwhelming attention to questions of power, globalization, and colonial and neocolonial ideologies at work in the production of knowledge through the digital humanities. It creates a dialogue between the global analyses of knowledge production and power from postcolonial studies and the proliferation of digital knowledge emerging from the growth of the digital humanities. Undeniably, the humanities in the digital age are being shaped by the development of digital humanities. Yet, they are, in turn, shaped by global flows and networks of capital, communication and power that threaten to rehearse colonial and imperial ways of knowing in the acceleration of knowledge production. Thus, among its concerns, postcolonial digital humanities brings to the issue of labour the perspective of the Global South. The technologies with which digital humanities projects engage are implicated in the relationship between globalization and technology. For example, among the labour practices employed within digital humanities is use of

Amazon Mechanical Turk. This service provides access to an anonymous, crowdsourced labour force whose workers are paid in cents for completing 'Human Intelligence Tasks' or HITs. The HITs for these projects include data entry or coding data. The majority of Amazon Mechanical Turk workers come from the Global South, particularly India. As a result, beyond the question of unethical and exploitative labour is the matter of cultural contexts the workers have (or lack) for the operations they are performing. For example, Ryan Heuser's *Emotions in Victorian London* is a data mining project that maps an emotional geography of London through sentiment analysis of 741 Victorian writers. The project's data was coded using Amazon Mechanical Turk HITs: workers identified sentiments associated with 167 London locations in more than 4,000 literary passages (e.g. 'Dreadful London' or 'London in the Light.'). Sentiment is both culturally and temporally constructed, so this case illustrates the pitfalls of relying on anonymous, crowdsourced labour when developing digital humanities projects.

Yet another concern of postcolonial digital humanities is access to digital knowledge and to the digital means of knowledge production around the world. Scholars developing methods for minimal computing are seeking to intervene in this area. Minimal computing emphasizes project design for low-bandwidth environments, reducing e-waste, conceptualizing digital humanities practices beyond high-powered desktop computing.[26] These include designing static HTML websites, digital platforms that can be run from thumb drives, and supporting open source platforms. In doing so, minimal computing embraces postcolonial critiques of globalization and technology and models responses to issues of access, wealth and uneven development.

Another dimension of postcolonial digital humanities is reconceptualizing the sub-field's focus on modelling. Matthew Kirschenbaum suggests that the digital humanities provides models of the world. He likens the act of programming to world-making, the coder positioned in the role of defining the rules and characteristics of the world as she articulates 'the behaviors of an object or a system from the ground up'.[27] Kirschenbaum argues that 'programming is about choices and constraints, and about how you choose to model some select slice of the world around you in the formal environment of the computer'.[28] In defining 'world', he is careful to distinguish between the world of the program and the world around us, 'something very much like a model, a selective and premeditated representation of reality, where some elements of the real are emphasized and exaggerated, others are distorted and caricatured, still others are absent altogether'.[29] He links the world-making of the program to that of literature through grammar – building blocks of syntax, actions, subjects, objects are the pretext for not only the development of a computer model of the world but also the plots of literature. The affordances of this act of world-making are the possibilities for the proliferation of many worlds, indicated by his suggestion that 'reality can be sliced and sampled in an infinite variety of ways'.[30] For Kirschenbaum, Jane Austen is 'one of our ultimate system builders and world-makers'.[31] In collapsing the distinction between the systems built for technological platforms and those invented by a writer, Kirschenbaum evokes Gayatri Spivak's critique of Austen's acts of white feminist world-making in *Jane Eyre*.[32] He is careful to remind that virtual worlds may be empirical but are not objective and they 'embody their authors' biases, blind spots, ideologies, prejudices, and opinions'.[33] Yet, they also embody the traces of colonialism and imperialism that have shaped not only literature, as postcolonial scholars have suggested, but also the rise of computing, a point amply made by Harding, Irani et al. and Ali. Approaching modelling as a form of world-making begs the question of earlier forms: settler colonies, maps, colonial archives, new legal systems, literature and colonizing of the mind. Colonialism has not only built the contemporary world but also created the ways we know the world; these legacies become implicit in digital knowledge production without explicit intervention.

Such concerns speak to the need for approaches to the digital humanities that write back to the traditional conceptions of individual projects and global power within the sub-field. Doing so actively resists reproducing imperial formations, conditions of production, biases and epistemologies in the digital humanities. For example, conventional maps of the digital humanities depict concentrations of digital humanities centres in the United States, Canada and the United Kingdom.[34] They elide the global picture of the digital humanities, much of which takes place at the peripheries. The *Around Digital Humanities in 80 Days* project writes back to this narrative. For eighty days, project director Alex Gil and a team of editors produced descriptions of digital humanities projects from around the world, generating a map that depicts a global model of the digital humanities.[35] It disrupts the centre narrative, pushing back against the distribution of power in the digital humanities in relation to the academies of the Global North and Global South. Yet, intervention is also needed at the broader scale of digital knowledge production. Further possibilities for such approaches are visible in the practices of postcolonial digital archiving and the possibilities of computational textual analysis for postcolonial digital humanities.

Postcolonial digital humanities archives and computational textual analysis

One significant intervention in postcolonial approaches to digital humanities is rethinking digital archives. Among the affordances of the digital humanities and participatory cultures of Web 2.0 is the relative ease of creating new archives using open source tools. For postcolonial studies, there is great promise in the possibility of developing archives that write back to colonial histories and fill the gaps of knowledge that remain a legacy of colonialism. With ready access to the internet in many parts of the world, the means of archival production seem limited only to bandwidth, server space and the labour needed to undertake digitization projects that intervene in both historical and literary archival silences. A postcolonial digital archive, then, takes advantage of the availability of emerging technologies with relatively low learning curves to write back to dominant narratives. They hold possibilities for giving voice to new stories that reshape the dynamics of power that shape the relationship between centre and periphery. With the availability of these technologies it is easy to succumb to the lure of techno-utopianism and to see technology as the answer to the problems of the colonial archive. If, in fact, that were the case, we would not see absences in digital archives that are reminiscent of those that exist in print forms of knowledge.

As a result, the postcolonial digital archive is more than mere addition and requires interrogating the structure of archives themselves. Like all digital archives, postcolonial digital archives offer ways of preserving and disseminating knowledge but are also implicated in creating and structuring knowledge. Avoiding reproducing existing inequalities in regimes of knowledge requires attending to postcolonial critiques of the archive. Postcolonial scholars have articulated the necessity of reading the imperial archive critically to identify countercurrents within dominant historical narratives. The colonial archive itself shapes the dimensions of who counts or is represented in colonial history. Durba Ghosh, for example, has argued that colonial archives have successfully managed to keep indigenous women's voices out,[36] and the same case has been made about other subaltern voices. Recovery of those voices omitted from the archive has been essential to postcolonial studies in general and subaltern studies in particular. Gyan Prakash argues that subaltern studies historians must read colonial and national archives against the grain, 'focusing on their blind-spots, silences, and anxieties'.[37] To read the archive critically is to see it not as a textual collection but as what Thomas Richards has described as 'the collectively imagined junction of all that was known or knowable, a fantastic representation of an epistemological master pattern, a virtual focal point for the heterogeneous local knowledge of metropolis and empire'.[38] The imperial archive belies a relationship between knowledge production, preservation and the colonial apparatus. The archive itself is a dynamic force in the production, distribution and consumption of history. Rather than 'a store of transparent sources from which histories recover a total image of the ... past', the archive is 'a site saturated by power, a dense but uneven body of knowledge scarred by the cultural struggles and violence'.[39] As such the archive itself is constitutive not only of colonial structures of the past but also how colonial pasts are perceived in the present.

Therefore, creating postcolonial digital archives requires attending to considerations that ensure the archive is actively resisting colonialism and neocolonial patterns of knowledge. Elizabeth Povinelli describes considerations such as 'the material conditions that allow something to be archived and archivable', 'compulsions and desires that conjure the appearance or disappearance of objects, knowledges, and socialities within an archive' and 'cultures of circulation, manipulation, and management that allow an object to enter the archive and thus contribute to the endurance of specific social formations'.[40] Martha Nell Smith argues that postcolonial digital archives must attend to the ways that social relations may be frozen in the production of digital archives:

> Makers and users of postcolonial digital archives should take care to recognize that there tends to be an amnesia or blindness to the fact ... that 'Systems of classifications (and of standardization) form a juncture of social organisation, moral order, and layers of technical integration. Each subsystem inherits, increasingly as it scales up, the inertia of the installed base systems that have come before'. Tools cannot be separated from the knowledge systems in which they have been imagined and made.[41]

Such issues are perhaps most clear in the case of *Aluka*, the transnational African digital archive available in JSTOR. The origins of the project are in international, South-to-South collaboration intended to build a digital library for southern Africa. Material in the archive emphasizes cultural heritage sites and freedom struggles, representing the work of both local and international scholars. Advocates argue that histories contained in the archive shed new light on narratives that that might be misread in national contexts when they are transnational in nature. Yet, *Aluka* has raised many issues among stakeholders, from concerns about intellectual property to misappropriation of national heritage. Because of the profit that the JSTOR database generates, the commodity value of national heritage through *Aluka* has been raised as well, along with the ethical dimensions of selling the database to a US-centred entity that profits off information. The project creators rationalize the choice by noting that 'the digitization process places contested archives in a cyberspace that is highly commodified'.[42] In his work on postcolonial digital archives in Alaska, Matthew Kurtz identifies tensions between institutional practice and postcolonial theory, particularly the decentring of power advocated by postcolonial thought and the geographical centring implied in the construction of the archive.[43] Designing archives as flexible, open, decentralized and optimized for worldwide access can actively resist such inscriptions.

Digital literary archives have made further progress on this matter, emphasizing both digitizing literary texts to make them openly available, strengthening regional language traditions and challenging the dominance of Anglophone writing in the digital literary sphere. A number of projects seek to strengthen Urdu, Tibetan and other literary traditions, believing that representation of the literatures online is essential to their survival.[44] The *Bichitra Online Tagore Variorum* project, housed at Jadavpur University, is perhaps the best developed of such projects and offers insight on the affordances and challenges of postcolonial digital literary archives. The project has digitized over 47,000 manuscript pages and over 91,000 pages of Rabindranath Tagore's books and journals in Bengali and English and is currently the most substantial archive of any author to date, anywhere and in any language.[45] Several features of the project speak to the critical practices of postcolonial digital humanities. For example, in the process of constructing the archive, its creators also designed new tools intended to help users navigate the archive. The collation tool *Prabhed* allows users to compare versions of the texts in the archive at macro and micro-levels. While there are any number of freely available tools that could be used for comparison, the creation of *Prabhed* for this archive in particular – to meet the challenge of bilingualism and the many genres in which Tagore wrote – suggests that digital tools for literary analysis are not universal and that there are benefits to designing ones that respond to the particularity of the archive and the unique characteristics of Tagore's oeuvre. Moreover, the project was made possible through collaborations with Santiniketan, the school Tagore founded; Calcutta University; Tagore collectors; and Harvard University. This last speaks to a phenomenon that often seems to be the case for digital humanities projects housed at institutions in the Global South: they frequently involve collaborations with universities around the world, usually ones in the United States or United Kingdom. Sometimes, as is the case with the Tagore archive, the collaboration is simply intended to source material from international archives. In other cases, funding is provided or exchanged, raising concerns about dynamics of neocolonialism or undue cultural influence in international collaborations between Global North and Global South. Moreover, the fact that the largest digital literary archive is on Tagore, arguably one of India's most famous writers, betrays a preference for canonicity even in a postcolonial context.

Yet, ongoing development of digital literary archives is central to computational textual analysis, as it presupposes the existence of electronic texts for analysis. While textual analysis is the primary methodology employed in literary studies, computer-assisted textual analysis allows users to engage with texts in new ways. Tools that assist with textual analysis afford opportunities not practically achievable without the aid of computers: conducting complex searches; generating topics lists; interacting with a text through word clouds, keywords in context, and word trends; and searching lengthy texts quickly.[46] While these forms of computer-aided textual analysis hold great promise for quantification and interpretation of texts, the main challenges for postcolonial literary studies are copyright law and uneven digitization of literary texts – Anglophone texts of US and British origin form a significant majority of digitized literatures. Producing electronic versions of postcolonial texts still within copyright, which is certainly the case for most of them, requires time-intensive running of optical character recognition (OCR) software and manually rekeying a print edition or scraping data from eBook editions – this is a project in and of itself and may be outside the bounds of fair use and legality.

Until we have more easily accessible digitized material from the postcolonial world, computer-aided textual analysis remains useful for postcolonial approaches to eighteenth- and nineteenth-century British and

American literature. Project Gutenberg offers full-text access to 49,000 public domain texts, while HathiTrust, a large-scale multi-institutional repository of digitized texts includes 10 million. *A Distant Reading of Empire*, a project by Mae Capozzi and Scott Enderle, demonstrates the use of such forms of analysis for postcolonial studies. Capozzi and Enderle created a corpus of 2,500 eighteenth-century texts that appeared between 1757 and 1795 from HathiTrust. Using the Java-based Machine Learning for Language Toolkit (MALLET), statistics-based natural language processing software, they engaged in topic modelling, a form of text-mining that groups words in a corpus into topics. Their goal was to look for relationships between Britain and India within the texts. MALLET processed the corpus and produced a list of topics, which Capozzi and Enderle then interpreted. When they looked at the topic that pertained to India, they noticed that two of the first few words ('company' and 'nabob') indicated a colonial dimension to the relationship between India and Britain in the eighteenth-century texts represented in the corpus. Additional data from the topic further supported the colonial connection. Their analysis uncovered linguistic issues with MALLET as well, namely that it was built for Anglophone corpora; if it encounters words from languages other than English, MALLET groups those words into language-based topics without further refinement.[47] The implications of Capozzi and Enderle's study for postcolonial studies are significant. While postcolonial literary scholars have used close reading to make claims about the relationship between colonialism, eighteenth- and nineteenth-century British literature, and representation, these conclusions are generally supported through analysis of a limited number of texts. Computer-assisted textual analysis, on the other hand, offers the opportunity of examining whether assertions that hold true for small corpora are borne out through macroanalysis across the larger literary landscape of the time.

Another approach to textual analysis that is easier to negotiate uses out-of-the-box tools to process data. The open source textual analysis tool *Voyant*, designed by Stéfan Sinclair and Geoffrey Rockwell, provides a web-based reading environment for electronic texts.[48] Users upload or copy and paste an electronic text into the tool, which then processes the material to produce a visualization of contextual keywords, word clouds and word frequencies. Google Ngrams offers a way of conducting distant reading 'lite' – understanding literature not through close reading but by looking for patterns shaping periods or recurring in genres, as Moretti proposes. He argues that distance 'is a condition of knowledge: it allows you to focus on units that are much smaller or much larger than the text: devices, themes, tropes – or genres and systems'.[49] Google Ngrams examine word and short phrase frequencies through yearly units, called n-grams, from print sources that appeared between 1800 and 2012. The tool offers an interesting perspective on language and its change and usage over time. Feeding a word or phrase into the tool produces a chart that visualizes the relationship between the word and the approximately 5.2 million texts in the Google database. A search for 'India,' for example, shows peak frequency around 1880, an interesting correlation with the fact that Queen Victoria took on the title of Empress of India in 1876. While 'colony' shows several peaks around 1820, 1840 and 1890, certainly bearing relationship to historical dimensions of colonization, 'colonialism' peaks in the late 1960s, late 1980s and early 2000s, shedding light on the connection between histories of colonization and the emergence of theoretical and political language to discuss the effects of colonization. There are rich possibilities here for the kinds of analyses of language undertaken at smaller scales in postcolonial literary scholarship. This includes considering why certain words appear more frequently in particular historical contexts and examining correlations between related terms. Certainly, there are limitations to this approach. For example, the dataset is limited to texts in Google Books, which replicates the issue of silences in the digitized literary archive. Critics have further suggested that the OCR of the texts may not be accurate and that texts may not be dated correctly. Yet, particularly for teaching and for qualitative data analysis and interpretation, Google Ngrams offers the possibility of informally gauging the popularity of particular words, terms or concepts over time and supplementing the act of close reading. As efforts to develop literary archives of the postcolonial world and digital tools that navigate the particular challenges of these archives persist, the possibilities for computational analysis of postcolonial literature will only grow.

While postcolonial approaches to digital humanities are still in the early stages, they are necessary to both the growth of the digital humanities and full of potential for the future of postcolonial studies. More than ever, we need attention to the role of technology in constructing channels of capital, knowledge and power, in which both postcolonial studies and the digital humanities are implicated. As during temporal modes of colonialism, links between textuality and power are amply present in the digital milieu. Just as writing has been marshalled in the service of power in the colonial past, it remains significant to geopolitical dynamics of the present. The power to colonize was linked to the power to write. The power to write offered the power to shape the history of modernity. The power to shape modernity is the power that shapes the present. Greater attention to digital humanities practices informed by a postcolonial approach shed needed light on the connections between colonial and neocolonial formations of knowledge that subtend the digital humanities. Meanwhile, the methodologies of digital humanities hold promise for the practice of postcolonial scholars and offer rich possibilities for further exploring the theoretical dimensions of postcoloniality. Through these interventions, we might create new models of scholarship for postcolonial studies in the digital age.

Notes

1. Andrew Lopez, Fred Rowland and Kathleen Fitzpatrick, 'On Scholarly Communication and the Digital Humanities: An Interview with Kathleen Fitzpatrick', *In the Library with the Lead Pipe*, http://www.inthelibrarywiththeleadpipe.org/2015/on-scholarly-communication-and-the-digital-humanities-an-interview-with-kathleen-fitzpatrick/ (accessed 8 September 2015).
2. Roopika Risam and Adeline Koh, 'Mission Statement', *Postcolonial Digital Humanities*, http://dhpoco.org/mission-statement-postcolonial-digital-humanities/ (accessed 9 September 2015).
3. *Postcolonial Studies at Emory* (scholarblogs.emory.edu/postcolonialstudies); *Postcolonial and Postimperial Literature* (www.postcolonialweb.org); *Postcolonial Space* (postcolonial.net/about).
4. *The Diverse History of Digital Humanities* (dhhistory.blogspot.com).
5. Deepika Bahri, 'About This Site', *Postcolonial Studies @ Emory*, https://scholarblogs.emory.edu/postcolonialstudies/about-this-site/ (accessed 8 September 2015).
6. Sandra Harding, *Is Science Multicultural?: Postcolonialisms, Feminisms, and Epistemologies* (Bloomington: Indiana University Press, 1998), 4.
7. Sandra Harding, *Sciences from Below: Feminisms, Postcolonialisms, and Modernities* (Durham: Duke University Press, 2008), 8.
8. Warwick Anderson, 'Postcolonial Technoscience', *Social Studies of Science* 32, no. 5–6 (2002): 643.
9. Itty Abraham, 'The Contradictory Spaces of Postcolonial Techno-Science', *Economic and Political Weekly* 41, no. 3 (2006): 211.
10. Amit Prasad, *Imperial Technoscience: Transnational Histories of MRI in the United States, Britain, and India* (Cambridge, MA: MIT Press, 2014), 2.
11. Susan Dray et al. 'Human-Computer Interaction for Development: Changing Human-Computer Interaction to Change the World', in *Human*

Computer Interaction Handbook, eds. Andrew Sears and Julie A. Jacko (Boca Raton: CRC Press), 1385.
12 Kavita Philip, Lilly Irani and Paul Dourish, 'Postcolonial Computing: A Tactical Survey', *Science, Technology, Human Values* 40 (2015): 800.
13 Charles Wade Mills, *The Racial Contract* (Ithaca: Cornell University Press, 1997), 10.
14 Walter Mignolo, 'DELINKING: The Rhetoric of Modernity, the Logic of Coloniality and the Grammar of De-Coloniality', *Cultural Studies* 21, no. 2 (2007): 450.
15 Syed Mustafa Ali, 'Towards a Decolonial Computing', *Open Research Online*, http://oro.open.ac.uk/41372/ (accessed 13 September 2015).
16 Ali, 'Towards a Decolonial Computing'.
17 Wendy Chun, 'Scenes of Empowerment: Virtual Racial Diversity and Digital Divides', *New Formations* 45 (2001): 170.
18 Lisa Nakamura, *Cybertypes: Race, Ethnicity, and Identity on the Internet* (New York: Routledge, 2002), 4.
19 See Anna Everett, 'The Revolution Will Be Digitized: Afrocentricity and the Digital Public Sphere', *Social Text* 20, no. 2 (2002): 126; Anna Everett, *Digital Diaspora: A Race for Cyberspace* (Albany, NY: State University of New York Press, 2009), 10; Anna Everett, Alexander Champlin, and John Vanderhoef, 'Race, Space, and Digital Games: An Interview with Anna Everett', *Media Fields Journal* 8 (2014).
20 Radhika Gajjala, *Cyberculture and the Subaltern* (Lanham: Lexington Books, 2012), 15.
21 Isabella Rigoni, 'Intersectionality and Mediated Cultural Production in a Globalized Post-Colonial World,' *Ethnic and Racial Studies* 35, no. 5 (2002): 835.
22 María Fernández, 'Postcolonial Media Theory,' *Art Journal* 58, no. 3 (1999): 60.
23 Pramod Nayar, 'The Digital Dalit: Subalternity and Cyberspace', *The Sri Lanka Journal of the Humanities* 37, no. 1–2 (2011): 70.
24 See Alan Liu, 'Where Is Cultural Criticism in Digital Humanities', in *Debates in the Digital Humanities*, ed. Matthew K. Gold (Minneapolis: University of Minnesota Press, 2013), 490; Tara McPherson, 'Why Are the Digital Humanities So White? or Thinking the Histories of Race and Computation', in *Debates in the Digital Humanities*, ed. Matthew K. Gold (Minneapolis: University of Minnesota Press, 2013), 139; Amy Earhart, 'Can Information Be Unfettered? Race and the New Digital Humanities Canon', in *Debates in the Digital Humanities*, ed. Matthew K. Gold (Minneapolis: University of Minnesota Press, 2013), 309.
25 Julia Flanders, 'The Literary, the Humanistic, the Digital: Toward a Research Agenda for Digital Literary Studies', *Literary Studies in the Digital*

Age: An Evolving Anthology, https://dlsanthology.commons.mla.org/the-literary-the-humanistic-the-digital/ (accessed 12 September 2015).
26 'What Is Minimal Computing?' *Minimal Computing*, http://go-dh.github.io/mincomp/about/ (accessed 10 September 2015).
27 Matthew Kirschenbaum, 'Hello Worlds', *The Chronicle of Higher Education*, January 23, 2009, http://chronicle.com/article/Hello-Worlds/5476 (accessed 5 September 2015).
28 Kirschenbaum, 'Hello Worlds'.
29 Ibid.
30 Ibid.
31 Ibid.
32 Gayatri Chakravorty Spivak, 'Three Women's Texts and a Critique of Imperialism', *Critical Inquiry* 12, no. 1 (1985): 245.
33 Kirschenbaum, 'Hello Worlds'.
34 Melissa Terras, 'Infographic: Quantifying Digital Humanities', *UCL Centre for Digital Humanities*, http://blogs.ucl.ac.uk/dh/2012/01/20/infographic-quantifying-digital-humanities/ (accessed 11 September 2015).
35 *Around Digital Humanities in 80 Days* (arounddh.org) (accessed 7 September 2015).
36 Durba Ghosh, *Sex and the Family in Colonial India: The Making of Empire* (Cambridge: Cambridge University Press, 2006), 17.
37 Gyan Prakash, 'Postcolonial Criticism and Indian Historiography', *Social Text* 31/32 (1992): 9.
38 Thomas Richards, *The Imperial Archive: Knowledge and the Fantasy of Empire* (London: Verso, 1993), 11.
39 Tony Ballantyne, *Webs of Empire: Locating New Zealand's Colonial Past* (Vancouver: University of British Columbia Press, 2014), 102.
40 Elizabeth A. Povinelli, 'The Woman on the Other Side of the Wall: Archiving the Otherwise in Postcolonial Digital Archives', *Differences* 22, no. 1 (2011): 154–5.
41 Martha Nell Smith, 'Frozen Social Relations and Time for a Thaw: Visibilities, Exclusions, and Considerations for Postcolonial Digital Archives', *Journal of Victorian Culture* 19, no. 3 (2014): 408.
42 Allen Isaacman, Premesh Lalu and Thomas Nygren, 'Digitization, History, and the Making of Postcolonial Archive of Southern African Liberation Struggles: The Aluka Project', *Africa Today* 52, no. 2 (2005): 70.
43 Matthew Kurtz, 'A Postcolonial Archive? On the Paradox of Practice in a Northwest Alaska Project', *Archivaria: The Journal of the Association of Canadian Archivists* 60 (2007): 81.
44 Projects such as *Nitartha Digital Tibetan* (www.nitartha.org/digital_texts.html), *Allama Iqbal Urdu Cyber Library* (www.iqbalcyberlibrary.net), *Rekhta* (rekhta.org) and *Umang* امنگ (umangpoetry.org) are additional examples.

45 *Bichitra Online Tagore Variorium* (bichitra.jdvu.ac.in/index.php) (accessed 11 September 2015).
46 Stéfan Sinclair and Geoffrey Rockwell, 'Teaching Computer Assisted Text Analysis: Approaches to Learning New Methodologies', in *Digital Humanities Pedagogy: Practices, Principles, and Politics,* ed. Brett D. Hirsch (Cambridge: Open Book Publishers, 2012), 242.
47 Mae Capozzi and Scott Enderle, *A Distant Reading of Empire* (http://readingfromadistance.wordpress.com (accessed 10 September 2015).
48 Voyant Tools (voyant-tools.org).
49 Franco Moretti, *Distant Reading* (New York: Verso, 2013), 57.

Part II

New Narratives

8 Postcolonial Poetry
9 Postcolonial Noncitizenship in Australian Theatre and Performance: Twenty-First-Century Paradigms
10 Graphic History: Postcolonial Texts and Contexts
11 Postcolonial Life-Writing
12 Decolonization and Postcolonial Cinema in Canada, Brazil, Australia and Nigeria
13 Postcolonial Gaming: An Interview with Seth Alter, creator of *Neocolonialism: Ruin Everything* (Subaltern Games)

8

Postcolonial Poetry

Emma Bird

Postcolonial poetry, like fiction, drama and film, engages with the impact and effects of colonialism. It can be characterized as writing which 'critically or subversively scrutinizes the colonial relationship' and its legacy, and which rewrites the myths and narratives on which colonialism relied.[1] This chapter is primarily concerned with poetry written after decolonization, and focuses on a selection of Indian poets writing in English. However, colonial poets have also engaged closely with empire, producing poems that variously reinforced or challenged colonial hegemony. Hence, in one of his most anthologized poems, Rudyard Kipling wrote of empire as a necessary and righteous 'white man's burden' in 1899, promoting a deeply ideological and benevolent vision of British colonialism.[2] Other poets expressed a more complex view of colonial rule. Toru Dutt, for instance, the first Indian woman to publish a collection of poetry in English, composed sonnets about the Indian landscape, using the language and style of colonial English. Her poems, full of 'graceful tamarinds', 'mango clumps' and 'bamboos', thus pre-empt many later postcolonial writers' attempts to refashion English in order to represent their own locale and experience.[3] Indeed, in much colonial poetry we can identify many concerns of later postcolonial writing, including an engagement with colonial history and its founding myths and an attempt to find an appropriate form and language in which to express personal and national experience. As Elleke Boehmer reminds us, 'the inventive energies and resistances we now value in postcolonial writing did not begin yesterday'.[4]

However, in postcolonial literary studies, poetry occupies a distinctly peripheral position. Writing in 2001, Jahan Ramazani found 'no books on postcolonial poetry of the Third World', remarking that university literature courses, postcolonial anthologies and academic volumes of essays tend to ignore or side-line poetry entirely.[5] The poet Manohar Shetty observes the economic divides separating poets from novelists in this short satirical verse: 'prose is horizontal / poetry vertical / they get the fat advances / we take our slim chances'.[6] Shetty's words resonate with many poets today, especially since the high profile commercial successes of postcolonial novelists. While Anita Desai, Salman Rushdie and Arundhati Roy have achieved wide acclaim, poets including Arun Kolatkar, Agha Shahad Ali and Eunice de Souza remain much less widely known. In India, this is especially surprising, given that India's first Nobel Prize for Literature was awarded to Rabindranath Tagore in 1913, for *Gitanjali* – his book of poems in English. This chapter begins by considering why postcolonial criticism has so often neglected to engage with a rich tradition of postcolonial poetry. It then proceeds to discuss the relationship between poetry and postcoloniality, reflecting on its engagement with and representation of the nation, language and cultural hybridity. However, to examine the postcolonial poem only insofar as it engages with certain themes is to perpetuate a narrow and limiting focus on the text. The second section thus considers how the poem can exceed the very terms and vocabularies of postcolonial analysis. This discussion focuses on the bilingual Marathi/English poet Arun Kolatkar, whose work consistently reveals the multiple and conflicting traditions to which the poet lays claim.

Poetry and postcolonial theory

Postcolonial studies has been 'monopolized by the aesthetics of prose', with numerous publications confirming the continuing critical interest in novels.[7] One reason for this may be that novels are much more commercially successful, and reach a wider audience. As Graham Huggan and Sarah Brouillette have shown, the Indian novel in English has been especially prominent in the global literary marketplace, accruing prestigious international awards.[8] By comparison, poets have typically largely published in local literary magazines or with small presses, and have reached fewer readers. Even well known figures have published primarily with smaller presses: Adil Jussawalla, who recently won the Sahitya Akademi Award, has published his poetry entirely with Indian based small publishing houses, and this has necessarily limited the size of his readership. Moreover, as Ramazani observes, as 'critical interest in poetry has suffered a general decline', even more mainstream publishers are unable to issue as many volumes.[9] Oxford University Press, for instance, which was enthusiastic in publishing poets from the Caribbean, West Africa and India during the 1970s, has more recently stopped issuing new volumes by individual poets, choosing instead to publish anthologies or collections by established figures. Scholarship on postcolonial poetry must therefore contend with its particular material conditions, and limitations on its availability.

The case of Arun Kolatkar is suggestive of the challenges involved in publishing and circulating poetry. Kolatkar's debut volume in English, *Jejuri*, was published in 1976 by the small press Clearing House, and was awarded the Commonwealth Poetry Prize in 1977. Clearing House was only able to issue a small number of copies, however, and its books did not circulate widely. Hence, while poems from *Jejuri* have been available in magazines and anthologies since the 1970s, it has only been accessible to a wider reading public in its entirety relatively recently, since it was reissued by NYRB in 2005 along with a critical introduction by Amit Chaudhuri.[10] This process remains ongoing, with the publication of Kolatkar's *Collected Poems in English* by Bloodaxe in 2010 further widening his potential readership.[11]

At the same time, postcolonial criticism has been slow to respond to the interpretive opportunities and aesthetic inventiveness of poetry, and has instead tended to focus its energies on the novel. This may be, in part, because of the institutional history of postcolonial studies, which Deepika Bahri points out, emerged first not in literary departments but in African American, feminist and Commonwealth studies.[12] Consequently, according to Bahri, postcolonial literature has suffered from readings that privilege its subject matter over its inventiveness and style. Certain kinds of writing have thus become especially prominent in the field – specifically texts that engage directly with issues such as colonial history or the nation. Furthermore, since the publication of Edward Said's *Orientalism* in 1978, readers have been encouraged to locate in these texts underlying strategies of resistance to colonial and neocolonial hegemony – which has helped to reinforce a certain interpretive attitude towards postcolonial literature. In their influential book *The Empire Writes Back*, for instance, Bill Ashcroft, Helen Tiffin and Gareth Griffiths declare that 'the most significant feature' of postcolonial literature is its ability to abrogate and appropriate colonial hegemony, often through being marked by the colonial experience.[13]

The novel is further envisaged as the literary form most responsive to representing and negotiating the nation. Following Fredric Jameson's provocative declaration that 'All third-world texts are necessarily [...] allegorical', critics have turned to the postcolonial novel as a textual manifestation of national conflict.[14] In an Indian context, this is especially pronounced: many well-known novelists have negotiated the demands of representing the nation using techniques such as realism, magical realism and hyperbole, producing a literary incarnation of the larger than life dimension of India itself.

If, as Ramazani suggests then, postcolonial criticism has been 'grounded in mimetic suppositions about literature', it is not surprising to find poetry relegated to the periphery.[15] The poem, which derives much of its singularity from formal density and figurative language, seems incompatible with such pragmatic and pedagogic approaches to literature. Indeed, from as far back as the European romantic period, critics have argued that poetry engages with an entirely different realm of experience, one that is subjective, personal, intimate and disengaged from the macro-sphere of politics.[16] Much more recently, Mikhail Bakhtin differentiated between dialogic and monologic forms of literature, arguing that poetry was by very definition a 'singular and unitary' genre 'outside of which nothing else exists and nothing else is needed'.[17] As Akshaya Kumar comments, the ongoing impact of such views has been the depoliticization of poetry, and the widespread belief that 'poetry is a discourse of un-negotiated rootedness'.[18]

Contrary to such a preconception, postcolonial poetry has been shaped and informed by the violence, ruptures and historical legacies of colonialism, just like prose. Poets writing in the aftermath of decolonization, and educated within a colonial system, faced what is by now a familiar challenge: how to come to terms with their divided cultural and historical inheritance; how to give voice to historical and contemporary injustices in the idiom, or the language, of the former colonial oppressor; how to mediate between the contested realm of the traditional and the modern. As Ramazani reminds us, poets have been subjected to the same experiences as novelists and must negotiate some of the key concerns common to postcolonial literature, including colonial history, nationalism, identity and the politics of language: 'postcolonial poets have been unhoused by modernity, by war and politics, by education and travel'.[19] Poetry responds too to new forms and manifestations of power in a global context, its forms, languages and imagery offering a revealing insight into an increasingly mobile and transnational world. As Rajeev S. Patke argues, then, poetry is not antithetical to postcolonial critique, but rather 'enriches the connotations of "postcolonial"' in significant ways.[20]

Poetry and postcoloniality

Given the uneven experiences and manifestations of colonial rule, postcolonial texts responded in various ways to decolonization. However, Elleke Boehmer identifies a shift during the 1950s and 1960s, as writers from decolonizing nations sought to differentiate their work from that produced in the colonial period, and to forge cultural links with the new nation.[21] This desire to formulate an independent idiom is often accompanied by the introduction of indigenous forms, locations, stories and references, allowing poets to celebrate the distinctiveness of their own cultural heritage while dispelling the impositions of colonial culture: 'nativist and nationalist reclamation is a strong impetus' in much postcolonial poetry of this period.[22]

In India, poets working in English were not likely to align themselves overtly with the nationalist movement. However, their work is no less concerned with representing and reimagining the nation, and with calling into question their own relationship to this entity. Dom Moraes, for example, had a difficult relationship to India: the only child of journalist Francis Moraes and clinical researcher Beryl D'Monte, Moraes was part of a small, English speaking cultural elite in Bombay, well connected to many leading writers and intellectuals. However, his childhood was lonely, exacerbated by his mother's deteriorating mental health and eventual institutionalization. Moraes renounced Indian citizenship for a long period, and spent much of his early adulthood in London. In 'Letter to My Mother', the poet personalizes his discomfort with India by imagining it as his own troubled mother:

> Your eyes are like mine.
> When I last looked in them
> I saw my whole country,
> A defeated dream [23]

Like his mother, with whom he can never have a fulfilling relationship, India is out of reach, 'A population of corpses' and disillusionments: 'You know I will not return', the poem concludes.[24]

Another poet whose work explores the precariousness of belonging in postcolonial India is Nissim Ezekiel, whose writing career began almost contemporaneously with India's independence. Unlike Moraes, Ezekiel chose to remain in India, negotiating its challenges from within. As a secular, middle-class, Jewish poet writing in English, Ezekiel existed at an angle from mainstream Hindu culture, and his poetry is inflected with a sense of the vulnerability of the marginal subject: 'I went to Roman Catholic school, / A mugging Jew among the wolves'.[25]

Throughout this autobiographical poem, Ezekiel's persona is figured as out of place, an imposter: 'A poet-rascal-clown' with a 'borrowed top'.[26] It is only towards the end that the narrator finds a sense of belonging in a newly independent India:

> I have made my commitments now.
> This is one: to stay where I am,
> As others choose to give themselves
> To some remote and backward place,
> My backward place is where I am.[27]

Ezekiel made his 'commitments' to India through the creation of a distinctly modern poetic voice: unsentimental, ironic and with a preference for closed formal structures. Ezekiel's poetry makes a clear departure from the kind of writing produced by Indians during the colonial period – which tended to draw on religious myths, or deployed the romantic and sentimental imagery of European romanticism. Indeed, one of his major contributions to Indian poetry in English was his cultivation of a new, dispassionate style – one that would allow him to capture what he calls in 'On An African Mask' 'the equilibrium of art'.[28]

As Akshaya Kumar observes, poets of Ezekiel's generation were more likely to display an anxiety about India than poets writing since the 1990s.[29] Indeed, many more contemporary poets celebrate the porosity of national boundaries in an increasingly mobile world – or else focus on the fluidity of diasporic identities. In the introduction to his 2002 anthology *Reasons for Belonging*, Ranjit Hoskote describes modern Indian poets as being more 'at ease' than their forebears, and more cosmopolitan in their styles: 'their poetry is refreshingly free of the excess ideological baggage of Indianness that encumbered the earlier generation'.[30] In Meena

Alexander's 'Gold Horizon', for instance, the poet celebrates the flexible connotations of 'home':

> Place names splinter
> on my tongue and flee:
> Allahabad, Tiruvella, Kozhencheri,
> Khartoum, Nottingham, New Delhi,
> Hyderabad, New York [31]

For Alexander, the search for a national identity no longer assumes prominence. Instead, she negotiates her place in a global landscape, which demands increasingly dispersed modes of habitation. Hence in her poem, the accumulation of place names – in India and across the globe – reveals how far travel and migration has transformed the relationship between poets like Alexander, and the idea of home and nation. Unlike Ezekiel, Alexander moves freely between different locales. As Akshaya Kumar notes of poets of Alexander's generation, their work renegotiates the nation, often incorporating images of flight, dispersal, travel and transit, as the very idea of India 'takes on a multi-scalar character'.[32]

Language

The use of English and its traditions has been a source of tension in the work of many postcolonial writers. In India, English was the language of colonial education, but as the nationalist movement gathered momentum, it came to be greeted with suspicion and 'animosity'.[33] After independence, poets often showed a marked anxiety about the relationship between English and notions of privilege, authenticity and tradition. For some, like R. Parthasarathy, writing in English constituted a form of betrayal to ones' local roots. In *Rough Passage*, he famously depicted his 'tongue in English chains',[34] creating a protagonist who 'spent his youth whoring / after English gods'.[35] Parthasarathy, who would later stop writing poetry in English altogether, imagines a clear relationship between language and belonging: 'language is a tree, loses colour / under another sky'.[36]

Most poets, however, have acknowledged the risks involved in using English even while exploring its creative opportunities. Indeed, they can be seen to have taken up the challenge, articulated by Adil Jussawalla in 1974, when he argued that the 'Indian writer's relevance to his own people depends on what he does to language – the degree to which he may break out of a classical mould'.³⁷ Jussawalla's own *Missing Person*, does precisely this by incorporating conflicting images, registers and traditions, and by foregoing a linear narrative structure in favour of a fragmentary accumulation of scenes. Violent imagery reminds the reader of the risk involved in every act of creation: English is 'bright as a butterfly's wing / or a piece of tin / aimed at your throat'.³⁸ Other creative strategies include the use of non-Standard English and the replication of the way the language is spoken; code switching; and the incorporation of untranslated words and phrases, all of which demonstrate the creative energies of the English language.

The anxiety over English, and the desire to prove its credentials, has gradually given way to a growing ease with the language. For Amit Chaudhuri, it is poets' everyday use of English that gives it its 'peculiar excitement'.³⁹ When poets 'used ordinary English words like "door", "window", "bus", "doctor", "dentist", "station", to suggest a way of life', he suggests, they implicitly reject the notion that English is a foreign language at all.⁴⁰ Instead, it 'was already theirs', and 'had less to do with the colonizer than with modern Indians' exploration, and rewriting, of themselves'.⁴¹ As Kamala Das declares, language gives substance to individual identity:

> The language I speak
> Becomes mine, its distortions, its queernesses
> All mine, mine alone. It is half English, half
> Indian, funny perhaps, but it is honest ⁴²

Poets have not only shown an increasing confidence with the language, but have also transformed canonical texts, forms and traditions. Eunice de Souza and Melanie Silgardo, for example, make use of the confessional mode of mid twentieth-century poets, using its formal intimacy to explore women's experiences in suburban Bombay; Arvind Krishna Mehrotra's early poetry was influenced by European surrealism; and Arun Kolatkar transposed the colloquial language and informal style of the American beats into an urban Indian milieu. For these poets, the English language – and western literary forms– has proven deeply enabling.

Translation

At the same time, 'Multilingualism is an inevitable way of life' for most Indian poets, who typically have access to at least two or three languages.⁴³ For poets writing soon after independence, this could sometimes prove a source of unease: hence in A.K Ramanujan's 'Letter To A Friend', the poet presents the tension between English, which has a formal, public function, and Kannada and Tamil, which are the languages of intimacy and childhood: 'Between official letters, I doodle the wet / wild tendrils of a familiar alphabet'.[44] However, as Rajeev S. Patke contends, multilingualism has 'kept English interactive with the local linguistic environment:' postcolonial poetry in English, he shows, is deeply enriched by the presence of multiple languages, formal patterns and styles.[45] Ramanujan's English poems are thus shaped by his South Indian heritage, both in subject matter and style.

Indian poetry is full of such instances, as regional heritages and forms influence poems written in English. Hence the Kashmiri poet Agha Shahid Ali alluded to Urdu, Persian and Arabic cultural forms in his poetry, and 'brings an Islamic tradition of high lyricism into English'.[46] Ali is especially well known for his extensive use of the ghazal form, using this structure to negotiate his own multilingualism and diasporic identity. Similarly, medieval bhakti poetry has also significantly shaped the English writings of many poets: Akshaya Kumar identifies these forebears as an important presence in poems by Ramanujan, Kolatkar, Dilip Chitre, Arvind Krishna Mehrotra and others.[47] The laid-back style, irreverent attitude, religious iconoclasm and direct mode of address found in Kolatkar's English poems, for instance, bears resemblances with the work of Tukaram, and his poetry also often features well-known figures from bhakti narratives, relocating them into a contemporary setting. In *Kala Ghoda Poems*, Kolatkar depicts a street cleaner at work, but reimagines her as an incarnation of the female saint poet Meerabai: as the cleaner begins to compress the piles of rubbish, he sees her as 'a Meera before her Lord, / a Meera / with a broomstick for a lute'.[48] Kolatkar's English poem, then, set in downtown Bombay, in one of India's most Westernized of cities, is shaped and enriched by much earlier regional traditions and tropes.

The postcolonial poem can be considered as a palimpsest, shaped by the simultaneous accumulation of regional, colonial and world histories. As A.K. Ramanujan notes in his famous poem 'Small Scale Reflections on a Great House', the 'ancestral house' of a single family –an allegory for the postcolonial poem too – is created from an accumulation of objects, things, events and traditions, each leaving their mark:

nothing
that ever comes into this house
goes out. Things come in every day
to lose themselves among other things

> lost long ago among
> other things lost long ago[49]

The postcolonial poem serves as a formal manifestation of the historical forces and effects of colonialism, decolonization and globalization. The individual poem – in its themes, language and form – thus provides insight into the changes occurring in the wider social, economic and political sphere.

Limitations of the postcolonial

At the same time, poetry can enunciate an experience of history, place and language that exceeds the terms of postcolonial analysis. Indeed, while critics like Patke and Ramazani have done much to reorient attention to the postcolonial saliences of poetry, it is important to remain alert to the limitations of such an approach. As Patke points out, 'most poets are impatient with the term "postcolonial"', arguing that it is responsible for interpreting texts in a homogenous and deterministic way.[50] As some critics have suggested too, postcolonial literary analyses risk overlooking forms of oppression that have nothing to do with colonial power, and of ignoring the complex ways in which writers engage with ongoing forms of class, gender or caste discrimination. For Aijaz Ahmad, for instance, 'class and gender formations' remain largely excluded from much postcolonial criticism, which tends instead to focus on colonial history, decolonization and the nation.[51]

Hence, we might consider Eunice de Souza's poetry, which engages with female experience. Her poems enact a strident critique not of colonial society, but more particularly, of forms of patriarchy found in the Catholic Goan communities of suburban Bombay. In 'Sweet Sixteen', for instance, the poet depicts the hypocrisy of convent schools, which deliberately kept girls in a state of sexual naivety: 'Mamas never mentioned menses', the speaker declares; a nun 'pinned paper sleeves / onto our sleeveless dresses;' and the 'preacher thundered' at them, 'Never go with a man alone / Never alone'.[52]

In other poems, de Souza exposes the invasive cultural practices inflicted on the female body by a deeply gendered society. In 'Marriages are Made', she portrays the preparations for a cousin's wedding, which sees her family and body scrutinized:

her father declared solvent
her eyes examined for squints
her teeth for cavities
her stools for the possible
non-Brahmin worm[53]

Her body, which is 'not quite tall enough / and not quite full enough', is violated by this process of cataloguing, suggesting the loss of individuality entailed by patriarchal practices in contemporary India.[54]

If de Souza's poems bring women's experiences to the fore, Arun Kolatkar's *Kala Ghoda Poems* directs attention to contemporary subjects whose poverty or caste exclude them from society. These poems are set on a traffic island in downtown Bombay, and depict the people, animals and objects rendered extraneous to the city's official history. Over recent decades, and particularly since it was renamed Mumbai in 1995, the city has been claimed by right wing Hindu ideologues as a space belonging exclusively to Marathi speaking Hindus. At the same time, in many popular cultural accounts, Bombay is presented as an alluring and spectacular city – a city of fabulous wealth and opportunity. Kolatkar's poem challenges both conceptions, by incorporating precisely those figures excluded by political and cultural hegemony. Hence, he writes of the migrants, transients, drug dealers, shoe-shine boys, discarded bicycle tyres – calling into question the authority of those narratives that would keep them hidden.

Kolatkar's poetry also alerts us to the ephemeral and non-deterministic qualities of poetic language. Indeed, one of the characteristic features of his work is its commitment to detailing the smallest and briefest of moments, experiences and events, preserving them and allowing the reader to experience them too. For many poets, it is precisely this quality of language that becomes lost by postcolonial discourse, which some argue 'pushes literary uniqueness into a ghetto'.[55] Postcolonial poetry is not only insightful for its themes but also meditative, experimental and deeply affective – attributes that criticism must work hard to acknowledge.

In 'The Butterfly', the poem that appears in the centre of Kolatkar's *Jejuri*, the poet depicts the sudden appearance of a small butterfly, paying particular attention to the transience of this moment: 'It is split like a second. / It hinges around itself'.[56] The butterfly is not used as a metaphor: 'There is no story behind it', we are told, 'It is pinned down to no past'.[57] Instead, the butterfly functions as 'a pun on the present' – a brief reminder of the richness of the everyday and its contingencies, and of the challenge of representing this:

'Just a pinch of yellow, / it opens before it closes / and closes before it o'.[58] The poem finishes, or rather breaks off, as the butterfly disappears.

Throughout *Kala Ghoda Poems* too, Kolatkar recreates ephemeral experiences and impressions. From the smell of cheap tobacco, the sensation of rubbish between the street cleaner's toes, or a flower brushing softly against the skin of a young woman, Kolatkar's poems are concerned with the sensory realm. He is alert to the small interruptions of daily life, and to how these can transform a space. Hence in 'Watermelons', the appearance of a watermelon vendor makes time stand still for the people on the street:

> The city holds its breath
> as the cart goes click-clack,
> prolonging the road,
> stretching the morning
> to eternity[59]

The watermelon cart is inconsequential in a political, historical sense: like the little yellow butterfly, it has no impact on the events of the day. However, Kolatkar captures the brevity of the moment it occupies, and in doing so, critiques what Bahri refers to as the 'standardization of expectations and responses' to postcolonial literature.[60] The challenge for the reader then, is to remain alert to these moments, and to poetry's specific capacity to 'convey muted experiences and structures of feeling that exist outside of normative contexts'.[61] To do so is not to separate poetry from politics; on the contrary, it is to acknowledge the complex relationship between aesthetics and politics, and to recognize that texts operate in multiple ways.

Notes

1. Elleke Boehmer, *Colonial and Postcolonial Literature: Migrant Metaphors* (Oxford: Oxford University Press, 2005), 3.
2. 'The White Man's Burden'. Elleke Boehmer, *Empire Writing: An Anthology of Colonial Literatures, 1970–1918* (Oxford: Oxford University Press, 1998), 273.
3. 'Sonnet – Baugmaree'. Boehmer, *Empire Writing*, 70.
4. Ibid., xxxvi.
5. Jahan Ramazani, *The Hybrid Muse: Postcolonial Poetry in English* (Chicago: University of Chicago Press, 2001), 3.
6. Manohar Shetty, 'Vertical'. *Sunday Deccan Herald*, Bangalore, 25 January 2009, n.p.

7   Akshaya Kumar, *Poetry, Politics and Culture: Essays on Indian Texts and Contexts* (New Delhi and Abingdon: Routledge, 2009), 1.
8   Brouillette, *Postcolonial Writers in the Global Literary*; Huggan, *The Postcolonial Exotic*.
9   Ramazani, *The Hybrid Muse*, 3.
10 Arun Kolatkar, *Jejuri* (New York: New York Review Books, 2005).
11 Arun Kolatkar, *Collected Poems in English*, ed. Arvind Krishna Mehrotra (Tarset: Bloodaxe, 2010).
12 Deepika Bahri, *Native Intelligence: Aesthetics, Politics, and Postcolonial Literature* (Minneapolis: University of Minnesota Press, 2003), 4.
13 Bill Ashcroft, Helen Tiffin and Gareth Griffiths, eds., *The Empire Writes Back: Theory and Practice in Postcolonial Literatures* (London and New York: Routledge, 2002), 6.
14 Fredric Jameson, 'Third World Literature in the Era of Multinational Capitalism', *Social Text* 15 (1986): 69.
15 Ramazani, *The Hybrid Muse*, 4.
16 Ibid., 2.
17 Mikhail Bakhtin, 'Discourse in the Novel', in *The Dialogic Imagination: Four Essays*, ed. Michael Holquist. Trans Caryl Emerson and Michael Holquist (Austin and London: University of Texas Press, 1981), 286.
18 Kumar, *Poetry, Politics and Culture*, 11.
19 Ramazani, *The Hybrid Muse*, 12.
20 Rajeev S. Patke, *Postcolonial Poetry in English* (Oxford: Oxford University Press, 2006), 14.
21 Boehmer, *Migrant Metaphors*, 173.
22 Jahan Ramazani, 'Poetry and Postcolonialism', *The Cambridge Companion to Postcolonial Literatures*, ed. Ato Quayson (Cambridge: Cambridge University Press, 2012), 939.
23 Dom Moraes, 'Letter to My Mother' in *Selected Poems*, ed. Ranjit Hoskote (New Delhi: Penguin Books, 2012), 70.
24 Moraes, 'Letter to My Mother', 71.
25 Nissim Ezekiel, 'Background Casually', in *Nissim Ezekiel Collected Poems*, 2nd edn. (New Delhi: Oxford University Press, 2005), 179.
26 Ezekiel, 'Background Casually', 179.
27 Ibid., 181.
28 Ezekiel, 'On an African Mask', ibid., 6.
29 Kumar, *Poetry, Politics and Culture*, 114.
30 Ranjit Hoskote, 'Introduction', in *Reasons for Belonging: Fourteen Contemporary Indian Poets*, ed. Ranjit Hoskote (New Delhi: Viking Penguin Books, 2002), xiv.
31 Meena Alexander 'Gold Horizon', in *Meena Alexander, Illiterate Heart* (Evanston: triquarterly Books, Northwestern Press, 2002), 49.

32 Kumar, *Poetry, Politics and Culture*, 114.
33 Arvind Krishna Mehrotra, 'Introduction', in *A History of Indian Literature in English*, ed. Arvind Krishna Mehrotra (London: Hurst and Company, 2003), 20.
34 R. Parthasarathy, *Rough Passage* (New Delhi: Oxford University Press, 1977), 49.
35 Parthasarathy, *Rough Passage*, 17.
36 Ibid.
37 Adil Jussawalla, 'Introduction', in *New Writing in India*, ed. Adil Jussawalla (New Delhi: Penguin Books, 1974), 19.
38 Adil Jussawalla, *Missing Person* (Bombay: Clearing House, 1976), 14.
39 Amit Chaudhuri 'Huge Baggy Monster: Mimetic Theories of the Indian Novel after Rushdie', in *Clearing a Space: Reflections on India, Literature and Culture*, ed. Amit Chaudhuri (Oxford: Peter Lang, 2008), 118.
40 Chaudhuri 'Huge Baggy Monster', 118.
41 Ibid.
42 Kamala Das, 'An Introduction', in *Summer in Calcutta*, ed. Kamala Das (Bedford, Philadelphia: Everett Press, 1965), 59.
43 Laetitia Zecchini, *Arun Kolatkar and Literary Modernism in India* (London and New York: Bloomsbury, 2014), 65.
44 A. K. Ramanujan, 'To a Friend Far Away', in *A.K. Ramanujan Collected Poems* (New Delhi: Oxford University Press, 1995), 268.
45 Patke, *Postcolonial Poetry in English*, 61.
46 Bruce King, *Modern Indian Poetry in English*, 2nd edn (New Delhi: Oxford University Press, 2001), 274
47 Kumar, *Poetry, Politics and Culture*, 182.
48 Kolatkar, 'Meera', *Collected Poems*, 87.
49 A. K. Ramanujan, 'Small Scale Reflections on a Great House', *Collected Poems*, 96.
50 Patke, *Postcolonial Poetry in English*, 12.
51 Aijaz Ahmad, *In Theory: Nations, Classes, Literature* (London: Verso, 1992), 92.
52 Eunice de Souza, 'Sweet Sixteen', in *A Necklace of Skulls: Collected Poems*, ed. Eunice de Souza (New Delhi: Penguin Books, 2009), 6.
53 Ibid., 'Marriages Are Made', 4.
54 Ibid.
55 Patke, *Postcolonial Poetry in English*, 12.
56 Arun Kolatkar 'The Butterfly', in *Jejuri*, ed. Arun Kolatkar (New York: New York Review Books, 2005), 21.
57 Kolatkar 'The Butterfly', 21.
58 Ibid.

59 Kolatkar, 'Watermelons', *Collected Poems*, 150.
60 Bahri, *Native Intelligence*, 34
61 Françoise Lionnet, 'New World Exiles and Ironists from Évariste Parny to Ananda Devi', in *Postcolonial Poetics: Genre and Form*, eds. Patrick Crowley and Jane Hiddleston (Liverpool: Liverpool University Press, 2011), 14.

9

Postcolonial Noncitizenship in Australian Theatre and Performance: Twenty-First-Century Paradigms

Emma Cox

In the early twenty-first century, the robustness of state mechanisms for conferring belonging is increasingly indexed to the movements of particular kinds of noncitizen outsiders: individuals whose transnational mobility is 'unauthorized', but who are vulnerable to intense surveillance, military interception, detention and deportation. The question of whether this global predicament takes on a particular inflection or even urgency in settler colonial states is a complex one. Across the formerly colonized world, the last century was a period of nation building characterized by the successive unbinding of ties with Europe and the legislative formalization as well as cultural embedding of new citizenships. In Australia, the focus of this discussion, such embedding has always been tied to intractable national anxieties concerning the problem of settler autochthony in an invaded land.[1] It is nebulous (though tempting) to attribute Australia's hard-line repudiation of noncitizen outsiders to the dubious circumstances of its founding (by 'unauthorized' Europeans); at the same time, the solidarity in certain activist contexts of Aboriginal Australians with asylum seekers against the nation's punitive asylum frameworks is both significant and telling.[2] But that is not to say that the unauthorized arrival of persecuted and disenfranchised individuals reconstitutes the prevailing logic of sovereignty (as distinct from its biopolitical implementation), postcolonial or otherwise.

Today, illegitimate border crossings – or failed *attempts* – are effectively 'choreographed' by the political leaders of nation states who continually devise new means to intercept and corral unruly, undocumented bodies. Nowhere is this more the case than in Australia, a nation whose asylum policies (central to which is the mandatory, indefinite detention of all unauthorized noncitizens) have been characterized as 'the most parsimonious […] in the western world'.[3] Theatre and performance, modes of cultural practice that are of course first and foremost *embodied*, have a capacity and a responsibility to register and illuminate this state choreography and its wider consequences. The aim of my discussion here is to survey and analyse some of the ways in which theatre and performance in twenty-first-century Australia has engaged with the hotly contested subject of asylum, and to connect this artistic field with its overlapping social fields – chiefly, the character and effect of responses by western leaders and western media to the transnational movements of asylum seekers. Specifically, my reading will examine three key performance traditions in Australia's postmillennial theatre and performance of non-citizenship, namely verbatim theatre, refugee performance and the site-based performance of live art and protest. In each instance, I will focus on issues around embodiment and representation, suggesting in particular how Australia's postcolonial theatre of non-citizenship challenges prevailing political and media-related discourses surrounding the asylum seeker and/ or refugee.

A postcolonial theatre of non-citizenship seeks to intervene critically and ethically in the dominant discourses, frameworks, and practices concerning which bodies have the *capacity to do* (specifically 'move freely' or not) as a result of their legal status. I consider the stages of mobility and stasis that typically instantiate the asylum-seeking process to offer ways of reading and rearticulating its embodied cartographies: forced departure, journey, detection or evasion, detention or clandestine movement, waiting for status resolution, resettlement or deportation. One of the rights ostensibly conferred by citizenship is freedom of movement, which entails the right to enter other countries and return to one's own. Of course, temporally limited rights to move to and within a nation are also conferred by 'lesser' forms of authorized noncitizenship, including limited or permanent leave to remain, student visas, tourist visas and so on. Article 13 of the Universal Declaration of Human Rights identifies the right to move as applicable to the citizen; in practice, however, certain citizenships permit greater mobility than others, as do certain methods of arrival and their accompanying documentation (this is before we even take into account the precarious condition of statelessness). One of the most marked results of the right to move being a legislated and policed capability has been the aggressive politicization of the *manner of arrival* of unauthorized asylum seekers (or would-be refugees). In Australia, the state prevention of asylum seekers' access to national territory rests upon a formidable suite of apparatuses including detention camps (many of them extra-territorial and located on remote islands), maritime deterrence and interception. The main consequence of this is biopolitical: the state's coercion, often outside the perimeters of its own territory, of (non) arriving bodies.[4]

I use the term 'choreography' to describe the artful design of bodily sequences and appearances (individually or *en masse*). Its application in the context of forced migration casts in a new light the embodied consequences, and possible 'artfulness', of state border mechanisms. A border comes into use, or is activated, at the moment in which an attempted border-crosser appears and encounters its authoritarian logic; Sophie Nield articulates this lucidly in terms of what she calls the 'border machine', which, by disaggregating the body from its representation in the form of identity documentation, 'creates the condition of being "beside oneself", life disaggregated into presence and its proof. The machine of appearance demands that we perform ourselves before the law, in that no-man's land on the border between the body and its representation'.[5] To the extent that state organization of bodies can be understood as choreographic, it is a choreography that involves the management of how and where bodies will 'appear' as political life, be halted, subject to questioning, searched and identified (or not). Co-constitutively with its coercive function as political machine, the border manifests as a field of hyper-visibility (as bodies staggering from boats, clustering along roadsides, or railways, or pressing up against wire fences); while it is clear that space exists for journalism to underscore or to interrogate the tenor and rationale of governmental administration, crucially, statist and media domains function in such a way as to co-assemble a choreography. In using the term 'choreography', I do not mean to suggest that the organization of asylum seekers' lives is reducible to aesthetic representation. Instead, I propose that the administration and the spectacularization of irregular movement are together crucial to the emergence of an embodied politics.

The postmillennial period, in particular, has seen the emergence of a new discourse of what I term 'malcitizenship', which amplifies a perceived contiguity between categories of 'asylum seeker' and 'criminal suspect'. Katja Franco Aas highlights the increasing intertwining or convergence of criminal and migration jurisdictions, a set of discursive and legal slippages that she theorizes with reference to Juliet P. Stumpf's terminology on 'crimmigrant' bodies. Aas observes that '[t]he discursive and political coupling of migration and crime is creating a specific dynamic of social exclusion' centred around 'an *illegalized* global underclass, whose control is a driving force behind the formation of many of the transnational surveillance networks'.[6] As well as placing points of interference in the path of the illegitimate migrant, popular emphases on the latter take shape as a clearing of the path of its privileged other, setting in opposition 'crimmigrants and bona fide travelers'[7] and casting differential moral tinges upon their respective experiences of and rights to trans-territorial movement. In Australia, the federal government's discourses and actions convey an explicitly militaristic rationale surrounding the nation's successive immigration and border protection mechanisms: 'The Pacific Solution', 'Operation Relex', 'Operation Resolute', 'Operation Sovereign Borders'.

The use of the term 'malcitizen' refers to persons whose citizenship is perceived to have been broken or malfunctioned, such that they are expelled from the legal domain of rights and the social domain of civility. In recent years, malcitizens of the United States, the United Kingdom and elsewhere have been identified for extrajudicial imprisonment as part of the 'War on Terror', or execution by targeted drone strike in pre-emptive engagements. Australia's most widely known case of malcitizenship is that of David Hicks, who spent more than five years imprisoned at Guantanamo Bay detention camp after 9/11 and whose conviction for terrorist offences has now been struck down. Sometimes the categorization of malcitizen misfires, as in the case of Cornelia Rau, a German citizen and Australian permanent resident who was unlawfully detained for several months in an Australian immigration detention centre between 2004 and 2005. Occasionally, the categories of 'refugee' and 'terrorist malcitizen' come into convergence with stunning optics, as in December 2014 when the Iranian extremist, Man Haron Monis, a refugee who had been granted Australian citizenship some years prior, carried out an armed hostage siege at a café in central Sydney; Monis and two hostages died during the siege. At the time of writing, the Australian government is taking advice from a parliamentary committee on proposed legislation that would strip dual nationals of Australian citizenship if they have been convicted of terrorist offences.

One of the capacities of theatre and performance concerned with forced migration is to use narrative and embodied imaginative techniques to show what the convergences and interdependencies between 'crimmigrant' and 'bona fide' categories of human might look like in particular moments or contexts, and in this way to scrutinize the basis of the distinction. Future theatrical projects will undoubtedly need to take into account this emerging paradigm and its effects. It is a paradigm that in postcolonial nations like Australia evidences a shift in orientation from understanding the power dynamics undergirding access to citizenship as inflected by colonial legacies to understanding citizenship itself as inflected by a troubled new cosmopolitanism. Performance opens spaces for stories and also for practical convergences where socio-political exclusion and division may be typical. As such, it can intervene politically on behalf of those denied status and representation. Next, I look at the contributions of verbatim theatre, refugee performers, and site-responsive performance, showing how these embodied practices can challenge the prevailing choreographies of non-citizenship and projections of malcitizenship.

Verbatim theatre: Narrative, validation and innocence

In near retrospect, the rise to prominence of verbatim theatre in the UK, North America and Australia in the late 1990s and early 2000s[8] seems symptomatic of profound and rapid changes to the way digital technology mediates events, experiences and recollective capacities (individual and cultural). A subset of documentary theatre devised wholly or in part from the words of real people, verbatim theatre owes an obvious debt to the valorized domain of the law, which has oral testimony at its heart, and artistically to agitprop traditions, but it is perhaps more than anything else the product of a networked and rapidly globalized culture of recording. A culture of recording is one that atomizes events, isolates and disseminates details and ultimately attributes relative capital to human experience; in an artistic context, all of this contributes to verbatim theatre's purchase. Practitioners of the form often regard their work as intervening in the public record, offering new or alternative accounts of events. In Australia, the precipitous politicization of unauthorized asylum seekers or 'boatpeople' from 2001 onwards fitted quite neatly into a verbatim theatre paradigm because of the readiness with which the issue could be timelined in an event-based way. The relevant 'events' of 2001 have been repeatedly documented: they include the Tampa affair, in which the Australian government refused entry into territorial waters to the Norwegian ship, *MV Tampa*, that had rescued several hundred asylum seekers; the 'children overboard' scandal, in which government ministers, the Prime Minister and Navy personnel wrongly accused asylum seekers of throwing children into the sea in order to prevent pushback to Indonesia; and the SIEV X disaster, in which 353 asylum seekers drowned in waters between Indonesia and Australia.

Caroline Wake notes that verbatim theatre has been 'by far the largest subgenre' of theatre in Australia produced in response to immediate asylum seeker debates and narratives.[9] Verbatim productions made in Australia from 2001 generally utilized testimony drawn from interviews with asylum seekers and refugees; these include *Asylum*, produced by Urban Theatre Projects and directed by Claudia Chidiac (2001); *Club Refuge*, produced by the activist network Actors for Refugees (2002); Sidetrack Theatre's *Citizen X* (2002); Michael Gurr's *Something to Declare*, produced by Actors for Refugees (2003); Ros Horin's *Through the Wire* (2004); and *In Our Name*, created by director Nigel Jamieson in collaboration with the Al Abbadi family (2004). The overriding aims of these works concerned authenticity: the imperative of truth telling, approached in the context of unjustly marginalized or disbelieved stories (that were also positioned as representative of refugee stories *per se*). The plays had as a common starting point the idea that proximity to refugees' words (and those of their supporters) lent the narratives a certain ethicality. In practical terms, there are a host of problems with this, not least the dilemma of theatrical embodiment: who can perform as a refugee, and in what manner (naturalistic, or as reportage)? What are the risks, on the other hand, of a refugee playing him or herself, as occurred in *Through the Wire* with Iranian theatre maker Shahin Shafaei, who struggled with his self-enactment within the creative frame of his Australian director.[10] The broad rationale of these verbatim plays – to open up affective spaces that validated refugees' deservingness of protection in Australia – meant that they sometimes tended towards political and emotional myopia. Agnes Woolley reminds us that the words of refugees are so closely tied to concepts of evidence that their scope for differentiated (self-)representation is curtailed: '[i]f, as is usually the case, "well-founded" is interpreted as a demand for proof or evidence of the persecution from which the refugee is fleeing, then the current and prevailing concept of the refugee is rooted in the idea of a validating narrative'.[11] This impacts upon the moral dimensions of theatrical characterization; as I have argued elsewhere, 'the expectation that when a refugee speaks he or she is "giving evidence" is so pervasive that it becomes exceedingly difficult to ethically circumvent constructions of refugees as innocent individuals'.[12] I would contend that most verbatim theatre productions about refugees in Australia to date have triangulated, to a greater or lesser extent, three elements, narrative, validation and innocence (in the sense of ambition as well as morality[13]), in order to situate refugees within what is essentially a humanizing paradigm, and to open up possibilities for imaginative audience engagement with refugee experiences.

It was, in the end, in circumvention of this politico-aesthetic triangulation that one of the most interesting verbatim refugee-responsive productions of the post-2001 era emerged in Australia. *CMI (A Certain Maritime Incident)*[14] (Sydney and Canberra, 2004) was devised from Hansard transcripts of the Senate Select Committee on A Certain Maritime Incident (2002), which investigated events of 6–8 October 2001, during which an Australian Navy vessel intercepted the distressed people smuggling boat SIEV 4 (Suspected Illegal Entry Vessel 4) and rescued its passengers. This event came to be known as the 'children overboard affair' and *CMI (A Certain Maritime Incident)* is concerned with the ways in which discourses of witnessing are deployed and redeployed in such a way as to construct a political mirage of half-truths and convenient lies. The production was superficially akin to a mode of verbatim theatre that has come to be known as 'tribunal theatre', which is devised from verbatim records of formal hearings, depositions or court cases. But in sharp contrast the genre-defining tribunal verbatim plays staged at London's Tricycle Theatre from 1994 to 2012,[15] *CMI (A Certain Maritime Incident)* radically questioned its capacity to recuperate the truth of recent events by stitching together already-problematic verbatim accounts and using an interlocking series of distancing strategies such as cross-casting, child casting, ironic delivery, digital delivery as well as hyperbolic aesthetic eruptions. It also departed from the ethos of recuperative verbatim theatre in its rehearsal of several kinds of false witnessing, something Wake traces deftly in her discussion of the play and its implications for our understanding of witnessing.[16] In *CMI (A Certain Maritime Incident)*, the 'new' narrative with which the theatre makers were most concerned was not to do with the lives of asylum seekers or refugees, but rather, the Australian political class and their insufficiency as transparent representatives in a liberal democracy. If the play didn't seek to 'set the record straight', it was nonetheless revelatory in its doggedness: what it revealed was power's obfuscatory relationship to language; the tenacity of lines connecting vested interests in the Navy and in government; and ultimately, the unaccountability of power when it is applied quite literally to the 'unlawful' bodies of vulnerable people. To the extent that its starting point was its practitioners' ethical incapacity to speak for noncitizen others across vast power differentials, I would suggest that *CMI (A Certain Maritime Incident)* might be an exemplary postcolonial play.

Refugee performers and participatory environments

There are fairly obvious practical and ethical reasons why theatrical productions that engage with traumatic or politically contentious subject matter are not often enacted by those whose lives they dramatize. When refugees do participate as performers, whether 'as themselves' or in a generic capacity as a refugee character, a key purpose can often be broadly pedagogic (concerned with capacity building or engaging with community perceptions); the context of the performance is often in and for a close-knit support or activist community. Refugee performers may have a not-always-acknowledged purpose of 'authenticating' the work in which they appear, or of affirming the ethicality of its enactments. This is often the case in works that find their way into professional or semi-professional theatres, and was effectively the function Shahin Shafaei ended up having in *Through the Wire*, a rare example of a professional documentary theatre production in which a refugee performed as himself (see above). The professional career of another Melbourne-based actor and filmmaker from a recent refugee background, Iraqi Australian Majid Shokor, has been less firmly yoked to identity politics: while Shokor's appearance in Bagryana Popov's *Subclass26A* (2005), a movement-based work that integrated sections of dialogue, was interpreted to a certain extent in authenticating terms, it was not a piece in which he performed his own 'refugee story'. Moreover, Shokor's role in Michael James Rowland's feature film *Lucky Miles* (2007) was not autobiographical (though he did play a refugee character); most recently, Shokor has appeared in and co-produced with director Marsha Emerman a documentary film on the history and development of Iraqi music, *On the Banks of the Tigris* (2015).[17]

In a small number of cases, new refugees in Australia have written and performed their own solo theatrical works. These include *There is Nothing Here* by Afshin Nikosouresht (Melbourne, 2002), *Refugitive* by Shahin Shafaei (touring, 2002–03) and *Nothing But Nothing* by Towfiq Al-Qady (Brisbane, 2005). In each case, the inherent intensity of solo performance came into convergence with a certain fascination with the 'authentic' refugee body, generating theatrical moments that were both narrative-based and concerned with performer-audience exchange. The works differed in their emphases and concerns with selfhood – Al-Qady's was explicitly autobiographical while Nikosouresht's and Shafaei's were abstracted from the authors' experiences in immigration detention. Their thematic concerns and theatrical techniques, though, including representations of detainee distress and self-harm, the use of direct audience address, and the addition of post-show Q&As, highlighted the meaningfulness of the convergence between refugee presence and performative appearance.

Most often, theatrical projects in Australia in which refugees participate as performers are collectively enacted, typically with non-refugee performers. They are usually directed and facilitated within an educational or community setting. In some contexts, performance works are given a staging in professional venues, whilst in others, the project culminates in community showcases. Works staged in the first few years of the twenty-first century were often concerned with the immediate issue of prolonged detention, emerging as they did in the years that saw a rapid consolidation of detention architectures as well as a series of high-profile scandals involving harsh treatment or repudiation of asylum seekers. Sometimes the process of creating these works involved contact with detainees; Linda Jaivin's two-hander about two young men in detention, *Halal-el-Mashakel* (first staged as a double bill with Shafaei's *Refugitive*), emerged out of Jaivin's regular visits to Villawood detention centre in Sydney. In a 2004 restaging one of the refugees upon whom the story was based, Iranian Morteza Poorvadi, performed one of the roles. In recent years, a detectable trend within participatory projects has been a move away from the preoccupation with documenting detainees' experiences and a growing interest in non-narrative performance modes, the transplantation and survival of creative traditions and an engagement with wider aspects of refugees' communities and psychological lives. A prominent example is *The Baulkham Hills African Ladies Troupe* (Sydney, 2013), a work that integrated testimonies derived from participating women's lives with song, dance and video.

A feature of some participatory projects in Australia is an interest in resettlement and wider issues of social cohesion in everyday life – this concern distinguishes such works from narrative refugee theatre concerned with the moment of arrival (or failed arrival), or with the politics of immigration detention. Catherine Simmonds's project with the Asylum Seeker Resource Centre in Melbourne, *Journey of Asylum – Waiting* (2010), involved refugees and asylum seekers at various stages of their resettlement process. It presented a series of vignettes which sought to convey the multiplicity of trajectories and experiences that make up the nominal subject position of 'refugee'. The work was a devised piece responsive to the backgrounds and characteristics of its participants, and its large cast of characters were listed as refugee 'protagonist' and non-refugee 'collaborator' categories. For the most part, real names remained unchanged, which generated a slippage between individuals and the various roles they played during the performance, as well as highlighting the degree to which interactions between asylum seekers and those from whom they seek assistance or protection follow a predictable script.[18] *Journey of Asylum – Waiting* was underpinned by Simmonds's awareness of the risks involved in the re-telling or enacting of trauma, and the tendency for refugees to be reduced to their 'story'. In one of the vignettes, a refugee-performer expressed weariness at being required to 'talk talk talk talk talk' (the very thing, of course, his presence in the play required of him). In another scene, a refugee-performer, lying in a mock-seductive pose in a Perspex box, teased with a sly satire the relationship between refugees and theatre audiences: 'Give me a banana and I will tell you a story. Give me two bananas and I'll tell you my story, but maybe you won't sleep for the rest of your life'. The effectiveness of these scenes, the second of which enacted the caging of its protagonist simultaneously with his ironic self-exposure, underscores Alison Jeffers's argument that close attention to the proxemics of participatory theatre involving refugees – what she describes in terms of 'bodies and space and the intersubjective relationships that develop through distance, proximity and the gaze in that space'[19] – can be the basis for a more nuanced understanding of the practice of being an audience member. This practice, Jeffers reminds us, may represent a form of 'civil listening' in which a 'shoulder-to-shoulder' relation with other audience members is a way of challenging simplistic claims to togetherness-through-theatre.

Site responsive performance, live art and protest

Performance that takes as a point of departure the site(s) in which it occurs, foregrounding relationships between performing bodies, spectators and sites, brings artistic endeavour and the embodied cartographies of asylum into most immediate convergence. That is, site-responsive performance, live art and public protest are forms that whilst internally diverse, can be characterized by their typical subordination of narrative representation to the orders and contingencies of social space. A prevailing technique of such work in Australia has been to intervene in citizens' relationships to the public places in which they move. The examples that I refer to here took place outside theatre buildings and for this reason they both circumvent the commonly noted challenge of refugee theatre as preaching to the converted, and raise new ethical and communicative challenges. As Jeffers notes, refugee-responsive art or protest in open public spaces situates spectators to a certain extent in a relation of compulsion, whereby they are 'are co-opted into witnessing, willingly or not', and consequently, 'the most common phrases used against it are couched in the language of physical violation'.[20]

Responsiveness to space and site in this context may enlist audience-participants in practices of mobility, or crossings. One recent Australian production that was conceived site-responsively as a mobile or promenade piece is *Origin-Transit-Destination* (2015) by Casula Powerhouse Arts Centre and Australian Performance Exchange. This free, immersive work, which was devised in part by refugees, was oriented around a bus tour with song and storytelling. It departed from Auburn, an area of western Sydney with a proportionally high refugee population, travelling to various locations including the vicinity of a detention centre, before finishing at the Casula Powerhouse Arts Centre. The work had the overt purpose of inviting its audience-participants to experience something akin to what asylum seekers encounter by embodying or re-mapping coerced trajectories. It articulates wider trends in immersive refugee-responsive theatre, of which Clare Bayley's production in a shipping container about refugees in Europe, *The Container*,[21] is a prominent example. But unlike Bayley's piece, *Origin-Transit-Destination* did not seek to put audience members in a state of physical or psychological discomfort, but rather to explore the potential of mobile performance, whereby being taken on a journey might be a means of enacting an interpersonal and political openness to grasping the remnants and traces of refugees' embodied predicaments.

A more extreme mode of work that operates at the interstices of live art and protest is performance that involves visceral bodily investment and intensification. Mike Parr's 2002 piece at the Monash University Museum of Art, *Close the Concentration Camps*, saw the artist appear with his mouth and eyelids sewn together and his trouser leg ripped open at the thigh, upon which the word 'alien' had been branded. This work occupies a genealogy of live art practices of which Parr has long been part, and is at the same time a direct response to the modes of self-injury that detained asylum seekers were undertaking at the time of the performance (and have done since). The same year, Mireille Astore presented her eighteen-day site-responsive work, *Tampa*, at the upmarket Tamarama Beach in Sydney, as an intervention that referenced the Australian government's refusal the previous year to permit into its waters the *MV Tampa* cargo vessel (see above). Astore's occupancy of a cage-like structure modelled on an asylum seeker boat was meant to explicitly reference sociologist Ghassan Hage's concept of ethnic caging, and thereby sought to provoke reflection upon the racialized effects of immigration detention.[22] The technique of modelling the physical suffering or deprivation of incarcerated asylum seekers was echoed in a series of solidarity fasts that took place in Australia between 2002 and 2005, many of them involving public figures, and in most cases taking place in public square or major shopping districts. Performance of this kind places the body in a state of discomfort and turns this discomfort into a public spectacle.[23]

Self-injury by detained asylum seekers has at various times been widespread in Australian detention centres, but it is by no means isolated to this geopolitical context. Jenny Edkins and Véronique Pin-Fat's analysis of self-injury as response to traumas of immigration detention and imminent deportation references cases from the UK, the Netherlands and Australia. Their key argument is that these self-injuries instantiate sovereignty's underlying structure as a 'relation of violence',[24] but that within the brutal terms of this relation, self-injury can take us 'beyond the impasse'[25] that is implied by an Agambenian reading of sovereign power as total. Self-injury offers spaces for resistance, 'first, in a refusal to "draw the line" or make distinctions between forms of life of the type upon which sovereign power relies; and, second, in what we call *the assumption of bare life*, that is, the taking on of the very form of life that sovereign power seeks to impose'.[26] While the resistant potential of detainee self-injury is clear, it remains vital to draw a distinction between the representational and symbolic power that accrues to self-injury as a phenomena, especially in carceral systems, and capacities in terms of selfhood and subjecthood implied by the idea of a volitional, political 'taking on' of forms of life. In other words, the meaning of self-injury needs to be disentangled from its temporal consequence as intense bodily suffering of the kind that, as Elaine Scarry suggests, has an 'unmaking' or world-reducing effect.[27]

A related mode of performative engagement by citizens in this context is the protest that interrupts the symbolic order of civic spaces. An increasingly prominent form is the 'die-in' protest at refugee support rallies, which has been seen across Europe and in the United States in the context of migrant crises and race relations, respectively. A notable Australian iteration of pro-refugee engagement in civic space has a distinctly postcolonial inflection: in Melbourne in 2010, Aboriginal activist Robbie Thorpe (who also identifies by the tribal name, Djuran Bunjileenee), reoriented a protest document first devised in the context of Aboriginal sovereignty activism, the Original Nation Passport. He undertook a public signing of a stack of these documents for the members of a group of Sri Lankan asylum seekers whose entry to Australia had been prevented by the Rudd Labor government. The asylum seekers were at the time refusing to disembark from the Indonesian port to which they had been forcibly returned by Indonesian authorities, at Australia's insistence. At the signing of passports, staged outside Melbourne's Trades Hall and recorded for public dissemination, Thorpe announced: 'we want to make it clear that the Aboriginal people, the true sovereigns of this land, are offering them a passport to enter into our territorial waters, and our land', adding, 'we're the colonized refugees'.[28]

Site-responsive, live art and civic protest interventions explicitly confront the biopolitics of Australian asylum legislation. In some cases, they test performers' physical limits as well as the limits of what a spectator is willing to watch. At their extreme end, they gesture towards the zone of the necropolitical: the paradigmatic power of sovereign governments to mandate death, or to oversee apparatuses that will lead to an undetermined number of deaths. The drowned asylum seeker and the detained asylum seeker exist as two contingent bodies along the embodied continuum of irregular noncitizen movement. In Australia, as in Europe, migrant arrival and death are closely imbricated with maritime zones. The co-occurrence of mass deaths at sea and the mass mobility of subaltern bodies opens up a fraught colonial legacy; Jenna Brager characterizes the historical link between undocumented maritime deaths and the hierarchies inaugurated by global capitalism:

The oceans are full of bodies – the waters speak of the necropolitical creation of disposable classes that are subject to vanishing. The boundaries are made clear, between the privileged class of the human and its other. The ritual of body disposal, which prevents or makes ghosts, is at the foundation of political community.[29]

Brager's observation brings us back to the core paradox with which theatre and performance makers concerned with asylum must grapple: the human beings with which they are concerned are those whose bodies are simultaneously 'subject to vanishing' and intensively watched, placed in containers, held aside.

Conclusion: Citizens and 'new subalterns'

Postcolonial perspectives can shed light on the political and aesthetic discourses, representations and choreographies associated with asylum in the twenty-first century. Performance can go a long way towards communicating the effects that exclusion from belonging and territoriality have on identity and personhood. It can point to ways in which belonging is racialized and illuminate the historical formations and legacies that underpin this racialization. Twenty-first-century noncitizenship is a legislated and embodied capacity that requires us to recast certain aspects of postcolonial critique. Similarly, the dynamics of asylum this century both reflect and exceed the global legacies of colonialism. David Farrier takes seriously the 'asylum seeker's candidacy as the new subaltern who initiates the step beyond postcolonial discourse – both describing its limitations in relation to the new globalized formation and indicating the direction of its advance, redrawing lines of engagement with deterritorialized sovereignty'.[30]

Because they function as both representation and as social practice, theatre and performance are important means by which to respond to the politics and experiences of noncitizenship. They have the capacity to probe the limits and crisis points of new transnational relationships and power dynamics. In this chapter I have sought to offer a survey and to loosely classify key modes of performance in Australia that have been responsive to the nation's uncompromising stance on human movements deemed irregular, unauthorized or unlawful. The extent and variety of artistic responses, along with the immediacy of ongoing debates, make Australia an important global entry point for understanding how relationships between asylum seekers and their would-be hosts are being registered in contemporary nations still occupying positions of privilege. At the same time, Australia's refugee-responsive performance culture rehearses troubled versions of citizenship – they manifest the desires, shame, pride, anxiety and resistance of people already 'here' within the nation, people who have the opportunity to claim or contest their own relative belonging, a belonging ultimately still cast in opposition to the embodied capacities of so many who are caught in an extended process of arrival.

Notes

1   Emma Cox, *Theatre & Migration* (Basingstoke: Palgrave, 2014), 36–39.
2   Emma Cox, *Performing Noncitizenship: Asylum Seekers in Australian Theatre, Film and Activism* (London: Anthem, 2015), chapter 5; Emma Cox, 'Sovereign Ontologies in Australia and Aotearoa–New Zealand: Indigenous Responses to Asylum Seekers, Refugees and Overstayers', in *Knowing Differently: The Cognitive Challenge of the Indigenous*, eds. G. N. Devy, Geoffrey V. Davis and K. K. Chakravarty (London: Routledge, 2013); Emma Cox, 'Welcome to Country? Aboriginal Sovereignties and Asylum Seekers', *Australian Studies* 3 (2011), http:/www.nla.gov.au/openpublish/index.php/australian-studies (accessed 1 October 2015).
3   David Farrier and Patricia Tuitt, 'Beyond Biopolitics: Agamben, Asylum, and Postcolonial Critique', in *The Oxford Handbook of Postcolonial Studies*, ed. Graham Huggan (Oxford: Oxford University Press, 2013), 263.
4   Australia's most recent extra-territorial strategies involved the commissioning of shipbuilder Dragon Industries Asia to build boats for maritime pushbacks to refugee source or transit countries in Southeast Asia.
5   Sophie Nield, 'The Proteus Cabinet, or "We Are Here but Not Here"', *RIDE: Research in Drama Education* 13, no. 2 (2008), 143–44.
6   Katja Franco Aas, '"Crimmigrant" Bodies and Bona Fide Travelers: Surveillance, Citizenship and Global Governance', *Theoretical Criminology* 15, no. 3 (2011), 337.
7   Franco Aas, '"Crimmigrant" Bodies', 338.
8   'Theater making that engages with people's personal stories has become mainstream, almost trendy'. Julie Salverson, 'Change on Whose Terms? Testimony and an Erotics of Injury', *Theater* 31, no. 3 (2001), 119–25, 119.

9   Caroline Wake, 'To Witness Mimesis: the Politics, Ethics and Aesthetics of Testimonial Theatre in *Through the Wire*', *Modern Drama* 56, no. 1 (2013), 102–25, 102.
10 For discussions of *Through the Wire*, and of Shahin Shafaei's performance, see Wake, 'To Witness'; Cox, *Performing Noncitizenship*, chapter 1.
11 Agnes Woolley, *Contemporary Asylum Narratives: Representing Refugees in the Twenty-First Century* (Houndmills, Basingstoke: Palgrave Macmillan, 2014), 124.
12 Cox, *Performing Noncitizenship*, 29.
13 See Cox, *Performing Noncitizenship*, chapter 1, for fuller discussion.
14 The texts of *CMI (A Certain Maritime Incident)*, Towfiq Al-Qady's *Nothing But Nothing* and Catherine Simmonds' *Journey of Asylum – Waiting* appear in Emma Cox (ed.), *Staging Asylum: Contemporary Australian Plays about Refugees* (Sydney: Currency, 2013).
15 These Tricycle Theatre productions include: *Half the Picture*, *Nuremberg*, *Srebrenica*, *The Colour of Justice: The Stephen Lawrence Enquiry*, *Justifying War*, *Guantanamo*, *Bloody Sunday*, *Called to Account*, *Tactical Questioning* and *The Riots*.
16 See Caroline Wake, 'Caveat Spectator: Juridical, Political and Ontological False Witnessing in *CMI (A Certain Maritime Incident)*', *Law Text Culture* 14, no. 1 (2010), 160–87.
17 Drawn in part from my unpublished interviews with Shahin Shafaei and Majid Shokor in Melbourne in 2008 and 2011, respectively.
18 For further discussion of *Journey of Asylum – Waiting*, see Cox, *Performing Noncitizenship*, chapter 1.
19 Alison Jeffers, 'Hospitable Stages and Civil Listening: Being an Audience for Participatory Refugee Theatre', in *Refugee Performance: Practical Encounters*, ed. Michael Balfour (Chicago: Intellect, 2013), 299.
20 Alison Jeffers, *Refugees, Theatre and Crisis: Performing Global Identities* (Basingstoke: Palgrave Macmillan, 2012), 90.
21 Clare Bayley's shipping container play *The Container* has been performed in a number of cities since its 2007 Edinburgh premiere: London, 2009; Denver, 2010; Cardiff, 2011; Washington, DC, 2013; Melbourne, 2013; Toronto, 2014; Calgary, 2015.
22 Mireille Astore, 'When the Artwork Takes the Pictures', *Law Text Culture* 10 (2006), 239–58, 248–50.
23 For further discussion of representations of refugee self-harm in Australian performance art and protest, see Cox, *Performing Noncitizenship*, chapter 4.
24 Jenny Edkins and Véronique Pin-Fat, 'Through the Wire: Relations of Power and Relations of Violence', *Millennium: Journal of International Studies* 34, no. 1 (2005), 1–24, 1.

25 Edkins and Pin-Fat, 'Through the Wire', 3.
26 Ibid.
27 Elaine Scarry, *The Body in Pain: The Making and Unmaking of the World* (Oxford: Oxford University Press), 1985.
28 'Aboriginal Passports Issued to Asylum Seekers Prevented from Entering Australia', The Juice Media, https://www.youtube.com/watch?v=XkjJpz7nxWM (accessed 25 May 2010).
29 Jenna Brager, 'Bodies of Water', *The New Inquiry*, thenewinquiry.com/essays/bodies-of-water/ (accessed 12 May 2015).
30 David Farrier, *Postcolonial Asylum: Seeking Sanctuary before the Law* (Liverpool: Liverpool University Press, 2011), 5.

10

Graphic History: Postcolonial Texts and Contexts

Binita Mehta and Pia Mukherji

Modern graphic formats, narratives and cultures have long been defined by emphasizing text/image multimodalities as primary constructive frames.[1] While early semiotic studies of comics examined graphic narratologies, image-structures and grammars, these comics codes were later characterized variously as 'ideological, deep or (de)constructive' by Marxist, psychoanalytic or postmodern theoretical revisions.[2] Elaborating on critical assumptions that thus describe comics-texts and vocabularies as both meaningful and political, this essay seeks to demonstrate that graphic writing may be read as an effective category of 'postcolonial textuality' (that) 'enters colonial discourse deconstructively, inhabiting its ambiguities and fissures', and thus initiates a 'persistent questioning of the frame, which at one level, is the space of representation, and at another level, the frame of western modernity itself'.[3] Specifically, we will examine how graphic writing, the use of text and image, lends itself particularly well to the elucidation of public and private colonial and postcolonial history.

In our analysis of the two graphic narratives that follow, one, Olivia Burton's *L'Algérie c'est beau comme l'Amérique* (2015) [Algeria is beautiful like America], examines the colonial and postcolonial relationship between Algeria and France. This is exemplified in the history of the pieds-noirs (literally black feet), the term used to refer to the white colonial settlers in Algeria that included not only people of French ancestry but also Italians and Maltese who settled in Algeria and became French citizens. The second focuses on the legacies of the South Asian Partition of 1947 as narrated in the graphic collection *This Side,*

That Side: Restorying Partition (2013), edited by Vishwajyoti Ghosh. Before examining the texts closely, we will provide a historicist frame for each reading. *L'Algérie c'est beau comme l'Amérique* will be contextualized historically, through a brief discussion of colonial Algeria, the complexities of the Algerian war, and post-independence Algeria. *This Side that Side: Restorying Partition* will be introduced by a review of comics-production history, with a specific focus on a post-independence Indian comics genealogy.

Jean-Paul Gabilliet's comprehensive study of the 'forms of modern comic art'[4] examines American comics history in the context of mass publishing and print cultures, and describes 'comics as a medium (defined by) a multiplicity of endogenic (aesthetic) and exogenic (technological, economic, social) factors.'[5] Gabilliet's constructivist method of comics definition helps us think about how postcolonial comics cultures coincide with the theoretical expression of a particular political category, that of 'public culture' as a condition of modernity, specifically in the postcolony. A discussion of the visual modalities of the 'postcolonial public' is summarized by Arjun Appadurai and Carol A. Breckenridge: 'Drawing on recent studies on South Asian public culture as a late modern formation distinct from western histories of mass and popular cultures, ... current transnational comics scenes may be contextualized within "new public modernities"'[6] which particularly emphasize cultural registers such as the circulation of images, the political roles of visuality, 'the importance of symbolic actions (and) the emancipatory dimensions of art, display and performance.'[7] The reconstitution of new visual grammars, iconographies and performances appears central to the projects of postcolonial public cultures. From this critical perspective, our readings of graphic Pied Noir/Partition histories in this essay are framed by a particular interpretation of, following Appadurai and Breckenridge, 'the idiomatic, political, and situated' aspects of postcolonial comics texts and histories: (as expressions of) emergent public cultures that demonstrate how modernity can become a 'diversely appropriated experience'[8] in different (post)national imaginaries.

Reading *L'Algérie c'est beau comme l'Amérique:* The Algerian War and pied-noir identity

Burton's graphic novel is one of several that have been written by children and grandchildren of those who are affiliated in some way to Algeria. In an article in *Le Monde*, the historian Benjamin Stora comments on how the younger generation, the children of French soldiers, immigrants and harkis, Algerian soldiers who fought with the French, 'éprouvent le besoin de s'inscrire dans une généalogie, une filiation, de savoir, quelle a été l'attitude du père ou du grand-père dans cette guerre'⁹ [feel the need to subscribe to a genealogy, a filiation, to know of the attitude of the father or the grandfather in that war]. Although Stora does not specifically mention the children and grandchildren of pied-noirs, they too can be included the groups that have 'felt the need' to trace their family genealogies.

The French colonized Algeria from 1830 to 1962. Although the move towards independence started earlier, the war lasted from 1954 to 1962 as different factions vied for power. The *Front de Libération nationale* (FLN) was composed of a group of young Algerian nationalist militants who wanted Algeria to be independent from French rule. In 1958, the French army in Algeria, who by 1957 numbered 450,000 troops, fearful that Algeria would settle with the FLN, tried to stage a coup d'état. General Charles de Gaulle was called in to deal with the situation and although he had earlier supported French occupation of Algeria by uttering the words, 'Vive l'Algérie française'[Long live French Algeria], he decided that the only solution at that time was independence. He was opposed by a group of dissident generals and settlers who formed the *Organisation de l'armée secrete* (OAS), and soon launched a terror campaign. The war of independence, or *la guerre sans nom* [the war without name], was a bloody one with violence committed by both the French army and the FLN. In France, Algerian immigrants who supported independence were harassed by the police and in the demonstration in Paris in October 1961, several were killed and their bodies thrown into the Seine.[10]

As Benjamin Stora notes, a number of factions were affected by the Algerian war and continued to face discrimination afterwards. Our focus is on one group, the pied-noirs. In her graphic narrative, Burton ruminates about the still-debated origins of the term pied-noir. Her ruminations are accompanied in her graphic novel by images of the various theories about the term's origins: the black boots the French soldiers wore during the 1830 war of conquest of Algeria in 1830; the colour of the feet of the cultivators who crushed grapes; the nickname that the French who were hostile to Moroccan independence gave themselves in 1956; and finally, next to the image of a Native American chief in full headdress, she suggests a reference to the Native American Blackfoot tribe. Ironically, she adds, the Black Feet in the French-Algerian context were the white colonizers, not the indigenous population.[11]

In late 1961 and early 1962, at the end of the Algerian war, there was a mass exodus of pied-noirs from Algeria to France. They were demonized by the metropolitan French, especially, as Todd Shepard informs us, by the new left. Shepard writes: 'Writers of the new left recentered their antifascism ... on the OAS and, in an easy elision, on the "Europeans of Algeria".' This buttressed a growing assumption that pied-noirs – like all people from Algeria – were not French and that it was their irrationality and violence that had produced 'French' wartime abuses such as torture.[12] Stora mentions that despite the psychological, social and economic struggles of the pied-noirs when they first arrived in large numbers to France in 1962, they were able to show a united front in their search for compensation for material possessions left behind. Although they will never fully be compensated either for their material possessions, nor for the memories of their lives in Algeria, they have been able to move out of ghettos in which they were housed when they first arrived.[13] Stora contrasts the progress of pied-noirs and their descendants to the harkis and their progeny who continue to live in ghettos. His sympathies appear to lie with the harkis who were also never accepted as French citizens.[14]

Given historical, stereotypical views of pied-noirs as perpetrators of violence because of their association with the OAS, and as different from the metropolitan French, fictional and documentary narratives based on pied-noir memories are valid and relevant and provide a complex and nuanced picture of colonial Algeria. In his book, *Redrawing French Empire in Comics*, Mark McKinney discusses graphic novels about the Algerian war, as well as those that trace familial genealogies:

> The history of the Algerian War is in many ways a family story ... Most of the recent comics about the Algerian War were created by artists with a family connection ... to the colonization of Algeria and the Algerian War. Many such cartoonists inject personal or family experiences into their representations of the Algerian War and its aftermath.[15]

McKinney describes the predominant focus of pied-noir graphic narratives as a 'nostalgic longing for a lost country and community' and claims that he found only one pied-noir narrative to have an 'unapologetic colonialist perspective'. Others about the Algerian war by authors of pied-noir heritage 'critique various forms of French colonial violence'.[16] Although Burton learns about colonial Algeria through conversations with her grandmother and about the Algerian war from her extended family, she does, against her family's wishes, visit the ancestral home in Algeria. Her 'second-hand' knowledge of the Algeria is translated into first-hand knowledge of post-independence Algeria during her visit in 2010.

From pied-noir Algeria to postcolonial Algeria

Part memoir, part travelogue, Olivia Burton's graphic novel[17] is a personal quest for the author's roots, as a descendant of a pied-noir family, written with the eye of a documentarian (the author has also made two documentaries). At the same time it discusses the private history within the public history of the colonial and postcolonial period in Algeria.[18] The form and content of the graphic novel – text by Burton, drawings by Mahi Grand, drawn in black and white with some images in colour taken during her visit to Algeria – is interspersed with flashbacks that include discussions with family members who repatriated to France at the end of the Algerian war in 1962. It includes memories of their life in Algeria before and during the war, as well as the author's return to Algeria in 2010 to visit her family's ancestral homes in the region of Aurès, as well as their apartment in Algiers where they took refuge during the war. Personal and public histories intertwine as Burton attempts to explore her family's pied-noir genealogy and to better understand their lives in Algeria. She has to engage with Algeria's colonial history, including the war of independence, and to come to terms with her own family's role as white settlers in Algeria. In the personal quest for her family's roots in Algeria, Burton moves from nostalgia to guilt, and finally to acceptance of her family's background and role during France's colonization of Algeria.

Burton's graphic novel divided into seven parts. Of those, Part I, the longest, entitled, *Je vais enfin voir* [I will finally see] sets up the context for her graphic novel. It opens with the author at the airport in Paris going through security on her way to Algeria. As she sits in her window seat in her plane, she reflects, through a series of frames drawn as flashbacks, on how she got to this point. Her grandmother was the conduit through which the she had learned about her family's pied-noir history. Until the day she died, the grandmother was nostalgic for her family home in Algeria and filled her granddaughter's head with colourful stories about life in Algeria where they were farmers. On her return to France, her grandmother made her home in Bandol, on the *Côte d'Azur*, the French Riviera, because the landscape most closely resembled their home in Algeria. Burton includes black and white photographs of their life there: grand balls with women and men dressed in elegant clothes, tennis games and family portraits. After her death, her grandmother leaves Burton a journal of memories of their life in Algeria that she takes with her to Algeria.

Over meals with her extended family, Burton learns about seminal events that occurred during the Algerian war that lasted from 1958 to 1962. She hears about the deaths that occurred during the war: 'Une rivière de sang y avait dans la rue' [There was a river of blood on the road].[19] Family members talked about mutilated soldiers, desecrated cemeteries, told stories about the barbarism of the indigenous population, but also stories about those who saved and helped some of the pieds-noirs, especially one, a member of the FLN, who had saved the author's grandfather's life. There was resentment towards General de Gaulle, who they felt had betrayed them.[20] Her mother is more reticent about discussing her life in Algeria, but does so with other pied-noir friends. She also mentions the ignorance of the metropolitan French about pieds-noirs, who perceived them as boorish colonizers.[21]

The author became acutely aware of her pied-noir heritage, or, her 'postcard' view of Algeria 'exploded' when she entered high school. The first incident she describes was when her friend Florence interrogates the author's grandmother about their lives in Algeria. When her grandmother answers that they were farmers, Florence retorts: 'Vous étiez des colons'[22] [You were colonizers]. Unsettled by Florence's hostility, her grandmother asserts that they worked hard and treated their workers well. That leads Burton to question not only what her grandparents had really done in Algeria, but also the ignorance of her friends who often said to her, 'Ben tu n'as pas l'air d'une Arabe!' [But, you don't look like an Arab] when she explained that her mother was a Pied-Noir.[23] At university, the students were even more vocal about their revulsion of pieds-noirs whom they called 'des exploitateurs racistes, des fachos, et même des tortionnaires'[24] [racist exploiters, fascists and even torturers]. Although the author finds it difficult recognize her family in such descriptions, she is nevertheless ashamed of them and their customs, including the food they ate – garlic, olive oil and hot peppers – unfashionable foods in the 1970s. As she remarks: 'Je suis partagée entre la rage et la honte'[25] [I am torn between rage and shame]. Forced to defend her family when attacked by outsiders, but judging them harshly at home, Burton describes her behaviour as schizophrenic.

An image covering an entire page of the comic book shows the author swinging on a branch of her family tree, unable to extricate herself, yet eager to distance herself from her family. In the following pages, the author condemns the French government, like she does her own family, for being deaf to the violence in their ex-colonies in Africa during the 1990s regarding the civil war in Algeria and the Rwandan genocide. As she observes cynically: 'Ils sont basanés ou carrément noirs, laissons-les se massacrer entre eux.'[26] [They are dark-skinned, or entirely black, let them kill each other]. Her critique of the French authorities is clear. They care little if the brown and black citizens of their ex-colonies kill each other. Their lives do not matter. The author's grief is accentuated by her grandmother's death. On her deathbed she asks Burton to sprinkle a sachet of dirt that she brought with her to France from the ancestral home, the village of Bernelle in the Aurès, on her coffin.

Arriving in Algeria and after a short stay in capital, Algiers, Burton takes a road trip to visit her grandparent's home.[27] It is during the road trip to Merouana (formerly Corneille), the village in the Aurès region in Algeria, where the paternal great-grandfather, Hippolyte Fabry, had arrived in 1900, that we reach the heart of the narrative, a confrontation between private and public history. In a discussion with her Algerian guide, Djaffar, whom she had met in Algiers through mutual friends in France, she confesses her feelings of guilt about being the grandchild of pieds-noirs, just like her grandparents had had a hard time accepting that fact that they were on the 'mauvais côté de l'histoire' [wrong side of history] and that they and constructed their whole life on 'une injustice de fond'.[28] [a basic injustice]. As they drive through the lush mountainous landscape of the Aurès, Burton imagines herself in the American West. In one frame, we see drawings of cowboys on horseback on a distant mountain; in next frame, they escort a covered wagon as they make their way west for a better life, just like her own ancestors moved to Algeria from nineteenth-century France for a better life. While Burton compares the landscape of the Aurès region with the landscape of the American West, McKinney speaks about the rapport between the conquest of Algeria and the American West: 'The irony is that in some sense the cartoonists do celebrate the Algerian War as epic history – France's Western adventure in Africa – weaving it together with fictional elements to create a narrative meant to be thrillingly authentic.'[29]

Burton is understandably nervous about how she would be received by villagers who had known her family. Djaffar reacts angrily to her self-identifying as a grandchild of a pied-noir. For him, it was an artificial identity that included Jews, Italians, Spaniards, as well as her grandfather who moved to Algeria from the Isère department in France. He adds that nobody in France today would define himself as 'le fils de collabo', the child of a collaborator, referring to the period of the Nazi occupation of France during the Second World War. For Djaffar, Burton's family was not pied-noir. They were Algerians since, as he remarks, they were born and raised in that country that they loved.[30] Does Djaffar's explanation of her grandparents' identity as Algerians assuage Burton's guilt about being the descendant of Pieds-Noirs? And, does his assertion that her family was Algerian let Burton off the hook?

The last two pages of her graphic novel are an attempt to realize peace and reconciliation between past and present, between private and the public history, between the pieds-noirs and the indigenous Algerian population. Seated in a metro car in Paris, Burton exchanges smiles with a young North African woman wearing a headscarf. We then see two sets of frames that represent the past and the present. The first frame of the first set shows an immigrant family waiting at the Belleville metro station. Belleville is an area in northern Paris where many North African immigrants live. The second frame shows newly arrived immigrants, presumably in the 1960s, standing next to a boat that had brought them to France. The first frame of the second set shows a North African man, perhaps an Algerian, seated next to a white Frenchman, while the following frame anachronistically transports us to the period of the Algerian war with the same two men, one dressed as a French solider holding a gun and the other a Algerian independence fighter, a *fellagha*, also with a gun.[31] In the author's imagination, the war is finally over and all factions are living together in harmony. The final frame of the graphic novel shows Burton looking out of the window of the metro car, a smile of satisfaction on her face.

Reading *This Side That Side:* *Restorying Partition*

Abhijit Gupta's periodization of the 'postcolonial popular'[32] describes the production of the Anglophone-Indian 'literary' as a popular format within post-independence networks of publishing and distribution that comprise new markets, readerships and genres. In summary, it examines a modern production history of genres that moves from the 'national', then to the 'metropolitan', and eventually to a 'globalized' popular. As a counterpoint to current American and Anglo-European scholarship that typically describes comics history in terms of a progression from a body of European pretexts leading to a largely American-influenced inventory of modern graphic cultures,[33] the 'postcolonial popular' offers an alternative approach. It charts a specific comics genealogy[34] of South Asian comics production, 'historically, (as) periods of breaks and discontinuities: illuminating the points where patterns or relations are reshaped or transformed (within) inventories of popular culture'.[35] This present brief summary of the institutionalization of Indian graphic writing is necessarily a partial gesture. Attending to the protocols and themes of the process, particularly those moments that unsettle the changing Indian comics scene, must also remind us of a transnational range of postcolonial graphic histories, a 'global circulation of narratives mapping both individual lives and world-historical events'.[36] An emergent critical field that includes the work of John A. Lent, Nancy Rose Hunt, Veronique Bragard, Fedwa Malti-Douglas, Massimo Repetti and Ann Miller, among others, investigates transformations within post-independence and diasporic graphic writing cultures in contemporary Francophone African, Arab-eastern,[37] and Southeast Asian settings. The overlaps and divergences between these distinct locations are noticeable, in each case, in their regional aesthetics, historical influences and socio-political environments. However, such evolving patterns of comics production typically include some common phases in their broad trajectories. These include state-directed educational and social instructional publication, market-driven 'national' comics production, avant-garde experimental comics publishing and contemporary political graphic writing that often uses transnational or digital platforms.

Comics historians have published systematic overviews of the post-independence Indian comics industry, identifying the stages and ideological shifts that mark its emergence and gradual establishment.[38] With the publication of Anant Pai's *Amar Chitra Katha* series by India Book House in 1967, a newly minted indigenous genre arrived, diversifying from nationalist and conservative history writing in *ACK* to the development of local super-heroic and comic character based franchises. These texts by independent publishing houses in the 1980s sold alongside popular Western-imported comics serials and pseudo-educational children's comics. Eventually, the industry shifted its cultural location to an established and contemporary Delhi-based graphic-novel industry. Partly politically engaged, progressive and experimental,[39] and partly global-consumer-culture driven and market-oriented, the industry sold exotica, orientalized mythology and localized-noir urban storyworlds via new technology platforms and international corporate collaborations.[40] Vishyajyoti Ghosh's 'curated' anthology, *This Side that Side: Restorying Partition* (2013) is an example of the new Indian graphic-novel and its revisionary agendas.

(Re)Drawing partition

Urvashi Butalia, recalling absent women's stories erased from 'incomplete' narratives of the Indian Partition, writes: 'There are, of course, no complete pictures ... Everyone who makes one draws it afresh. Each time, retrospectively, the picture changes.'[41] *This Side That Side: Restorying Partition* can be described variously: as a picture-anthology, a political collaboration, an imagined archive. In each case, it presents a compelling example of 'dialogic' postcolonial work[42] particularly relevant in the context of contemporary 'post-national' globalization, one that is characterized by an ethics of cross-locational conversation and speaking beyond differences. The collection of graphic (re)stories in this compilation takes as its subject a singular event of decolonization: the Partition of the South Asian subcontinent in 1947 to establish the free nation states of Pakistan and India after three centuries of colonial control, and eventually, the formation of Bangladesh in 1971, following the Indo-Pakistan and Bangladesh Liberation Wars. The bloody migration in 1947, of Hindu, Sikh and Muslim populations crossing border territories, left fifteen million citizens exiled and homeless, and one million killed by extreme sectarian violence. The legacies of these events persist not only in present-day conditions of national conflict and deprivation in the subcontinent but also within intimate histories, continuing displacements and repressed traumas that affect survivor communities. 'Historical wounds' inflicted by the practices of colonialism are impact events that exceed 'historical truths', according to historian Dipesh Chakrabarty, in that their status relies on the political recognition of suffering that is remembered, felt and lived through, and not found in objective or verifiable record. *Restorying Partition* attempts to 'speak of such a wound, or speak in its name'⁴³ by a method particular to the requirements of a 'postcolonial manifesto', that is, by 'diversifying its mode of address [...] to facilitate a democratic colloquium between antagonistic inheritors of the colonial aftermath'.⁴⁴

As an assembly of short graphic stories that are each crafted from collaborations – between artists and writers across South Asian borders and between story/image/document within texts – the collection establishes a creative colloquium, and traces multiple partition genealogies. In this sense, it may be read as a reconstructed archive, one that uses a variety of voices (intimate, allegorical, historical, domestic) to describe emblematic, relational, fragmented journeys and lives and employs colour-free visual styles including photographic, naturalistic, ligne-clear, caricature, cartoon, abstract, poster art, folk motifs, calligraphy, silhouette. The politics of the archive has been variously theorized by post-structuralist and postcolonial philosophers as enabling interventions within public history. Homi Bhabha, for example, has explored the strategic utility, in a postcolonial context, of Foucault's rejection of the archive 'as (inert) documents attesting to (a cultural) past; or as evidence of a continuing identity [...] The archive is the first law of what can be said, the system that governs the appearance of statements as unique event'.⁴⁵ The imagined archive in *Restorying Partition* presents, as preserved documents, lost and concealed partition stories that dramatize extreme violence – pathological, bodily, surgical mutilations of land, people and history, traumas of exile and homelessness. These fictions infiltrate an official national narrative: that of a hard-won and peaceful transfer of power, a procedural and rational division of territories based on majority representation of resident citizens, and the establishment of independent nation states and modern citizen identities in such a newly inaugurated postcolonial history.

In this sense, the interstitial and hidden histories articulated in this collection primarily challenge a dominant notion of the nation state as the most desirable form of political community, exemplifying progressive Western modernity and the principles of liberal democracy, an idea that was widely inherited by the constructive agendas of 'decolonized' territories in the aftermath of colonialism. *Restorying Partition* is self-consciously performative and revisionary, disrupting familiar registers of place, time and address that comprise conventional histories of nationalism, which then designate these as progressive, unified and the basis of individual and collective consciousness.

Drawing borders

'An Old Fable', by Tabish Khair and Priya Kurien, introduces the borderline as a foundational theme in historical record and narrative accounts of the Partition of 1947. The Indo-Pakistan border was famously mapped in forty days preceding the transfer of power, in a climate of gathering communal violence and British political disengagement, as a final colonial commission, 'an exercise that had to be executed in the right spirit of democracy, an institution ... set up back home'.[46] 'An Old Fable' dramatizes the absurdity of the political division that underwrote a 'decolonized' nationalism informed by inherited ideologies of progressive Western modernity, already historically complicit with imperial interests. The satirical monograph reworks the old Solomon myth, as Reason, Logic and Law determine a just English resolution to the competing claims of two mothers, clad in the religious colours of Saffron and Green, on a single child. The body of the child must be divided exactly, both horizontally and vertically, the reasonable and lawful verdict demands. The cruel inadequacy of the partition-borders to settle the claims of location and identity within the borders of the postcolonial nation are tied to a disruptive effect. Constitutive dualities and bifurcations – home/elsewhere, self/other, this side/that side – are, in fact, carried within the intimate certainties of home, self, belonging, and are thus recast entirely for those who stay within as well as those who leave.

Several stories ('Border', 'FaultLine', 'Which Side?') explore various aspects of post-partition margins: linguistic, symbolic, psychic, embodied. The haunting fragment 'Border' – composed using a mix of naturalistic and impressionistic styles by Kaisar Haq and artist Hemant Puri – introduces two recurring motifs that anchor testaments of partition border-crossings: the often feminized and sometimes erotic embodiment of land that has been divided or lost, and the psychoses that a separation from such homelands and histories induces. 'Let us say you dream of a woman, and because she isn't anywhere around, imagine her across the border', the narrative speculates.[47] The obsession impels you to travel to a 'squalid frontier town' where 'instead of crossing over, you lie dreaming of the woman and the border: perfect knife that slices through the earth without the earth's knowing, and severs and joins at the same instant.... You lie down on the fateful line under a livid moon. You and your desire and the border are now one'.[48] The uncanny history traced in 'Water Stories' (Arundhati Ghosh and Appupen) connects the final suicide of the protagonist with a sequence of past events of 'death by water', that of her grandmother and her mother, recalled by her father's memories of their East Bengal village by the Padma river, left behind in the post-partition migration. The river, mythically irrigating community life during years of settlement, turns inimical, implacable in these stories of the remembered land, especially towards women who would leave her: 'the river came through my memory and entered your mother's heart, freezing it in her chill embrace'.[49]

The long summer of 1947, staging the Partition, is also, crucially, a moment of 'anniversary remembrance' for the nations of India and Pakistan. Berger and Niven describe 'the anthropomorphic notion of a point of birth or emergence' that a 'national project needs' and commemorates as a basis for continuing 'memory cultures and national histories'.[50] *Restorying Partition* visualizes how counter-memories of the Partition infiltrate and unravel national 'anniversarism' to interrupt projects of historical continuities and community consolidations, and significantly, to displace notions of settled location. 'In-between' and untethered sites recur on the postcolonial map, exceeding prescriptions set by 'national' geopolitical determinants. Refugee camps, established as post-1947 receiving and rehabilitation centres or as temporary enclaves for second wave 'displaced' peoples in post-1971 Pakistan and Bangladesh (Muslims originally from India or else the 'other' Pakistan), become the subject of several stories that detail the uncertain status of these enclaves, stranded by history in unfamiliar provinces.[51] And Kashmir, in 'Tamasha-e-Tetwal', remains the territorial archetype of a 'union, unmade in spirit'[52] encompassing the long consequential effects of postcolonial historical trauma contained in the symptomatic divisions of the Partition that endure.

The scenes of Partition and its aftermath in *Restorying Partition* include compensatory moments in stories of reconstruction, often found in political gestures, art and individual attempts at renewed connections – evidence of 'postmemorial' work, whose more immediate 'connection to the source is mediated not through recollection but through imaginative investment and creation'.[53] Particularly, the imaginative appropriation of visual style or performance modes appears to support such expressive narratives as historical counterpoints. In 'Know Directions Home?', Nina Sabnani employs the voice of a displaced craftswoman, who, having 'learned to do Suf embroidery from my grandmother', successfully participates in the resettlement of her refugee community in the barren Kutch, who use their art as a collective resource. Pictured as an evocative Suf tapestry, the narrative closes with an assertion of identity and an address: 'Today we are a collective and we use our art, not only to support ourselves but also to tell our stories – Raniben Ratilal Bhanani, Kala Raksha Parkar Vas, Sumrasar Sheik, Bhuj Taluka, Gujrat'.[54]

Eventually, however, partition narratives tend, perhaps inevitably, to testify to the many forms of violence particular to the exigencies of 'border imperialism'. The storied crimes of 1947 – mass massacres, rape, torture, mutilations – are made explicitly graphic in just one of the twenty-eight accounts present in this anthology, indicative of the long historical silence on the subject in South Asian public culture and private testimony. Attending to a story of a survivor's crossing through a 'country littered with the dead, the tragic harvest of partition', the narrator in 'I Too Have Seen Lahore' speculates, 'Sixty two and four years had passed ... but the harrowing journey in August 1947 (had not) left him. Surely he would have preserved those memories by telling his stories to his children? But deep inside, Darshan Singh's connection with Klasswala is perhaps a tenuous one and exists only in his mind.'[55] The issue remains the difficulty of articulation of an incommunicable history that must find its mode of address outside the language of institutionalized systems. Border violence is theorized by Agamben as a state of exception in relation to law-establishing (imperial) boundaries, where the division between a 'bare life' and a 'political life' is enforced in a 'no man's land between public law and political fact'.[56] The border space of the state of exception therefore, 'concerns a threshold, or a zone of indifference, where inside and outside do not exclude each other but rather blur with one another'[57] and where the exiled, stripped of all legal and political attributes, are subjected to violence that has shed every relation to law. Crimes of the partition have been precisely thus sanctioned, produced and made unspeakable by their exceptionalism, a version of a larger narrative of imperial discipline and its historical consequences. Etienne Balibar has described the widespread nineteenth-century colonial practice of drawing territorial borders as 'at once a way to organize the world's exploitation and to export the "border-form" to the periphery, in an attempt to transform the whole universe into an extension of Europe'.[58] The landscape of decolonization, therefore, as the scene of 'drawn' nation states fashioned as European prototypes, inescapably becomes a theatre of border-conflicts that illustrate the spectacular failures of colonial legacies. *Restorying Partition*, as a graphic statement of one such inheritance, attempts to document the specific imperatives and consequences of postcolonial border history.

The graphic texts examined in this essay, Burton's *L'Algérie c'est beau comme l'Amérique* and the texts in *Restorying Partition*, rely on image/

text collaborations to illuminate critical moments in postcolonial political histories. In Burton's text, the use of family albums, photographs and maps become important visual indicators of private history during the colonial period and provide clues for tracing family genealogies and reconciliations with the colonial past in the postcolonial period. The compendium of (post) partition scenes in *Restorying Partition* bears witness to the vivid persistence of collective trauma in postcolonial testimony and public history. In both instances, the most effective interventions seem to proceed from a recognition, as Stephen Slemon has observed, of the colonial aftermath both as 'a set of political relations and as a signifying system (marked by the) ambivalent structural relations'[59] that underwrite (post)imperial historical discourse.

Notes

1   See, for example, Will Eisner's classic description of the comics medium: 'The format of comics presents a montage of both words and image, and the reader is thus required to exercise both visual and verbal interpretive skills. The regimens of art (perspective, symmetry, line) and the regimens of literature (grammar, plot, syntax) become superimposed upon each other.... And it is this disciplined application that creates the grammar of sequential art.' Will Eisner, *Comics and Sequential Art* (New York: Norton, 2008), 2. Other picture-narrative models include texts characterized by sequential images (McCloud 1993), the 'arthology' of symbolic/iconic images and panels (Groensteen 2007), or interactive multi-modal text-image exchanges (Harvey 2001).
2   Binita Mehta and Pia Mukherji, 'Introduction', *Postcolonial Comics: Texts, Events, Identities* (New York and London: Routledge, 2015), 1. For an overview of such comics criticism and theoretical fields, see Mehta and Mukherji, 'Introduction', 15, 16.
3   Stephen Slemon, 'The Scramble for Postcolonialism', in *De-Scribing Empire: Post-Colonialism and Textuality*, eds. Chris Tiffin and Alan Lawson (London: Routledge, 1994), 15–30.
4   Jean-Paul Gabilliet, *Of Comics and Men: A Cultural History of American Comic Books*, trans. Bart Beaty and Nick Nguyen (Jackson: University Press of Mississippi, 2005), xi.
5   Gabilliet, *Of Comics and Men*, xi.
6   Arjun Appadurai and Carol A. Breckenridge, 'Public Modernities in India', in *Consuming Modernity: Public Culture in a South Asian World*, ed. Carol

A. Breckenridge (Minneapolis: University of Minnesota Press, 1995), 1–19. 10.
7　Appadurai and Breckenridge, 'Public Modernities in India', 3.
8　Ibid., 4.
9　Benjamin Stora, 'Algérie-France, mémoires sous tension.' *Le Monde. fr.* 18 Mar 2010. Web. 7 August 2015, http://www.lemonde.fr/afrique/article/2012/03/18/algerie-france-memoires-sous-tension_1669417_3212.html. Translations our own.
10　Ann Miller, *Reading 'bande dessinée': Critical Approaches to French-Language Comic Strip* (Bristol: Intellect Ltd, 2007), 166, 167.
11　Olivia Burton and Mahi Grand, *L'Algérie c'est beau comme l'Amérique* (Paris: Steinkis editions, 2015), 30, 31.
12　Todd Shepard, *The Invention of Decolonization The Algerian War and the Remaking of France* (Ithaca and London: Cornell University Press, 2006), 193.
13　Benjamin Stora, *La gangrène et l'oubli La memoire de la guerre d'Algérie* (Paris: Éditions La Découverte & Syros, 1998), 258–260.
14　Stora, *La gangrène et l'oubli La memoire de la guerre d'Algérie*, 164, 165.
15　Mark McKinney, *Redrawing French Empire in Comics* (Columbus: The Ohio State University Press, 2013), 147.
16　McKinney, *Redrawing French Empire in Comics*, 172.
17　Interviewed on TV5 Monde, the author says that although based on documentary materials, some characters are a fiction.
18　A review describes it as a 'road-movie existential dans lequel des trois générations disent leurs espoirs et leurs déceptions [an existential road movie in which three generations discuss their hopes and their disappointments]'. Nicolas Michel, http://www.jeuneafrique.com/mag/252776/culture/lalgerie-cest-beau-comme-lamerique-une-bande-dessinee-en-nuances-sur-la-nostalgerie/ (accessed 10 October 2015).
19　Burton and Grand. *L'Algérie c'est beau comme l'Amérique*, 15.
20　Ibid.
21　Ibid., 21.
22　Ibid., 25.
23　Ibid., 26.
24　Ibid., 27.
25　Ibid., 29
26　Ibid., 38.
27　Ibid., 50–52.
28　Ibid., 138.
29　McKinney, *Redrawing French Empire in Comics*, 161.
30　Burton and Grand. *L'Algérie c'est beau comme l'Amérique*, 80–83.

31 Ibid., 170, 171.
32 Abhijit Gupta, 'Popular Writing in India', in *The Cambridge History of Postcolonial Literature*, vol. II, ed. Ato Quayson (Cambridge: Cambridge University Press, 2011), 1023–1038.
33 For scholarship on social histories of comic traditions, see David Kunzle, Jean-Paul Gabilliet, R. C. Harvey, Bradford Wright, Bart H. Beaty, Stephen Weiner.
34 The scope of this study does not allow an examination of parallel, diverse and related histories of post-independence regional language-based print cultures.
35 Stuart Hall, 'Popular Culture and the State', in *Popular Culture and Social Relations*, eds. Tony Bennett, Colin Mercer and Janet Woollacott (Milton Keynes: Open University Press, 1986), 22–50, 23.
36 Hilary Chute and Marjorie Dekoven, 'Comic Books and Graphic Novels', in *The Cambridge Introduction to Popular Culture*, eds. David Glover and Scott McCracken (Cambridge: Cambridge University Press, 2012), 187–94, 194.
37 For genealogies of the current Middle Eastern comics scene, see essays by Massimo Di Ricco and Lena Merhej in Mehta and Mukherji.
38 See O. P. Joshi, 'Contents, Consumers and Creators of Comics in India', in *Comics and Visual Culture: Research Studies from Ten Countries*, eds. Alphons Silbermann and H. D. Dyroff (Munich: K. G. Saur: 1986); Aruna Rao, 'From Self Knowledge to Superheroes: The Story of Indian Comics', *Illustrating Asia: Comics, Humor Magazines and Picture Books*, ed. John A. Lent (Richmond, Surrey: Curzon Press, 2001), 37–63; Jeremy Stoll, 'A Creator's History of the Comics Medium in India', *International Journal of Comic Art* 15. no. 1 (Spring 2013): 363–83.
39 Graphic novelists in this space include Sarnath Banerjee, Orijit Sen, Amruta Patil, Vishwajyoti Ghosh, Naseer Ahmed, Samhita Arni, Parismita Singh, Appupen.
40 See the corporate profile and online catalogues of Graphic India, Liquid comics, Campfire Graphic Novels.
41 Urvashi Butalia, *The Other Side of Silence: Voices from the Partition* (Durham: Duke University Press, 2000), 100.
42 See Dipesh Chakrabarty's description of the postcolonial dialogic mode in 'An Anti-colonial History of the Postcolonial Turn: An Essay in Memory of Greg Dunning', *Melbourne Historical Journal* 37 (2009): http://www.mhj.net.au/.
43 Dipesh Chakrabarty, 'History and the Politics of Representation', in *Manifestoes for History*, eds. Keith Jenkins, Sue Morgan and Alan Munslow (London: Routledge, 2007), 77.
44 Leela Gandhi, *Postcolonial Theory: A Critical Introduction* (New South Wales: Allen and Unwin, 1988), ix–x.

45 Michel Foucault, *The Archeology of Knowledge*, trans. A. N. Sheridan Smith (London: Routledge, 1977), 129.
46 Vishwajyoti Ghosh, *This Side That Side: Restorying Partition* (New Delhi: Yoda Press, 2013), 11.
47 Ghosh, *This Side That Side: Restorying Partition* (*TSTS*), 44.
48 Ibid., 44–49.
49 Ibid., 132, 133.
50 Stefan Berger and Bill Niven. 'Writing the History of National Memory', in *Writing the History of Memory*, eds. Stefan Breger and Bill Niven (London: Bloomsbury, 2014), 146–151.
51 See 'Know Directions Home', 'A Good Education', 'Taboo', 'Welcome To Geneva Camp', 'Little Women'.
52 Ghosh, *TSTS*, 120.
53 Marianne Hirsch, *Narrative Frames: Photography, Narrative and Postmemory* (Cambridge, MA.: Harvard University Press, 1997), 22.
54 Ghosh, *TSTS*, 111.
55 Ibid., 218.
56 Agamben, *State of Exception*, 1.
57 Ibid., 59.
58 Etienne Balibar, *We, The People of Europe? Reflections on Transnational Community* (Princeton: Princeton University Press, 2004), 7.
59 Slemon, 'The Scramble for Postcolonialism', 22.

11

Postcolonial Life-Writing

Jocelyn Stitt

Postcolonial life-writing comprises texts ranging from personal narratives by colonizers, travellers and the enslaved, to archival documents such as letters and journals, to recent accounts of individual and community life experiences.[1] Scholars such as Sidonie Smith, Julia Watson and Julie Rak have commented on the 'boom' in life-writing in the UK and North America in the last twenty-five years. Postcolonial writers have participated in this boom, creating luminous reworkings of the genre. Life narratives by writers such as Marjane Satrapi, Patrick Chamoiseau, Binyavanga Wainaina, Pumla Gobodo-Madikizela, Lorna Goodison and Dionne Brand, tell new narratives of personal experience interwoven with global perspectives on colonialism, independence movements and the emergence of postcolonial nations. Dionne Brand uses the elasticity of the genre to give voice to postcolonial subjectivity. 'To the descendants of the nineteenth-century Indian and African Diaspora, a nervous temporariness is our existential dilemma, our descent quicker, our decay faster, our existence far more tenuous; the routine of life is continually upheaved by colonial troublings.'[2] Given the wealth of texts to consider the genre of life-writing is relatively underexamined within the field of postcolonial studies, where the novel is often considered to be the central literary form.[3] In turn, some scholars charge that autobiography studies has not fully engaged with postcolonial life-writing.[4]

This chapter argues that postcolonial life-writing, embedded as it is in generic expectations of telling a 'true' story, can serve as a proving ground for some of the central debates and themes within postcolonial studies. These include issues of truth and authenticity, reworkings of European genres, showing the gendered nature of nationalism, the importance of the bildungsroman and as a narrative way to theorize history and memory. We then turn to life-writing's reception within postcolonial literary criticism, which cautions against Global North interpretations of the genre as non-literary and as objectively representative of a larger culture or people. Finally, using Caribbean literature as examples, the chapter interrogates the methodology of postcolonial life-writing criticism. By concluding with a focus on one region, this chapter hopes to make the case that postcolonial life-writings demand to be read within their own literary traditions as an important addition to the focus on cross-cultural scholarship.

Overview: Contemporary postcolonial life-writing

To take up the topic of postcolonial life-writing is to engage with issues of genre. How might life-writing be defined and used by postcolonial studies? What genres are privileged within postcolonial literary studies and why? Philip Lejeune defines autobiography as a 'retrospective prose narrative written by a real person concerning his own existence'.[5] Lejeune observes that our expectations as readers of autobiography (as opposed to fiction) include a reliance on the coterminous identity of the name on the title page, the main protagonist of the text and the narrator. He calls this the autobiographical pact – an understanding on the part of the reader that the events discussed in the text are those experienced by the author and that they are recounted truthfully by the narrator/protagonist.[6] The connection between author and text, although modified by postmodern ideas of subjectivity, has arguably only increased in importance in interpreting contemporary life-writing. James Olney traces a movement from the earliest examples of autobiography centred on 'bios' or life events to an emphasis on the 'auto' or self of first-person narrative, especially in the twentieth century.[7] In the contemporary moment, despite the postmodern destabilization of the authority of the author, expectations of authenticity in the genre of life-writing remain. Readers of life-writing, as reoccurring literary scandals about authorship and the veracity of representations of experience demonstrate, continue to expect a relationship between the author's 'real' identity and the events portrayed in the narrative.[8]

Thinking through genres of postcolonial literature raises important questions of what work we expect them to do.[9] Postcolonial literature and criticism highlights the experiences of colonized and formerly colonized peoples. The subaltern speaks and represents her own experience, culture and critique of imperialism. If this version of postcolonial literature as a mode of contrapuntal resistance to imperialism based on experience and identity (although often contested and precarious) sounds familiar, we might find it surprising that life-writing is not more central to postcolonial literary studies. Indeed, fictional narrative and autobiography share projects of telling an individual story that can be understood as representative of the lives, histories and social conditions of others.

Even with ongoing debates in postcolonial and autobiography studies about authenticity, identity and 'truth', generic expectations of a factually based narrative enables postcolonial life-writing to perform cultural work different from poetry or fiction. Later in the chapter I explore some of the dangers in interpreting postcolonial life-writing as transparently 'authentic' or 'true'. However, with roots in a genre concerned with making truth claims, postcolonial life-writing can powerfully describe social conditions in the service of decolonization and social justice. This is not to say that life-writing does not have creative elements or that every depicted event is factual, but that a major narrative strategy in postcolonial life-writing is what Philip Holden calls 'the historical emplacement of culture'.[10] Decolonization, Frantz Fanon argued, can only be accomplished through discarding claims to the universal and instead turning to multiple marginalized viewpoints. 'Challenging the colonial world is not a rational confrontation of viewpoints. It is not a discourse on the universal, but the impassioned claim by the colonized that their world is fundamentally different'.[11] Thus, postcolonial life-writing creates space for testimony, witnessing and archiving personal, community and national histories.

Traditional definitions of autobiography, focused on a single self and his individual life, have been critiqued by feminist and postcolonial theorists Caren Kaplan, Sidonie Smith, Julia Watson and Bart Moore-Gilbert as masculinist and Eurocentric. Although traditional autobiography may be rooted in European cultural forms, postcolonial life-writing often innovatively recreates and creolizes that genre. Whether written by the colonized themselves, or settler colonists, even early life-writing from the colonial contact zone utilizes strategies that may seem almost postmodern. Questions of audience come to the fore, as authors acknowledge writing for both insiders and outsiders to their experience. The double consciousness of writing for a potentially hostile audience is especially relevant in slave narratives. Indeed, in Olaudah Equiano's *Interesting Narrative* (1789) his authorship is emphasized within the narrative to reassure his readers of the authenticity of the experiences he relates.

The capaciousness of life-writing allows postcolonial authors to refashion the genre to create hybrid or creolized forms that can be understood as archives of experience and memory. Genre and form are reworked through the use of fragmented stories, combining multiple genres in one text, such as letters, legal documents, maps, photographs, drawings and personal narrative. Phillip Holden states that although postcolonial life-writing may have been seen by early critics as derivative of European modes, multiple texts demonstrate that 'it was possible to take a template, and to use it to produce something that resisted colonial power, or spoke of the possibility of something entirely new'.[12] *Persepolis* by Marjane Satrapi creates a visual vocabulary of oppression in the aftermath of the Iranian revolution by using the graphic novel as a form of life-writing. Trinidadian V. S. Naipaul works with colonial tropes of mapping and describing landscape. *The Enigma of Arrival* uses narrative strategies of uncertainty and spatial disconnection from the English landscape to mark the dislocations of emigration. These generic choices differ from the confidence and geographical certainties of Naipaul's previous non-fiction writing.[13]

In comparison to understandings of the novel as the vehicle for expressing postcolonial subjectivity and the emerging nation, Elleke Boehmer argues that novels *and* autobiographies are 'central vehicles in the imaginative constructions of new nation' and that 'gender plays a central, formative role in that construction'.[14] In important contributions to postcolonial life-writing studies, Javed Majeed and Philip Holden argue that gender and nation are written through the lens of the national father. Autobiographies produced by national leaders, such as Jawaharlal Nehru's *Autobiography* (1962), Kwame Nkrumah's *Ghana: The Autobiography of Kwame Nkrumah* (1979) and Nelson Mandela's *Long Walk to Freedom* (1994) not only exemplify the use of this genre in creating the postcolonial nation, they often gain a much larger readership than novels, which have been seen as the primary genre of writing postcoloniality.

First person testimonial narratives display another aspect of the cultural and political work performed by life writing. In these works in particular, life-writing becomes a means of theorizing postcolonial histories and subjectivities. Gillian Whitlock sees history and memory as complexly linked in postcolonial life-writing. Her most recent work uses the framework of testimony to engage with much of postcolonial life-writing's emphasis on bearing witness to colonialism and its aftermath. Whitlock sees testimony not so much as a break with Western modes of writing the self, but rather of reworking them. 'For testimonial narrative in particular, Enlightenment thinking on the emotions – sympathy, pity and compassion – and on the human – human, humanism and human rights – produced new possibilities for social activism'.[15] Pumla Gobodo-Madikizela creates just such a social justice testimony, combining personal and prison narratives in interviews with Eugene de Kock, the commander of an apartheid era commander of a death squad. Writing from her perspective as a psychologist, she reflects on de Kock's self-representation as seeking forgiveness for the unforgiveable, while testifying to the ongoing trauma he caused in the lives of others. Postcolonial life-writing holds out radical possibilities for understanding subjectivity outside of a Western framework. Jamaican poet Lorna Goodison, for example, plays with expectations of who should be the subject of life-writing, creating a narrative subjectivity that expansively includes sections written from her mother and other ancestors' points of view: *From Harvey River: A Portrait of My Mother and Her Island* (2007) incorporates photographs, family trees, historical writing and detailed descriptions of landscape to create a multi-faceted portrait of her family in the century after Emancipation.

The *bildungsroman* is another major point of connection between postcolonial literature, life-writing and the importance of subjectivity and history to both genres. Postcolonial coming of age narratives, whether prose or poetry, allow authors to couple the development of a child with the rise of independence struggles or postcolonial nations. Writing from a child's perspective gives readers insight into the intrusions of colonialism in traditional aspects of culture such as an author's mother tongue, gender roles in the family and conflicts over European methods of education. Martinican novelist Patrick Chamoiseau in *Childhood* (1999) and Kenyan essayist Binyavanga Wainaina in *One Day I Will Write About this Place* (2011) write impressionistic coming of age narratives, focalized through boyhood perceptions of their families, the environment and post/colonial society. Importantly, their narratives do not replicate the mid-century anti-colonial nationalist assumptions that the boy will become the embodiment of the ideal (male) citizen. Instead, gender, family and nation blur uncertainly together in the formation of the narrator's identity.

Genre debates within postcolonial studies

Given the many conjunctions of autobiographical and postcolonial theory, it is intriguing that the novel has been the focus of postcolonial literary studies. Why should the novel be so central to postcolonial literary criticism? A telling example comes from *Culture and Imperialism* (1993) where Edward Said argues for the novel as 'Immensely important in the formation of imperial attitudes, references and experiences. I do not mean that only the novel was important, but that I consider it *the* aesthetic object whose connection to the expanding societies of Britain and France is particularly interesting to study'.[16] Said's intervention urges us to reconsider the relationship of European cultural productions such as Jane Austen's *Mansfield Park* to the economics and ideologies of empire. Literary scholarship was thus poised to rethink European literature as intertwined with empire.

A concomitant project to studying the presence of imperial themes within European literature focused on the novel, and secondarily poetry, as vehicles for writing postcoloniality and establishing national identities.[17] In his own autobiography, C. L. R. James writes that an essay topic given to him as a schoolboy 'The Novel as Instrument of Reform' remained a topic he returned to often in his long writing career.[18] Peter Hitchcock echoes Said: 'We know almost instinctually that there is at least one genre of postcoloniality: this genre is the novel'.[19] Akin Adesocan confirms the centrality of the novel when he argues that in postcolonial studies 'the novel is unusually privileged in an array of literary forms'.[20] Scholars focused on the intertextual postcolonial novel as evidence of 'writing back to the centre', to use a foundational postcolonial studies phrase. Life-writing has long been seen as a lesser form. The kinds of life-writing and memoir produced in colonial contact zones, such as diaries, travel narratives and slave narratives, were categorized in the nineteenth century, Linda Anderson notes, as genres possessing less artistic merit and cultural capital than autobiographies produced by men who had distinguished themselves and who were often European, educated and privileged. In spite of the status of life-writing, important theorists have produced autobiographies themselves: examples include Edward Said's *Out of Place* (2000) and Sara Suleri's *Meatless Days* (1999). Indeed, a fruitful study could be made of the rhetorics of self-representation within these foundational theoretical texts.

Secondly, postcolonial scholars and writers may have been cautious of foregrounding life-writing because of the danger of conflating the individual and particular with the communal and political. Postcolonial life-writing marketed to the Global North risks literary texts being interpreted as transparently representative of their authors' culture rather than as crafted works of art, as Arif Dirlik argues. Early in the development of postcolonial autobiographical theory, Gayatri Spivak cautioned, 'I am guarded and watchful of the autobiographical impulse within postcoloniality. The line between aesthetics and politics is not necessarily programmed by the authority of the author'.[21] Spivak reminds us that acts of postcolonial life-writing may be circulated globally as testimony based on the dominant culture's interpellation of them as sharing a recognizable 'truth' that does not challenge the status quo.[22]

The highly visible juxtaposition of the personal, the artistic and the political in one text, is precisely one of the major contributions life-writing makes to postcolonial literary studies. Indeed, David Huddart noted in 2001 that autobiography theory 'exerted constant pressure' on postcolonial studies.[23] Certainly postcolonial theory from the 1980s and 1990s did not often attend to genre. Widely used theoretical anthologies such as *Colonial Discourse and Postcolonial Theory: A Reader* (1994), *The Postcolonial Studies Reader* (1995), and *Postcolonialisms: An Anthology of Cultural Theory and Criticism* (2005) used themes rather than genre as organizing principles. Walter Goebel and Saskia Schabio recently argued that postcolonial critics' privileging of cultural identity as expressed within the novel has resulted in a lack of attention to issues of aesthetics and formal choices, which can be explored through an examination of literary genres, such as autobiography, the short story or the folktale.

Perhaps in response to an emerging 'generic turn', *Literature for Our Times: Postcolonial Studies for the Twenty-First Century* (2012) includes several essays focused on genre and on life-writing. So while I would not confidently proclaim as Holden does that 'from the margins of postcolonial literary studies, auto/biography now seems to have travelled to centre stage', I would assert that autobiography studies and postcolonial studies have begun speaking to each other.[24] The past fifteen years have produced several monographs devoted to life-writing produced within colonial and postcolonial contexts. I explore some of these below to set the stage for an exploration of life-writing methodologies through the example of the circulation of Caribbean life-writing.

Methodologies: The Caribbean as case study

The previous two sections dwelt upon definitions of genre, identifying the 'work' performed by postcolonial life-writing and the relationship between postcolonial and autobiography studies. The question now arises: what methodologies are available to us for interpreting life-writing? If the novel in the past was seen as *the* postcolonial genre, this chapter argues that life-writing should understood as a genre equally invested in writing postcoloniality. If so, what methodology(ies) are most useful for analysing and making meaning out of texts that are already devoted to analysing and making meaning out of life stories? This section focuses on Caribbean life-writing for two reasons: the region has produced some of the most canonized postcolonial life-writing texts and theory, including works by Frantz Fanon, C. L. R James and George Lamming. Some of the most globally popular life-writing authors such as Derek Walcott in poetry and Jamaica Kincaid and Edwidge Danticat in prose come from the Caribbean.

Methodologies for postcolonial life-writing as a whole might gain from an understanding of how the Caribbean literatures circulate in the public sphere of the nineteenth-century, modern popular cultures and in literary criticism. For instance, there are signal differences between nineteenth-century Caribbean life-writing and that produced by African Americans within the same time period. Nellie McKay argues that the foundations of African American literature rest on life-writing, since it was this genre that first as circulated through abolitionist presses and newspapers. In contrast, Raphael Dalleo notes in his study of Caribbean literary public spheres, that the French, Spanish and British exerted control over colonial newspapers and presses, so that life-writings were published in Europe and largely aimed at metropolitan audiences.

Sarah Brouillette and Elena Machado Sáez remind us that complicating a discussion of colonial reading publics are issues of contemporary market demands for postcolonial texts that capitalize on the exotic, traumatic or resistance to oppression. Again, in distinction to African American literature, Jamaican scholar and writer Ifeoma Fulani outlines how emerging Caribbean writers struggle with small reading publics in their countries of origin and a lack of publication opportunities. Intriguingly, the Caribbean primary texts that are so widely discussed often come from a limited pool that unwittingly replicates a contested understanding of the

Anglophone Caribbean canon. Much of what we think of as Caribbean literature is structured around Olaudah Equiano, Mary Prince and Mary Seacole as representative of writing of the eighteenth and nineteenth centuries. Mid-century male authors, often those who studied and lived in Europe, such as Fanon, James, Lamming, Naipaul and Walcott comprise another source for scholars of Caribbean life-writing. Lastly, writers from the upsurge in women's writing from the 1980s and 1990s such as Edwidge Danticat and Jamaica Kincaid are well represented in autobiographical scholarship.

Much postcolonial literary criticism using Caribbean texts does not address the gaps in this periodization. It does not question, as Evelyn O'Callaghan insists we do, what was published between Mary Seacole's publication of her *Wonderful Adventures* in 1857 and the emergence of women's writing in the 1930s. Indeed, the canonical gaps between Mary Seacole, mid-century male writers and female writers in the 1980s have been under debate within Caribbean studies for the past decade. Alison Donnell states that in choosing to research Caribbean women's writing before the 1950s, she not only picked obscure texts, but ones that 'were almost unknowable to the frameworks and pathways that had then been established for reading Caribbean Literature'.[25] Leah Rosenberg argues that only very recently have scholars begun to critique the idea that the Caribbean literary tradition started with male novelists in the 1940s and that women writers only became visible in the 1980s and 1990s.[26] During the early 2000s scholars questioned the supremacy of masculinist and exclusionary versions of nationalism in mid-century writing that glorify the folk and motherhood without portraying women as having agency.[27] The nationalist project of reclaiming masculinity through the production of 'high literature' (i.e. the novel) occluded the contribution of women and Indo-Caribbean writers generally, but also the presence of other genres within the Caribbean literary tradition.

Rosenberg's examples of writing excluded from the canon include the early nineteenth-century autobiographical writings by two free women of colour: Anne Hart Gilbert and Elizabeth Hart Thwaites. Sue Thomas provides convincing evidence that the Hart sisters' narratives and other spiritual life-writings such as Robert Wedderburn's (1817) have been marginalized within the canon. Works such as *The Autobiography of Anna Mahase Snr* (1992) published in Trinidad and detailing the years between 1935 and 1967 of an Indo-Caribbean teacher and proponent of girls' education are seldom part of the circulation of twentieth-century texts. This is perhaps because they do not conform to narratives of anti-colonialism and emergent nationalism as the preeminent subjects of postcolonial literature, or because they do not fit with the chronology that Caribbean literature emerged in the mid-century.

Beyond considerations of reading publics, tracing the presence of Caribbean life-writing in recent monographs helps us recognize how these texts move within the academic world. I identify three main modes of analysis. Overall, the method employed thus far has been largely comparativist. A common mode of interpretation is reading Caribbean texts that share thematic or ideological elements with texts from the Global North. A major subset of this methodology is the use of Caribbean women's texts in studies of women's writing, as in Whitlock's *An Intimate Empire: Reading Women's Identity* (2000) and Moira Ferguson's *East Caribbean: Gender and Colonial Relations from Mary Wollstonecraft to Jamaica Kincaid* (1993). Marketable established writers such as Edwidge Danticat and Jamaica Kincaid may seem overexposed in contrast to Caribbean writers who are unpublished in the UK or US or who do not treat themes of overcoming adversity or trauma.

Widely discussed Antiguan author Jamaica Kincaid features in several life-writing monographs such as J. Brooks Bouson's *Jamaica Kincaid Writing Memory, Writing Back to the Mother* (2006), and Jana Evans Brazile's *Caribbean Genesis: Jamaica Kincaid and the Writing of New Worlds* (2009) as well as those not dedicated to postcolonial writers as in Jo Malin's *The Voice of the Mother: Embedded Maternal Narratives in Twentieth-Century Women's Autobiographies* (2000), Leigh Gilmore's *The Limits of Autobiography: Trauma and Testimony* (2001) and Eva C. Karapinski's *Borrowed Tongues: Life Writing, Migration, and Translation (2011)*. In an interview about her novel *See Now Then* (2013), Kincaid argues that her life-writing is held up as proof of her lack of artistic achievement as well as critiqued for not portraying the expected 'travails of the black woman'.[28] In her mélange of memoir and political essay, *Create Dangerously* (2010), Danticat addresses that she is simultaneously a figurehead for the Haitian diaspora in the United States and perceived as a 'parasite' by some in Haiti. Danticat is at once representative and inauthentic. That Kincaid and Danticat insist on their 'difference' within accepted discourses about postcolonial writers strongly suggests that categories we may believe have been evacuated by postmodern theory: authenticity, essential selves and pure national cultures, remain a contested site for postcolonial authors in the global literary marketplace.

A second methodology involves comparing postcolonial texts across regions and time periods. The texts studied share commonalties such as political agendas, as in Philip Holden's *Autobiography and Decolonization: Modernity, Masculinity, and the Nation-State* (2008) that looks at autobiographical texts written by postcolonial national leaders, including a section on Marcus Garvey. Some postcolonial scholars use cross-cultural comparisons to identify common characteristics of life-writing. Writing about the legacies of French colonialism, Edgard Sankara juxtaposes contemporary Francophone texts from Africa and the Caribbean to understand why African writers faithfully try to reproduce French life-writing norms while Caribbean writers try to usurp them. Bart Moore-Gilbert's *Postcolonial Life-Writing* (2009) uses Fanon as a touchstone as he analyses how the characteristics of Euro-American women's life-writing might be applicable to postcolonial writing by men and women, including Caribbean life narratives by Mary Prince and C. L. R. James.

Comparativist and thematic approaches are important life-writing methodologies. James Olney identifies this methodology as producing the best theoretical models. 'It has long been my conviction that theory of life-writing is best derived from major instances of the mode rather than from interchange with other critics'.[29] In other words, reading multiple life-writing texts together produces a better understanding of the practices, themes and fissures in a particular corpus. As for postcolonial theory, Robert Young argues that there can be no postcolonial literature without comparison; comparison is embedded in the project to write back to an already existing European literature.[30] This is not to say that critics using comparativist approaches are theorizing life-writing incorrectly, but rather that these wide ranging studies need to be complemented by analysis of life-writings created in specific cultural contexts, often for national or regional audiences.

Leigh Gilmore argues that a central question for autobiography studies is 'the limits of representativeness, with its compulsory inflation of the self to stand in for others'.[31] These questions, rather than discrete categorizations, propel Caribbean autobiography studies published in the last fifteen years. Sandra Pouchet Paquet's *Caribbean Autobiography: Cultural Identity and Self-representation* (2002) was the first monograph on Caribbean life-writing and marked a turning point of Caribbean studies scholars reading life-writing through the lens of Caribbean literary history. While Paquet's focus was largely on mid-century writers, publications by Evelyn O'Callaghan and Sue Thomas delve deeper into life-writing published before the 1940s. Louise Hardwick examines narratives of childhood, building on the transnational

Francophone work of Françoise Lionnet in the first monograph solely on the French Caribbean. *The Routledge Companion to Anglophone Caribbean Literature* (2011), edited by Michael Bucknor and Alison Donnell, signals a new recognition of genre studies by devoting a section generic innovations. Lisa R. Brown's chapter in this work understands Caribbean life-writing not as a set of texts engaged in the same ideological project, but rather a broad based genre for exploring identity and history in the region.

As a genre grounded in truth claims, postcolonial life-writing takes on different cultural work than fiction and poetry. Life-writing is thus as an important genre for documenting and testifying about the conditions and subjectivities generated by European imperialism and its aftermath. This chapter hopes to contribute to a new narrative of postcolonial life-writing by rethinking the tradition of privileging of the novel. Tracing the circulation of Caribbean life-writing within contemporary criticism can tell us much about gaps and marginalizations of primary texts within the field and how scholars might productively study life-writing within regional and national cultures as well as cross-culturally. Postcolonial life-writing represents a vibrant corpus of texts that have the potential to significantly increase our understanding of the role genre plays in mosaic postcolonial literatures.

Notes

1. I use the term 'life-writing' rather than the narrower term 'memoir' or 'autobiography'.
2. Dionne Brand, *A Map to the Door of No Return: Notes to Belonging* (Toronto: Random House Canada, 2001), 61.
3. Timothy Brennan, 'The National Longing for Form', in *Nation and Narration*, ed. H. Bhabha (London and New York: Routledge, 1990); David Huddart, 'Postcolonialism', in *Encyclopedia of Life Writing: Autobiographical and Biographical Forms*, ed. M. Jolly (London and New York: Routledge, 2001); Lisa R. Brown, 'Caribbean Life-Writing and Performative Liberation', in *The Routledge Companion to Anglophone Caribbean Literature*, eds. M. Bucknor and A. Donnell (London and New York: Routledge, 2011).
4. Huddart, 'Postcolonialism'; Bart Moore-Gilbert, *Postcolonial Life-Writing: Culture, Politics, and Self-Representation* (London and New York: Routledge, 2009).

5   Philip Lejeune, *On Autobiography*, ed. P. J. Eakin, trans. Katherine Leary (Minneapolis: University of Minnesota Press, 1989), 4.
6   Lejeune, *On Autobiography*, 4.
7   James Olney, *Memory and Narrative: The Weave of Life Writing* (Chicago: University of Chicago Press, 1998), xv.
8   Sidonie Smith and Julia Watson, 'Witness or False Witness: Metrics of Authenticity, Collective I-Formations, and the Ethic of Verification in First-Person Testimony', *Biography* 35, no. 4 (2012); Rak, *Boom!*; Leigh Gilmore, 'Boom|lash: Fact-Checking, Suicide, and the Lifespan of a Genre', *a/b: Autobiography Studies* 29, no. 2 (2014): 212–224.
9   See Nicolas Harrison on the centrality of the novel to the 'work' of postcolonial literature, *Postcolonial Criticism: History, Theory, and the Work of Fiction* (Cambridge: Polity Press, 2003).
10 Philip Holden, 'Postcolonial Auto/Biography', in *The Cambridge History of Postcolonial Literature Vol. 1*, ed. A. Quayson (Cambridge: Cambridge University Press, 2011), 120.
11 Frantz Fanon, *The Wretched of the Earth* (New York: Grove Press, 1994), 120.
12 Holden, 'Postcolonial Auto/Biography', 110.
13 Samjay Krishnan, 'Formative Dislocations in V. S. Naipaul's *The Enigma of Arrival*', *MFS Modern Fiction Studies* 59, no. 3 (2013): 619.
14 Elleke Boehmer, *Stories of Women: Gender and Narrative in the Postcolonial Nation* (Manchester: Manchester University Press, 2005), 14.
15 Gillian Whitlock, *Postcolonial Life Narratives: Testimonial Transactions* (Oxford: Oxford University Press, 2015), 5.
16 Edward Said, *Culture and Imperialism* (New York: Vintage, 1993), xii.
17 For more on theoretical approaches to studying Empire and the cultural productions and resistance practices of colonized and postcolonial subjects, see Simon Gikandi in Patricia Yaeger, 'Editor's Column: The End of Postcolonial Theory? A Roundtable with Sunil Agani, Fernando Coronil, Gaurav Desai, Mamadou Diouf, Simon Gikandi, Susie Tharu, and Jennifer Wenzel', *PMLA* 122, no. 3 (2007): 633–51.
18 C. L. R. James, *Beyond a Boundary* (Durham: Duke University Press, 2013), 19.
19 Peter Hitchcock, 'The Genre of Postcoloniality', *New Literary History* 34, no. 2 (2003): 302.
20 Akin Adesocan, 'New African Writing and the Question of Audience', *Research in African Literatures* 43, no. 3 (2012): 2.
21 Gayatri Spivak, 'Three Women's Texts and Circumfession', in *Postcolonialism & Autobiography: Michelle Cliff, David Dabydeen, Opal Palmer Adisa*, eds. Alfred Horung and Ernstpeter Ruhe (Amsterdam and Atlanta: Rodopoi 1998), 21.
22 Spivak, 'Three Women's Texts and Circumfession', 9.

23 Huddart, 'Postcolonialism', 253.
24 Holden, 'Postcolonial Auto/Biography', 108.
25 Alison Donnell, *Twentieth-Century Caribbean Literature: Critical Moments in Anglophone Literary History* (London and New York: Routledge, 2006), 11.
26 Leah Rosenberg, 'Anglophone Caribbean Literature and the Canon', in *The Routledge Companion to Anglophone Caribbean Literature*, eds. Michael Bucknor and Alison Donnell (New York: Routledge, 2011), 353.
27 Donnell, *Twentieth-Century Caribbean Literature*; Jocelyn Stitt, 'Gendered Legacies of Romantic Nationalism in the Works of Michelle Cliff', *Small Axe* 24 (2007): 52–72.
28 National Public Radio, 'Time rules in Jamaica Kindcaid's new novel, 'See Now Then' (2013), http://www.npr.org/2013/03/03/173086194/time-rules-in-jamaica-kincaids-new-novel-see-now-then (accessed 25 June 2014).
29 Olney, *Memory and Narrative*, xii.
30 Robert J. C. Young, 'The Postcolonial Comparative', *PMLA* 128, no. 3 (2013): 688.
31 Leigh Gilmore, *The Limits of Autobiography: Trauma and Testimony* (Ithaca: Cornell University Press), 5.

12

Decolonization and Postcolonial Cinema in Canada, Brazil, Australia and Nigeria

Kerstin Knopf

The representation of postcolonial non-European cultures in Western mainstream media – print, television, radio, feature films and ethnographic films – is often a neocolonial discourse fraught with ethnocentrism, prejudice, distortion and stereotypes. With Michel Foucault we might understand this media discourse as a 'gaze of power'. Neocolonial discourses have created myths of Indigenous and local people embedded in the semantics of exoticism, primitivism and savagery, which, in turn, have shored up Eurocentric cultural hegemonies, generated racialized thought and cemented 'naturalized' Eurocentric cultural, political and economic domination of subaltern people. Indigenous and subaltern film directors and producers around the world have started to battle this politics of representation by creating a decolonized film discourse. Notably, the last decade has seen an immense development in Indigenous and postcolonial feature film production which shows in the ever-growing Indigenous and African film festivals.

The decolonization of neocolonial film discourses

Michel Foucault has described the disciplinary power of the observing and objectifying gaze that he equates with language and thought.[1] Martin Jay explains: 'what is in fact "seen" is not a given, objective reality open to an innocent eye. Rather, it is an epistemic field, constructed as much linguistically as visually, which is no more or less close to the "truth" than what it replaced'.[2] Thus, aural and visual discourses necessarily deviate from the 'truth' of their objects; representation and discourses are epistemological constructs of the represented. Foucault further delineates discourse and scientific/academic qualification as phenomena of power. It follows that whoever is in power has control over discourse and wields power through discourse. This discourse is carried and distributed through political and governmental bodies, the judicial and executive system, educational institutions, publishing houses and the like. Hence we might understand the authorial and objectifying gaze as a 'gaze of power'. Foucault's ideas applied to settler colonial and other colonial nations presents the neocolonial Western gaze through film, photography and television as 'inferior others' through what Ann Kaplan calls 'the imperial gaze'.[3] Following Jay, this neocolonial lens or discourse, informed by cultural hegemonies, represents 'truths' about or images of its colonized objects that severely deviate from self-perceived 'truths' or images.[4] Homi Bhabha argues that both the colonizer and colonized are implicated in the colonial gaze and that its projection of 'otherness' reflects back on the colonial culture. To him the returned gaze of the colonized, the 'gaze of otherness', destabilizes through its mimicry and re-articulation of subjectivities of observer and observed: 'the look of surveillance returns as the displacing gaze of the disciplined, where the observer becomes the observed and the "partial" representation rearticulates the whole notion of identity and alienates it from essence'.[5]

Himani Bannerji's and Kaplan's concepts of 'returning or reversing the gaze'[6] applied to the works of postcolonial visual artists, filmmakers and media creators clarifies the process of visual and aural self-representation as metaphorically returning or reversing the neocolonial gaze, because the artists appropriate the formerly colonialist means of media production to create works that look critically at colonialist images and discourse. These postcolonial media artists decolonize the neocolonial media and 'lens/

gaze of power' by interrogating the neocolonial imaginary, intercepting neocolonial politics of representing, stereotyping and objectifying 'the other', asserting a postcolonial voice and control over the products and generating decolonized subjectivities – with their own independent film production companies or in collaboration with mainstream media creators. Much like the postcolonial 'writing back', they correct the representations of colonized cultures in Western historiographic, ethnographic and dramatic films and thus disengage their images from such neocolonial representational contexts. They unveil and critique racist and hegemonic thought and representational practices and question Eurocentric assumptions of universality in historic, socio-political, legal, economic, literary, art and media discourses. They correct misrepresentations, appropriate canonical neocolonial texts, translate them into their own cultural context, and use them for their own purposes. Bill Ashcroft explains: 'Canonical literary [and visual] texts are "consumed" in such a way that they become the basis for resistant, appropriated versions which subtly subvert the values and political assumptions of the originals'.[7] This appropriating, deferring, deconstructing neocolonial master narratives manifests as decolonization of print, film and media discourses.[8]

Postcolonial film in Canada

Canada has a developed output of postcolonial film and mediamaking with Indigenous radio stations across the nation, the first Indigenous television station in the world with a country-wide broadcast licence, APTN, and an average annual output of two Indigenous dramatic feature films and numerous short and documentary films. In this chapter Indigenous Canadian film is included alongside film from more commonly considered postcolonial locations. While acknowledging First Nations Canadian novelist Thomas King's critique of postcolonialism as an approach that reinstates colonialism as the prime organizer of Native people's experience, and his assertion instead that indigenous Canadian creative output has a separate context, the inclusion of indigenous Canadian film is an important way to access the broader contexts of postcolonial and neocolonial studies, and offers a way to begins a comparison between colonial and neocolonial effects on the landscape. Outstanding filmmakers are Alanis Obomsawin and Zacharias Kunuk, both trailblazers for Indigenous documentary and dramatic filmmaking, as well as Shirley Cheechoo, Shelley Niro and directors Sonia Boileau and Adam Garnet Jones, whose first features (*Le Dep*; *Fire Song*) premiered at the 2015 ImagineNATIVE Film and Media Arts Festival in Toronto.

Shirley Cheechoo (Cree) began her career as actress, playwright and visual artist before venturing into film; she has now three feature films to her credit (*Bearwalker*, 2003; *Johnny Tootall*, 2005; *Moose River Crossing*, 2013). *Johnny Tootall*, which won 'Best Film' honours at the 2005 American Indian Film Festival in San Francisco, is set in the community of Ahousaht First Nations. The eponymous hero is destined to become Nuu-chah-nulth hereditary chief after his father. He is however not interested in Indigenous traditions, leaves the community and joins the Canadian Forces. Johnny returns to Ahousaht after twelve years, suffering from post-traumatic stress disorder because he has accidentally killed a young boy in the Bosnian war. His younger brother RT, who very much respects his father, cultural traditions, and land, is now married to Johnny's former love Serena and they have a daughter Tiffany. RT has organized a road blockade in order to protest against clear-cutting of their rainforest and to block the logging trucks from taking away the valuable wood. The community is split over the issue, because some non-Indigenous families depend upon an income through truck driving and Indigenous people want to prevent logging on their traditional land close to the community and a sacred shrine. After one police officer and RT are shot dead at the blockade, RT's spirit leads Johnny to the sacred shrine with carved Nuu-chah-nulth figures. Only RT's pressure, the spirit of their passed father, and a wolf spirit called by their mother drive Johnny to support the blockade and acknowledge Nuu-chah-nulth traditions in the end. Shawn A-in-chut Atleo, Nuu-chah-nulth hereditary chief and former National Chief of the Assembly of First Nations, has supported this film as story advisor and with a short cameo as one of the protestors.

The film begins with shots of cedar trees that are threatened to be cut, and it shows the intrusion of settler culture in the form of destroyed and clear-cut forest. Accompanying Johnny on his last leg of the trip home, the camera shows the coastal landscape, minke whales, Nuu-chah-nulth masks and welcoming figures, the wolf spirit, and the Ahousaht community. The film thus introduces traditional key elements right at the beginning, however, intercut with shots of chain saws and heavy machinery cutting trees, shots describing Johnny's war experience and trauma, and shots showing the protest site. It thus pinpoints settler colonial relationships in Canada as well as Indigenous modernity that is generated from traditions, modern lifestyles, entanglements in the economics and politics of a capitalist nation as well as resistance towards them. West Coast people have lived with clear-cutting and consequential bare landscapes, soil erosion and deterioration of wildlife habitats and fish populations since the late nineteenth century. Their protests have culminated in the biggest protest against clear-cutting, the 1993 Clayoquot Sound protests, an area surrounding Ahousaht. Setting her film in Ahousaht, Cheechoo makes direct filmic references to these protests and critiques the long-lasting and destructive settler colonial geopolitics in this area. The film focuses on symbolic and physical acts of protecting traditional Indigenous territory and reclaiming Indigenous sovereignty, sustained by the banner on the trees, reading OURS!, which repeats similar images from Nuu-chah-nulth protests. Much of the dramatic action is set in the rain forest underlining the importance of land and old growth forest for the Nuu-chah-nulth people and visually supporting assertion of Indigenous sovereignty. The film takes great care to present the plot from an Indigenous perspective: it gives more screen time to Indigenous presence, it features reserve life, places much of the drama within the Tootall family and the conflict between the brothers, and includes a number of cultural and spiritual Nuu-chah-nulth elements, avoiding cliché. Furthermore the film dialogues include Nuu-chah-nulth terms such as *hahuuthi*, meaning 'responsible stewardship of the land'. The film has a composed traditional musical score, which further supports the Indigenous perspective.

With the character of Johnny Tootall, Cheechoo complicates a number of aspects of Indigenous presence in the modern global world. Most obviously Johnny's participation in the Bosnian war raises not only questions about Canada's involvement in peacekeeping missions with possible human rights violations and the killing of civilians, but also sharpens the focus on Indigenous participation in such militarist endeavours that allow drawing parallels to colonialist military occupation of Indigenous lands. This idea is prominently voiced by RT accusing his brother of 'occupying other peoples' sacred lands'.

Postcolonial film in Brazil

The Brazilian film industry is the biggest in Latin America. While it is difficult to define postcolonial cinema in Brazil, there are noteworthy examples: *favela* films (situated in Brazil's urban slum quarters), such as *City of God* (Fernando Meirelles, 2002) and *City of Men* (Paulo Morelli, 2007), Glauber Rocha's socio-political *Cinema Nuevo*, José Mojica Marins's neo-gothic horror cinema centring on the iconic Zé (the evil gothic figure that embodies a deep anarchic outrage against the corrupt and exploitive trinity of church, politics and the police),[9] and films dealing with Indigenous struggles, of which *Birdwatchers* is an excellent example.

Birdwatchers [*La terra degli uomini rossi*] (2008) was directed by Marco Bechis, who is of Chilean-Italian ancestry, grew up in Buenos Aires, and has lived in Los Angeles, New York, Paris and Milan. He was imprisoned and tortured under Videla's military dictatorship in Argentina, which influenced his award-winning films *Garage Olimpo* (1999) and *Figli/Hijos* (2001). *Birdwatchers* competed for the Golden Lion at the 2008 Venice Film Festival and won the One World Media Award in 2010. The film deals with the dispossession of Indigenous people in Brazil by land-grabbing landowners and multinational corporations and represents the *retomadas*, the growing Indigenous land reclamation movement. Viewers learn that the Guarani-Kaiowá are dispossessed of their land and live in abject poverty on small reserves. After two girls commit suicide, one community decides to relocate to their traditional land since they cannot be a healthy community apart from their *tekohà* [home land]. They establish a makeshift camp on the road side beside farmer Dimas's field – their ancestral lands, where they are harassed by armed guards and planes spraying pesticides. More and more Guarani arrive and support the movement to reclaim their traditional land. Yet they have to make a living and a few go work as farm hands, while Osvaldo starts learning how to become a shaman. Alcohol, internal struggles and another suicide weaken the *retomada* movement. When the Guarani-Kaiowá occupy the farm field, farmers hire henchmen to kill the cacique Nádio to intimidate the Guarani. Osvaldo, who is in love with Dimas's daughter Maria, is also driven to suicide by the evil spirit *Anguè* but resists.

Bechis's extraordinary film takes issue with the ongoing colonization of Indigenous peoples in Latin America and with their continuing dehumanization, impoverishment and paternalist treatment through neocolonial societies. Clear-cutting of rainforests, business interests of multinational corporations, and the world's hunger for beef, sugar, soy, wood and bio fuels only intensify their plight. *Birdwatchers* unrelentingly presents the daily reality of the Guarani-Kaiowá, who have lost their entire homeland during the last one-hundred years. Survival International states that Guarani are the largest Indigenous group in Brazil. Some live in tiny reservations surrounded by cattle ranches, sugar cane and soy fields, and some in makeshift plastic tents beside freeways and roads in squalid conditions. Malnutrition, diseases and youth suicide are rampant in these devastated communities. Wild animal populations are decimated, the Guarani cannot go hunting; and those who take part in the *retomadas* live under constant threat to their lives. The Takuára leader Marcos Vernon was beaten to death by farm helpers in January 2003; in August 2015 another Guarani group that re-occupied their traditional lands was attacked by ranchers' henchman, people were injured, and their leader Semião Vilhalva shot dead.[10] This is the daily reality of only one dispossessed Indigenous group in Latin America, one that has found a political voice and international recognition through Bechis's film.

In a pivotal scene that re-enacts *retomadas*, the Guarani-Kaiowá move onto their ancestral land, which Dimas claims as his. In an extreme long shot, which frames the field in the foreground and the forest in the background, we see Guarani men literally emerging out of the green forest and moving onto the reddish field. Also from the road camp, men, women, children and elders move onto the field. A shaman plants a feathered stick in order to manifest their reclaiming the land. In this scene, the Indigenous people are portrayed as embedded in the land: they emerge from the forest, they move onto the land mainly with traditional weapons and they are aligned with the land through careful colour composition. The organic green, reddish, brown and ochre tones of the forest, river and soil echo the skin of the *Indígenas*, their red and black face paint, and their clothing, which is often coated in dust that transforms denim blue and reddish shirts into organic colour. When the people occupy the field, the camera places the land and the feathered stick in the foreground in low-angle shots. It creates a compelling effect filming the silent defiant faces of the men before they disarm the farmer's guard. In a climactic face-off, Dimas takes red soil into his hand claiming he owns the land for two generations, while Nádio eats some of the soil, expressing that he and his people are of the land that nourishes them.

Birdwatchers is a very local, low–budget film, without technical devices and produced in close cooperation with the Guarani-Kaiowá, who were non-professional actors and cultural advisors. Although Bechis is not an Indigenous director, he transmits the struggles of the Guarani-Kaiowá for physical and cultural survival and against encroaching big landowners. His filmmaking style is adjusted to the local Indigenous people. He employs their perspective, filming from within the community, observing their daily lives, and he aligns the camera with the land and its subdued colours when filming the people as opposed to the bright, artificial blue, green and red colours of things related to the farmer's family and Western society, who thus appear as intruders in the world of the Guarani-Kaiowá. The film has a slow pace with longer takes and no fast cuts. The soundtrack mixes the soundscape of the rain forest, maraca rattles, the noises of an industrialized country, and the accentuated placement of Italian baroque music, which stresses colonization and the changes in Indigenous lives. Moreover, all dialogue among the *Indígenas* is presented in the Guarani language.

In the end, Dimas and the Guarani are not reconciled, the land conflict will be settled in court. The film thus calls to mind that in the twenty-first-century Indigenous people still face difficult living conditions and many are under various threats from neocolonial settler societies and world trade that all Western industrialized countries are part of.

Postcolonial films in Australia

Australia has the most vibrant and diverse Indigenous film industry in the world with a production of two to three dramatic feature films per year in genres like road movies, youth movies, comedies, musicals, mystery thrillers and human relations stories. Most outstanding directors are Rachel Perkins, Ivan Sen, Tracey Moffatt, Warwick Thornton and Beck Cole, Perkins being the most accomplished with three major documentaries and five feature films so far to her credit.

Richard J. Frankland, of Gunditjmara ancestry, is a singer, writer and director; the comedy *Stone Bros.* (2009) is his feature debut. *Stone Bros.* is fast and loud and employs the road movie genre surely and effortlessly; it thus continues the tradition of Indigenous road movies that was begun in Australia with *Backroads* (Phillip Noyce, 1977), made in close collaboration with activist, actor and writer, Gary Foley, and *Beneath Clouds* (Ivan Sen, 2002).[11] It shares similarities with the first US-American Indigenous road movie *Smoke Signals* (Chris Eyre, 1998). In *Stone Bros.*, the cousins Eddie and Charlie return home to Kalgoorlie after some unsuccessful years in Perth, also to bring home two sacred rocks their uncle gave them when they left. Charlie, responsible for Eddie losing his rock and his job as a cleaner in the Perth Museum, is a mischievous companion, taking 186 pre-rolled joints as provision, hence the title. In adapted picaresque fashion, the two have some genuine and funny adventures that serve Frankland well to paint a charming and self-ironic picture of Indigenous society in its relation to 'white' Australia. Stoned,[12] the cousins pick up a girl who turns out to be an Italian metal guitarist, flee panic-stricken from a tarantula, get imprisoned, meet their transgender cousin Regina, gatecrash a wedding party, fight a killer terrier and show up half-naked in a small-town museum to retrieve said rock.

Foremost, the film wants to entertain and counter the media images of Indigenous Australians that often associate them with politics, crime, poverty and socio-economic issues. Frankland achieves a cathartic relief from such ever-pressing issues through Indigenous humour, physical comedy and hilarious situations. While the film keeps us busy laughing, it also tells a story set in contemporary Indigenous culture beyond stereotypes and political and social clichés. In fact, it effectively undermines nostalgic stereotypes of traditional Indigenous Australian life and spirituality Westerners 'learn' in mainstream museums, print, film and media cultures.

In the Perth Museum scene, Charlie and Eddie observe Indigenous artefacts but know next to nothing about traditional Australians. Opposite a black-and-white image of an ancestor standing on one leg supported by a walking stick, Eddie tries to imitate the now stereotypical posture that supports the visual trope of the primitive Aborigine: dark-skinned, mystical, outback, loin-clothed.[13] Eddie, who is at least interested in 'that culture stuff', is almost a modern reflection of this image, but inveterate Charlie reminds him that he uses a mop as a 'walking stick'. He thus humorously deconstructs the posture, or better, a Western and Indigenous nostalgic reverence for 'typically' Indigenous postures and 'authentic' Indigeneity, evident in the work of early twentieth-century photographers like Donald Thomson and strengthened by films like *Walkabout* (Nicolas Roeg, 1971). The men's humorous engagement with their ancestor also makes fun of Western museum culture, which often mis/represents Indigenous cultures, exoticizes and mystifies traditional Indigenous life, locates Indigeneity predominantly in a nostalgic past and thus cancels modern Indigenous identity. Hence larrikin Charlie declares, 'This place gives me the creeps'. The climax of this scene is clumsy Charlie triggering the standing portraits of Australia's prime ministers to fall down in a domino-effect, where the museum guard's cat ends up flattened under

John Howard. This slapstick comedy element is visual deconstruction of partial Australian historiography *par excellence* and reminds us that it needs revision from an Indigenous perspective.

In the same ridiculous manner the film deconstructs the cliché of the traditional nature-loving Aborigine when Charlie and Eddie scream bloody murder and scramble away from a tarantula in their car and when Charlie curses magpies as 'skinny-legged bastards;' also both men have lost the skill to hunt kangaroos but run over one with their car, which they then roast. In the same manner, Frankland mocks a New Age cop and his 'dreaming', his cultural appropriation of traditional Indigenous culture. Hilariously, he has Mark run into the desert shedding his clothes until completely naked – he is not outright dismissed but laughed at in a benevolent way. Likewise, the film treats Regina, working as a drag queen, very respectfully, having the cousins accept her new identity. In the end, the Italian musician dates Regina, a plot turn that undermines compulsory heteronormativity and presents transgender identities as ordinary. Furthermore, the film parodies inter- and intracultural colour coding when Charlie and Eddie argue who is blacker than the other and would thus have more success with women.

The film begins with Eddie looking intently at a special rock in the Perth Museum; the plot is dynamized by Eddie and Charlie bringing home their sacred rocks, and, at the end, they retrieve Eddie's rock from a small-town exhibition, pretending to be hired dancers, dressed-up traditionally with painted faces and bodies. They thus emphasize the film's decolonizing approach to contemporary Indigenous identities that move freely between tradition and modernity. The moment when they smash the showcase with traditional pounding sticks and take the rock is a cinematic analogy to decolonizing acts of repatriating Indigenous artefacts from museums and scientific collections. That they are successful only in a small-town museum and not in Perth only signals that reparation work has a long way to go.

Postcolonial films in Nigeria

In 1979 Alfred E. Opubor et al. held that film was the least developed mass media in Nigeria and saw potential for a Nigerian film development in terms of education, bringing African cultures and values into the medium as well as job opportunities for filmmakers and auxiliary industries.[14] Contested indigenizing measures following a devastating civil war caused Hollywood to cease distribution and created a cinematic gap. New Nigerian film institutions, destabilized by alleged corruption and profligacy, were unable to develop coherent strategies to establish a national film industry. Instead, an era of 'pirate infrastructure' and rampant bootlegging followed, abetted by successive military governments, swinging between supporting cinema and documentary film, as well as rising urban crime rates, discouraging millions of Nigerians from going to the movies in the dark hours. Thus since the 1980s, Nigeria has seen a rapid reduction of cinemas and decline of state film funding, while inexpensive video technology in the 1990s triggered a booming video film industry – Nollywood, a 'self-supporting African success story'.[15] The Nollywood concept is as uncomplicated as incredible to most cineastes: within two to three weeks a complete film was shot on video, with often inexperienced or time-pressed actors, and a budget of 15,000–50,000 dollars. Scriptwriters churned out scripts without much care; often there was no script at all but a vague scenario. The film was released on a video cassette or later DVD for around five dollars on local markets; pirate copies appeared shortly after. These cheap films achieved incredible popularity and were soon exported into the sub-Saharan continent and African diasporas in the Caribbean, Brazil, North America and Europe. Some cable channels in the UK and the United States show exclusively Nollywood films and specific websites allow live streams. At times, Nollywood produced 2,000 to 3,000 films annually with up to 30,000 copies each, employed 300,000 Nigerians, and generated 250 million dollars. Profits were made through the massive sales numbers and video piracy. Accordingly, the quality of the films was low, with a poor soundtrack, wooden acting, cheap technical effects, and the like. No Nollywood film made it into African or other international film festivals. Even now the lowest technical and acting level is accepted as long as the story is exciting.[16] Nollywood is no emulation of Hollywood at all;[17] rather it exists independent of the global Western-dominated film industry – a decolonizing factor in itself.

Nollywood films focus on African life, everyday problems, moral offences, criminality, success stories, spiritual and magical practices; dialogue-intensity and meandering narration go back to African oral traditions; film aesthetics and production values ignore Western film standards. But the plots satisfy Nigerian longing for success and prosperity; many films are set in higher class circles with luxurious houses, cars and people, which counters stereotypes of Africa being a hotbed of wars, poverty, hunger, illegal migration, drugs and corruption. Nollywood thus circulates transcultural stories mixing African traditions and modernity, influenced by oral traditions, Yoruba travelling theatre, and non-African cinemas and values. Today the state controls production numbers, increasing the quality of script and cinematography; and Nollywood films gradually appear at international film festivals.

A number of filmmakers work in this liminal zone between African arthouse cinema, the global film industry, and Nollywood, for example Kenneth Nnebue, Tunde Kelani, Lancelot Oduwa Imasuen and Kunle Afolayan.[18] Tunde Kelani has made already eighteen films, *Thunderbolt [Magun]* (2000) was probably the most successful with a love story involving tensions between Igbo and Yoruba cultures, evil witchery and traditional healing vis-á-vis modern medicine. *Maami* (2011) won several awards at the 2012 ZUMA Film Festival and the 2013 Nollywood Movies Awards. It narrates the story of Kashimawo, a Nigerian soccer star playing for Arsenal, who returns to Nigeria shortly before the World Cup in 2006. Indeed the Nigerian soccer association assumes he came home to play for Nigeria in the cup, but Kashy has private reasons to return since it is the tenth anniversary of a fateful birthday. In flashbacks the film recounts Kashy's childhood with a loving mother, braving extreme poverty with wit and resourcefulness. On his tenth birthday, Kashy wishes for nothing more than a good meal with meat, which Maami tries to procure the money for; having lost all money and gifts from people she brings Kashy into his father's house unnoticed where he sees things that will haunt him forever. Both barely escaping from the house, Maami dies in a road accident. Maami is the true heroine of this film; she once abducted Kashy from their rich home in order to protect him from a father who had already sacrificed his brother and other boys to his occultist practices. These are portrayed as backwards and dangerous as much as wealth and fame is transient (in *Thunderbolt*, African healing practices are represented as a beneficial complements to modern medicine). *Maami* owes much to the performance of Funke Akindele as Maami, her bravery, witty dialogue, affectionate and sharing personality – all presented as Kashy's childhood memories.

The film works with oppositions between Kashy's prosperity, fame, and elitist surroundings and the poverty and hardships of the people he came from, also supported by filming in English and Yoruba respectively. Kashy visits his former orphanage and neighbourhood and participates in dances, while his manager is completely alienated from poorer and more traditional parts of society. The film thus brings into sharp relief widespread poverty, superficial Western lifestyles, corruption and cruelty of those in power, but also warmth and generosity of the poorer Nigerians. Kashy's openhanded donations, his unrelenting judgement of his now old and sick father, and the melodramatic scene at his mother's grave mean the film tends towards moralizing, but these aspects integrate it perfectly into Nollywood tradition where good always wins against evil.

The films discussed display a variety of decolonizing strategies, above all, self-controlled decolonial media production, aligning cinematic perspectives with subaltern subjects and thus channelling audience sympathies, adapting film styles to presented cultures and traditional narrating patterns, filming in Indigenous languages when possible, using local finance systems and low budgets, critiquing exploitation of natural resources and Indigenous people, appropriating Western film genres, and parodying settler colonial historiography and representational practices. In this way, postcolonial cinema undermines the ubiquitous dominance of Eurocentric film discourses and autonomously and self-confidently presents postcolonial cultures and modern life worlds.

Notes

1 Michel Foucault, *The Birth of the Clinic: An Archaeology of Medical Perception* (New York: Pantheon Books, 1973), 115.
2 Martin Jay, 'In the Empire of the Gaze: Foucault and the Denigration of Vision in Twentieth-Century French Thought', in *Michel Foucault: Critical Assessments*, Vol. 1, ed. Barry Smart (New York and London: Routledge, 1994), 206.
3 E. Ann Kaplan, *Looking for the Other: Feminism, Film, and the Imperial Gaze* (London and New York: Routledge, 1997).
4 For a more comprehensive discussion of Foucault's 'gaze of power' and the notion of 'decolonizing film', cf. Kerstin Knopf, *Decolonizing the Lens of Power: Indigenous Films in North America* (Amsterdam and New York: Rodopi, 2008), 1–7.
5 Bhabha, *The Location of Culture*, 17, 127.
6 Himani Bannerji, 'Returning the Gaze: An Introduction', in *Returning the Gaze: Essays on Racism, Feminism and Politics*, ed. Himani Bannerji (Toronto: Sister Vision Press, 1993), xxii–xxiii; Kaplan, *Looking*, 295–99.
7 Bill Ashcroft, *Post-Colonial Transformation* (London and New York: Routledge, 2001), 33.
8 Cf. Randolph Lewis' concept of 'representational sovereignty' and Michelle Raheja's 'visual sovereignty'; Randolph Lewis, *Alanis Obomsawin: The Vision of a Native Filmmaker* (Lincoln and London: University of Nebraska

Press, 2006), 175; Michelle H. Raheja. *Reservation Reelism: Redfacing, Visual Sovereignty, and Representations of Native Americans in Film* (Lincoln and London: University of Nebraska Press, 2010), 193–205.

9. Christoph Huber, 'Mythos, Müll und Marginalia: José Mohica Marins, Prophet von Brasiliens Neuem Kino', in *Spuren eines Dritten Kinos: Zu Ästhetik, Politik und Ökonomie des World Cinema*, eds. Lukas Foerster et al. (Bielefeld: transcript, 2013), 235.

10. Survival International, http://www.survivalinternational.org/tribes/guarani (accessed 10 October 2014).

11. Felicity Collins and Therese Davis, *Australian Cinema after* Mabo (Cambridge: Cambridge University Press, 2004), 165.

12. Cf. Pauline Marsh's discussion of various connotations of 'stone' in the film. Marsh, 'The Primitive, the Sacred and the Stoned in Richard J. Frankland's *Stone Bros*' Studies in Australasian Cinema 6, no. 1 (2012): 31–33.

13. Gordon Waitt quoted in Marsh, 'The Primitive', 31.

14. Alfred E. Opubor et al., 'The Status, Role and Future of the Film Industry in Nigeria', in *The Development and Growth of the Film Industry in Nigeria*, eds. Alfred E. Opubor and Onura E. Nwuneli (Lagos: Third Press International, 1979), 1–22.

15. Noah A. Tsika, *Nollywood Stars: Media and Migration in West Africa and the Diaspora* (Bloomington and Indianapolis: Indiana University Press, 2015), 6, 3–6.

16. Jonathan Haynes, 'African Cinema and Nollywood: Contradictions', *Situations: Project of the Radical Imagination* 4, no. 1 (2011): 72–74; Peter Böhm, 'Nollywood', *taz*, 25 June 2008, http://www.taz.de/!5179955/(accessed 19 April 2015).

17. Haynes, 'African Cinema', 85.

18. Tsika, *Nollywood Stars*, xvi.

13

Postcolonial Gaming: An Interview with Seth Alter, creator of *Neocolonialism: Ruin Everything* (Subaltern Games)

Seth Alter and Jenni Ramone

When computer games are so prevalent, perhaps it is inevitable that independent programmes will emerge that engage with postcolonial subjects. Seth Alter's *Neocolonialism*[1] addresses the phenomenon of neoliberal capitalism and invites the player to reconsider their part in the global economic system. Matthew Rosegreen explains that '*Neocolonialism* is a strategy game based around the impact of neocolonialism and globalization. However, while most game developers would look at this as inspiration for a game in the style of SimCity that relies on the player maintaining a healthy economy, Subaltern Games invites the player to exploit it by becoming a world leader and then making self-serving business decisions', and suggests 'the way that the game approaches the issue of global capitalism is not unlike the delivery of similar topics on other media platforms such as films, television or fictional publications'.[2] However, games have a different target audience from the audiences of these forms, and a different mode of engagement, so I spoke to Seth Alter to find out what he hoped to achieve with *Neocolonialism*, as well as to find out more about the decisions he made in constructing the game.

J.R.: Please introduce yourself! How did you start creating games? What is your background?
S.A.: I am Seth Alter. I run Subaltern Games, a small games studio based in Boston.

I have always loved playing games, telling stories and teaching. I graduated from Wesleyan University with a History B.A. in 2011. While looking for employment, I began to develop Neocolonialism – I had taken a few computer science courses in my Freshman year, but otherwise had never coded before. I was briefly a teacher in 2012, quit that job in October of that year, and have been working full-time on games ever since. The video game industry is usually divided into two categories. AAA studios make high-budget games like *Grand Theft Auto* or *Call of Duty*, and are analogous to Hollywood. Indie studios have far smaller budgets, and are generally known only to the enthusiasts. There is a vast gulf between AAA and indie; virtually all studios fall into one category or the other. There is also a small but growing movement of 'alt games', which are more artsy and experimental than indie games and are not necessarily made with profit in mind.[3] My studio is an indie studio. I released *Neocolonialism* in November 2013. I am currently working on my second project, *No Pineapple Left Behind*.

J.R.: Could you describe the concept of No Pineapple Left Behind?
S.A.: In *No Pineapple Left Behind*, you have to run a school full of children. Children have lots of wants, needs and feelings. That's a problem, because if they get don't pay attention in class and get low grades, your school loses money. However, you can turn children into pineapples. All that pineapples do is take tests and get grades. They do not have feelings and are not people, but they are much simpler to handle, and therefore much cheaper.[4]

J.R.: What is the idea behind the game Neocolonialism?
S.A.: *Neocolonialism* is a video game about ruining the world via unchecked capitalism. You and up to six other people play as bankers. You buy and sell government votes, vote on free trade agreements, manipulate the IMF and attempt to siphon money into your secret Swiss bank account. *Neocolonialism* is meant to be a sort of proof-of-concept that a video game with otherwise familiar systems, coupled with a powerful and intentional message, can be far more compelling than one without such a message. Reciprocally, I wanted to challenge the broader societal notion that all games are intrinsically shallow. That being said, since I started working on

Neocolonialism in late 2011, there has been a surge of very introspective and thoughtful indie games.

J.R.: Could you describe how you play it?
S.A.: *Neocolonialism* is a 'turn-based strategy' game. The world (depicted as an upside-down map) is divided into discrete sub-regions, each with 'tokens' representing regional infrastructure. A player will enact a series of decisions, and then it will be the next player's turn and so on. *Neocolonialism* is intentionally similar to games like Risk in certain respects and includes mechanics (rules, strategies, etc.) that turn-based strategy fans would be familiar with. However, the unusual politics of the game yielded both new mechanics, and twists on existing ones.

I gave a talk at Indiecade East 2015 about how *Neocolonialism* deconstructs the standard turn-based strategy game. My talk was about 4X games, a sub-genre of strategy games. 4X games are generally empire-building simulators. '4X' refers to an acronym of four verbs – Explore, Expand, Exploit, Exterminate – which broadly define the arc of most of these games.

4X have a few well-known titles such as the Civilization series, but in general they are more obscure than shooters and role-playing games. They tend to take a long time to play (I once had a Civilization game that lasted 22 hours) and have a very methodical pacing.

Initially in most 4X games, you (the player) start with a small patch of territory on a broader map. The map is often initially obscured, so you must explore the map for useful resources, rival factions, etc. The map is usually divided into discrete sub-regions (like in Risk), and your people are divided into discrete 'units' (like chess pieces). Once you have explored and have a better sense of the surrounding terrain, it is time to expand. You capture provinces, peacefully or otherwise, and move your faction's borders outwards. Once you have sufficient territory, you can begin to exploit the terrain. Each region has a set of resources (common ones include wealth, minerals, wood, etc.) that you can accumulate over time. You use resources to build. 'Build' in 4X games means enhancing existing territory. Perhaps with enough wood, for example, you can build a bank, which increases the output of wealth. This is also how you build military units. A strong military is important because 4X surround you with rivals that are vying for power. Often, there is a way to win a 4X game without resorting to war, but in practice, genocide is a very effective path to victory.

Neocolonialism is in many ways an anti-4X game. It offers exploration only in the most abstract sense, by inverting the map of the world and forcing players to rethink their assumptions about it. In most 4X games, expansion is considered to be essentially moral (in that you are bringing the light of civilization or whatever to the wilderness), but in *Neocolonialism* you are clearly not helping anyone – in fact, one of the best strategies in my game involves keeping most of the world poor. *Neocolonialism* allows you to exploit the world like other 4X games, but makes it clear that you are only doing so for your personal benefit. Your secret Swiss bank account money will never be re-distributed throughout the globe, and everyone is probably worse off thanks to your meddling. Essentially, *Neocolonialism* is on the surface the same as a standard 4X game, except that it takes pains to make the amorality of your actions abundantly clear rather than rewarding you in any sense for developing a mighty empire.

Unlike shooter games, turn-based strategy games are generally not mainstream hits. *Neocolonialism* is simple for a turn-based strategy game, but very complicated for video games in general. *Neocolonialism* requires a great deal of negotiating and back-stabbing between its players. In many cases, players stand to benefit from cooperating with each other (some will benefit more than others). But ultimately, there is only one winner.

There are twelve regions in the game. Each region can have Mines and/or Factories, as well as free trade agreements. These structures affect the price of a region's vote. There are twelve turns in the game, each divided into three phases. In the Investment Phase, players take turns buying and selling votes in regional parliaments. Each region has ten votes up for purchasing. If players, working together, purchase at least three votes in a region, they will trigger elections for a prime minister. Votes are crucial because they are the only way to win the game, and because they are the player's source of income; they pay out 1/3 of their price at the start of the Investment Phase.

In the Policy Phase, each region with a prime minister takes a turn (if there is no prime minister, there are elections between the players). The prime minister then proposes a new economic policy, upon which then everyone else with purchased votes will vote. A prime minister can also choose to Bank, which converts their votes into money and siphons it into their secret Swiss bank account. The player cannot use this money ever again, but whoever has the most Swiss money is the winner. In the IMF Phase, a random crisis (such as a worker's strike) threatens a random region.

One player (rotating per turn) is the IMF Managing Director, and can enact a unilateral economic policy in that region.

J.R.: You have included phrases from theory and philosophical thinking: is this a unique aspect of the game?
S.A.: No. Such quotes are called 'flavour text' and are fairly ubiquitous. *Neocolonialism's* quotes are far more ironic than is usual.

J.R.: Could you elaborate on 'flavour text' – what exactly does this mean?
S.A.: Flavour text embellishes thematic elements of the game rather than clarifying its rules.

J.R.: Do you think it's always clear to players that your 'flavour text' is more ironic than usual?
S.A.: NO! The store page includes a negative review from a player who took offense at a truly stupid Donald Trump quote. As a side note, in general it is very clear to people that the game itself is ironic.

J.R.: Have you had many comments on the flavour text?
S.A.: People have remarked on it, but that review is the only one that makes significant mention of it. Here and elsewhere, flavour text is meant to be supplementary to the game, not a main focus. I am curious though why you are asking about flavour text. In video games, it is as standard as text in a movie telling the viewer where the scene is ('PARIS: FRANCE. TWO YEARS EARLIER'). How does flavour text appear to an outsider?
J.R.: I suppose, from the perspective of someone who hasn't played videogames, it seems to do more than just set the scene because it's a creative use of text – sometimes in film the use of text like 'two years later' seems clunky and points to a narrative that isn't clear, whereas the text in videogames like this seems to operate like an extra creative part of the experience. I can see how it functions now you've explained it to me, but it seems to create relationships – especially with quotations from philosophy which are normally read in printed materials – and to extend the boundaries of the game. It almost feels like the game is closer to digital literature than I expected it to be. Flavour text feels like something that can be analysed further. Perhaps it forces the player to be more aware of the external world and the way the game is not a fantasy with no relevance to or impact on the real world.

S.A.: It is relatively unusual to quote outside sources in flavour text. Often, the format is used for in-game explanations. As an example, if your character in a Lord of the Rings-esque game found a magic sword, it might have associated text like:

> ATTACK: 7
> SPEED: 6
> SPECIAL: Fire damage +1
> *This sword was crafted by Elves in the First Age of the world.*

In this mock example, the *last* line is the flavour text, since it doesn't inform the player of the practical functionality of the magical sword. Alternatively, if this was a game based on *Lord of the Rings* – and there are some of those – maybe the designers would quote Tolkien directly. But, *Neocolonialism* is meant to reflect the real world rather than a fantasy world, so I suppose that is why my quotes are pulled from the real world.

J.R.: Are there any similar games which tackle themes such as colonialism and neocolonialism? If so, in what ways is your game different?
S.A.: There are a handful of games that directly challenge colonialism or neo-colonialism. Again, *Neocolonialism* is rather unique, but here are a few: *80 Days*; *Phone Story*; *The Cat and the Coup*.[5] While I do not have any hard evidence of this, I suspect that it is difficult for developers to accumulate a sufficient budget to make such a game, particularly if they are living in the poorer areas of the world. *Neocolonialism* is very unusual in that it is a turn-based strategy game (a genre heavily associated with narratives of colonial conquest), and that it is far larger and more sophisticated than most games with similar politics. It also forces the player to play the antagonist rather than allowing for a more optimistic narrative. There are MANY games that address colonialism in unintentional or problematic ways. For example, protagonists of *Call of Duty: Modern Warfare* are US soldiers combating brown-skinned terrorists in fictional desert countries.

J.R.: Have you had discussions with people (other developers, or people who use games) about Call of Duty: Modern Warfare and its problematic aspects? Do you think it's widely perceived as problematic?
S.A.: This question is sort of a can of worms because since August 2014 there has been an ongoing enormous and very scary cultural war about video games called Gamergate. Gamergate is hard to explain succinctly.[6] The shared world of video game journalists, developers and miscellaneous major

personalities is relatively small and highly interconnected. Within that, there is a large minority that is very vocal about the problems of *Call of Duty*, and virtually everyone is aware of the ongoing conversation. In general, members of the indie community are more likely than the corporate AAA community to speak out against Call of Duty and its ilk.

J.R.: What is your typical player like? Is there an ideal audience for this game?
S.A.: Most people who play the game are strategy gamers, which is to say white men. Strategy gaming is a niche within a niche, requiring a particular support of cerebral mentality, and cherished by a small, insular fanbase. Which is to say, not only are strategy games not for everyone, but the community can be difficult to break into, especially if you do not match the demographic majority. *Neocolonialism* is modelled on some of my personal favourite games, but making it a strategy game restricted its potential for broader appeal. It is a core design decision that I regret.

J.R.: Do you think videogames perform a different role in culture from films, art, literature, graphic novels? Do they make people think or feel or experience ideas in different ways from other art and cultural forms?
S.A.: Insofar as films play a different role from literature, and so on, yes. Video games are very new (games in general are of course ancient) and as such are still immature. Most top-selling games are focused on verisimilitude and graphical fidelity rather than the story they are telling. There is no '*Citizen Kane*' of the games world (though there probably does not need to be one). Video games are far more ubiquitous than they were as recent as ten years ago, and have decisively transitioned from being a niche art form to a global one.

Games almost always involve a degree of 'role playing' in which a player is acting out a role, whether it is a US soldier or a mighty warrior. They thus have the potential to put the player directly (and literally!) in the shoes of someone else, allowing them to see the world from a new perspective. When people talk about games, they almost do so in terms of what they 'did' rather than observed from afar and often will retain a shared set of experiences. For example, people who have played Mass Effect (a hugely popular series) will talk to each other about decisions that *they* made or how *they* resolved plot lines. In *Neocolonialism*, you *are* a banker, and the ruination of the world is *your* doing.

J.R.: Is it possible to change society if enough people engage with videogames like this one? What message do you hope people will take away from the game Neocolonialism?

S.A.: You actually have to get out and enact change in order to change society. Video games can't change the world any more than books or movies can. But they can change how someone perceives the world. If a gamer plays *Neocolonialism* and walks away from the experience with new-found misgivings about how the global economy is structured, then the game has fulfilled its task.

Notes

1. http://store.steampowered.com/app/333540/ (accessed 15 June 2015).
2. Matthew Rosegreen, 'Review: Neocolonialism – Subaltern Games', https://postcolonialstudiescentre.wordpress.com/2015/11/12/review-rosegreen/2015 (accessed 19 November 2015).
3. Note: the industry and the labels it uses to define itself change frequently and swiftly. Seth Alter states that by the time you read this, either label may have fallen into disuse, become blurred with each other, or morphed into something else.
4. See the game trailer online: https://www.youtube.com/watch?v=twimJX7O7H4 (accessed 15 June 2015).
5. 80 Days, http://www.frogwares.com/game/80days.html; Phone Story http://www.phonestory.org/; The Cat and the Coup, http://www.thecatandthecoup.com/
6. For further details on Gamergate, see http://www.theestablishment.co/2015/11/18/gamergate-alison-prime-trolling/ or the gamer-targeted discussion here: http://rationalwiki.org/wiki/Gamergate

Part III

New Debates

14 Postcolonial Refugees, Displacement, Dispossession and Economies of Abandonment in the Capitalist World System
15 Postcolonial Sexualities and the Intelligibility of Dissidence
16 Contemporary Migration and Diaspora Studies: Current Debates and the Role of Literature
17 Postcolonialism and African American Literature
18 Faith, Secularism and Community in Womanist Literature from the Neocolonial Caribbean
19 Secularism in India: Principles and Policies

14

Postcolonial Refugees, Displacement, Dispossession and Economies of Abandonment in the Capitalist World System

Stephen Morton

In a central sequence in Abderrahmane Sissako's 2006 film *Bamako*, a young man called Madou Keita delivers a testimony about his experiences of the socio-economic impact of the World Bank's structural adjustment policies on Mali. Recounting his attempt to leave the country in search of a better life in Europe, Keita describes how he and the group of migrants he was travelling with were abandoned in the Sahara desert and shot at by a group of people he believes to be Algerians.[1] Keita's testimony raises profound questions about the political and economic legacy of imperialism for understanding the dynamics of migration and the transnational movement of people. What light can the narratives of postcolonial refugees such as Keita shed on the violence of imperialism and its economies of dispossession and abandonment, particularly in postcolonial contexts? How might a consideration of the relationship between the policies of financial institutions such as the World Bank and the plight of contemporary refugees question and complicate the predominant distinction in contemporary European political discourse between legitimate asylum seekers and supposedly illegitimate economic migrants? In what ways might the experiences and narratives of postcolonial refugees recalibrate theories of sovereignty and biopower in such a way that takes account of the histories of dispossession and abandonment associated with the global expansion of capitalism? And what forms of agency and resistance are available to postcolonial refugees to contest the political and economic forces that have precipitated their displacement?

One of the earliest thinkers to address the relationship between European imperialism and the figure of the refugee was the German Jewish political philosopher Hannah Arendt. In her book, *The Origins of Totalitarianism* (1951), Arendt argued that the figure of the refugee is a subject who is deprived of the right to have rights. Arendt was thinking in particular of the ways in which the anti-semitic policies of Nazi Germany had effectively stripped the European Jewish population of their citizenship, thereby defining them as stateless peoples or refugees. Yet Arendt also suggested that the historical events leading to the Holocaust could be traced back in part to the violent formations of European colonial sovereignty that operated in South Africa, German South-East Africa and King Leopold's Belgian Congo. Just as the bureaucracies of European colonial governments had dehumanized the native populations of African societies through the pseudo-scientific language of racism to justify the exploitation of African labour power, so European nation states defined Jewish immigrants as aliens, who could be stripped of the rights associated with citizenship.

Arendt's reflections on the historical relationship between racism, anti-semitism and the refugee may seem to prefigure the more recent reflections on biopolitics in the work of Michel Foucault and Giorgio Agamben. In his posthumously published lecture series *Society Must Be Defended* (1997), Foucault considered how racism and race thinking sheds light on the biopolitical functioning of power. Like Arendt, Foucault suggested that racism is bound up with the history of European colonialism and the Nazi genocide of European Jews. As Foucault put it, 'Racism first develops with colonization, or in other words, with colonizing genocide'.[2] In terms that were quite different from those of Arendt, however, Foucault also suggested that racism needed to be understood in terms of a change in the function of power from one of sovereignty to one of biopower. One of the defining characteristics of sovereignty for Foucault was the right of life and death. The sovereign was the figure who had the right to take the life of one of their subjects. As Foucault put it: 'The very essence of the right of life and death is actually the right to kill: it is at the moment when the sovereign can kill that he exercises his right over life. It is essentially the right of the sword'.[3] During the eighteenth and nineteenth -centuries, however, Foucault identified the emergence of a new right in technologies of political power: 'the power to "make" live and "let" die'.[4] This power did not simply take the place of sovereignty, but rather complemented it. With this shift in the emphasis of the power associated with liberal governmentality, Foucault suggested that there was a parallel shift in the mode and scale of power: from the individual human body of the condemned subject to the life of the human population. It is at this point, Foucault claims, 'that racism intervenes'. In a conceptual move that expands and develops his account of biopolitics, Foucault argues that racism is 'primarily a way of introducing a break into the domain of life that is under power's control: the break between what must live and what must die'.[5]

Foucault does not specifically discuss the figure of the refugee in his reflections on racism. Yet his account of how biopower distinguishes between human populations that must live and those who must die has significant implications for understanding the conditions that lead to the forced migration of human populations. It is worth noting too that what Foucault means by letting die has far reaching implications. 'When I say "killing"', Foucault says, 'I obviously do not mean simply murder as such, but also every form of indirect murder: the fact of exposing someone to death, increasing the risk of death for some people, or, quite simply, political death, expulsion, rejection, and so on'.[6] While letting die can entail being put to death in certain circumstances, it can also mean being abandoned by the state. Letting die can mean losing access to food, clean water, healthcare, housing, private property or a living wage, but it can also mean loss of protection from racial, ethnic or religious violence and persecution.

The expansive connotations of letting die have been the source of considerable debate among some of Foucault's critical commentators, most notably the Italian legal philosopher Giorgio Agamben. For Agamben, there is a blind spot in Foucault's account of the shift from sovereignty to biopower that elides the way in which the biopolitical body has always been at the foundation of sovereign power. As Agamben puts it, '[...] *the production of a biopolitical body is the original activity of sovereign power*. In this sense, biopolitics is at least as old as its sovereign exception'.[7] At stake in Agamben's critique of Foucault is the suggestion that the formation of sovereign power from ancient Greece to contemporary political democracies such as the United States have been founded on an exceptional violence in which the bare life of the citizen can be killed by the state. For Agamben, this sovereign power of the state is epitomized in the classical political thought of the Romans. In classical Roman law, the figure of *homo sacer*, or the *man* who could be killed without being sacrificed exemplifies the hidden foundation of the political. In Agamben's formulation, *homo sacer* denotes a figure of human life that is included in the political order and can be killed without reference to the rule of law. That is to say, it is the 'capacity' of human life 'to be killed' that forms the 'first foundation of political life' for Agamben.[8] In the modern nation state, by contrast, Agamben argues that the figure of bare life has been incorporated into a political discourse of citizenship. Yet this collapsing of the distinction between bare life and citizenship does not mean that the citizen is necessarily protected from the exigencies of sovereign power in the modern nation state. Against the common assumption that state terror and genocide such as the Jewish holocaust is an aberration or exceptional case of human atrocity, Agamben argues that the modern nation state is founded on a 'state of exception', where it is possible to define a group of citizens as bare life, or people who can be killed without bring sacrificed. 'At once excluding bare life from and capturing it within the political order, the state of exception actually constituted, in its very separateness, the hidden foundation on which the entire political system [of the modern nation state] rested'.[9]

For Agamben, the space of the camp exemplifies this 'state of exception' because it exposes the hidden foundations of the nation state and its sovereign power over the life and death of its citizens. Significantly, he argues that the first appearance of the 'state of exception' is in the context of European colonialism: he cites the establishment of camps by the Spanish in Cuba in 1896 to suppress the insurrection of its colonized subjects and by the English in South Africa during the Boer war. What is crucial for Agamben is that 'the camp opens up when the state of exception starts to become the rule'.[10] The fact that some of the first camps were founded in colonial states certainly exposes the violence associated with the civilizing mission of European colonialism – even if considerations of colonial sovereignty are not explicitly addressed at the forefront of Agamben's work.

It is also worth pausing to reflect on the implications of Agamben's reflections on the sovereign ban for the condition of the postcolonial refugee. In Agamben's formulation, the ban denotes a relation of semantic and conceptual ambiguity between the sovereign and the person who is banned or banished from the borders of a political territory. In the legal and philosophical traditions of ancient Greece and Rome, Agamben claims that to be banned 'originally meant both "at the mercy of" and "out of free will, freely", both "excluded, banned" and "open to all, free".[11] Significantly, Agamben also suggests that the figure of the exile exemplifies the very condition of abandonment – an observation that can shed significant light on the false dichotomy between the (legitimate) asylum seeker and the (illegitimate) economic migrant in contemporary political discourse.

A consideration of the relationship between the uneven development of capitalism and the dynamics of transnational migration may not feature at the forefront of Agamben's reflections on sovereignty and exceptional violence. Yet his account of the sovereign ban could be seen to complement Hannah Arendt's preoccupation with superfluous life in her speculations on totalitarianism. Echoing Karl Marx's reflections on the unemployed and the pauper, Arendt noted how the rise of European imperialism had defined certain people as superfluous – a term which itself suggests that certain people's lives were deemed worthless or without value. As she puts it:

> The impetus and what is more important, the silent consent to such unprecedented conditions are the products of those events which in a period of political disintegration suddenly and unexpectedly made hundreds of thousands of human beings homeless, stateless, outlawed and unwanted, while millions of human beings were made economically superfluous and socially burdensome by unemployment.[12]

In the context of the 1930s, the events which precipitated mass unemployment, homelessness and statelessness may have appeared sudden and unexpected; with the benefit of hindsight, however, Arendt implies that such events were a logical outcome of imperialist policies. From Arendt's specific historical perspective in the post-war period, the tendency to define certain people as 'superfluous' varied between different European colonial powers. 'The so-called hypocrisy of British policies', argued Arendt, 'was the result of the good sense of English statesmen who drew a sharp line between colonial methods and normal domestic policies, thereby avoiding with considerable success the feared boomerang effect of imperialism upon the homeland'. In Arendt's view, this so-called 'boomerang effect' was more pronounced in Germany, Austria and to a lesser extent, France, where the whole nation was organized according to imperialist principles – 'for the looting of foreign territories and the permanent degradation of alien peoples'.[13] This is not to suggest, however, that the racist thinking associated with colonialism did not influence Britain's domestic policies towards immigrants. As David Glover

(2012) has argued, the passing of the Aliens Act in 1905 set a new precedent for immigration control by excluding so-called 'undesirable aliens'.[14] In the dominant British cultural imagination of the time, 'the word "alien" [...] had become a popular synonym for East European Jews'.[15]

The Aliens Act certainly exemplified the way in which immigration law provided a technique for discriminating between human life that was deemed superfluous to the economy and cultural identity of a nation state and that which was deemed to be valuable and desirable. Yet the exclusionary forms of nationalism that statutes such as the Aliens Act symbolized were not of course confined to European imperial powers such as Britain. In her comments on the formation of Israel in 1948, Arendt noted how the formation of the state of Israel created another population of Palestinian refugees at the very moment it attempted to find a political solution to the Jewish refugee crisis. Arendt's brief yet critical reflections on Israel/Palestine have important implications for understanding the ways in which the exclusionary foundations of the colonial state provided a political template for the formation of postcolonial states, as commentators such as Achille Mbembe, Giorgio Agamben and Judith Butler have noted. A critical assessment of the conceptual limits of such exclusionary forms of sovereignty can help to elucidate the forms of hospitality and agency that are available to postcolonial refugees, as we will see.

In a powerful analysis of colonial and postcolonial forms of sovereignty, Achille Mbembe has argued that it is the colony that represents the site where sovereignty consists fundamentally in the exercise of a power outside the law and where 'peace' is more likely to take on the face of a 'war without end'. In this colonial state of exception, the native is represented as 'another form of animal life', who shares no human bond with the conqueror.[16] The sovereign power of the colonizer is thus defined by his capacity to subject, control and even kill the colonized. In a radical reframing of Foucault's account of biopolitics, Mbembe emphasizes that colonial sovereignty is inherently necropolitical: it distinguishes between human populations who are disposable and those who are not. Two examples that Mbembe cites to support his thesis about the way in which necropower operates are the South African township under apartheid and the occupied territories of Palestine. In each of these cases, it is the spatial annexation of the colonial territory that makes possible the exercise of necropower and the violent assertion of colonial sovereignty. A consideration of the postcolonial refugee does not figure in Mbembe's discussion of necropolitics. Yet it is not difficult to see how the necropolitical logic of disposability that Mbembe attributes to colonial and postcolonial states also impacts on the forced movement of people. Indeed, the contemporary spectacle of Syrian refugees drowning in the Mediterranean ocean in a desperate attempt to escape from a long-running civil war is but one harrowing example of the ways in which a necropolitical logic of disposability shapes and determines the lives and deaths of the dispossessed.

If necropolitics can help to make sense of both the spectacular and quotidian forms of violence and abandonment associated with colonial and postcolonial state formations, this is not to suggest that death is the only form of sovereignty and agency available to postcolonial refugees. In a short response to Hannah Arendt's reflections on the refugee in *The Origins of Totalitarianism*, Giorgio Agamben argues that 'the refugee is the sole category in which it is possible today to perceive the forms and limits of a political community to come'.[17] For Agamben, the figure of the refugee calls into question the universal claims of human rights declarations by 'breaking up' the assumption that the 1789 Declaration of the Rights of Man and the Citizen includes human subjects who are not citizens. What is more, the refugee highlights the fiction that national belonging is guaranteed by nativity or birth, and thereby 'throws into crisis the original fiction of sovereignty'.[18] For Agamben as for Arendt, it is the Nazi holocaust of the European Jews that clearly exemplifies the failure of universal human rights declarations to protect the rights of human populations. Yet Agamben's argument also has important implications for understanding the condition of the postcolonial refugee. For just as Arendt predicted in *The Origins of Totalitarianism* that the formation of the state of Israel would create a new population of Palestinian refugees and a new regime of violent political sovereignty, so Agamben suggests that the 'four hundred and twenty-five Palestinians who were expelled by the state of Israel' in the early 1990s and 'dwell in a sort of no-man's-land between Lebanon and Israel' constitute what Hannah Arendt termed '"the avant-garde of their people"'.[19] Crucially for Agamben, Arendt's term 'does not necessarily or only mean' that these Palestinian refugees 'might form the original nucleus of a future national state'. For such a political solution 'would probably resolve the Palestinian problem just as inadequately as Israel has resolved the Jewish question'. Instead, Agamben argues that the 'no-man's-land' where the Palestinians have found refuge offers a means of altering the political territory in such a way that 'the citizen will have learned to acknowledge the refugee that he himself [sic] is'.[20]

Agamben's speculations on the possibilities of imagining a form of political life that would render inoperable the exclusionary categories of the nation state are certainly thought provoking. Yet his discussion does not address the socio-economic circumstances of the 425 Palestinian refugees he invokes. Such a consideration is particularly important for understanding the plight of postcolonial refugees, as the Palestinian writer, Ghassan Kanafani, demonstrates in his novella *Men in the Sun* (1956). Located on the border between Iraq and Kuwait, *Men in the Sun* is focalized through the consciousness of three Palestinian refugees, who travel to Kuwait in search of a better life. Structured through a series of flashbacks, the novella documents the tragic failure of the three men to cross the border illegally from Iraq into Kuwait. As each of these flashbacks suggest, the particular circumstances that precipitated the displacement of the three men can be traced back to the *nakba* or catastrophe of 1948, when an estimated 750,000 people were forced to leave their land. For this reason, the novella is often read as a complex allegory of the stateless Palestinian nation – a nation that is both imagined and defined by a diasporic population that was displaced by the events of 1948. Joe Cleary, for example, has suggested that the setting of the story dramatizes the constitutive impossibility of writing a straightforward national allegory of Palestine: 'The immediate absence of Palestine from Kanafani's novel ought to be read […] as a fundamental preoccupation and dilemma: the difficulty of representing a land that has no official existence'.[21] Yet at the same time, the novella also documents the material conditions of dispossession that forced each of the three men to make the perilous journey from Palestine to Kuwait and to put their lives and livelihoods in further jeopardy. In this respect, the novella suggests that the material circumstances of dispossession cannot be separated from the political conditions of Palestinian displacement. Kanafani's evocation of life as a Palestinian refugee is brief yet poignant. We learn how the dispossessed peasant Abu Quais waited ten years 'squatting like an old dog in a miserable hut' to be convinced that he had lost his land, his youth, his house and his village.[22] If Quais is slow to recognize the material conditions of his dispossession, this slowness also tells us something about the interminable legacy of Palestinian dispossession. The promise of relative prosperity that he associates with migrant labour interrupts the interminable poverty of dispossession and displacement. In Quais' mind, the experiences of his neighbour, Saad, who returned with sacks of money from Kuwait after working in that country as a driver, come to symbolize the utopian possibilities that the petro-capitalism of the Gulf states appear to offer. Yet his failed attempt to cross the border between Iraq and Kuwait in the back of a water tanker along with two other refugees exemplifies the ways in which the settler-colonial history of capitalist modernity in Israel/Palestine is bound up with the dispossession and abandonment of the Palestinian population. Such a relationship is grimly exemplified in the novel's closing scene, where the Palestinian lorry driver and smuggler, Abul Khaizuran, disposes of the corpses of the three men in a local municipal rubbish dump, after they suffocate in the back of his water truck. This untimely ending of the refugees' lives may be read as a comment on the time of the Palestinian nation. Indeed, Cleary has suggested that Marwan's broken watch can be read as 'a metaphor for the termination of Palestinian time'.[23] Yet this figure of dead time also foregrounds the specific ways in which the temporal logic of capitalist modernity is bound up with the dispossession and abandonment of human populations.

The disposability of the three male protagonists at the end of *Men in the Sun* and the suggestion that they are excluded from the temporality of capitalist modernity raise profound questions about the forms of political agency and representation that are available to postcolonial refugees. In what ways might the diasporic perspective of the refugee alter our understanding of the nation as the horizon for political struggle and change? How might we begin to imagine an idea of the nation that is not bound up with exclusionary ideas of sovereignty and possessive individualism? And what light can refugee narratives shed on the gendered foundations of national sovereignty?

The limits of nationalism as a political horizon were partially addressed in Hannah Arendt's political thought. Towards the end of the chapter on 'Decline of the Nation State; End of the Rights of Man' in *The Origins of Totalitarianism*, Arendt reflects on the position of minorities and refugees in relation to the structure of the European nation state. Citing the historical experience of the Jewish population in Nazi Germany, Arendt describes how 'Hitler's solution of the German Jewish problem' was 'first to reduce the German Jews to a nonrecognized minority in Germany, then to drive them as stateless people across the borders, and finally to gather them back from everywhere in order to ship them to extermination camps'. As a counterpoint to what she calls the "liquidation" (a term she leaves in inverted commas) of 'all problems of minorities and stateless' – Arendt turns to the formation of the state of Israel in 1948 and queries whether this nation state formation – which was established 'by means of a colonized and then conquered territory' – really 'solved' the Jewish question. In the terms of Arendt's argument, this appears to be a rhetorical question. For, as Arendt proceeds to explain, 'the solution of the Jewish question merely produced a new category of refugees, the Arabs, thereby increasing the number of stateless and rightless, by another 700,000 to 800,000 people'. Almost as an afterthought, Arendt adds that 'what happened in Palestine within the smallest territory and in terms of hundreds of thousands was then repeated in India on a large scale involving many millions of people'.[24]

In historical terms, Arendt's suggestion that the partition of India and the creation of the Islamic Republic of Pakistan *repeated* the formation of the State of Israel, and the partition of Palestine may seem inaccurate since these two events happened more or less simultaneously in very different cultural and political spaces. Yet in other respects, Arendt's suggestion that there are structural similarities between the partition of India-Pakistan and Israel-Palestine is thought provoking. The parallel that Arendt draws here can tell us something about partition and the forced migration it often entails as a technique of late colonial sovereignty. Joe Cleary has suggested that partition was one of the political means by which some former British colonial governments managed the transition from colonial sovereignty to postcoloniality. This is not to say that partition was directly attributable to a colonial power; for as Cleary points out, 'the impetus for partition stemmed from a minority community within the colonial state that feared the anti-colonial national movements about to assume power would imperil their interests and identity'.[25] In this respect, partition also produces challenges for postcolonial sovereignty. The UN partition plan for Palestine of 1947 laid the ground for a conflict in which the Palestinian population was effectively denied sovereignty over their land and territory. And the partition of India and Pakistan in 1947 created a situation in which statelessness became the groundless ground of the postcolonial nation.

In the context of India's national independence, Aamer Mufti has argued that the 'abstract, "secular" citizen has its *Enstehung*, its moment of emergence, in a violent redistribution of religious identities and populations'.[26] The foundation of India's postcolonial sovereignty, in other words, is inextricably intertwined with partition, and the violent re-ordering of the political geography of the Indian subcontinent. In the wake of partition, the establishment of Indian sovereignty can then be understood as a historically specific instance of what Walter Benjamin has called law-making violence. For the legal constitution of India and Pakistan as sovereign territories in the aftermath of British colonial rule paradoxically involved the suspension of the normal rule of law, which nominally guaranteed the rights of all citizens, regardless of their religious identity. More specifically, the suspension of the normal rule of law that was coeval with the reordering of India's political geography in 1947 and 1948 also exposed the violent patriarchal and communal foundations of the postcolonial nation, which often inscribed the sovereignty of the emerging nations on the bodies of women. This is not to say that women were the exclusive victims of communal violence during the partition of India, and its aftermath. Yet a focus on the gendered dimension of partition can shed light on the ways in which partition has been commemorated, and its place in the predominant national narratives of India and Pakistan.[27] Such a focus can also help to illuminate some of the blindspots and lacunae in the critical thought of Hannah Arendt and Giorgio Agamben with respect to the history and historiography of postcolonial refugees.

At the end of Bapsi Sidhwa's novel *Cracking India* (1991), the child-narrator Lenny describes how her Godmother helps Lenny's Hindu Ayah, Shanta, to return from Lahore to her family in Amritsar in the violent aftermath of partition. In response to Shanta's demand to return to her family in India, Lenny's Godmother questions whether her family will take her back.[28] By asking this question, Lenny's Godmother foregrounds the tensions between a patriarchal communalist discourse of cultural purity and honour and a secular discourse of citizenship that constitutes the national imaginary after the partition of India and the formation of Pakistan. What is more, this question emphasizes how Shanta's understanding of her home as a place of refuge is inextricably bound to gendered narratives of national belonging and ethnic identity. In the aftermath of India's partition, the Abducted Persons Act of 1949 defined home in terms of religious affiliation and cultural purity rather than a place of habitation. As the feminist historians Ritu Menon and Kamla Bhasin have argued, 'The Abducted Person's Act was remarkable for the impunity with which it violated every principle of citizenship, fundamental rights and access to justice'.[29] More specifically, the practice of recovering abducted citizens from either India or Pakistan centred on the 'proper regulation of women's sexuality' within patriarchal communalist discourses of national honour and cultural purity.[30]

The national framing of women refugees as abducted citizens who needed to be recovered presents significant critical challenges to the accounts of the refugee offered in the thought of Arendt and Agamben. Part of the difficulty lies in the terms and concepts such thinkers have mobilized in appeals to the humanity of stateless peoples. For Arendt, dignity was an 'essential quality' of the human – a term that is freighted with ambivalent and contradictory meanings. On the one hand, dignity is associated with

Immanuel Kant's formulation of an exceptional and self-legislating human morality that is to be sharply distinguished from monetary worth; on the other hand, dignity can mean the quality of being worthy or honourable. As Ranjana Khanna has suggested, appeals to dignity in the aftermath of the violence associated with South Asia's partition shed light on the patriarchal and communalist terms in which national honour or dignity has been defined and delimited.[31]

If Arendt's appeal to the dignity of stateless peoples overlooks the specific ways in which this concept was also mobilized to effectively foreclose experiences of gendered violence and violation, Agamben's reflections on the refugee and the state of exception ignore the gendered dimensions of sovereign power altogether. For the most part, Agamben's account of bare life and the state of exception centres on the masculine figure *homo sacer* as if it were universal. Furthermore, with the exception of a passing reference to colonialism, most of Agamben's examples are taken from the history of European nation states. For these reasons Agamben's account of the camp and the refugee might seem rather limited and inappropriate to address the specificities of South Asian women's narratives in the aftermath of partition. One of the problems with Agamben's universalizing use of the masculine form *homo sacer* to describe all human life that is subject to the violence of sovereign power is that it ignores the significance of the gendered body in the foundation of sovereign power and in challenges to political sovereignty, as scholars such as Ronit Lentin and Cristina Masters have argued. In the Aristotlean account of political life that is central to Agamben's understanding of the political, gender has been crucial in defining distinctions between the public and the private, the political and the non-political.[32] What is more, the experiences of women in conflict zones and colonial wars reveals how the bodies of gendered refugees are subjected to particular forms of violence that are made possible by a state of exception.[33] If the state of exception is a law that suspends the normal rule of law, it also consolidates the patriarchal order that underpins national sovereignty. By attempting to document and commemorate the ways in which women refugees experienced communal violence differently during India's partition, South Asian writers have contributed to a more nuanced understanding of the gendered dimensions of sovereignty and the state of exception – as the next section of this chapter suggests.

There is a certain sense in which Agamben's account of the 'state of exception' as the hidden foundation of the nation state may shed light on the formation of the Indian nation state and the subsequent partition of India and Pakistan. As many commentators have suggested, partition effectively involved a temporary suspension of the law as millions of people were forced to leave their homes in India or Pakistan. Vazira Fazila-Yacoobali Zamindar, for example, argues that the 'Transfer of power took place from colonial rule to national rule in what was a crisis, a state of emergency. Both postcolonial states were formed from a divided albeit unchanged colonial structure of governance and had to restage the modern state on behalf of the nation'. This restaging took the form of both the Indian and Pakistani governments establishing 'Emergency Committees of the Cabinet to bring "law and order" in murder-cleaved Punjab and Delhi, as well as the Ministries of Relief and Rehabilitation to "manage" the well-being of the millions displaced'.³⁴ For Menon and Bhasin, this temporary suspension of the law led to the massacre and violation of millions of people:

> The Boundary Commission announced its awards on August 16. Within a week, about one million Hindus and Sikhs has crossed over from West to East Punjab, and in the week following, another two and a half million had collected in refugee camps in West Punjab. [...] By the time the exodus was finally over, about eight to ten million people had crossed over from Punjab and Bengal .... and about 500,000–1,000,000 had perished.³⁵

Against the rational claims of the nationalist elite and the outgoing colonial administration that partition would resolve what it described as the problem of communalism and work to unify the nation along religious lines, Menon and Bhasin observe a contradiction between the secular rhetoric of citizenship and the religious rhetoric of communalism that underpinned the discourse of national belonging in South Asia. Such a contradiction could be seen to manifest the sovereign power of the late colonial state over the lives and deaths of the population.

In the territorial re-ordering of postcolonial South Asia that followed independence, the transfer of people across the boundary lines between India and Pakistan revealed how the British colonial state had effectively abandoned the population to a condition of lawlessness, communal violence and looting. In the Foucauldian terms of biopolitics, the divide and exit strategy of the British colonial administration could be understood as a particular form of letting die. As the historian Neeti Nair puts it, the 'failure' of the British colonial administration 'to impose martial law and [their] unwillingness to stay until proper power-sharing arrangements were negotiated between the Congress and the League endows them with much of the responsibility for the hundreds of lives lost'.³⁶ In this sense, the abdication of colonial sovereignty can itself be understood as an act of sovereignty that transfers modes of knowledge, subjectivity and governance – modes which in turn define and delimit the meanings of freedom after the act of national liberation.

One of the legacies of the British colonial administration in South Asia was that it contributed to the production of modern political identities and national geographies in India by documenting in minute detail social phenomena such as village settlement patterns, types of cottages, staple diet, fats and oils used, kinds of oil presses, types of ploughs, types of husking and so on.[37] In doing so, it brought together territory and population in ways that both constituted and consolidated colonial sovereignty. Yet this form of colonial sovereignty also produced fault lines in the geographic and demographic imagination of the postcolony. Brian Keith Axel has noted how the Survey of India (1767) has been framed as the authoritative historical source for national cartography in the postcolonial era. In the attempt to shore up the territorial integrity of the postcolonial Indian nation state, for example, the Government of India demanded that the population submit to a particular idea of unity in diversity that entails what Jawaharlal Nehru called the surrender and obliteration of difference.[38] Yet the formal definition and classification of differences in language, culture and religion that were part of the British colonial administration's will to know and control the subject population also served to divide that population along communal lines. Writing of the colonial representation of 'Hindu-Muslim strife' in nineteenth-century Banaras, Gyanendra Pandey notes how violent stereotypes of Muslims and Hindus were mobilized to describe and know the 'native' character.[39] Such ethnographic stereotypes simultaneously worked to define and constitute the terms in which national subjectivity was made intelligible.

To make sense of the violent social and political forces that led to the displacement and dispossession of postcolonial refugees, it is certainly helpful to consider the role of the colonial state in the construction of cultural and political identities. In his study of the genocide in Rwanda, *When Victims Become Killers*, Mahmood Mamdani argued that the violence of the Hutus against the Tutsis can be traced back to the formation of 'political identities in the context of modern colonialism'.[40] For Mamdani, the construction of racial and ethnic identities by colonial law led to the production of a bifurcated concept of postcolonial citizenship that distinguished between natives and settlers along ethnic lines. It is of course true that Mamdani's analysis of the political categories that underpin definitions of native and settler in postcolonial Rwanda cannot account for the specific religious, communal and gendered dynamics of partition in postcolonial South Asia. Yet, Mamdani's analysis of the ways in which the colonial construction of political identity worked to constitute ethnic identities in the postcolony has important implications for understanding the dynamics of communal violence and displacement in South Asia. As the historians Sukeshi Kamra and Gyanendra Pandey have emphasized, the communal violence that followed India's partition was partly a consequence of the British divide and rule policy that had exploited communal differences between Hindus, Muslims and Sikhs. The construction of communal identities in British colonial discourse seemed to further exacerbate these communal tensions after independence rather than fostering reconciliation between different ethnic groups.

The gap between the promise of India's national sovereignty and the communalist violence that followed partition is foregrounded in Bapsi Sidhwa's novel *Cracking India*.

Employing the device of a child narrator, Sidhwa intimates that there is a connection between the decision of the political elite 'to break a country' and the production of communal identities.[41] The metonymic list of names that Lenny hears highlights the privileging of dominant political figures including 'Gandhi, Jinnah, Nehru, Iqbal, Tara Singh, Mountbatten' in public discourse and histories of partition. Yet Lenny's repetition of these names also foregrounds the distance between these elite political figures and the subsequent production of ethnic identities along religious lines. In doing so, Lenny highlights the gap between the official discourse of the state and the lived experience of genocide, violation and displacement that constituted partition. What's more, Lenny's observation that her friends 'shrink' and 'dwindle' into symbols or communal identities exposes the vulnerability of the people to the ethnic and communal violence that followed the abdication of colonial sovereignty.

What is crucial in *Cracking India*, moreover, is the attempt by Sidhwa to register the traumatic histories of partition from the standpoint of South Asian women who were victims of sexual violation perpetrated by men against women of different ethnicities. Indeed, as Menon and Bhasin note, 'the reconfiguration of relationships between communities, the state and women in the wake of a bitter and violent conflict amongst Hindus, Muslims and Sikhs took place in part around the body and being of the abducted woman of all three communities'.[42] The concern with the body of the violated and abducted woman is a narrative thread that runs through *Cracking India*.

Near the beginning of the novel, which is set during the end of British colonial rule, the child-narrator describes how her Hindu maid, Shanta, is the object of the masculine gaze during their walks in a local park in Lahore; later in the text, Lenny emphasizes that Shanta's Hindu, Sikh and Muslim admirers are 'unified around her'.[43] Such passages serve to foreshadow Shanta's status as a symbolic figure who embodies the gendered dynamics of communal violence in the text. For later in the text, Shanta is abducted and raped by her former Muslim admirer Ice Candy Man, who forces her to change her name to Mumtaz and work as a prostitute in Lahore's red light district.

It is primarily through the character of Shanta that Sidhwa reveals the ways in which women were at the centre of communalist violence during and after the partition of India. In a related discussion, Menon and Bhasin note, the 'range of sexual violation explicit in [many women's testimonials] ... is shocking not only for its savagery, but for what it tells us about women as objects in male constructions of their own honour'.[44] In light of this observation, the abduction and violation of Lenny's Hindu Ayah at the end of the novel can be interpreted as an act of communal violence, which foregrounds the ways in which the bodies of women refugees became a sign of dispossession and disposability.

In *Cracking India* it is generally the child narrator Lenny who mediates the representation of sexual and physical violence against women, and this narrative device clearly distinguishes the text from the testimonials and interviews that constitute much recent scholarship on women's partition narratives. In chapter eighteen, for instance, the narrator describes the massacre of Muslims on a train from Gurduspur and the monstrous spectacle of a gunny sack full of dismembered women's breasts through the reported speech of the Muslim character Ice Candy Man. Such a re-presentation of violence and bodily dismemberment may seem distanced from the events themselves.

While at times Sidhwa's narrative does pose questions about the implications of partition for the safety of her Parsee family in Lahore, for the most part the narrative focuses on communal violence between Hindus, Sikhs and Muslims. The effect of this narrative perspective is that the narrator and her family seem to inhabit a relatively secure and privileged perspective that 'insists on ethnic neutrality as a basis for contesting both Indian and Pakistani nationalist discourses founded upon religious identity'.[45] Yet Sidhwa also highlights the complicity and responsibility of Lenny and her family in partition and communal violence. When Shanta is apprehended by a mob of angry Muslim men, Lenny feels guilty for inadvertently revealing

Shanta's hiding place to the mob. Furthermore, as the critic Sangeeta Ray has suggested in an illuminating reading of the novel, the involvement of Lenny's mother and aunt in the project of recovering women refugees from the camp for fallen women and returning them to their home where they may not be welcomed is a highly dubious one.[46] Although their involvement in the recovery process might seem like a worthy cause that counteracts the abduction and violation of women refugees, it is also complicit in the maintenance of national boundaries and discourses of ethnic purity.

In his controversial essay, 'Third World Literature in an Era of Multinational Capitalism', Fredric Jameson (1986) tried to develop a materialist account of 'Third World' cultural production that situated questions of cultural form and meaning in relation to the global economic system. Critics of Jameson's essay have tended to focus on his 'sweeping hypothesis' that 'all Third World texts are to be read as national allegories' – a hypothesis that seems both reductive and generalizing.[47] More specifically, Jameson's suggestion that the private lives of Third World fiction's protagonists symbolically represent the social, political and economic conflicts in the public sphere of a Third World nation runs the risk of repeating the framing of women's bodies and histories as a passive vehicle in patriarchal discourses of the nation. As a consequence, Jameson also misses the opportunity to reflect on the ways in which a consideration of national allegory might also elucidate the ways in which gender and sexuality are bound up with the histories of dispossession and abandonment that are coeval with the uneven development of capitalist modernity. If women's bodies were symbolically framed as a sign of honour and shame in patriarchal discourses of the South Asian nation during and after partition, such moral terms cannot be separated from the logic of possessive individualism that shaped the territorial and demographic re-ordering of South Asia after partition. This is not to suggest, however, that the body of the gendered postcolonial refugee is simply or only a passive vehicle for pre-dominant economic discourses (in much the same way that the gendered body is framed as a figure of national honour or shame). Against such logic, women's narratives of dispossession and disposability can certainly shed light on the limits of freedom after the act of national liberation; but they also foreground the ways in which gender and sexuality are implicated in capitalism's economic logic of dispossession and abandonment.

Hannah Arendt has written that 'the first loss which the rightless suffered was the loss of their homes, and this meant the loss of the entire social texture into which they were born and in which they established for themselves a distinct place in the world'.[48] It is partly this sense of loss and dispossession that haunts South Asian women's writing about partition. If the commemoration of such a loss is to avoid perpetuating the violence associated with national sovereignty and communal identification, it is crucial that we acknowledge the way in which gendered practices of communal violence are part of the foundation of the postcolonial South Asian nation rather than an aberration or exception. To paraphrase Bhaskar Sarkar in his study of Indian cinema in the wake of partition, South Asian women's writing can provide the conceptual resources for a critical mourning work that acknowledges the gendered dimension of trauma and communal violence that was coextensive with the reordering of the Indian subcontinent in 1947, and produces the 'intersubjective and ethical conditions for a critical secularism'.[49] Novels such as Bapsi Sidhwa's *Cracking India* do not simply commemorate the historical experience and traumatic memories of communal violence; they also raise questions about how the commemoration of home can work to aid and abet communal narratives of victimhood. And in so doing, such narratives foster a form of critical mourning work that persistently interrogates the violent, patriarchal foundations of the state.

Such a form of critical mourning work may question the constraints placed on postcolonial refugees from speaking about the conditions of statelessness. For Hannah Arendt, being deprived of the right to make public statements, or to hold opinions suggests that the stateless have no rhetorical space as legal subjects; they are, as Susannah Young-ah Gottlieb aptly puts it, 'statementless'.[50] And by denying the stateless rights that were deemed to be inalienable according to the language of the 1798 Declaration of the Rights of Man, the state revealed that human rights for the stateless were in practice contingent upon the sovereignty of a given political community. Indeed, it is the failure of human rights discourse to protect the rights of the stateless that prompts Arendt to resort to the use of a performative contradiction in which she, as a member of the stateless population she describes, declares that the refugee is denied the right to have rights. In so doing, Arendt asserts the right to have rights (such as the right to make speech acts) in spite of the state's denial of such rights to the stateless. If the legal constraints placed on the bodies of refugees have worked to silence them, it is also true that refugees have developed performative strategies to contest the biopolitical regimes of sovereign nation states that have deemed refugees to be a superfluous form of life that can be abandoned. In a discussion of the contemporary Australian state's asylum policies towards refugees from Afghanistan and Iraq, David Farrier and Patricia Tuitt have suggested that the desperate act of refugees sewing their lips together foregrounds the sovereign violence of laws and policies which fail to recognize the humanity of refugees.[51] Such desperate performative acts also work to contest the economies of abandonment that increasingly underpin contemporary asylum policies. In a related discussion of Australia's recent asylum policies, Elizabeth Povinelli has suggested that the policy of forcibly detaining Afghani asylum seekers fleeing the Taliban in fetid camps on bankrupt Pacific island states such as Nauru and Manus exemplifies how the neoliberal logic of the market has increasingly permeated the structure and ideology of late liberal societies – with particularly lethal consequences for refugees.[52]

Yet it is also important to emphasize that this neoliberal logic of the market has a history that is bound up with the uneven development of capitalism on a global scale – a history that was made possible by colonial techniques of sovereignty. As this chapter has suggested, the creation of refugee populations in emergent postcolonial states such as Israel/Palestine, India and Pakistan was not only a sign of the failure of nascent postcolonial nation states to protect the lives of its citizens after the British colonial state's final sovereign act of abdicating colonial sovereignty. It also discloses how colonial and neocolonial state formations have deemed superfluous the lives and livelihoods of people who are thought to be unprofitable to the financial interests of capital. It is in this respect that the economic logic of abandonment renders undecidable the distinction between the refugee and the economic migrant.

In the economic abandonment of human populations, refugees/migrants are often forced to seek even more exploitative and precarious forms of subsistence – from sex work to human organ donation. In Stephen Frears' feature length fiction film *Dirty Pretty Things* (2002), for example, a Turkish asylum seeker called Senay and Okwe, a medical doctor fleeing government persecution in Nigeria, find themselves embroiled in an underground organ trafficking business that is run out of a London hotel. The film's suggestion that the bodies and body parts of the world's poorest and most vulnerable migrants might be exchanged for a European passport may seem far-fetched. Yet the visual representation of the ways in which Okwe and Senay are encouraged to commodify their bodies in the film has significant implications for understanding the neoliberal logic at stake in the legal exclusion and economic abandonment of asylum seekers and refugees. As the critic Emily S. Davis puts it:

> *Dirty Pretty Things* allegorizes the plight of the migrant worker in the global city as a struggle not to be consumed by the excessive demands of capitalism in the age of globalization. Extending the premise that immigrants donate the invisible blood, sweat, and tears that prop up Western economics, the underlying theme in the film is that immigrants quite literally keep wealthy (and mostly, but not exclusively, Western) bodies going by selling their own.[53]

Davis' tantalizing suggestion that we read *Dirty Pretty Things* as an allegory for the 'plight of the migrant worker' is certainly thought provoking. Yet it also raises further questions about the ways in which narratives of postcolonial refugees might tell other stories about the precise ways in which the economic logic of abandonment itself creates further unregulated markets for exploitation. What does it mean to speak of such markets as illegal when they also benefit the laws of capitalism precisely by virtue of their exclusion from the formal rule of law and national body politic? In what ways might the rhetorical structure of allegory facilitate a better understanding of the ways in which postcolonial migrants and refugees are commodified even as they are excluded from and demonized by the national body politic as parasitical foreign bodies? How might refugee narratives of precarious forms of labour such as sex work shed light on the specific ways in which women's bodies are commodified and exploited in the capitalist world system? And what continuities exist between the displacement and dispossession of postcolonial refugees that took place in the aftermath of late colonial partition and contemporary regimes of sovereignty and forced migration? Such questions certainly foreground the importance of subjecting the terms in which postcolonial refugees have been framed and stereotyped as a disposable form of life to critical scrutiny. Yet they also necessitate a consideration of the ways in which narratives of postcolonial refugees can shed light on the colonial histories of dispossession, displacement and abandonment that have enabled the uneven and unequal development of capitalism on a global scale.

Notes

1. Abderrahmane Sissako (dir.), *Bamako*, Artificial Eye/New Yorker Films (2006).
2. Michel Foucault, *Society Must Be Defended: Lectures at the Collège de France 1975–76*, trans. David Macey (London: Allen Lane, 2003), 256.
3. Foucault, *Society Must Be Defended*, 240.

4   Ibid., 241.
5   Ibid., 242, 243.
6   Ibid., 256.
7   Giorgio Agamben, *Homo Sacer: Sovereign Power and Bare Life*, trans. Daniel Heller-Roazen (Stanford: Stanford University Press, 1998), 6.
8   Agamben, *Homo Sacer*, 89.
9   Ibid., 9.
10 Ibid., 38.
11 Ibid., 110.
12 Hannah Arendt, *Origins of Totalitarianism* (Cleveland and New York: Meridian Books, 1958), 447.
13 Arendt, *Origins of Totalitarianism*, 155.
14 David Glover, *Literature, immigration, and diaspora in fin-de-siècle England: A Cultural History of the 1905 Aliens Act* (Cambridge: Cambridge University Press, 2012), 1, 2.
15 Glover, *Literature, immigration, and diaspora*, 4.
16 Achille Mbembe, 'Necropolitics', *Public Culture* 15, no. 1 (2003): 23.
17 Giorgio Agamben, 'We Refugees', trans. Michael Rocke, http://www.egs.edu/faculty/agamben/agamben-we-refugees.html (accessed 8 April 2009).
18 Agamben, 'We Refugees'.
19 Ibid.
20 Ibid.
21 Joseph Cleary, *Literature, Partition and the Nation State* (Cambridge: Cambridge University Press, 2002), 199, 200.
22 Ghassan Kanafani, *Men in the Sun and Other Palestinian Stories*, trans. Hilary Kilpatrick (Boulder: Lynne Rienner, 1999), 26.
23 Cleary, *Literature, Partition and the Nation State*, 223.
24 Arendt, *Origins of Totalitarianism*, 290.
25 Cleary, *Literature, Partition and the Nation State*, 4.
26 Aamir Mufti, 'Auerbach in Istanbul: Edward Said, Secular Criticism, and the Question of Minority Culture', *Critical Inquiry* 25 (1998): 119.
27 Jill Didur, *Unsettling Partition: Literature, Gender, Memory* (Toronto: University of Toronto Press, 2006), 7, 11.
28 Bapsi Sidhwa, *Cracking India* (Minneapolis: Milkweed Editions, 1991), 274.
29 Ritu Menon and Kamla Bhasin (eds.), *Borders and Boundaries: Women in India's Partition* (New Brunswick: Rutgers University Press, 1998), 125.
30 Menon and Bhasin, *Borders and Boundaries*, 108.
31 Ranjana Khanna, 'Indignity', *positions: east asia cultures critique* 16, no. 1 (Spring 2008): 39–77.
32 Cristina Masters, 'Femina Sacra: The "War on/of Terror", Women and the Feminine,' *Security Dialogue* 40 (February 2009): 33.

33 Ronit Lentin, 'Femina Sacra: Gendered Memory and Political Violence', *Women's Studies International Forum* 29, no. 5 (2006): 465.
34 Vazira Fazila-Yacoobali Zamindar, *The Long Partition and the Making of Modern South Asia: Refugees, Boundaries, Histories* (New York: Columbia University Press, 2007), 6.
35 Menon and Bhasin, *Borders and Boundaries*, 35.
36 Neeti Nair, *Changing Homelands: Hindu Politics and the Partition of India* (Cambridge, MA: Harvard University Press, 2011), 9.
37 Brian Keith Axel, *The Nation's Tortured Body: Violence, Representation and the Formation of a Sikh Diaspora* (Durham: Duke University Press, 2001), 115.
38 Cited in Axel, *The Nation's Tortured Body*, 116.
39 Gyanendra Pandey, *The Construction of Communalism in Colonial North India* (New Delhi: Oxford University Press, 2012), 39–41.
40 Mahmood Mamdani, *When Victims Become Killers: Colonialism, Nativism and Genocide in Rwanda* (Princeton: Princeton University Press, 2001), 14.
41 Sidhwa, *Cracking India*, 101.
42 Menon and Bhasin, *Borders and Boundaries*, 109.
43 Ibid., 105.
44 Ibid., 43.
45 Ambreen Hai, 'Border Work, Border Trouble: Postcolonial Feminism and the Ayah in Bapsi Sidhwa's *Cracking India*', *Modern Fiction Studies* 46, no. 2 (2000): 389.
46 Sangeeta Ray, *Engendering India: Women and Nation in Colonial and Postcolonial Narratives* (Durham: Duke University Press, 2000), 126–47.
47 Jameson, 'Third World Literature in an Era of Multinational Capitalism', 69.
48 Arendt, *Origins of Totalitarianism*, 173.
49 Bhaskar Sakar, *Mourning the Nation: Indian Cinema in the Wake of Partition* (Durham: Duke University Press, 2009), 14.
50 Susannah Young-ah Gottlieb, *Regions of Sorrow: Anxiety and Messianism in Hannah Arendt and W.H. Auden* (Stanford: Stanford University Press, 2003), 34.
51 David Farrier and Patricia Tuitt, 'Beyond Biopolitics: Agamben, Asylum, and Postcolonial Critique', in *Oxford Handbook of Postcolonial Studies*, ed. Graham Huggan (Oxford: Oxford University Press, 2013), 253–70.
52 Elizabeth Povinelli, *Economies of Abandonment* (Durham: Duke University Press, 2011), 149–52.
53 Emily Davis, 'The Intimacies of Globalization: Bodies and Borders On-screen', *Camera obscura* 21, no. 2 (2006): 48.

15

Postcolonial Sexualities and the Intelligibility of Dissidence

Humaira Saeed

This chapter will make a case for the relationship between sexuality and (post)coloniality, and gesture towards what postcolonial literary scholarship might gain from engaging with representations of dissident sexualities. Through reference to Manju Kapur's *A Married Woman* (2003) and Shani Mootoo's *Cereus Blooms at Night* (1996), I will argue that postcolonial novels can make dissident sexuality intelligible through a rejection rather than adoption of Western colonial epistemologies. *Woman* is set in India and focuses on the story of Astha, a housewife and mother who embarks on a sexual relationship with the younger and politically engaged Pipileeka. *Cereus* takes place on the fictional Caribbean island of Lantacanamara, and centres on the overlapping stories of narrator Tyler and characters Otoh and Maya, all three of whom articulate non-normative sexualities. My analysis aims to demonstrate that postcolonial sexuality is not simply the addition of two terms, as it speaks to the ways in which gender and sexuality become figurations of colonial, imperial and racialized dynamics.

Anjali Arondekar and others have pointed out that the late nineteenth century and early twentieth century were marked by significant and intersecting developments in Western discourses of sexual dissidence and colonialism.[1] Indeed, the establishment of medical discourses on sex and sexuality,[2] developed alongside those of scientific racism, can be understood as informing justifications for colonial expansion.[3] As such it becomes clear, as Ann Laura Stoler has proposed, that the development of a European discourse on sexuality must be understood in direct relation to colonial enterprizes.[4] My discussion in this chapter follows Stoler's approach which, building on Foucault's historicization of sexuality, argues for 'race and sexuality as ordering mechanisms that shared their emergence with the bourgeois order of the early nineteenth century', emphasizing these as '*formative features* of modernity' rather than 'aberrant offshoots of them'.[5] As such, I consider sexuality to be as integral to discussions of postcolonialism as considerations of the nation state, the globalization of capital and the rise of secularism.

Recent theoretical developments in sexuality studies have seen postcolonial concepts such as diaspora uncritically adopted by critics in ways that reinscribe a universalized white Western experience at the heart of exile.[6] Yet alongside this, there is work that engages with sexuality in relation to the national and the transnational from a queer-of-colour perspective.[7] A number of critics have begun to think through global articulations of sexuality,[8] and collections of writings produced from grassroots organizations and from within activist communities have started to emerge, collections that span academic enquiry and fictional and artistic works.[9] Building on these ideas, this chapter will firstly offer a brief outline of the role of sexuality in colonial discourse and imperial structures, to then consider how postcolonial texts resist Western modes of sexual recognition and signification. Connor Murphy's interlude, included within this chapter, explores hybridity and metaphor as strategies deployed by postcolonial writer Rakesh Satyal in representing a diasporic sexuality beyond an epistemological identity framework.

Sexuality, colonial discourse and imperialism

Examining sexuality alongside and through colonial discourse is not a new intervention. Well-known studies by scholars such as Anne McClintock outlined the ways in which Victorian attitudes towards sexuality and domesticity informed systems of domination within the British Empire, and explored how feminized depictions of colonized peoples worked to justify imperial dominance.[10] Edward Said's pioneering *Orientalism* also had something to say about colonial rule and colonial space emerging through sexualized epistemologies, addressing how colonies were conceptualized as feminized spaces that required control.[11] Joseph Massad has built on Said's work, arguing that 'Europeans came to judge civilization and cultures along the vector of something called "sex", as well as its later derivative, "sexuality"'.[12] Phillipa Levine has argued that the colonial conquest was both structured and 'symbolised by white men's sexual relations with colonised women', and so sexual relations between colonized men and European women were feared as they threatened the dominance of both the colonial state and the supremacy of white men.[13] This fear was often communicated as the threat of sexual attack, and was integral to how indigenous males were constructed as primitive and therefore sexually threatening to European women, a crucial construction for justifying and maintaining the oppressiveness of colonial rule.[14]

Anxieties around power were played upon by anti-colonialists such as Frantz Fanon, for example in his framing of resistance to colonialism through recourse to sexual metaphor: 'I marry white culture, white beauty, white whiteness. When my restless hands caress those white breasts, they grasp white civilization and dignity and make them mine'.[15] Here, not only is racism shown to affect the experience of desire in colonial contexts, but the dominance of male over female is deployed to symbolize and express anti-colonial resistance, through offering an inverted sexual metaphor to that dynamic underpinning colonial systems. However, this inversion remains constrained within the logics of cross-sex desire, a limitation explored by Greg Mullins who argues that:

> Within the logic of patriarchy, binary relations of power between colonizer and colonized are quite easily mapped onto gender relations of male and female. Within the logic of heterosexuality, male sexual dominance of women becomes part of this mapping. But the potential for women to desire women, for men to desire men, and for any of a number of nonnormative sexual acts to take place outside a heterosexual configuration of power confuses the logic of allegory and the clarity of metaphor.[16]

For Mullins, there emerges an overreliance on structures of heterosexuality to metaphorically discuss dominance, meaning that non-heterosexual sex acts have disruptive potential. Levine concurs with this, proposing that male-male desire has the potential to 'wholly have undone the colonial hierarchies so carefully constructed and constrained by these gendered orders'.[17] Rather than reversing the gendered and sexualized power dynamic as Fanon moves to do above, Levine suggests that male-male desire would destabilize the very systems of domination upon which colonial rule was predicated. While this line of enquiry is appealing, both Mullins and Levine pursue a view of same-sex relations that is somewhat unconvincing in its utopianism. If, as Mullins suggests, colonial desire is structured through 'a preestablished stereotyped understanding of sex as a relation of domination and submission in which the exotic other is potently erotic,'[18] this gendered system of domination would not necessarily be overthrown due to same-sex relations. Indeed, as Robert Aldrich reluctantly acknowledges, the links 'between colonialism and homosexuality often seem a paradigm of European men taking advantage of the colonial situation,'[19] thus becoming complicit with the colonial enterprise: same-sex desire and acts do not necessarily mean radicalness.[20] Mullins himself argues, 'the potential for homosexuality to destabilize imperial or patriarchal relations of power, however, is not necessarily realized as an anti-imperial political position.'[21] I outline this to emphasize that an examination of same-sex desire in postcolonial contexts offers continuity with colonial discourse and not a break. While connections are mutable, imbrications prevail – from colonies being inscribed as sexually permissive, to the links being made between rights discourse and modernity.

Said's well-known discussion of constructed knowledges about the 'Orient' outlines how bourgeois modernity was organized through binaries of difference. Considering this alongside Eve Sedgewick's argument that the development of the binary of homosexual-heterosexual was key to understandings of how the Western-European self was established in modernity,[22] homosexuality as a category is bound up in Western epistemological structures.[23] Here I want to consider the connections between these constructions and the place of homosexuality and homophobia in globalization. The current conjuncture can be understood as one where the decriminalization of homosexuality or the awarding of LGBT human rights act as evidence of modernity.[24] Judith Butler has discussed the desire of the US LGBT rights movements to pursue state legitimation, or recognition for an intimate life that is not heterosexual.[25] The construction of LGBT people as subjects of rights can be seen in sharp distinction with the dynamic discussed earlier in this chapter whereby Western men tried to escape constraints on sexual freedoms by travelling to colonial sites. Jasbir Puar's influential work on the US context theorizes this shift through her concept of 'homonationalism', in which the nation state no longer excludes the homosexual by virtue of their sexuality. Resultantly, Puar argues that a normative homosexuality – or, homonormativity – has emerged that folds some queer subjects into the nation, as long as other subjects are repudiated.[26] That this repudiation is enacted along racial, religious and class lines explains how certain queer subjects can become part of the United States' imperial enterprise without necessitating an ethical shift to have taken place. In other words, the imperial enterprise adapts in order to maintain power through allowing certain minority groups to be part of its gains. This gestures towards how sexual dissidence in postcolonial contexts does not necessarily create liberation from colonial dynamics.

Sexually dissident subjects

Arondekar's *For The Record* raises the question of 'how sexuality is made visible in the colonial archive and of how this process paradoxically discloses the very limits of that visibility'.[27] She is concerned with the pattern whereby sexuality is understood as that which must be excavated, which must move from secrecy to disclosure, a progression popularized through the concept of coming out of the closet. As well as it following the Western model of the closet, Arondekar is critical of the way that the heterosexual-homosexual binary gets deployed to construct heterosexual as public and homosexual as private. The need to excavate the homosexual thus falls into a particular logic of recognition, which informs a desire to locate largely Western models of male homosexuality in history.[28] Tom Boellstorf and Martin Manalansan have also challenged the usefulness of frameworks such as the closet when looking at non-Western contexts and subjects. Not only because of the aforementioned binary of homosexual-heterosexual on which the closet relies, but also because the closet is understood in relation to notions of confession and self-declaration.[29] As such these frameworks and terms can have incredibly limited application and use due to their reliance on coming out narratives and the expectation that personal trajectories will be articulated in these terms.[30] In contrast, *Woman* offers a protagonist trajectory that allows postcolonial sexuality to come into view outside of such binarized notions. It can be noted that Astha's story is not pitched as a coming out narrative: there is no move across a binary divide from the heterosexual to the homosexual that seeks to make Astha intelligible through recourse to an identitarian journey. In Gopinath's words it 'refuses to subscribe to the notion that the proper manifestation of same-sex eroticism is within a politics of visibility and identity'.[31] Here I build on Hoad's argument that literary texts can show what exists at the limit of the imagination, and Rao's response that literary texts show the limits of what is imaginable, rather than directly representing the lived experience of queer bodies.[32] I hope to now put forward a postcolonial queer reading practice that explores further the implications and effects of how an 'Eastern sexuality that *exceeds representation*',[33] is made intelligible within literature, and in what ways postcolonial texts are beholden to identity categories that Massad rightly decries as created through Western ontology. In asking whether discussions of same-sex desire are invariably complicit in a form of epistemic violence, and how sexuality might be understood in localized material terms,[34] I argue that Anglophone postcolonial literature can find ways to represent sexual dissidence without recourse to terminology and tropes established through Western epistemological structures.

Rahul Rao has posited that sexual liberation becomes the means by which imperialism represents itself as the establisher of the good society, championing women and queers as objects of protection from their 'racial' and national kind,[35] observing that Spivak's oft-cited 'white men saving brown women from brown men', can now be reworked as 'white homosexuals saving brown homosexuals from brown homophobes'.[36] Massad, who also notes this shift, identifies that where 'the premodern West attacked the world of Islam's alleged sexual licentiousness, the modern West attacks its alleged *repression* of sexual freedoms', though evaluating the recognition of homosexual subjects by the postcolonial state.[37] Both Massad and Rao create arguments that consider the universalizing push of International NGOs such as the International Lesbian and Gay Association (ILGA). Massad terms such organizations and their attendant discourses the 'gay international',[38] arguing that they produce homosexual subjects where they do not exist, i.e. that they collapse all same-sex desire into the homosexual-heterosexual binary, and repress any same-sex desires that will not be assimilated into Western epistemologies of identity.[39] Sara Ahmed has called for an awareness of this tendency for Western institutions to universalize experience and speak for the 'other'. Ahmed calls this a fantasy of proximity, whereby one believes they know what the other needs or feels and can speak or act on their behalf.[40] This move to understand the other collapses the diversity of sexual expression, or polymorphous expressions, not only into the homosexual-heterosexual binary but into a Western homonormativity. The very terms of recognition being proposed by these human rights organizations, then, uses this fantasy of proximity to only recognize the postcolonial queer when it articulates itself as a copy of the Western homosexual. Furthermore, individuals' belief in the validity of their diverse forms of queerness can become reduced to instances when they mirror these tropes of recognition. This can be seen reflected in Murphy's analysis of *Blue Boy*, in which the pain and isolation experienced by protagonist Kiran develops in conjunction with an awareness that cannot recognize his hybridized self in the frames of reference of his peers.

During one particular excursion described in *Woman*, Pipileeka and Astha attend a programme of films as part of an International Gay and Lesbian film festival, which creates a relevant locus for thinking about the globalization of sexuality. The women's distinct responses to the transmission of globalized identity in the films are quite telling. Although Astha acknowledges the 'special relevance' the films might hold for her, during the screening she sits 'registering indifferently the men and women speaking broad American about the discrimination they faced as gays […] she could not connect to what she was seeing. Her own situation was different'.[41] The films have travelled and are being screened within India, but the American identities represented within these films bear little relevance to Astha's life or performance of sexuality. Astha finds the experience alienating and quickly makes excuses to go home and help her daughter with homework, whereas Pipileeka states, 'We have to struggle for acceptance and the right to love as we feel. Don't you think so?'[42] clearly attaching to the liberation narrative coming through in the films: her recourse to 'we' becomes indicative of a sense of collective identity and Pipileeka's recognition of herself in this.

Massad is dismissive of elite LGBT people in postcolonial contexts who adopt a homonormative model because they stand to gain as individuals if recognized by the state, arguing that are nothing more than imperial stooges. Pipileeka's engagement here would be dismissed by Massad, however, within the context of the novel, she acts as both interlocutor and foil against which we can access Astha's discomfort. Rao is again useful in examining their distinct responses, in particular his term 'homocapitalism', that 'builds on concepts like homonormativity and homonationalism to signify the selective incorporation of some race-, class- and gender-sanitized queers into capitalism and the disavowal of others through a liberal politics of recognition that obviates the need for [economic] redistribution'.⁴³ Here Rao highlights how state recognition becomes understood as the primary goal from which all other redistribution will follow. Again, this is based on a Western model of kinship whereby if the state recognizes the earning power of queer subjects, they will enjoy a wage premium based on the assumption that this will be a dual-income household with no children,⁴⁴ ignoring the 'web of [financial] obligations within which even professional middle-class nucleated family lives are lived'.⁴⁵ The imposition of a Western model, then, ignores local kinship structures and the material conditions within which people live. Looking again at Astha's discomfort means, on the one hand, that the novel does not homogenize her and Pipileeka's experiences in terms of identity to create an 'Indian lesbian novel' (whatever that might be), but rather shows the tensions that attempts at recognition can generate. On the other hand, it demonstrates that Astha is not in a position to embody this Western model of identity and recognition because of her kinship responsibilities and attachments – the fact that she is a mother – a significant material and affective distance between her and Pipileeka.

Rao's intervention also considers that when international financial institutions such as the World Bank make loans contingent on how far the state recognizes its LGBT population, finances become dependent on how far that population adopts the Western model: the very same institutions that create recognition as a prerequisite have the power to create heterosexuality as an economic imperative. The interventions of both Rao and Massad challenge the possibility of articulating queerness in localized postcolonial terms. There is a danger, then, that the only way to imagine a queer postcoloniality is through recourse to leaving postcolonial sites. In Rao's discussion of postcolonial texts, he critiques the ways that fantasies of escape entail creating a modern vision of capitalism as liberation from current conditions.⁴⁶ In this pattern, the promise of Western capitalist nations is tied up with the promise of sexual liberation, a trajectory that is both troubled and challenged in postcolonial articulations of sexuality. At the close of *Woman* Pipileeka moves to the United States to undertake a PhD, a move that mirrors her investment in Western liberal understandings of the self that are expressed at the film festival. However, Astha stays with her husband Hemant and two children, which can be read as a rejection of the liberation trajectory that requires leaving the postcolonial nation. Indeed, her decision to stay is reflective of how her local kinship structures are more important than an individualized sexual identity.

These negotiations between leaving and staying is also broached in *Cereus* where protagonist-narrator Tyler states that

> [a]fter much reflection I have come to discern that my desire to leave the shores of Lantanacamara had much to do with wanting to study abroad, but far more with wanting to be somewhere where my 'perversion', which I tried diligently as I could to shake, might be either invisible or of no consequence to people to whom my foreignness was what would be strange.[47]

Here, Tyler's queerness is the motivation for his leaving in order to study nursing in 'The Shivering Northern Wetlands' (which acts as a cipher for Britain), but this does not stop him from returning to Lantanacamara after his degree. The queer kinship without state recognition that he then establishes with Maya and Otoh is what creates the belonging and thus the condition for him staying in Lantanacamara. Each character has a form of queerness: Maya's experiences of incest, Tyler's femininity though assigned male, Otoh's transition from being understood as female to being understood as male, and Tyler and Otoh's sexual attraction for one another, yet the novel's close posits that 'being themselves' does not necessitate them leaving the Caribbean. Indeed, Otoh is told 'you are not the first or the only one of your kind in this place. You grow up here and you don't realize almost everybody in this place wish they could be somebody or something else? That is the story of life here in Lantanacamara.'[48] This suggests that the experience of difference, or of non-normativity, has as much of a place in the Caribbean as anywhere else.

Disidentification and postcoloniality: Decentring sexuality

In closing this chapter, I will be utilizing Jose Esteban Muñoz's theory of disidentification to point to how postcolonial literature can offer a representation of same-sex desire that simultaneously eschews identity categories. Muñoz develops an articulation of hybridity that resists the Western ontological structure that asserts that sexuality is at the core of the self.[49] I propose that the fiction discussed here posits instead a hybrid form of sexuality that 'disidentifies' from both hegemonic national identities and hegemonic gay identities, but without this being a place of loss. In considering what this might productively offer the practice of postcolonial literary analysis, I deploy the following from Judith Butler:

> An ethical query emerges in light of such an analysis: how might we encounter the difference that calls our grids of intelligibility into question without trying to foreclose the challenge that the difference delivers? What might it mean to learn to live in the anxiety of that challenge, to feel the surety of one's epistemological and ontological anchor go, but to be willing, in the name of the human, to allow the human to become something other than what it is traditionally assumed to be?[50]

Following this, we can identify a move towards an interpretative practice that encourages by refusing to be held down by epistemological and ontological anchors: in this case the Western model of LGBT identity, and the homosexual-heterosexual binary.

In departing from epistemological anchors, Muñoz's *Disidentifications* offers something of a conceptual road map. For Muñoz, it is imperative to move away from how sexuality is known to how it is performed and expressed; disidentification is a strategy of survival produced through such performance, rather than identity, which is a strategy of visibility (or recognition) that acts as a concluding epistemological category.[51] In *Cereus* the focus on performance and experience over identity is evident. Tyler and Otoh move between positions of gender, sexuality and name, the cumulative effects of which is that their identities remain indeterminate and in flux. While both characters are described as having non-normative genders and sexualities, this is not done through Western identity categories. Indeed, categories such as lesbian, gay or transgender, are never used in the novel, and the politics of naming are rejected in favour of references such as: 'my propensities', 'a curiosity', 'my own nature', 'my ways' and 'an outsider'.[52] The explicitness of the novel in this regard, 'the adult Tyler, who was neither properly man nor woman but some in-between, unnamed thing'[53] speaks directly to disidentification, which is never static, but always interactive and localized:

> To disidentify is to read oneself and one's own life narrative in a moment, object, or subject that is not culturally coded to 'connect' with the disidentifying subject. It is not to pick and choose what one takes out of an identification. It is not to willfully evacuate the politically dubious or shameful components within an identificatory locus. Rather, it is the reworking of those energies that do not elide the 'harmful' or contradictory components of any identity. It is an acceptance of the necessary interjection that has occurred in such situations.[54]

Muñoz's intervention here is reminiscent of Spivak's discussion of strategic essentialism as an 'enabling violation', in that there is an awareness that there are dubious and shameful components that attach to identity but that the negative elements can be reworked or reclaimed, and that there is always some level of antagonism to be negotiated. When Muñoz speaks of queers of colour, his words are usefully applied to postcolonial queer subjects, arguing that 'white normativity is as much of a site of antagonism as is heteronormativity'.[55] Identification with the Western identity model might require a counter-identification with heterosexual postcolonial communities, insisting that the sexual binary is the only struggle for postcolonial subjects, and that belongings of sexuality take primacy. Where this counter-identification might lead to a rejection of postcolonial communities, both texts under discussion here instead demonstrate a disidentification, as characters continue to negotiate and value their relationship with the local.

Conclusion

While Massad critiques fictional texts for creating identitarian views of sexuality in line with the gay international,[56] I have tried to offer a more recuperative reading that seeks to appraise texts, looking for what Rao outlines as 'the radical potential that we should assume exists everywhere oppression is felt'.[57] Considering Massad and Rao together, we can conclude that in order to be recognized as a global citizen of rights (which can be equated with being recognized as human),[58] one must have the economic autonomy to be able to articulate a Western model of desire and kinship; a homonormative identity, then, is not available to all, but it is desired due to the material promise it offers. In turn this homonormativity bolsters the creation of another repudiated 'other', that of the self 'whose ontological structure is not based on the hetero-homo binary',[59] and as such cannot be recognized and cannot access redistribution. When Butler asks 'Are there not other ways of feeling possible, intelligible, even real, apart from the sphere of state recognition? Should there not be other ways?'[60] we are pushed to consider how a queer postcolonial subject might emerge away from the universalizing push of global homosexuality. Further, how might a queer postcolonial subject exist autonomously against what Kobena Mercer and Isaac Julien have termed 'the privileged role of the singular agent of democratic revolution',[61] which in the context of an international gay-human rights, is embodied by the archetypal liberated, class-mobile white gay man. In this chapter I have sought to engage with these questions, arguing that the promulgation of identity categories in the current conjuncture can be effectively challenged with fiction, because of its performative ability to create selves whose 'relation to the social is not overdetermined by universalizing rhetorics of selfhood'.[62] The two novels under discussion here, and the analysis offered by Murphy, demonstrate that a postcolonial sexuality is more than sexuality within postcolonial locales, or of postcolonial subjects, but that this fiction has the potential to challenge the very tropes and terminologies that maintain global dominance in constructing epistemologies of sexuality.

Interlude: Recreating identities: Fire and sexuality in Rakesh Satyal's Blue Boy
Connor Murphy

The literal and symbolic use of fire in Rakesh Satyal's *Blue Boy* (2009) creates a dialogue for postcolonial sexuality; it functions as the metaphor through which desire is able to, as Gayatri Gopinath writes in *Impossible Desires*, 'erupt into the present'.[63]

Protagonist Kiran, the self-described 'Ohioan Indian'[64] undergoes, according to Satyal, a 'kind of crucible'[65] as he tries to decide 'which life of mine is normal, my school-bound American one or my party-bound Indian one'.[66] Throughout the novel, he struggles to realize his sexuality in a racist, homophobic school, where he is referred to as 'you people' and a 'feggit'.[67] Kiran's occupancy of a liminal space in society – a homosexual American child of Indian parentage – that is in turn informed by legacies of colonialism, leads to the suppression of his emerging desires, as he declares: '[I am] absolutely ashamed of who I am.'[68]

This doubly cruel marginalization leads Kiran to burn down his schoolteacher's classroom in an explosive fit of rage, 'flames licking at bulletin boards all over',[69] articulating what critic Rahul Gairola calls the 'fiery shame of desire'.[70] In turn this creates fire as a force that unveils, destroys and forges Kiran's sexual identity anew, in forms that honour his hybrid cultural, as well as sexual, identity.

At the school's talent show, Kiran attempts to unite his struggles with racial and sexual alienation by dressing up as Krishna, the Hindu god, while dancing to Whitney Houston's 'How Will I Know?' Kiran makes his 'entrance of a blue-flame boy into the world',[71] his solitary passion for both Eastern and Western culture overriding the 'collective hush'[72] which falls upon the audience. This oppressive silence, a metaphor for how he is treated in American society, is broken by his newfound, amalgamated identity. According to postcolonial theorist Homi K. Bhabha, this hybridized self alters 'conditions of dominance into the grounds of intervention';[73] Kiran claims a hybridized identity for himself, within which sexuality is integral, and enables self-determination to be born out of his liminal position.

If Kiran's journey to finding selfhood starts in fire, it is symbolically apt that it ends in water. The language of the elements allows Kiran to absolve his shame, as he proclaims at the novel's climax: 'I know what they mean by that – a boy who is so sissy he is "flaming gay". Perhaps I am, just not in the way that they think. They have no idea what sort of emotional flood rages in my every day, how alternately high and subtle my sexuality can be.'[74] The reclaiming of 'flaming gay', transforming this phrase from a slur into a source of empowerment, lets loose the 'flood' of his sexual identity, a form of self-expression that exceeds the limited frames of reference of his contemporaries. His difference is no longer a mark of humiliation, but a mark of uniqueness. What Satyal describes as Kiran's 'crucible' reforms him in a stronger image, as the novel concludes this metaphor in its closing lines: 'Sometimes we are so consumed by the flame, burning so painfully in its heat, that we can't see the utter gorgeousness of the fire.'[75] In *Blue Boy*, self-acceptance is an act of resistance, a continual process of recreation that recreates identities as fluid.

Notes

1   See Ronald Hyam, *Empire and Sexuality: The British Experience* (Manchester: Manchester University Press, 1990); Christopher Lane, *The Ruling Passion: British Colonial Allegory and the Paradox of Homosexual Desire* (Durham: Duke University Press, 1995) for discussion of the connections between Britain's imperial expansion and homosexuality. Anne Fausto-Sterling 'Gender, Race, and Nation: The Comparative Anatomy of "Hottentot" Women in Europe, 1815–1817', in *Deviant Bodies:*

     Critical Perspectives on Difference in Science and Popular Culture, eds. Jennifer Terry and Jacqueline Urla (Bloomington: Indiana University Press, 1995), 19–48, for an exploration of the ways in which colonial expansion was informed by a preoccupation with sex and sexual difference. Also see Robert J. C. Young, *Colonial Desire: Hybridity in Theory, Culture and Race* (London: Routledge, 1995).

2 See Michel Foucault, *The History of Sexuality: The Will to Knowledge* (London: Penguin, 1998).

3 Neville Hoad, 'Arrested Development or the Queerness of Savages: Resisting Evolutionary Narratives of Difference', *Postcolonial Studies* 3, no. 2 (2000): 133–58; Siobhan B. Sommerville, 'Scientific Racism and the Emergence of the Homosexual Body', *Journal of the History of Sexuality* 5, no. 2 (1994): 243–66, have argued for the ways in which evolutionary arguments were deployed in constructing both the homosexual and the colonized as primitive and savage beings.

4 Ann Laura Stoler, *Race and the Education of Desire: Foucault's History of Sexuality and the Colonial Order of Things* (Durham: Duke University Press, 1995)

5 Stoler, *Race and the Education of Desire*, 7–9. Foucault's foundational *History of Sexuality* failed to engage with colonialism at all.

6 See Anne-Marie Fortier, 'Queer Diasporas', in *Handbook of Lesbian and Gay Studies*, eds. Diane Richardson and Steven Seidman (London: Sage, 2002), 183–97; Gayatri Gopinath, *Impossible Desires: Queer Diasporas in South Asian Public Cultures* (Durham: Duke University Press, 2005).

7 See Martin Manalansan, 'In the Shadows of Stonewall: Examining Gay Transnational Politics and the Diasporic Dilemma', *GLQ* 2 (1995): 425–38; David L. Eng, *The Feeling of Kinship* (Durham: Duke University Press, 2010).

8 See Ruth Vanita (ed.), *Queering India: Same-Sex Love and Eroticism in Indian Culture and Society* (London: Routledge, 2002); William J. Spurlin, *Imperialism within the Margins: Queer Representation and the Politics of Culture in Southern Africa* (Basingstoke: Palgrave, 2006); Martin F. Manalansan, *Global Divas: Filipino Gay Men in the Diaspora* (Durham: Duke University Press, 2003); Arnaldo Cruz-Malavé and Martin F. Manalansan (eds.), *Queer Globalizations: Citizenship and the Afterlife of Colonialism* (New York: New York University Press, 2002).

9 See Sokari Ekine and Hakima Abbas (eds.), *Queer African Reader* (Oxford: Pambazuka Press, 2013); Thomas Glave (ed.), *Our Caribbean: A Gathering of Gay and Lesbian Writing from the Antilles* (Durham: Duke University Press, 2008). Both texts work to break the stereotype of homophobic nations/continents and speak to the diversity of queer lives in these locales,

as well as the diversity of struggles. They deserve a mention here if only to emphasize that the struggle for self-determination in terms of national and sexual autonomy continues to be taken on in many spheres.

10 Anne McClintock, *Imperial Leather: Race, Gender, and Sexuality in the Colonial Contest* (London: Routledge, 1995).
11 Edward Said, *Orientalism* (London: Penguin, 1995).
12 Joseph A. Massad, *Desiring Arabs* (Chicago: University of Chicago Press, 2007), 6; also see Joseph Boone 'Vacation Cruises: Or, the Homoerotics of Orientalism', *PMLA* 110, no. 1 (1995): 89–107, 92.
13 Philippa Levine 'Sexuality and Empire', in *At Home with the Empire: Metropolitan Culture and the Imperial World*, eds. Catherine Hall and Sonya O. Rose (Cambridge: Cambridge University Press, 2006): 122–42, 134– 35.
14 Sara Mills, *Gender and Colonial Space* (Manchester: Manchester University Press, 2005), 34–35; Joanne Sharp, *Geographies of Postcolonialism* (London: Sage, 2008), 37. Also see Levine, 'Sexuality and Empire', 134.
15 Frantz Fanon, *Black Skin, White Masks*, trans. C. L. Markmann (London: Pluto Press, 1986), 36.
16 Greg Mullins, *Colonial Affairs: Bowles, Burroughs, and Chester Write Tangier* (Madison: University of Wisconsin Press, 2002), 16.
17 Levine, 'Sexuality and Empire', 135.
18 Mullins, *Colonial Affairs*, 8.
19 Robert Aldrich, *Colonialism and Homosexuality* (London: Routledge, 2002), 367.
20 Aldrich has argued that certain colonies became known as sites where sexual inclinations that were constrained within European culture could be explored, in *Colonialism and Homosexuality*, 368. Boone offers a more complex picture, considering the interplay of privilege and oppression that such men brought to the colonies ('Vacation Cruises', 99–100).
21 Mullins, *Colonial Affairs*, 16.
22 Eve Sedgewick, *Epistemology of the Closet* (Berkeley: University of California Press, 1990).
23 See Philip Holden, 'Coda: Rethinking Colonial Discourse Analysis and Queer Studies', in *Imperial Desire: Dissident Sexuality and Colonial Literature*, eds. Philip Holden and Richard J. Ruppel (Minneapolis: University of Minnesota Press, 2003), 295–321.
24 Rahul Rao, 'Queer Questions', *International Feminist Journal of Politics* 16, no. 2 (2014): 199–217, 206; it should also be noted that this pattern of criminalizing homosexuality is a particular legacy of British colonialism.
25 Judith Butler, *Undoing Gender* (London: Routledge, 2004); see especially 'Beside Oneself'.

26 Jasbir K. Puar, *Terrorist Assemblages: Homonationalism in Queer Times*. (Durham: Duke University Press, 2007). Puar builds on Duggan who coined the term 'homonormativity' in *The Twilight of Equality*.
27 Anjali Arondekar, *For the Record: On Sexuality and the Colonial Archive in India* (Durham: Duke University Press, 2009), 3.
28 Arondekar, *For the Record*, 8, 9.
29 The discourses of both sexology and psychoanalysis were based on case studies with individuals, which followed the model of a confessional that could reach the 'truth' of the individual.
30 Manalansan, 'In the Shadows of Stonewall', 434. Manalansan quotes a Filipino man saying, 'I know who I am and most people, including my family, know about me – without any declaration,' emphasizing that identities do not have to be proclaimed out loud but can be felt, intuited and performed.
31 Gopinath, *Impossible Desires*, 155 (Gopinath is here referring to a different text).
32 Ibid.
33 Boone, 'Vacation Cruises', 90, my emphasis. Boone's use of 'Eastern' here is in reference to colonial discourse.
34 See Arondekar, *For the Record*; Massad's introduction to *Desiring Arabs*; Kobena Mercer and Isaac Julien, 'Race, Sexual Politics and Black Masculinity: A Dossier', in *Male Order: Unwrapping Masculinity*, eds. Rowena Chapman and Jonathan Rutherford, 97–164 (London: Lawrence & Wishart, 1988), 106–8; Holden and Ruppel, *Imperial Desire*.
35 Rao, 'Queer Questions', 203.
36 Ibid., 203.
37 Massad, *Desiring Arabs*, 37. Also see Jin Haritaworn, *Queer Lovers and Hateful Others: Regenerating Violent Times and Places* (London: Pluto Press, 2015). Haritaworn discusses how the homonormative subject has been developed through the construction of the 'homophobic Muslim'. Also see Said, *Orientalism*. Said argues that Islam has long been seen as belonging to the Orient, therefore structured as monolithic and threatening by the West.
38 Massad, *Desiring Arabs*, 161.
39 Ibid., 163.
40 Sara Ahmed, *Strange Encounters: Embodied Others in Post-Coloniality* (London: Routledge, 2000), 180.
41 Manju Kapur, *A Married Woman* (London: Faber and Faber, 2003), 237. The word lesbian is used only once in the novel, and to refer to the international film festival, rather than individual identity.
42 Ibid.
43 Rahul Rao, 'Global Homocapitalism', *Radical Philosophy* 194 (2015): 38–49, 47.

44 Although this terrain is shifting with more same-sex couples raising children, the structure is still expected to follow the dominant model of the nuclear family.
45 Rao, 'Global Homocapitalism'.
46 Rao, 'Queer Questions', 210 (Rao is here referring to a different text).
47 Shani Mootoo, *Cereus Blooms at Night* (London: Granta, 1998), 47, 48.
48 Mootoo, *Cereus Blooms at Night*, 237.
49 Gloria Anzaldúa, *Borderlands/La Frontera: The New Mestiza* (San Francisco: Aunt Lute Books, 1987). Anzaldúa's semi-autobiographical *Borderlands/La Frontera* offers one of the earliest theorizations of borders that are geographical and conceptual, such as between binary opposites: men and women, heterosexuals and homosexuals. In Anzaldúa's formulation, borderlands refer to spaces of hybridity, and she challenges the conception of a border as a simple divide, urging resistance to discourses that maintain and uphold such binaries.
50 Butler, *Undoing Gender*, 35.
51 Muñoz, *Disidentifications*, 5.
52 Mootoo, *Cereus Blooms at Night*, 22, 48, 10.
53 Ibid., 71.
54 Muñoz, *Disidentifications*, 12.
55 Ibid., 22.
56 Massad, *Desiring Arabs*, especially 'The Truth of Fictional Desires'.
57 Rao, 'Queer Questions', 202.
58 For further discussion, see Ferreira Da Silva Denise 'Toward a Critique of the Socio-Logos of Justice: The Analytics of Raciality and the Production of Universality', *Social Identities* 7, no. 3 (2001): 421–54.
59 Massad, *Desiring Arabs*, 40. Massad elaborates:While subjectivities in many non-Western contexts do not include heterosexuality and exclude homosexuality, as that very binarism is not part of their ontological structure, what the incitement and intervention of international human rights activism achieves is the replication of the every Euro-American human subjectivity its advocates challenge at home (41).
60 Butler, *Undoing Gender*, 114.
61 Mercer and Julien, 'Race, Sexual Politics and Black Masculinity', 102.
62 Ibid., 20.
63 Gopinath, *Impossible Desires*, 2.
64 Rakesh Satyal, *Blue Boy* (New York: Kensington Books, 2009), 36.
65 Rakesh Satyal, E-mail Interview, 28 August 2015.
66 Satyal, *Blue Boy*, 125.
67 Ibid., 106.
68 Ibid., 193.
69 Ibid., 236.

70 Rahul Gairola, 'Burning with Shame: Desire and South Asian Patriarchy, from Gayatri Spivak's "Can the Subaltern Speak?" to Deepa Mehta's *Fire*', *Comparative Literature* 54, no. 4 (2002), 307–24, 307.
71 Satyal, *Blue Boy*, 255.
72 Ibid., 254.
73 Homi K. Bhabha, 'Signs Taken for Wonders: Questions of Ambivalence and Authority under a Tree Outside Delhi, May 1987', *Critical Inquiry* 12, no. 1 (1985): 144–65.
74 Ibid., 224.
75 Ibid., 265.

16

Contemporary Migration and Diaspora Studies: Current Debates and the Role of Literature

Subha Xavier

In Robin Cohen's defining work on global diaspora he signals the marked entry of scholars of cultural studies and literature into the field of diaspora studies as 'assailants' and 'space invaders' in a field that was hitherto dominated by the social sciences.[1] Until recently, migration and diaspora were domains reserved for social scientists, who studied the movement and flow of people – first from the perspective of economics and sociology, then of political science, then anthropology and even ethics. With the dawn of a new century and a growing corpus of literary works about migration produced in all the major publishing centres of the world, scholars of literature and culture have recently carved a place for a different type of study of migration and diaspora, one focused around questions of poetics and cultural production as they intersect with the rights of exiles, migrants and the displaced more generally. This most recent expansion of the field favours interdisciplinary modes of scholarship that tackle the global dimensions of migration studies through the dialogue between work in literature and the humanities and the social sciences.

This chapter examines migration and diaspora studies in light of new forms of literary reading and writing. The two fields are presented here as distinct but overlapping disciplines in order to tease out some of the concerns that have arisen within the scope of each. Discussions of concepts in migration and diaspora studies are further augmented, in the pages that follow, by references to salient literary criticism as it thematically or methodologically intersects with the social sciences. The chapter proceeds in three main sections. First part, 'Migration Studies', offers a brief overview of foundational perspectives in the field in order to lay groundwork for one of the most pressing contemporary debates – concerning the increasing number of female migrants on the international stage, and their almost complete absence from the scholarly literature until the early 1980s. Second part performs a similar move for 'Diaspora Studies', first looking at the field's foundational texts and then, in a follow-up section, assessing its controversial relationship to emergent concepts of transnationalism which extend the term's scope in ways that trouble older paradigms. The third and final section of the chapter forges a place for literary expression in these overlapping fields of study by taking a closer look at the works of two writers of French-language works who engage these conceptual frameworks in obliquely poetic ways that forge openings for theoretical insights into the debates discussed earlier in the chapter. Specifically, the prose of Shan Sa's *La Joueuse de Go/The Girl Who Played Go* and the poetic writing of Dany Laferrière's *L'Énigme du retour/The Enigma of the Return* take centre stage in the final part of this chapter, as do the creative agency of two writers and the textual strategies they deploy to navigate multilingual and intercultural scenes within the vibrant contemporary literatures of migration and diaspora.

Migration studies: Foundational concepts

Migration studies begins in many ways with a reappropriation of Immanuel Wallerstein's World System Theory through the writing of sociologists like Saskia Sassen, and Douglas S. Massey et al., who recast international migration as a function of globalization and the dynamics of market creation. They emphasize the importance of transnational networks and institutions as well as the cumulative causation, whereby international immigration sustains and propagates itself within host countries. Sassen points to the magnetism of global cities in attracting immigrants and creating migrant networks that further spur movement towards the host country as a nexus of new economic, cultural and political capital. Sassen's work is then crucial to a nuanced understanding of the place of cultural production by immigrants and the prevalence of cities in the literature of migration.[2] Race and ethnicity play a critical role in sociological work on migration, which is acutely aware of societal inequities that result from the presence of immigrant populations. This is also perhaps the most recurrent thematic preoccupation of the literature of immigration in all languages and a significant point of intersection between sociological and literary studies of migration.[3]

The cultural impact of immigration was first addressed among sociologists in the writing of Roland Robertson on globalization. Robertson's world culture theory stems from his idea of globalization as 'a compression of the world and an intensification of consciousness of the world as whole'.[4] Robertson notes how an awareness of global interdependence gives rise to a new world culture and his later writing begins a complex dance between globalization and the socially constructed localities that comprise it, something we also see in the writing of sociologist Manuel Castells and the global versus local debate that ensued. Migrants are in many ways the purveyors of this interdependent reality and the reason why sociological models have failed to come up with any one coherent theory of migration. Since migration goes beyond the explanatory power of socio-economics in the sheer diversity of motivating factors and migratory experiences, the field as a whole has lent itself to increasing interdisciplinarity.

In the field of anthropology, scholars like Arjun Appadurai and James Clifford have made substantial contributions to the study of migration through their respective concepts of *ethnoscapes* and *routes* suggesting new ways of theorizing increased flows of people across nation states in the global age. Both scholars dismiss the heavy burden placed on localization and rootedness, favouring the prevalence of contact zones where migrant sensibilities – and the cultural production that ensues – come to fruition. The typical sites of anthropological enquiry have hence shifted over the last few decades to include the deterritorialized realities of the global age and the disjunctive economy and culture that results from the embattled relationship between states and nations as well as the movement of people, capital, technology, media and ideas across political boundaries of every kind.

Many contemporary literary scholars use these anthropological concepts to suggest further nuances to the theory. Leslie Adelson's study of the literature of Turkish migration to Germany, for instance, argues that this literature reconfigures the sign of ethnicity, which 'functions in the literature of migration as a construction zone where national and transnational ethnoscapes are so transformed that they become newly intelligible'.[5] Likewise, Nadje Al-Ali and Khalid Koser emphasize the transnational communities approach to migration, signalling how the very definition of 'home' has changed for international migrants as transnational practices redefine and create new spaces for connection. Al-Ali and Koser challenge the traditional dichotomy between an originating national space and singular ethno-national migrant communities through essays that uncover the processes whereby place and identity are socially constructed. Migrant cultural production increasingly engages with such transnational cultural spaces that go beyond a nation-to-nation, country of origin to host country, one-directional journey. Graziella Parati argues that migration literature in Italian for example describes 'movement from a multiplicity of "heres" to a multiplicity of "theres"'.[6]

Just as writing on globalization inevitably tackles the issue of immigration as a vital feature of the global age, so another body of theory around the concept of cosmopolitanism has taken on the ethical dimensions of migration in its relation to nationalism and questions of race and ethnicity. Of note here, is the work of Seyla Benhabib Seyla who invokes a Kantian ethics of hospitality as the driving force for human rights policy in the age of migration. Though Benhabib makes a clear distinction between refugees and immigrants, she advocates for a rethinking of cosmopolitan practice that goes beyond theory to address the individual needs of those who choose to cross borders today. Human rights have understandably become an important concern of migration studies, especially with deaths by the thousands occurring annually in the waters of the Mediterranean and boats full of people still making their way towards Northern shores against all odds.

Debate: A feminization of international migration?

As boatloads of migrants from Syria, most recently, and Libya, Morocco and Senegal for the past decade, have made headlines, it is the alarming number of women and children that are most capturing the attention of the international community. This worldwide interest in female migrants began with the launching of a UN working paper that was the first to suggest that the international migration of women in recent times was both new and unprecedented, coining the expression 'feminization of migration'. This, even though a 2002 UN extension of estimates of international migrants since 1960 had indicated that there have always been almost as many female migrants as male ones worldwide. In response to this report, a team of social scientists published a 2006 interdisciplinary study showing that since the 1980s, and with the increase in the number of female scholars of migration, gender as it intersects with migration studies has been thoroughly researched especially in fields such an anthropology. Still others, however, point to the paucity of equally distributed theoretical work on migration and gender in disciplines such as sociology. The place of female migrants, if studied, has been subject to some controversy, because their presence in the labour force has been read as secondary to that of their male counterparts. At the heart of these conflicting accounts of female migration is in fact a lack of attentiveness to data – both qualitative and quantitative – involving women and the challenge of accounting for gender differences through data, than any real lack of female migrants.[7] The debate that has ensued about whether in fact migration is becoming increasingly feminized has been best addressed by recent work by Katharine Donato and Donna Gabaccia in which they draw on interpretive angles taken both from the humanities as well as the social sciences to put into question how gender has been studied, analysed and categorized in its relationship to migration. Their exhaustive historical study departs from the category of sex ratios to discuss how gender is ideologically and culturally deployed to explain migration over four centuries of human history. Donata and Gabaccia signal various obstacles to the enumeration of migrants including record-keeping that is able to capture migrant illegality and irregularity, or differentiate between flows of people when movement is 'temporary, circular, repeated or multidirectional'.[8] Their study is global and comprehensive and notes that countries where there has been a feminization of migration, have been exceptions rather than the rule. Donato and Gabaccia point out that the history of twentieth- and twenty-first-century migrations has been one of a gradual, intermittent and ongoing global convergence towards gender balance. What is new, they argue is the discovery and naming of a feminization, as well as the resulting increase in concern over gender difference in migration.

In literary studies, the same period of heightened interest in the migration of women worldwide saw a significant proliferation of analyses of female migration in literature.[9] Female writers of migrant texts have certainly increased in numbers over the last thirty years as more and more immigrant women have taken up the pen from the 1980s onwards. In literature too, one may apply the *longue durée* approach to understanding how gender balance has been achieved over time with the increased global flows of educated women to countries with major publishing centres. Here again, it is less of a feminization of migration than a progression towards equal gender representation within the field of literature that scholars have capitalized on in recent times. Donato and Gabbacia in fact credit the humanities for the marked change in conceptual fluency around gender that has in turn spilled over into the social sciences.

Literature about the experience of women in migration takes on a vast array of questions, including that of violence against an often triply oppressed subject within the trauma of displacement and the confrontation of cultures, languages and/or ethnicities. Gender roles, moreover, are often portrayed within these texts as ideologically fluid, and socially constructed. This generation of women writers of migration, however, betray an investment in the financial success of their books alongside literary success, as they are keenly aware of the imperatives of the market. Carine Mardorossian's analyses of recent migrant fiction by Caribbean women writers points to instances where sexual violence is recast in almost sensationalist terms even while condemning patriarchal gender-based aggression. Similarly Nicki Hitchcott makes a case for violence, as it appears in the work of Franco-Cameroonian Calixthe Beyala, as a performative mode. I also argue elsewhere that Beyala's work vacillates between feminism and a certain degree of welcomed voyeurism.[10] Women's migrant textuality hence walks a fine line between feminist critique and market cunning, to denounce female oppression and often violence against women, in creative ways within the confines of global capital.

Diaspora studies: Foundational concepts

Though it dates back only to the mid-twentieth century as a formalized field of study, the concept of diaspora, as many scholars point out, first appeared in the Greek translation of the Hebrew scriptures to describe the plight of Jews living outside Palestine. As the term changed hands, first in the forced movement of Africans through transatlantic slave trade (sixteenth century onwards) and then in colonial-induced mass migrations (nineteenth century), diaspora has been largely defined in relation to modernity. Its current deployment in theory and practice owes to approaches taken from the social sciences (Safran; Cohen; Brah; Dufoix) as well as the humanities (Gilroy; Clifford; Hirsch). Together, these different methodologies for studying diaspora have opened up the field to a humanities inflected attention to 'the arts of memory, the dialectics of place, the affective economies of dispersal, the ethnographies of nostalgia, the intersubjectivities of social identity and the citational practices that ground senses of cultural particularity outside the homeland [...] along with social categories and identities'[11] Along these lines, most notable was Sudesh Mishra's coining of the term 'diaspoetics' to induct the field of diaspora criticism on its own terms and its extended usage as 'meta-critical art'.[12] Diaspoetics has exposed the study of diaspora to literary representation and criticism. Indeed diaspora literature has been a burgeoning area of study since the 1980s and critical writings have had to account for an ever-expanding canon of texts alongside a conceptual splitting of diaspora. In its ontological sense, it alludes to a geographic reality on the one hand, while its theoretical use has been extended onto an epistemological use of diaspora to include ways of 'thinking or representing the world'.[13] Of course, it is precisely such an extension of diaspora studies to what Radhakrishnan called a 'virtual theoretical consciousness'[14] that engendered the theory versus historicity debate within diaspora studies, expressing concerns over absent historical referents, material realities and group specificities of dispersal in broadened configurations of scholarship on diaspora.

Diaspoetics continues to occupy a great deal of scholarly attention, nonetheless, as literary critics increasingly deploy its analytical tools to study contemporary postcolonial writing. In the French-speaking world, work by Carmen Husti-Laboye and Joël Des Rosiers stands out as examples of innovative ways of negotiating the creative tension between the use of diaspora as a critical tool and as a historical experience. Recent collections of essays in English edited by Sukanya Banerjee et al., Ato Quayson and Girish Daswani as well as Asma Sayed continue to respond to the challenges posed by diaspoetics by considering diaspora from a multidisciplinary perspective with case studies anchored in the historical specificities of various diaspora communities from across the globe.

Debate: Are diasporas transnational?

In Ato Quayson and Girish Daswani's introduction to the *Blackwell Companion to Diaspora and Transnational Studies*, they present an increasingly globalized view of diaspora that accounts for its inherent differences that complicate any pretention to discrete homogeneity. They also rethink diaspora, firstly through Avtar Brah's notion of *diaspora space* – which points to the multivalent relationships between homelands and host nations as they shape today's diasporas – and secondly when paired with transnationalism. Transnational communities do not share ethnic or cultural forms of identification, but their connectedness at 'subnational levels' or in 'trans-social spaces' suggest a 'multiplicity of historical trajectories or *pathways* that affect people in different ways', argue Quayson and Daswani.[15] Through the transnational, diaspora subjects are distinguished from migrants who remain tied to the nations they leave and those they integrate. Migrants are thus often conceptualized in relation to the nation state, while transnational diasporas are in the words of Khachig Tölölyan: 'multilocal and polycentric in that what happens to kin communities in other areas of dispersion as well as in the homeland consistently matter to them'.[16]

Quayson and Daswani's position, however, is deliberately set against earlier work by Jana Evans Braziel and Anita Mannur who distinguish between diaspora and transnationalism though they concede that diasporas may be described as transnationalist.[17] Braziel and Mannur define diaspora as 'the movement – forced or voluntary – of people from one or more nation-states to another'.[18] They describe transnationalism as larger impersonal flows, which they align with globalization and global capitalism. For Braziel and Mannur, diaspora remains a human phenomenon whereas transnationalism involves both cybernetics as well as the movement of goods and products across geopolitical lines. They are willing to consider diaspora's valence in transnational settings, though they refuse to grant transnationalism a human dimension. Sukanya Banerjee's more recent collection of essays underscores Braziel and Mannur's position all the more. Banerjee contends that diaspora allows for configurations that are not simply about transcending nation-states, but also continental and regional divisions – as evidenced in African diaspora studies – and academic ways of separating the world that explore South-South relations for instance. Banerjee makes a case for the routing together of academic disciplines and their concomitant approaches to analyse diaspora as experience and as metaphor. Since academic work continues to be demarcated along national lines, she argues that the transnational reinforces these divisions even while purporting to surpass them. Banerjee, along with her co-editors Aims McGuinness and Steven Mckay, read transnationalism as intimately tied to globalization, which they argue has been mobilized as a teleological device in a linear conceptualization of history.[19] Diaspora, on the contrary, opens itself up to new temporal and spatial formations, especially when deployed as an approach to contesting historical practices, rather than as a typology.

For Quayson and Daswani, reimagining diaspora through transnationalism allows for new applications precisely within the reality of a globalized world where nation-states continue to play a preponderant role. Their edited volume rehearses diaspora's national longings within dispersed communities all the while creating new local alliances and possibilities. Quayson and Daswani's edited collection refuses to tease out the human from the economic, as the social and cultural dimensions of diaspora remain intricately woven into the ongoing processes of globalization, labour and trade migration, as well as resettlement.

Diaspora literature, as Carmen Husti-Laboye's work shows in the Afro-French context, is increasingly transnationally focused and looks to build bridges with broadly conceived diaspora communities beyond the borders of the formerly colonizing nation. Such is the work of Congolese writer Alain Mabanckou whose work deliberately crosses national lines, refusing on the one hand to situate many of his fictional texts within recognizable African boundaries, and through suggestive essays that make connections to issues of Black consciousness well beyond the scope of African diaspora fiction. Recent work on the literature of Edwidge Danticat, Dionne Brand and Chika Unigwe further distinguishes between different generations of diaspora writers and the younger generation's response to globalization through a cosmopolitan, transnational identification that resists European-centred assimilation. Globalization is thus acknowledged as a process that is intricately tied – if not causally linked – to the phenomenon of human dispersal and the literature that ensues is increasingly defined in its relation to the transnational networks that produce it. Moreover, as many scholars of postcolonial literature have signalled in recent times, diaspora writers are active participants in the transnational circulation of their work today and, as I argue elsewhere, negotiate their own way through global capital as agents of a literary market economy.[20] In the next section, we will discuss two such examples taken from the Chinese and Haitian diaspora respectively.

Case study: Contemporary French literature and migration – *Migrant Modes*

It may at first sight appear strange to align the work of Sino-French writer Shan Sa with that of Haitian-born Canadian writer Dany Laferrière. Nothing in their work compares on a thematic level other than the fact that they both write in French about cultures and experiences that are not French. What they share – on the surface – is a personal experience of migration (from China to France and Haiti to Canada respectively) that translates into different literary renditions of cross-cultural contact, multilingual writing and transnational peregrinations. Whether either one of these writers had any desire to integrate into the growing diasporic community in their respective country, both authors now see their work repeatedly summoned as somehow representative of the multitude of migrant experiences there. What is clear, in both cases, is that neither of them chose to write about a particular diaspora, privileging instead a writing of migration that disengages from speaking for just one community of people, recounting the personal itineraries of transnational subjects in continual flux.

In their deliberate blurring of lines between migration and diaspora, Shan Sa and Dany Laferrière complicate both the theory and practice of migration and diaspora studies by enacting just the very troubling of categories that we saw earlier in this chapter through our analysis of recent debates in both fields. The literature of Shan Sa tells the story of migration from a female point of view without ever really recounting the story of the author's own migration between China and France. Yet the feminization of the Sino-French text takes place in the way she mobilizes what I call a 'migrant mode' of writing in which she negotiates her identity as a female French writer through the Chinese medium. While Dany Laferrière's work, on the other hand, is heavily steeped in autobiography, his approach as scholar Jana Evans Braziel points out makes larger connections to Black diasporic identity, 'forcing the trope or the stereotype of the "Black male" itself into migration'.[21] Laferrière deploys a migrant mode of writing that can only be read as transnational both in its engagement with the processes of globalization that shape today's Black writer and the experience of living across several national spaces. In the pages that follow, we will examine the work of each of these two writers, revisiting recent debates in migration and diaspora studies that were discussed earlier, through the literary voices of two of the French-speaking world's most successful contemporary writers.

Shan Sa's migrant feminism

When Chinese poet Yan Ni decided to emigrate from her native China at the age of eighteen, after having witnessed the 1989 events of Tian'anmen Square first hand, she chose France not because she spoke the language, but because at the time her father was a professor at the Sorbonne. Like many female exiles, and as a young woman emigrating alone, it was inconceivable that she should choose a country in which she knew no one. Seven years after her arrival in Paris, under the pen name of Shan Sa, she published her first novel in French *Porte de la Paix Céleste*. The novel was not only an impressive testimony to Shan Sa's ability to learn and master the French language in so short a time, but it quickly set her on an unrivalled literary course, earning the prestigious *Goncourt du Premier Roman*/Goncourt Prize for the First Novel and two other awards in the same year. *La Porte de la Paix Céleste/The Gate of Celestial Peace* is the fictional narrative of a young fugitive woman named Ayamei, who is the student mastermind behind the demonstrations at Tian'anmen Square. After the bloody massacre that leaves her friend dead, Ayamei flees as Chinese soldiers lead by lieutenant Zhao pursue her into the mountains. Although this first novel has little of Shan Sa's signature French prose known today for its abundance of metaphor, the language is simple and direct as it has always remained. At the centre of this novel, as most other works of prose Shan Sa has authored, is a strong-willed idealist, a young woman who is critical of her own society, and who does not feel she belongs. Ayamei becomes a migrant in her own country, fleeing the Communist regime and its officers to whom she is known only as 'la criminelle' ['the criminal'], she becomes an eternal itinerant: 'Je m'en vais! Mon sang bouillonne. Je dois repartir. J'ai compris que je ne dois jamais m'arrêter. J'irai jusqu'au plus haut des sommets, jusqu'à la Porte Céleste.'[22] ['I am leaving! My blood boils. I have to leave again. I have understood that I must never stop. I will go to the highest peaks, up to the Celestial Gate.'][23] In this, like others of her most noteworthy novels, migrancy extends beyond the real world to the magical and fantastical realms.

Since *Porte de la Paix Céleste* in 1997, Shan Sa has published a total of seven other novels, along with several collections of poetry both in Chinese and French. She has earned numerous prizes including the *Prix Goncourt des Lycéens* for her third and most successful novel to date *La Joueuse de Go /The Girl who Played Go* published in 2001. Since its publication, this novel about a love story between a young Chinese go player and a Japanese spy during the second Sino-Japanese war has sold over 1 million copies in French and has been translated into nineteen different languages.[24] The immense success of *La Joueuse de Go* may be explained – at least in part – by the style of this novel. Rather than the straightforward prose of her first two novels, this and subsequent works engage in a linguistic play between Mandarin Chinese and French that relies on the translation of meanings and sounds from ideograms, replete in imagery, to a poetic arrangement of the French lexicon. Critic Sophie Croiset explains the generous use of rhetorical devices in Shan Sa's work as a marker of Chinese calligraphic influence. Sino-French poet François Cheng also notes that the Chinese semiotic system betrays a more intimate link to the real, since there is less of a rupture between the signifier and the signified.[25] Shan Sa's syntactical manoeuvring in French thus results in a migrant mode of heightened metaphoricity, which in turn is especially developed around her female characters.

The textual spaces of other novels by Shan Sa – such as *L'Impératrice* 2003/*Empress*, *Les Conspirateurs* 2005/*The Conspirators*, and *La Cithare nue* 2010/*The Naked Zither* – are equally inhabited by strong female characters, who migrate within and beyond China both spatially and temporally, crossing villages and cities, but also social hierarchies and even epochs in search of love, and more importantly their own emancipation. As a writer who revels in the historical romance genre set in China – but recounted in French – Shan Sa's female characters have something of a mythic quality, as though their presence in the French text goes well beyond the language's ability to hold them in. Allusions to Chinese painting, writing and calligraphy – as in the example discussed above – abound, and often provide the key to unlocking the mystery that underlies the character's profound unhappiness within the text. At the same time, Shan Sa's continued success, both in French and Chinese literary markets, suggests that she is able to walk the line between social critique and linguistic manipulation with subtlety and skill, somehow giving both French-speaking readers, and Chinese-speaking ones alike, the sense that it is in their respective language that the characters' real stories are told.

Dany Laferrière's transnational returns

The literary works of Haitian-Canadian writer Dany Laferrière – unlike that of Shan Sa for example – are consistently categorized as diaspora literature, a moniker the author himself struggles to accept.[26] Migrating to Quebec to escape the oppressive Duvalier regime in 1976, Laferrière joined an already growing diaspora in the United States and Canada, but also worldwide, that would henceforth cast its shadow on all his literary production. While Laferrière has published several novels about his own experiences of diaspora and about the politics of Haiti, he has also occupied a more transnational space as a writer from his very first novel in 1985 *Comment faire l'amour avec un nègre sans se fatiguer/How to Make Love to a Negro Without Getting Tired*, and its sequel of sorts two years later *Éroshima*, to *Je suis un écrivain japonais/I am a Japanese Writer* in 2008 and his most recent 2009 novel-poem *L'Énigme du retour/The Enigma of the Return*. While Laferrière's debut novel with its titillatingly provocative title launched Laferrière's career in Quebec, it is his most recent award-winning work *L'Énigme du retour* that has confirmed his transnational impact as an author. Selling 20,000 copies in Quebec and 15,000 copies in France within the first two months of publication, *L'Énigme du retour* earned Laferrière the prestigious *Prix Médicis* in France, an award given to a writer whose fame does not as yet match the level of his or her talent. The French prize thus sought to finally recognize Laferrière as a literary master in the French-language canon, an honour that was soon to be followed by his election onto France's illustrious Académie Française in 2012 as the institution's first Haitian, first Canadian, first Quebecer and only second Black member in its 380-year history. One may argue that Laferrière's prize-entrenched rise to fame was only due to a question of timing. Laferrière typically refuses to release any of his new works during the French prize season in the Autumn, and it was his editors that finally convinced him to launch *L'Énigme du retour* in September 2009. On the other hand, Laferrière has always been a savvy creator and marketer of his own literary works, ensuring the financial success of his career with remarkable craft within its publishing centres, while also nudging at stereotypical representations of Blackness worldwide.[27] In many ways, Laferrière has especially embraced a transnational positioning in his most successful works, both in terms of awakening critical racial consciousness and securing profits within a global capitalist marketplace. Interspersed between these more transnationally oriented texts are then those that fall more neatly within the scope of Haitian diaspora experience, those that have not made the bestseller lists or sparked international attention, but have secured a loyal readership over the years. *L'Énigme du retour* is thus the culmination of a carefully nurtured literary career, from survival as a Black immigrant writer in Quebec to fame as a Haitian-born writer of transnational literature in French.

L'Énigme du retour, written in the wake of Laferrière's father's passing in exile, is a poetic tribute to migration between Haiti and Canada, to the passing of time, to diaspora life and to Laferrière's own story. It is a work of mourning that takes the author from Montreal to New York and Port-au-Prince, a journey of exile-in-reverse that is now only the privilege of the transnational writer. Laferrière muses upon the realities of exile for most other migrants, in the novel's haiku-like form. He also reflects on his life of comfort in Montreal, recalling a time in Port-au-Prince when hunger dictated his every thought. The novel-poem is a meditation on the very journey of the diaspora writer and pain that even celebrity cannot assuage. When Laferrière's nephew Dany, who is an aspiring writer himself, asks his uncle for advice, the author responds with a reminder that 'glory' comes at great cost: 'La gloire viendra./ Trop tard./L'idéal sera alors/ une journée sans douleur.'[28] ['Glory will come./ Too late./ The ideal will then be/a day without pain.'] A few verses later, Laferrière makes a playful reference to his own story of success:

> Pour écrire un roman, j'explique à mon neveu,
> avec un sourire au coin,
> qu'il faut surtout de bonnes fesses
> car c'est un métier
> comme celui de couturière
> où l'on reste assis longtemps.[29]
> [To write a novel, I tell my nephew
> with a sly smile,
> what you really need is a good pair of buttocks
> because it's a job
> like the seamstress'
> where you spend a lot of time sitting down.]

While the 'sly smile' suggests he is referring to his debut novel *Comment faire l'amour avec un nègre sans se fatiguer* replete with sex scenes and an abundance of female bodies to behold, the verse quickly transforms the implied meaning to allude to the lonely, immobile task of the writer at his or her desk. Laferrière suggests that the use of sex in his early work was nothing other than a ploy to gain readers, to seduce a literary readership, and ensure sales. He insinuates that this strategy was one that was carefully conceived over time, one that involved hard work, as it did in those early years. Indeed, as I explain elsewhere, Laferrière worked tirelessly to attract readers to his first novel which when examined more closely is only superficially about sex (Xavier 2016). Instead, Laferrière informs his nephew that the vocation of the writer is more akin to that of a seamstress or – as he goes on – to that of a cook.

Negotiating the line between diaspora and transnational writer has been a lifelong pursuit for Dany Laferrière, but one that he has managed to blur time and time again. If he is today one of the French-speaking world's most successful writers, it is certainly because he has done so with poise, artfulness and patience. Mobilizing a migrant mode of writing that betrays the author's investment in the creation, production and distribution of his own literary success, while also engaging with the political realities of Blackness, neo-colonialism, dictatorships and diaspora, Laferrière's work is a testimony to perseverance.

Conclusion

As a recent philosophical study by Thomas Nail opens, 'the twenty-first century will be the century of migrant. At the turn of the century, there were more regional and international migrants than ever before in recorded history'.[30] As theoretical work endeavours to catch up to this ever-growing reality, it is now apparent that migration and diaspora studies will be the leading paradigms through which to reconfigure postcolonial studies for the new era. The literature of Shan Sa and Dany Laferrière both signal the exciting new directions that the study of migration and diaspora are taking today. In considering these specific literary case studies alongside debates in either field, this chapter adds to the burgeoning dialogue between literary studies and the social sciences in order to emphasize the ways in which migration and diaspora theory can and must be shaped by texts derived from different disciplines along with their concomitant methodologies. The increased movement of peoples brings with it challenges for reconceiving cross-cultural and multilingual conversations across academic fields of study, and yet literary works have already begun this crucial function for us. It is therefore in conjunction with literary forms that new histories, theories and studies must be imagined for the study of migration and diaspora in the twenty-first century.

Notes

1. Robin Cohen, *Global Diasporas* (New York: Routledge, 2008), 127.
2. See Odile Cazenave, *Afrique sur Seine: A New Generation of African Writers in Paris* (Lanham: Lexington, 2007); Adlai H. Murdoch, *Creolizing the Metropole: Migrant Caribbean Identities in Literature and Film* (Bloomington: Indiana University Press, 2013); Pascal De Souza and Adlai H. Murdoch (eds.), *Metropolitan Mosaics and Melting Pots: Paris and Montreal in Francophone Literatures* (Cambridge: Cambridge Scholars Publishing, 2013).
3. See James F. Hollifield, 'Immigration and the Republican Tradition in France'; J. F.Hollifield, P. L. Martin and P. M. Orrenius (eds.), *Controlling Immigration: A Global Perspective* (Stanford: Stanford University Press, 2014); Maha Marouan and Merinda K. Simmons, *Race and Displacement: Nation, Migration, and Identity in the Twenty-First Century* (Tuscaloosa: University of Alabama Press, 2013); Dominic Thomas, *Africa and France: Postcolonial Cultures, Migration, and Racism* (Bloomington: Indiana University Press, 2013); Noami Davidson, *Only Muslim: Embodying Islam in Twentieth Century France* (Cornell: Cornell University Press, 2012).
4. Roland Robertson, *Globalization* (London: Sage, 1992), 8.
5. Leslie Adelson, *The Turkish Turn in Contemporary German Literature* (London: Palgrave, 2005), 124.
6. Grazieala Parati, *Migration Italy* (Toronto: University of Toronto Press, 2005), 102.
7. This is changing thanks to the efforts of the International Migration Institute, set to release new quantitative data on global migration flows 2000–2010 in autumn 2015, and the recent book by Donato and Gabaccio (2015) discussed in this chapter.
8. Katherine M. Donato and Donna Gabbeccia, *Gender and International Migration* (New York: Russell Sage Foundation, 2015), 42.
9. See Meredith M. Gadsby, *Sucking Salt: Caribbean Women Writers, Migration and Survival* (Columbia: University of Missouri Press, 2006); Yasmin Hussein, *Writing Diaspora: South Asian Women, Culture and Ethnicity* (Aldershot: Ashgate, 2005); Merinda K. Simmons, *Changing the*

Subject: Writing Women across the African Diaspora (Columbus: Ohio State University Press, 2014).

10 Subha Xavier, "Entre féminisme et voyeurisme: L'éros migrant chez Calixthe Beyala", *Revue Zizanie* 1, no. 1 (2015).

11 Ato Quayson and Girish Daswani, *A Wiley Companion to Diaspora and Transnationalism* (Hoboken: Wiley Blackwell, 2013), 8.

12 https://ehlt.flinders.edu.au/ehlt/conference_archives/jandj2004/abstracts/Mishra,%20Sudesh.pdf (accessed 2 April 2015).

13 James Procter, 'Diaspora', in *The Routledge Companion to Postcolonial Studies*, ed. John McLeod (London: Routledge, 2007), 251.

14 R. Radhakrishnan, 'Postcoloniality and the Boundaries of Identity', *Callaloo* 16, no. 4 (1993): 750–71, 763.

15 Ato Qyason and Girish Dawani, *A Wiley Companion to Diaspora and Transnationalism* (Hoboken: Wiley Blackwell, 2013), 6.

16 Khachig Tölölyan, 'The Contemporary Discourse of Diaspora Studies', *Comparative Studies of South Asia, Africa and the Middle East* 9, no. 1 (2007): 107–36, 121.

17 Jana Evans Braziel and Anita Mannur, *Theorizing Diaspora* (Oxford: Blackwell, 2003), 8.

18 Braziel and Mannur, *Theorizing Diaspora*, 8.

19 Sukanya Banerjee, Aims McGuinness and Steven C. Mackay (eds.), *New Routes for Diaspora Studies* (Bloomington: Indiana University Press, 2012), 5, 231.

20 See Graham Huggan, *The Postcolonial Exotic: Marketing the Margins* (London: Routledge, 2001); Richard Watts, *Packaging Post/Coloniality: The Manufacture of Literature Identity in the Francophone World* (New York: Lexington Books, 2005); Sarah Brouillette, *Postcolonial Writers and the Global Literary Marketplace* (New York: Palgrave, 2007); Om Prakash Dwivedi and Lisa Lau (eds.), *Indian Writing in English and the Global Literary Marketplace* (New York: Palgrave, 2014); Subha Xavier, *The Migrant Text* (Montreal: McGill-Queen's University Press, 2016).

21 Jana Evans Braziel, *Artists, Performers, and Black Masculinity in the Haitian Diaspora* (Bloomington: Indiana University Press, 2008), 29.

22 Shan Sa, *La Joueuse de Go* (Paris: Gallimard 2001), 144.

23 Unless otherwise indicated, all translations are mine.

24 Statistics provided by French Marketing firm GFK show the book sold 1,619,475 between 2003 and 2012.

25 François Cheng, *L'écriture poétique chinoise, suivi d'une anthologie des poèmes des Tang* (Paris: Seuil, 2006), 13.

26 In an interview I conducted with Laferrière in July 2012, Laferrière expressed discomfort with the ways in which the Haitian community in Canada has both rejected some of his earlier work and claimed other works for the diaspora.
27 See my analysis of Laferrière's navigation of the literary marketplace in Xavier, *The Migrant Text*, 2016.
28 Dany Laferrière, *L'Énigme du retour* (Montréal: Boréal, 2009), 103.
29 Laferrière, *L'Énigme du retour,* 104.
30 Thomas Nail, *The Figure of the Migrant* (Stanford: Stanford University Press), 2015, 1.

17

Postcolonialism and African American Literature

John Cullen Gruesser

Widely credited with founding colonial discourse theory in *Orientalism* and thus paving the way for postcolonial studies, Edward Said went on, fifteen years later, to publish *Culture and Imperialism*, which seeks in part to reveal the reciprocity between colonialism and the English novel. In the latter book he draws attention to postcolonial 'responses' to colonial discourse, issuing a call for what he terms 'contrapuntal reading', a method requiring us to extend 'our reading of texts to include what was forcibly excluded'.[1] In *Playing in the Dark: Whiteness and the Literary Imagination* (1992), Toni Morrison analyses what she calls the 'Africanist' or shadowy black presence in canonical white American literature, contending that it has had profound and readily identifiable effects on this writing. In 'Unspeakable Things Unspoken: The Afro-American Presence in American Literature' (1989), an important precursor to *Playing in the Dark*, she asks, 'Is the text sabotaged by its own proclamations of "universality"? Are there ghosts in the machine? Active but unsummoned presences that can distort the workings of the machine and can also *make* it work?' As she goes on to remark, 'These kinds of questions have been consistently put by critics of Colonial Literature vis-à-vis Africa and India and other third world countries. American literature would benefit from similar critiques'.[2] Given the formidable similarities between postcolonial and African American literary criticism,

---

Material in this chapter appeared in different form in *Confluences: Postcolonialism, African American Literary Studies, and the Black Atlantic* (Athens: University of Georgia Press, 2005, 2007).

exemplified by but by no means limited to Said's and Morrison's projects, it is both surprising and regrettable that few postcolonial theorists have sufficiently accounted for black American literature and that African Americanists have in general been resistant to postcolonial theoretical concepts. By no means am I suggesting that the two fields can and should be conflated. The experiences and cultural productions of people of African descent in the United States differ markedly and profoundly from those of persons from colonized or formerly colonized lands. Yet throughout history theoretical concepts imported from one discipline or culture into another have resulted in important advances in critical praxis. My purpose is not to blur the distinctions between postcolonial and African American literary studies but rather to identify points of correspondence and build bridges between them so as to enrich both fields.

In 1985, Henry Louis Gates Jr. guest-edited a special issue of *Critical Inquiry* titled '*Race*', *Writing, and Difference* comprising fourteen essays by an impressive group of theorists and scholars, including Said, Homi Bhabha, Gayatri Spivak, Barbara Johnson, Jacques Derrida and Gates himself. The majority of the articles addressed subjects that would today be regarded as postcolonial while four others would be categorized as relating to African American scholarship. This special issue represents a key moment of confluence for a variety of theoretical and critical approaches to literature and culture, especially postcolonial and African American studies. In the ensuing years, both fields have grown considerably in terms of prominence and impact within and beyond the academy. Since its coalescence in the late 1980s and early 1990s, postcolonialism has been incredibly fecund, exerting an influence on areas as diverse as Native American, biblical and Shakespearean studies. Yet despite the precedent of Gates's *Critical Inquiry* issue and the striking points of intersection between the two fields, African American studies has not been significantly influenced by postcolonialism and postcolonial theorists and critics have tended not to explore the long history of African American engagement with issues such as colonialism, displacement and syncretism, and only occasionally have they chosen black American literature and culture as subjects for contemplation and analysis.

Because exceptions to the insularity or what might be called the territorialization of postcolonial and African American literary studies have been relatively infrequent, they are particularly noteworthy. In the introduction to *The Location of Culture*, a meditation on contemporary attempts to 'locate the question of culture in the realm of the *beyond*',

Homi Bhabha reads the 'freak social and cultural displacements' in the "'unhomely" fictions' of the African American and South African Nobel laureates Morrison and Nadine Gordimer.[3] Echoing Said and Morrison, Bhabha declares that the 'act of writing the world, of taking the measure of its dwelling, is magically caught in Morrison's description of her house of fiction – art as "the fully realized presence of a haunting" of history', adding, 'my translation of Morrison's phrase becomes a statement on the political responsibility of the critic. For the critic must attempt to fully realize, and take responsibility for, the unspoken, unrepresented pasts that haunt the historical present'.[4] Later in *Location*, a book that emphasizes the porous nature of the borders that separate people(s), Bhabha provides a concise description of postcoloniality that breaks down barriers that some postcolonial theorists have erected: 'Postcolonial perspectives emerge from the colonial testimony of Third World countries and the discourses of "minorities" within the geographical divisions of East and West, North and South'.[5] Despite its apparent simplicity, this description builds on Bhabha's highly nuanced conception of the term in 'DissemiNation', an essay that engages the work of Said, Benedict Anderson, Walter Benjamin, Jacques Derrida, Michel Foucault, Sigmund Freud, Julia Kristeva and others. Although some articles and essay collections, including those devoted to postcolonialism and the United States, embraced Bhabha's inclusive conception of postcoloniality, others expressed reservations about or openly rejected it.[6] Without question Paul Gilroy's ambitious black Atlantic project, outlined in 'Cultural Studies and Ethnic Absolutism' and elaborated in *The Black Atlantic: Modernity and Double Consciousness, Small Acts: Thoughts on the Politics of Black Cultures,* and 'Route Work: The Black Atlantic and the Politics of Exile', stands as the most profound attempt to correlate postcolonialism and African American studies. Gilroy's penetrating readings of black American texts indicate the advantages of using postcolonial theoretical concepts, discourse analysis and an expanded frame of reference to analyse African American literature.

In the pages that follow, my goals are, first, to provide concise introductions to three prominent and related theories of how marginalized peoples respond to dominant and dominating discourses for scholars, students and other interested readers who may not be well acquainted with one or more of them and, second, to assert the advantages of breaking down the boundaries separating postcolonial and African American literary studies.

Postcolonialism

People have been involved in what has been variously known as anticolonial, Third World and/or Commonwealth studies for many years. The demarcation of a codified domain of literary study now known as 'postcolonialism', however, is comparatively recent. In *Orientalism*, Edward Said builds on Michel Foucault's contention that discursive formations are systems of power that restrict the way people see and talk about things. Examining the West's depiction of the Orient, especially the Near East, from the early 1800s to the present as its own reverse image, Said asserts that the purpose and results of Orientalist discourse are hegemonic: 'My contention is that Orientalism is fundamentally a political doctrine willed over the Orient because the Orient was weaker than the West, which elided the Orient's difference with its weakness'.[7] Because of its delineation of colonialist discourse, against which postcolonial texts have been seen as reacting, *Orientalism* has come to occupy the position of an urtext for postcolonial studies. Most observers regard *The Empire Writes Back: Theory and Practice in Post-Colonial Literatures* (1989) as a groundbreaking publication in terms of codifying this new or newly renamed field. The title derives from a 1982 essay by Salman Rushdie and refers to how writers at the margins have responded to their colonized status and their exclusion from the literary canon. Not major theorists, along the lines of Said, Bhabha and Gayatri Spivak, but rather synthesizers, popularizers and disseminators of theory drawn from a variety of figures, regions and perspectives, the authors of this book, Bill Ashcroft, Gareth Griffiths and Helen Tiffin, are responsible to a degree for the widespread use of the term 'postcolonialism' today.

As the first major attempt to delimit postcolonial studies, *The Empire Writes Back* sparked considerable critical debate in academic journals during the 1990s, being the subject of numerous reviews, articles and review essays, some of which have had long-term ramifications for the field. The 1991 essay 'What Is Post(-)colonialism?' for example, welcomes the appearance of *The Empire Writes Back,* but the authors, Vijay Mishra and Bob Hodge, express certain reservations, particularly about its conflation of white settler countries (such as Australia) with formerly invaded countries (e.g., Nigeria) under the postcolonial rubric. 1993 saw the appearance of the first postcolonial anthology, Patrick Williams and Laura Chrisman's *Colonial Discourse and Postcolonial Theory: A Reader,* which criticizes *The Empire*

Writes Back's version of postcolonialism and features substantial selections from books and lengthy scholarly essays. This was followed a year later by Ashcroft, Griffiths and Tiffin's more comprehensive *Post-Colonial Studies Reader*, comprised of relatively brief excerpts from books and articles. In 1998, Ashcroft, Griffiths and Tiffin published their third book for Routledge (one of the leading presses in the field of postcolonial studies), a glossary of terms titled *Key Concepts in Post-Colonial Studies*, and in 2002 they brought out a second edition of *The Empire Writes Back*, which is identical to the first except for a new chapter and the addition of one paragraph to the Conclusion.[8]

The Empire Writes Back discusses three elemental concepts of postcolonial theory: the centre-periphery opposition, the displacement experienced by colonized persons, and the hybrid character of postcolonial writing.[9] The metropolitan center serves as the clearinghouse for not only colonial and imperial policy but also the English language and the literary canon. Politically, colonized people at the periphery of empire submit to, openly rebel against, or covertly subvert colonial and imperial strictures. Linguistically, writers in settler cultures in particular but also authors in invaded societies who choose to write in English transform the language into an 'english' of their own, which reflects the peculiarities of their environment. In the literary realm, because of their distance from the centre and their use of a unique english, writers at the margins are excluded from the canon to which their texts counter-discursively respond.

Ashcroft, Griffiths and Tiffin regard displacement as an integral component of the postcolonial condition, engendering 'the special post-colonial crisis of identity [..., i.e.,] the concern with the development or recovery of an effective identifying relationship between self and place'.[10] White settlers import and continue to speak the English language; however, they experience a spatial displacement from metropolitan culture. People in invaded societies do not suffer from geographic dislocation but have an alien language and culture forced on them, which results in linguistic displacement and cultural denigration. *The Empire Writes Back* acknowledges the limitations of the settler and invaded society models, citing their inability to describe the West Indian situation adequately. West Indians of African and Asian descent, like black Americans (about whom *The Empire Writes Back* is curiously reticent), experience a treble (spatial, linguistic and cultural) displacement.

One of the most striking ideas informing postcolonial literature, hybridity (often used interchangeably with the terms 'syncretism' and 'creolization') counterbalances the negative connotations of displacement and its attendant identity crisis. In the introduction to the section of *The Post-Colonial Studies Reader* devoted to hybridity, Ashcroft, Griffiths and Tiffin, summing up the work of Bhabha and others, assert that 'Most post-colonial writing has concerned itself with the hybridized nature of post-colonial culture as a strength rather than a weakness. Such writing focuses on the fact that the transaction of the post-colonial world is not a one-way process'.[11] A direct result of the experience of displacement, hybridity reflects the possession of a 'double vision' unavailable to those who have not been exposed to both metropolitan and peripheral culture, which, *The Empire Writes Back* notes approvingly, 'ensures that in all post-colonial cultures monolithic perceptions are less likely'.[12]

Despite significant similarities between the histories of and recent theories about African American and postcolonial literature, the Australian academics Ashcroft, Griffiths and Tiffin largely exclude black American writing from the seemingly all-inclusive realm of postcolonialism. Rather than limiting itself to postindependence writing, *The Empire Writes Back* defines its subject area as 'all the culture affected by the imperial process from the moment of colonization to the present day'.[13] As a result, American literature as a whole qualifies as postcolonial. *The Empire Writes Back*'s American examples, however, come exclusively from mainstream white writing: Charles Brockden Brown's late eighteenth-century gothic and sentimental novels reveal that he wrestled with questions about the adaptability of inherited forms to a postcolonial environment; a quotation from Mark Twain's *Adventures of Huckleberry Finn* illustrates how the vernacular is used to convert the English language into a distinctive 'english' in settler cultures; Henry James and T. S. Eliot exemplify the tendency of 'those from the periphery to immerse themselves in the imported culture, denying their origins in an attempt to become "more English than the English"'.[14]

Meanwhile, *Empire*, which rather arbitrarily limits itself to 'those peoples formerly colonized by Britain'[15] and thus concentrates on English language texts, denies the legitimacy of what it calls the 'Black writing' model, particularly as manifested in the francophone Negritude movement. Even though Ashcroft, Griffiths and Tiffin unite such disparate literatures as those of Singapore, Ghana and (white) America under the umbrella of postcolonialism, they contend that the 'Black writing' model founders because of the major difference between the experiences of African Americans and those of other peoples of African descent. Ashcroft et al.

do not devote any of the eighty-six selections in *The Post-Colonial Studies Reader* to African American literature.[16] Moreover, in an entry on 'African American and post-colonial studies' in *Key Concepts*, they claim that African American studies 'has had a widespread and often quite separate development from post-colonial studies, to which it is related only in a complex and ambiguous way'.[17] And yet to illustrate how writers in invaded societies have responded to linguistic alienation, in *The Empire Writes Back* they cite Chinua Achebe quoting James Baldwin to explain how marginalized authors transform the English language so it will '"bear the burden" of their experience'.[18]

In 'Re-thinking the Post-Colonial: Post-Colonialism in the Twenty-first Century', the new chapter appearing in the second edition of *The Empire Writes Back,* the authors raise but refrain from answering the key question 'Can we really say that slavery and its effects (e.g., the black diaspora) are not a legitimate element of the colonial and should not be part of what we study to try and understand how colonialism worked?'.[19] Although acknowledging a 'lively and argumentative' relationship between African American and postcolonial studies, especially in the work of 'bell hooks, Henry Louis Gates, and Cornell [sic] West', the authors of *The Empire Writes Back* contend that the former field is 'much larger' than the latter,[20] by which they presumably mean that African American studies concerns much more than the colonialism and neocolonialism of black Americans. However, even if African American studies encompasses histories and issues not directly connected to postcolonial studies, it does not follow that the fields should be seen as totally isolated from each other given the many areas where they do intersect.

With some justice, *The Empire Writes Back* criticizes Negritude for being essentialist and adopting the binarism of Western philosophy. However, it also presents a flawed history of the movement that reduces cross-cultural interactions between black American and African political and literary movements: 'the philosophy of Negritude has been most influential in its derivative form in the Afro-American Black consciousness movement. Senghor's influence in America can be traced to prominent Black intellectuals of the 1920s such as Langston Hughes and Richard Wright'.[21] However, Leopold Senghor and Aimé Césaire did not found Negritude until the 1930s, and the former not only openly acknowledged his movement's debt to African American writing, particularly that of Hughes, but also linked it to the turn-of-the-century anglophone African Personality movement.[22] Moreover, Wright, who was born in 1908, did not begin publishing until the 1930s. Although Ashcroft, Griffiths and Tiffin point out the continuing pursuit of a black aesthetic in African American criticism, they note approvingly the influence of structuralism and discourse analysis in the early 1980s on critics such as Houston Baker and Henry Louis Gates, whose literary critical approach they regard as a significant advancement over Negritude and the Black Arts movement.

Despite Ashcroft et al.'s attempt to exclude black American writing from their compendium of marginalized literatures, the similarities between certain aspects of their account of postcolonial discourse, on the one hand, and Gates's Signifyin(g), a major theory about black American literature by one of the best-known and most prolific African American literary critics, on the other, are striking. Just as postcolonial theory has transformed the extent to and ways in which the writings of colonized and formerly colonized people have been discussed and analysed, Gates's *Figures in Black: Words, Signs and the 'Racial' Self* (1987) and *The Signifying Monkey: A Theory of Afro-American Literary Criticism* (1988) have had a profound impact on the study of African American literature. In their efforts to transform their fields, Gates and many postcolonial theorists have made use of poststructuralism. Moreover, they also have proposed similar, politically tinged rhetorical strategies as their fields' signature gestures.

Reflecting the influence of Said, Rushdie, Spivak and others, Helen Tiffin argues in 'Post-Colonial Literatures and Counter-discourse' (1987) that postcoloniality neither simply responds to metropolitan culture and/or the literary canon (because a writer could be imitating colonial discourse without questioning its legitimacy) nor merely adopts an anticolonial political stance, which would raise the possibility of a white Briton writing postcolonial literature; rather, it subverts the dominant discourse while calling its own biases into question. Tiffin considers counter-discursiveness superior to other models that are based on nationality, race or culture, such as Negritude, because of its ability to account for not only a wide variety of literatures that write back to the metropolitan centre but also situations in which postcolonials themselves assume the role of colonizers: 'such a model can account for the ambiguous position of say, white Australians, who, though still colonised by Europe and European ideas, are themselves the continuing colonisers of the original inhabitants'.[23] Tiffin identifies two types of postcolonial counter-discourse. One responds to colonialism and colonialist literature in a general way. The second rewrites a specific, canonical colonialist text. For Tiffin all postcolonial texts are counter-discursive, yet some, such as Jean Rhys's re-vision of *Jane Eyre* in *Wide Sargasso Sea* and J. M. Coetzee's reworking of *Robinson Crusoe* in *Foe*, are more explicitly so than others.[24] It should be noted that Tiffin's assertion that postcolonial literatures can themselves be the object of counter-discourse appears to provide a model for thinking about black American literature's relationship to mainstream white literature; however, the authors of *The Empire Writes Back*, who firmly assert the counter-discursive nature of postcolonial writing in their conclusion, make no attempt to extend it to the American context.

Signifyin(g)

Gates's efforts to delineate the African American literary tradition resemble attempts to define postcolonial literature. He rejects the repudiative theories of African American literature proposed by Houston Baker and Robert Stepto as well as Addison Gayle's and Maulana Karenga's Black Aesthetic in favour of 'Signifyin(g)', a revisionary, double-voiced response to the 'discourse of the black', Gates's term for texts by both whites and people of African descent that portray black characters. His theory builds on Zora Neale Hurston's, Ralph Ellison's, Thomas Kochman's, Geneva Smitherman's, and especially Roger Abrahams's and Claudia Mitchell-Kernan's discussions of 'signifying' as a folkloric concept. In an effort to map out a tradition that is distinctively black but avoids the essentialism that characterizes Negritude, the Black Arts movement and Afrocentrism, Gates argues that black American writing is not simply a repudiation of assertions of black inferiority that either imitates white literature or refutes its assumptions, nor is it a reflection of a distinctive black essence; instead, it is a counter-discursive strategy associated with the African American trickster figure of the Signifying Monkey, which ultimately derives from the Yoruba trickster and messenger of the gods, Esu-Elegbara.

Conceived as companion volumes, Gates's *Figures in Black* relates African American literature to mainstream white literary theory, reviews the history of black literary criticism, and proposes a theory of Signifyin(g) rooted in the black vernacular tradition, while *The Signifying Monkey* elaborates, illustrates, and situates this theory in a specifically black (primarily African American but also, he asserts, African and diasporic) context. In *Figures* Gates laments and endeavours to remedy African Americans' aversion to theory, an aversion that, as he points out, is nevertheless readily understandable given the manner in which theory has for centuries victimized people of African descent. Rather than responding with a theory of their own, according to Gates, black American writers up until at least the Harlem Renaissance strived to counter accusations of black inferiority by demonstrating their literacy and rebutting the charges levelled against them. This involved writing texts that adhered to mainstream white formal and stylistic conventions, publishing biographies of blacks responsible for great achievements, and producing propagandistic literary works that had few if any aesthetic aspirations. The emphasis on content and disregard of form and technique continued in the 1930s, 1940s and 1950s when the influence of Marxist ideas resulted in what Gates punningly calls the 'race and superstructure' school of black literary criticism, reaching its 'zenith of influence and mystification' with the Black Arts movement in the 1960s.[25]

Gates focuses on two works of African American literary criticism from the 1970s that in different ways fall short of providing a rigorous and comprehensive theory of black American literature. The first is Houston Baker's *Long Black Song: Essays in Black American Literature and Culture* (1972), which asserts that white theories of culture were largely responsible for creating a distinct black American culture that arose to repudiate them. Baker also sees repudiation as characteristic of African American folklore and as a key feature distinguishing black and white American literature. Gates discerns two problems with the book's emphasis on repudiation. First, like African American literature and criticism generally, it focuses on the content of a literary work rather than its structure, technique and rhetoric. Second, by making black American writing dependent on the white theorizing about the culture to which it responds, rather than proposing an autonomous (black) source for African American literature, *Long Black Song* is doomed to go to battle against – and have its argument shaped by – those same assertions of black inferiority. Gates takes issue even more strongly with Addison Gayle's *The Way of the New World* (1975), which elaborates the Black Aesthetic. Once again content dominates over form in this strictly ideological criticism, which regards language and literature as expressions of a black essence. Gates laments Gayle's purely political criticism of writers such as James Baldwin and his literal approach to literature, which cannot do justice to a multivalent text like Ralph Ellison's *Invisible Man*. According to Gates, the major problem with Gayle's theory is its refusal to recognize that literature is a linguistic system and not an expression of external reality: '"Blackness" is not a material object, an absolute, or an event, but a trope; it does not have an "essence" as such but is defined by a network of relations that form a particular aesthetic unity'.[26]

Gates regards rigidly essentialized descriptions of African American literature as dead ends and he proposes a more theoretically rigorous alternative that combines aspects of each approach. After calling for 'attention to black figurative language, to the nature of black narrative forms, to the history and theory of Afro-American literary criticism, to the fundamental relation of form and content, and to the arbitrary relationship between the sign and its referent' as well as to the 'nature of intertextuality, that is, the nonthematic manner by which texts [...] respond to other texts'[27] – calling for attention, in short, to key concerns of traditional mainstream white literary criticism and poststructuralist theory that, prior to the 1980s, had rarely been broached by African American critics – he introduces his theory of Signifyin(g), which is intended to address these deficiencies. Unlike Baker's repudiation theory in which African American literature opposes but is nonetheless dependent on white literature, Gates asserts that Signifyin(g) 'is indigenously black and derives from the Signifying Monkey Tales', which themselves derive from the African trickster Esu-Elegbara.[28] Moreover, instead of being obsessively thematic like Baker's, Gayle's, and black American critical theories generally, 'Signifyin(g) is a uniquely black rhetorical concept, entirely textual or linguistic, by which a second statement or figure repeats, or tropes, or reverses the first', existing only 'in the realm of the intertextual relation'.[29]

Instead of concentrating on the content of African American literary texts that repudiate the assertions of white authors, Signifyin(g) focuses on the rhetorical strategies black American authors use to revise the discourse of the black. A major strength of Gates's theory is its ability to account for literary movements and genres that develop in response to earlier ones. Phillis Wheatley critically signifies on Milton's and Pope's poetry and Kant's and Hume's aesthetic theories, the slave narrators revise not only such sentimental figures as the noble Negro of texts like Aphra Behn's *Oronooko* and the 'Dying Negro' of the English Romantic poets but also the sentimental and the picaresque novel, and the authors associated with the Harlem Renaissance rewrite turn-of-the-century anti-Negro propaganda. The process does not work in only one direction, however, for Gates regards the plantation novel as a counter-discursive response to the slave narrative. Nor do black texts only signify on white ones and vice-versa. Gates describes Zora Neale Hurston's *Their Eyes Were Watching God* as a 'double-voiced' novel that blends African American oral tradition and the free indirect discourse used by European authors such as Gustave Flaubert and Virginia Woolf, and likewise reads Ishmael Reed's *Mumbo Jumbo* as a complex revision of white and black writers, particularly Wright and Ellison. Acknowledging that 'all texts Signify upon other texts' and suggesting that this intertextual, revisionary concept may be useful in studying other literatures, Gates nevertheless regards his notion of Signifyin(g), which graphically represents the linguistic difference between white and black pronunciations of the word 'signifying', as distinctively black because he believes that 'black writers, both explicitly and implicitly, turn to the vernacular in various formal ways to inform their creation of written fictions. To do so, it seems to me, is to ground one's literary practice outside the Western tradition', adding, 'black writers most certainly revise texts in the Western tradition, [yet] they often seek to do so "authentically", with a black difference, a compelling sense of difference based on the black vernacular'.[30]

In *The Signifying Monkey*, Gates makes a useful distinction between motivated and unmotivated Signifyin(g), associating the former with parody and the latter with pastiche. He explains that '[b]y motivation I do not mean to suggest the lack of intention, for parody and pastiche imply intention, ranging from severe critique to acknowledgment and placement within a literary tradition'.[31] Both types of literary signification can appear in a single, 'double-voiced' text: 'Literary echoes, or pastiche, as found in Ellison's *Invisible Man*, of signal tropes found in Emerson, Eliot, Joyce, Crane, or Melville (among others) constitute one mode of Signifyin(g). But so does Ellison's implicit rhetorical critique of the conventions of realism' in the texts of Richard Wright.[32] To 'Signify', then, is to repeat with 'a black difference'.[33] To do so in the context of a negative critique is to engage in motivated Signifyin(g), as '[w]hen Sterling A. Brown riffs on Robert Penn Warren's line from "Pondy Woods" (1945) – "Nigger, your breed ain't metaphysical" – with "Cracker, your breed ain't exegetical"'.[34] To do so without the critique, either as a loving act of bonding, as Gates argues Alice Walker does in *The Color Purple* vis-à-vis Zora Neale Hurston's *Their Eyes Were Watching God*, or 'without sufficient revision', as he asserts Paul Laurence Dunbar does in some of his dialect poems in relation to James Whitcomb Riley, is to practice unmotivated Signifyin(g).[35]

Despite the similarities between postcolonial counter-discourse and Signifyin(g), many postcolonial theorists have chosen not to correlate African American and postcolonial literature. Gates also chooses not to pursue such connections. Although he pinpoints an African origin for Signifyin(g) in Esu-Elegbara and magnanimously offers 'Signifying' (without the 'g' in parenthesis) to 'critics of other literatures [who may] find this theory useful as they attempt to account for the configuration of the texts in their traditions',[36] he chooses to restrict his focus to African American oral and written literature and does not explicitly relate his theory to the literatures of (other) colonized peoples. However, this can and should be done.

The black Atlantic

Like postcolonial theorists and Gates, Paul Gilroy proposes a counter-discourse that is neither completely rhetorical nor rigidly essentialist in his pathbreaking book *The Black Atlantic: Modernity and Double Consciousness* (1993). Engaging with philosophical, sociological, historical, political, as well as literary issues, Gilroy explains that he borrowed the term 'black Atlantic' from African art history and histories of mercantilism because he 'wanted to supplement the diaspora idea with a concept that emphasized the in-between and the intercultural'.[37] Although he rejects the essentialism that characterizes Negritude and Afrocentrism in favour of a plural (but nevertheless historically grounded) diasporic approach, his theory of the black Atlantic is itself a black writing model, albeit a selective one. Gilroy's subtitle refers to W. E. B. Du Bois's famous concept of African American 'twoness'. However, his theoretical model is not fully Pan-African. Associated with Du Bois who played a role at all six of the Pan-African meetings that took place between 1900 and 1945, the term refers to the recognition of a shared heritage and common political interests among people of African descent throughout the world. The black Atlantic, defined as 'a deterritorialised multiplex and anti-national basis for the affinity or "identity of passions" between diverse black populations',[38] is predicated on the experience and/or memory of new world slavery, which links African Americans, black Britons and West Indians of African descent but does not include other colonized peoples, Africans (with the exception of Sierra Leoneans and Liberians, many of whom are descendants of freed slaves), apparently, among them.

The black Atlantic model is valuable for four major reasons. First, Gilroy's brave attempt to rewrite the history of modernity to include slavery and its attendant racist ideology raises important questions that theorists and historians of the modern era have long needed to address. Second, the black

Atlantic accounts for and underscores the many cross-cultural interactions among black American, black British, black West Indian and to a lesser extent African philosophy, music, literature and political discourse that a sizable portion of postcolonial theorists have chosen not to emphasize. Third, Gilroy convincingly argues that transatlantic (particularly European) travel profoundly influenced the political stances of key African American figures. Finally, he effectively employs postcolonial theoretical concepts in his often brilliant readings of the texts of these black Americans.

Residing 'in but not necessarily of the modern, Western world'[39] and thus possessing what Gilroy calls a 'striking doubleness', black Atlantic peoples share more than a collective history of victimization; they have an ambivalent perspective on modernism and Western notions of progress that differs significantly from that of ruling white populations. Seeing slavery and its attendant horrors as connected to rather than divorced from the Enlightenment ideas associated with modernism, black Atlantic peoples constructed what Gilroy calls a 'counterculture of modernity'.[40] Echoing postcolonial theorists, Gilroy regards the black Atlantic experience of displacement and its 'unashamedly hybrid character' as potential sources of strength 'capable of conferring insight' rather than unmitigated detriments 'precipitating anxiety'.[41] However, Gilroy regards movement through space as more significant than place and displacement, a shift that is nicely expressed through his emphasis on 'routes' rather than 'roots'. For this reason, maritime travel and trade figure prominently in his black Atlantic model: 'It should be emphasized that ships were the living means by which the points within th[e] Atlantic world were joined. They were mobile elements that stood for the shifting spaces in between the fixed places that they connected', making them 'cultural and political units', conduits for 'political dissent' and 'cultural production'.[42]

Gilroy not only uses postcolonial theoretical terminology to delimit the black Atlantic world and characterize its counter-discourse to modernism but also applies it to African American literature, to which he consistently turns (rather than the literary productions of black Britons and West Indians of African descent) to illustrate his points. For over two centuries, black Americans have been acutely aware of their peculiar situation, frequently conceiving themselves as the vanguard of the black race, the people most qualified to lead Africa and other members of the diaspora to freedom and prosperity. This is the belief Gilroy identifies as African American exceptionalism, a viewpoint that his emphasis on African American travel and the cross-cultural interactions among black Atlantic peoples works to problematize.⁴³ He remarks in 'Cultural Studies and Ethnic Absolutism' that 'much of the precious political, cultural, and intellectual legacy claimed by Afro-American intellectuals is in fact only partly their "ethnic" property. There are other claims to it which can be based on the structure of the Atlantic diaspora.'⁴⁴ In illustrating his theory in *The Black Atlantic*, Gilroy chooses to concentrate on texts by black American men who traveled across the Atlantic to Europe and sometimes Africa. He pinpoints Du Bois's *The Souls of Black Folk* (1903) as 'the first place where a diasporic global perspective on the politics of racism and its overcoming interrupted the smooth flow of African American exceptionalism'⁴⁵ and asserts that this foreign experience significantly influenced other key African American figures, altering 'their perceptions of America and racial domination'⁴⁶ and often converting them from an exceptionalist position to either a Pan-African or an internationalist outlook.

My intention in this chapter has not been to argue that African American literature should be regarded as postcolonial but rather to contend that certain concepts of postcolonial literary theory can usefully be applied to African American literary studies, as Gilroy's *The Black Atlantic* vividly illustrates and vice versa. Despite differences in scope and objectives among them, postcolonial theory, Signifyin(g), and the black Atlantic offer valuable and far-reaching critical insights. Each uses the concept of a historically and politically grounded counter-discourse to describe the process by which one or more marginalized peoples rewrite the dominant discourse imposed on them. Moreover, each of these three influential, revisionary theories devotes attention to the ambivalent, 'double' or hybrid position marginalized persons occupy within specific societies. Although this experience of two or more cultures can produce anxieties about identity in the subject, it also confers on him or her a unique perspective that can be advantageous in some contexts. Postcolonialism's stress on place and displacement helps to make comprehensible the attractions and repulsions that African Americans, who like black West Indians are spatially, linguistically and culturally displaced from their ancestral home, have felt towards Africans and other people of the diaspora. Signifyin(g)'s ability to account for genres and countergenres greatly assists in understanding the relationship between black American literary productions and mainstream, white literature, particularly the ways in which specific genres have long been used to caricature or otherwise stereotype black characters and the means by which African American writers have responded to this. The black Atlantic model not only explores some of the common ground between postcolonial and African American literary studies, but its stress on movement through space also promotes the discovery of cross-cultural influences among peoples of African descent. Acknowledging the numerous and significant differences between the experiences of blacks in the United States and people in colonized and formerly colonized nations, I continue to believe that African Americanists and postcolonial theorists and critics would do well to consider the histories and cultural productions of black Americans vis-à-vis those of postcolonial persons more comprehensively than they may have done heretofore.

Notes

1. Said, *Culture and Imperialism*, 66, 67.
2. Toni Morrison, *Playing in the Dark: Whiteness and the Literary Imagination* (New York: Vintage, 1993), 211, 212.
3. Bhabha, *The Location of Culture*, 1, 12.
4. Ibid., 12.
5. Ibid., 171
6. See Deborah Madsen, 'The (mis) Uses of Cannibalism in Contemporary Cultural Critique', *Diacritics* 30, no. 1 (1999): 509–17; C. Richard King, 'Hawthorne's Puritans: From Fact to Fiction', *Journal of American Studies* 33, no. 3 (2000): 106–23; A. Singh, P. Schmidt and L. Buell, *Postcolonial Theory and the United States: Race, Ethnicity, and Literature* (Jackson: University Press of Mississippi, 2000).
7. Edward Said, *Orientalism* (New York: Vintage, 1979), 204.
8. Page references here are to the second edition of *Empire*.
9. These are by no means the only subjects discussed in *Empire*, which strives to codify the field by making connections among and imposing order on a wide variety of postcolonial theories.
10. B. Ashcroft, G. Griffiths and H. Tiffin, *The Empire Writes Back*, 2nd edn. (New York: Routledge, 2002), 8.
11. B. Ashcroft, G. Griffiths and H. Tiffin, *The Post-Colonial Studies Reader* (New York: Routledge, 1995), 183.
12. Ashcroft et al., *Empire*, 36.
13. Ibid., 2.
14. Ibid., 15, 56, 4.
15. Ibid., 1.
16. Although a few African American literary critics are included, their selections are devoted to theory and colonial discourse, not black American literature.

17 B. Ashcroft, G. Griffiths and H. Tiffin *Key Concepts in Post-Colonial Studies* (New York: Routledge, 1998), 6.
18 Ashcroft et al., *Empire*, 10.
19 Ibid., 200.
20 Ibid., 202.
21 Ibid., 21.
22 See Senghor's 1966 speech 'Negritude' and Hughes's 'The Twenties', in which the latter claims, 'Had the word *negritude* been in use in Harlem in the twenties, Cullen, as well as McKay, Johnson, Toomer, and I might have been called poets of *negritude*' (p. 32).
23 Helen Tiffin, 'Post-Colonial Literatures and Counter-Discourse', in *The Post-Colonial Studies Reader*, eds. B. Ashcroft, G. Griffiths and H. Tiffin (New York: Routledge, 1995), 96.
24 Although it and the book it responds to (Camus's *L'Étranger*) are written in French, Kamel Daoud's *Meursault, contre-enquête* (2013) is a notable recent example.
25 H. L. Gates, *Figures in Black: Words, Signs, and the "Racial" Self* (New York: Oxford University Press, 1989), 31.
26 Gates, *Figures in Black*, 40. Gates rejects Baker's repudiative theory and the Black Aesthetic, and also, like the authors of *Empire*, Negritude, which he sees as possessing the flaws of both.
27 Ibid., 41.
28 Ibid., 48.
29 Ibid., 49.
30 H. L. Gates, *The Signifying Monkey: A Theory of Afro-American Literary Criticism* (New York: Oxford University Press, 1988) xxiv, xxii.
31 Gates, *The Signifying Monkey*, xxvii.
32 Ibid., xxvii.
33 Ibid., xxii–xxiii.
34 Ibid., 122.
35 Ibid., xxvii, 113, 120.
36 Ibid., xxv.
37 Paul Gilroy, *Small Acts: Thoughts on the Politics of Black Culture* (New York: Serpent's Tail, 1993), 208.
38 Paul Gilroy, 'Route Work: The Black Atlantic and the Politics of Exile', in *The Post-Colonial Question: Common Skies, Divided Horizons*, eds. I. Chambers and L. Curti (New York: Routledge, 1996), 18.
39 Gilroy, *Small Acts*, p. 120
40 Paul Gilroy, *The Black Atlantic: Modernity and Double Consciousness* (Cambridge: Harvard University Press, 1993), 37.
41 Gilroy, 'Route Work', 22.
42 Gilroy, *Black Atlantic*, 16, 17.

43 Despite Gilroy's frequently expressed opposition to African American exceptionalism, his preference for black American literary texts might be seen as perpetuating it. For a discussion of African American exceptionalism, see John Cullen Gruesser, *Black on Black: Twentieth-Century African American Writing about Africa* (Lexington: University of Kentucky Press, 2000), 13–14.
44 Paul Gilroy, 'Cultural Studies and Ethnic Absolutism', in *Cultural Studies*, eds. L. Grossberg, C. Nelson and P. Treichler (New York: Routledge, 1992), 192
45 Gilroy, *Black Atlantic*, 120.
46 Ibid., 17.

18

Faith, Secularism and Community in Womanist Literature from the Neocolonial Caribbean

Dawn Miranda Sherratt-Bado

This chapter examines the relationship between neoimperial state discourses of secular national community and diasporic spiritual conceptions of community in womanist literature from the neocolonial Caribbean.[1] Such a study is pertinent to the current moment when neoimperial state logic continues to equate the Caribbean spiritual practice of obeah with obscurantism and barbarity. As a case study of dialogic tension and resistance, the neocolonial Caribbean is particularly apposite due to the creolization processes that have historically sustained its diverse spiritual communities in the face of state oppression. I will consider the ways in which these discourses intertwine within the narrative framework of texts by contemporary Afro-Caribbean writers Jamaica Kincaid, Gisèle Pineau and Erna Brodber. Namely, I will focus on their respective portrayals of obeah and its derivatives, quimbois and myalism, in the context of the Western realist bildungsroman tradition with which these authors engage.[2] This study traces the formative effects of diasporic belief systems on the developing consciousness of the young Afro-Caribbean woman – a figure who is the focalizing perspective for all three authors. I will begin with Jamaica Kincaid's *Annie John* (1983), a novella set in colonial Antigua during the 1950s and 1960s which depicts the individuation from the mother that occurs during the transition from girlhood into adolescence.[3] Next I will analyse Gisèle Pineau's novel *Exile according to Julia* (1996, translated into English in 2003), an exploration of adolescence that takes place in Paris during the 1960s and 1970s.[4] Finally, I will discuss Erna Brodber's novella *Myal* (1988), a story of young womanhood and collapsed marriage that is set in Jamaica in 1919.[5] All three books are set in the authors' respective birthplaces and centre on the protagonist's journey to womanhood within the context of Caribbean colonialism and its coexisting discourses of faith and secularism.

I argue that as neocolonial subjects, Kincaid, Pineau and Brodber write from womanist authorial perspectives and portray syncretic belief systems as inclusive networks that link Caribbean diasporic communities more effectively than the coercive British Commonwealth or French DOM matrices.[6] Their novels indicate that the superstructural unitary, secular national identity which defines ostensibly 'collective' citizenship within the contemporary neoimperial world order is in fact built upon a base of combined and uneven development.[7] This emphasis on combined and uneven development is allegorically encoded in their chosen framework of the bildungsroman – a genre that narrativizes the *development* of the protagonist from childhood to adulthood. The traditional Western bildungsroman served to consolidate national identity through the experiences and impressions of the young (heteronormative white European male) protagonist. In the novels analysed here, however, Kincaid, Pineau and Brodber focus on the young black woman, a marginalized figure from the island colony. These novels allegorize colonial (under)development into modernity through a womanist lens. During this period of transition, the protagonist suffers from colonial zombification, encoded as a mysterious illness that colonizes her body and restricts its movements. This contributes to her sense of schizophrenia and separation from herself which, Kincaid, Pineau and Brodber suggest, can only be cured by the collective effort of the surrounding diasporic spiritual community. They illustrate that the structuring state discourses of the British Commonwealth and the French DOMs are predicated upon faith in a national collective that promises equal citizenship to its constitutive populations, and yet these linear, universalizing discourses also overwrite racial, gender and religious difference. By focalizing their narratives through young Afro-Caribbean women who are supported by the connective web of a diasporic spiritual community, Kincaid, Pineau and Brodber instantiate womanist writing praxes that manifest within their narratological forms.

Creolized belief systems

Obeah is a syncretic form of folk medicine and religion that originated in the seventeenth century with the cultural creolization of enslaved West Africans in the colonial Caribbean plantation space. In the colonial era, obeah quickly grew beyond a spiritual practice and evolved into an outright political phenomenon. Obeahmen and -women were repeatedly counted among the leaders of slave rebellions as their cultural prestige meant they had extensive influence over their fellow slaves, and consequently they were able to motivate them to direct action against their oppressors. From its very inception obeah functioned as a powerful form of cultural resistance in the Caribbean, and it continues to do so today. Contemporary variations of obeah are still practised among Afro-Caribbean communities in archipelagic and continental Caribbean nation states, including Antigua, Guadeloupe and Jamaica, the respective homelands of authors Jamaica Kincaid, Gisèle Pineau and Erna Brodber.[8] This comes despite the fact that obeah in its various forms was outlawed in both the British and French West Indies by the colonial authorities and it is still illegal throughout the neocolonial Caribbean today. In the French Antilles a portion of the Afro-Caribbean population (mainly in Guadeloupe and Martinique) practise a version of obeah called quimbois that features 'a set of practices related to magic and sorcery with roots in African religiosity'.[9] Myalism (also called myal) is a version of obeah practised solely in Jamaica which 'retains aspects of African-derived religiosity that have been lost in other parts of the Anglophone Caribbean'.[10] Obeah has been demonized by the West since the early colonial period when it was first discursively constructed as a crime by the British and French plantocracies, who used the term indiscriminately to condemn any mystical or mystifying activities by African slaves as 'black magic'. Negative associations with obeah were perpetuated throughout history by both the colonizers and the colonized due to its criminalization by colonial authorities. This effect persists within contemporary neocolonial Caribbean society and much of the current legislation on obeah barely deviates from its original colonial wording.

This study adduces passages from Kincaid, Pineau and Brodber's novels in order to demonstrate that obeah, quimbois and myalism serve as counter-narratives of identificatory development. These de-essentialized discourses resist totalizing (neo)imperial state narratives of secular identity and community. Furthermore, the interweaving of realist exposition and the interjection of the numinous in descriptions of everyday life within these novels reworks and expands the bildungsroman through dialogic interdiscursivity. This is a formal approach whereby an utterance is irreducible to a singular, received form of representation. In interviews these authors have confirmed that obeah, quimbois and myalism are ordinary aspects of life in the Caribbean – modes of being-in-the world that blur the distinction between the sacred and the secular. Their oeuvres feature creolized spiritual practices prominently, portraying them as diasporic epistemes that challenge Western conceptions of lived reality. By making the young Afro-Caribbean woman the focalizing perspective of the novel and by moving obeah, quimbois and myalism to the centre of their narratives, these authors craft new, womanist forms of the bildungsroman, thereby displacing recolonizing imperialist models.

Obeah and the maternal matrix in *Annie John*

Kincaid's *Annie John* is an autofictional tale of a young Antiguan girl's journey from girlhood to adolescence. During this transition the eponymous protagonist suffers from a period of infirmity, the cause of which remains unidentified in the text. Since Annie is also the narrator of the novella, we are inside her consciousness as she endures a mysterious, prolonged bout of illness. Her actual malady and treatment intertwine with her muddled thoughts in an abstract, dreamlike vision. The majority of critics tend to link this incident to the onset of puberty and individuation from the mother since when Annie recovers, she finds that she has grown taller and possesses a more independent demeanour. Annie falls ill 'during the rains', as Selwyn Cudjoe puts it, which is typically a period of growth for the island's vegetation.[11] It is possible that Kincaid uses an overt ecological metaphor here to connote a time of 'budding' young womanhood. Annie's enigmatic condition coincides with a period called 'The Long Rain', as Kincaid entitles this chapter of the book.[12] The chapter's title alludes to the Antiguan climate, which follows a cycle that alternates between the wet and dry seasons, the rainy season lasting for months at a time before returning to a state of drought. Then again, I would argue that it is overly facile and rather reductive to conjecture that Kincaid describes this event in such an incredibly complex, multivalent manner simply to illustrate the confusion of pubescence.

Kincaid portrays this occurrence in a highly maternally inflected passage in which Annie's worried mother, Mrs John, summons Annie's maternal grandmother Ma Chess – a Carib obeahwoman from Dominica – to aid in rehabilitating Annie using traditional obeah methods, along with (grand) motherly care.[13] Initially, Ma Chess suggests that Annie's mother call on the help of Ma Jolie, a local obeahwoman. At first Mrs. John declines, knowing that Annie's stepfather Alexander, a devout Anglican, would object. Instead she opts to take Annie into town to see the doctor, an Englishman named Dr Stephens. However, upon examination, Annie states that 'he could find nothing much wrong, except that he thought I might be a little run-down. My mother asked herself out loud, "How could that be?"'[14] Annie is soon bedridden, and her condition worsens.

Her mother sends for Ma Jolie, who performs several obeah rituals and produces herbal tinctures which she administers to Annie. In spite of this, Annie's health continues to deteriorate. She recounts, 'I don't know how long it was after this that Ma Chess appeared. I heard my mother and father wonder to each other how she came to us, for she appeared on a day when the steamer was not due, and so they didn't go to meet her at the jetty.'[15] Ma Chess suddenly materializes at the John residence, all the way from Dominica and completely unannounced, and Kincaid never reveals her mode of transportation. As a result, she instantly enshrouds the character of Ma Chess in an air of mystery and enchantment, and illustrates her connection to the world of spirits. Annie's encounter with her grandmother is a heightened sensory experience as if, like a new born, she is discovering her maternal figure for the first time. She notes, 'When Ma Chess leaned over me, she smelled of many different things, all of them more abominable than the black sachet Ma Jolie had pinned to my nightie. Whatever Ma Jolie knew, my grandmother knew at least ten times more. How she regretted that my mother didn't take more of an interest in obeah things.'[16] Ma Chess wishes that Annie's mother would follow in her footsteps and become an obeahwoman, but she does not share the same level of devotion to its practice. Consequently, Mrs. John is unequipped to assist in Annie's recuperation as it requires expertise in obeah and is a task which Ma Chess must undertake alone.

Annie's grandmother steps into the maternal role, as Mrs. John is forced to defer to her greater knowledge of obeah and can only stand aside and watch helplessly. In an incredibly poignant and carefully nuanced passage, Ma Chess seemingly regestates the frightened and delirious Annie, who recalls:

> Sometimes at night, when I would feel that I was all locked up in the warm falling soot and could not find my way out, Ma Chess would come into my bed with me and stay until I was myself – whatever that had come to be by then – again. I would lie on my side, curled up like a little comma, and Ma Chess would lie next to me, curled up like a bigger comma, into which I fit.[17]

Annie coils into the foetal position in moments of intense suffering and dread, and Ma Chess instinctively re-envelops her in a womb of (grand) motherly nurturing and love. It is significant that her protective, swathing presence restores her granddaughter to her essential self – as Annie states, Ma Chess maintains a state of amniotic cohesion with her 'until I was myself – whatever that had come to be by then – again'.[18] When read more meticulously, this scene reveals its intricate political undertones. I agree that it can be read as limning Annie's individuation from her mother, as the majority of critics propound, but I would also venture that Kincaid portrays this event on a decidedly more politically charged, even polemical, scale. Correspondingly, Mrs. John can be read as a Westernized half-Carib, half-African woman who functions as an allegorical sign for the colonial (mother) island. In this scenario, the colonial mother-island is incapable of sufficiently caring for its children, the contemporary Antiguan population, whom Annie John embodies via her multiracial heritage. Furthermore, Annie John shares the exact same name as her mother and thus represents the potential for a newly embodied version of the Caribbean populace – one which is closer to its precolonial roots. As a figuration of the Caribbean child Annie must therefore return to the primal scene of her formation, which is the site of her originary culture(s). Kincaid links Ma Chess to autochthonous Caribbean culture and ancient African culture, respectively, as she is both a full-blooded Caribbean indigene and an authority on obeah. Hence, the author identifies Ma Chess as the natural locus for this allegorical rebirthing process. Here Kincaid simultaneously associates obeah with maternality and metonymizes the wisdoms of originary mother culture(s) which predate those of Western medicine and scientific knowledge in the sagacious, instinctual character of Ma Chess. Additionally, obeahwomen are traditionally given the affectionate title 'Ma', a term of endearment conventionally used for grandmothers in Caribbean culture, and Kincaid infers the existence of an entire motherly matrix of obeahwomen such as Ma Chess and Ma Jolie who unite in order to preserve the well-being of their community.

The author reaffirms the rhizomic structure of this network by not only demonstrating its inter-island marine root/route system, but also its interethnic composition, as women from the Carib community such as Ma Chess also adopt African-derived obeah customs, which complement native Caribbean spiritual practices such as animism and shamanism. This serves to reinforce the creolized constitution of obeah, in addition to the shared cultural history of the African slaves and the indigenous Caribbean peoples. Kincaid alludes to their shared oppression as cultural groups which were subjugated and enslaved by the European invaders; but at the same time, she also elucidates a positive outcome of this painful history in the form of obeah. For example, Nicolas Saunders remarks:

> It was one of many ironic coincidences of Caribbean history that the great number of enslaved African peoples transported across the Atlantic to work on Caribbean plantations possessed animistic religions similar to those of the Taíno and Carib. When African slaves escaped to the mountains or otherwise came into contact with remaining Amerindians, their worldview was probably a point of spiritual connection, despite different languages, cultures, appearances, and traditions.[19]

Kincaid also highlights obeah as a means of cultural resistance to Western colonialism and its patriarchal hegemony by juxtaposing maternal obeah healing practices with patriarchal Western medicine. This is evident when Annie says of Ma Jolie, 'She gave my mother some little vials filled with fluids to rub on me at different times of the day. My mother placed them on my shelf, right alongside the bottles of compounds of vitamins that Dr. Stephens had prescribed.'[20] Kincaid employs symbolic imagery in this scene, metaphorizing an ideological comparison via the physical placement of the two healing methods beside each other on the shelf. This sight proves greatly displeasing to Annie's stepfather, whom she identifies as her father figure. She states, 'When my father came in to see me, he looked at all my medicines – Dr. Stephens's and Ma Jolie's – lined up side by side and screwed up his face, the way he did when he didn't like what he saw.'[21] Accordingly, Kincaid aligns Western medicine with the anglicized male figures in the novel – the English physician Dr Stephens, and Annie's Afro-Caribbean stepfather Alexander, who is a staunch Anglican. The fact that Annie identifies her stepfather as her actual father can be seen as alluding to the intrusion of the colonial Father and attendant paternalistic, colonizing discourses upon non-Western domesticity. Moreover, Kincaid implicitly links Alexander John's Anglicanism with his belief in Western science, thereby underscoring the connection between Western religion and medicine as twinned hegemonic ideologies that impinge on non-Western belief systems. Kincaid seems to suggest that although Western and creolized ideologies coexist within the British West Indies, they do not do so harmoniously. The same can be said for the frictile comingling of quimbois and Western ideologies in the French Antillean context, as Pineau demonstrates in her novel.

Quimbois and the Émigrée in *Exile according to Julia*

Originally published in French as *L'Exil selon Julia* (1996) and translated into English in 2003, *Exile according to Julia* is a semi-autobiographical tale based on Gisèle Pineau's doubly diasporic experience growing up in cultural exile in France during the 1950s and 1960s. Her family was part of the massive transplantation of Caribbean people who migrated to European metropoles following the Second World War in search of work and better prospects for their children. Pineau's father enlisted in the French army and moved their family from Guadeloupe to Paris, where she was born and raised. She did not visit her family's homeland until 1970, when as an adolescent she joined them on their return to the French Antilles. Pineau explains how she reimagines her grandmother's traumatic displacement:

> I tell the story of my grandmother, the six years she spent in France. [...] I lived in France an exile by proxy, at my grandmother's side because it was she who really was an exile. She had not chosen to come to France. She came because my father wanted to save her from the brutality of her husband who beat her [...] I was searching for a hospitable country, and I recognized this country in my grandmother's stories. I longed to belong to this country, to say to myself: 'Yes, I am from Guadeloupe, me too.'[22]

Exile according to Julia tells the tale of the narrator Marie and, concurrently, that of her grandmother Julia.[23] In Pineau's book the family absconds with Marie's grandmother to Paris in order to rescue her from her abusive husband Asdrubal, whom they call 'The Torturer'. The family address Marie's grandmother affectionately in Creole as *Man Ya* (short for 'Ma Julia'), and she comes to serve as an important cultural link to Guadeloupe since Marie's parents have all but abandoned their Creole legacy in an attempt at assimilation.

In her novel Pineau examines the exilic predicament of the doubly displaced Caribbean subject in the imperial centre. Man Ya suffers from a kind of zombification that her family terms '*la maladie de l'exil*', which translates as 'exile sickness'.[24] However, as Pineau indicates, Marie also experiences this psychological condition at a profound level. She is affected by her exilic position more deeply than her family, who repress their feelings of cultural estrangement and even make light of Man Ya's suffering. When they snatch Man Ya from Guadeloupe and bring her to Paris, she exclaims, 'These children look on me as a strange creature. The whole blessed day they speak with RRRR in their mouth. I don't understand their language. And there are only whites in France. And I don't understand why blacks go to lose themselves in that country.'[25] She feels that her family have 'lost themselves' and their sense of identity in moving to France. However, she soon comprehends that they can rediscover their Creole inheritance by hearing stories of home and through her quimbois teachings. This diasporic spiritual practice enables her to 'stand upright in this land', thereby taking a step in colonizing the metropole.[26] In so doing, she reasserts diasporic presence while working to disembed monolithic Western presence from a parcel of the metropolitan landscape.

Through her vivid descriptions of the island world of quimbois, Man Ya's storytelling infuses her grandchildren with vital knowledge of their homeland and thus, their heritage. Her actions serve as an example to Marie's mother Daisy, who finally tells the children about her hometown. Daisy exclaims, 'Routhiers is a place... how can I describe it... Woods! At the foot of the Carbet Falls. Interminable mist and drizzle. Rich black earth. You throw a seed, and from it grows a forest that holds wicked zombies and witches' magic.'[27] Man Ya realizes that such tales of supernatural creatures frighten the children and she reassures them with stories of her garden in Guadeloupe, which she limns as a safe haven that will protect them from malignant beings and spells. Marie recounts:

> But all at once, she takes us back to her garden, and we escape from the bad men. Even more than her house in Routhiers, she misses her garden. She pictures it for us, a wonderful place where all kinds of trees, plants and flowers grow in abundance in an overwhelming green, an almost miraculous

verdure, dappled here and there with a silver light that shines nowhere else but in the heart of Routhiers. [...] We see it all through her eyes and believe her as one believes in Heaven, wavering endlessly between suspicion and deep conviction.[28]

Man Ya's imaging of her garden allows her grandchildren to feel transported to another world as they are captivated by her storytelling, which enlivens every contour of the landscape. The intensity of her sentiment when she reminisces about her garden almost renders the Guadeloupean environment palpable for her grandchildren, despite the fact that they have never seen it. The children come to know the whole of the island terrain as well as its flora and fauna through imagined sensory experience. In hearing her stories, these terrestrial features become so utterly intertwined with Man Ya's identity that the children conflate the two within their psyche and begin to view her as an embodiment of the Guadeloupean hinterland. Marie describes her grandmother as a kind of sorceress who is able to 'conjure up' Guadeloupean topography with her very words as though she is casting a spell. Her storytelling mesmerizes the children, and Man Ya reveals herself as a *quimboiseuse*, or obeahwoman. Indeed, at other points in the novel she tells the children how her garden in Guadeloupe not only 'gives her food' but also 'herbs' which she uses for quimbois practices.[29] She pledges to teach them 'the herbs for healing, the medicine-roots, the blessed barks', to show them 'the secrets of bushes' and how 'to recognize the jagged edges, the lacy shapes and the scents, the feel and the right use'.[30] Like the obeahwomen in Kincaid's text, Man Ya is a compelling maternal figure whose knowledge of quimbois spiritual practices brings healing to the family and draws them closer together, reinforcing the bonds of diasporic community.

Myalism and Grove Town in *Myal*

Erna Brodber's novella *Myal* is set in 1919 – a significant moment in Jamaican history as it marks the year when the West India regiment returned from fighting on behalf of Great Britain in the First World War. Waves of labour strikes and riots erupted throughout the island but were crushed quickly by colonial forces. These circumstances prompted various Jamaican independence movements and fostered a renewed sense of solidarity among the diverse local population. Part of the novel takes place in Morant Bay, a setting which evokes this milieu of political foment as it alludes to the 1865 Morant Bay Rebellion, a major turning point in Jamaican history. As Brodber writes, 'The half has never been told', 'there was need for action'.[31] She portrays this reawakening into political consciousness through the experiences of the protagonist, Ella O'Grady, a young woman from Grove Town whose mixed racial ancestry reflects the creolized cultural heritage of Jamaica. The daughter of an Irish policeman and his Afro-Jamaican maid, Ella is a light-skinned, ginger-haired woman who ascends from poverty to the mulatto middle class. Nevertheless, in spite of her privileged social status, Brodber alerts us to Ella's paralysing zombification from the outset. Ella's illness is the narrative locus – much like Annie John's affliction and Marie's *maladie de l'exil*. Accordingly, *Myal* opens with the proclamation:

> Curing the body is nothing. Touching the peace of those she must touch and those who must touch her is the hard part. And you can't do that unless you can touch their spirits. My people woulda humble them spirit and let me reach them: but this kind of people,…spirit too sekkle pekkle. Best let them keep their distance after all.[32]

Here Brodber indicates that the only way to cure colonial zombification and schizophrenia is by touching the spirit of not only the individual, but also that of the surrounding community. As Shalini Puri argues, 'in *Myal*, resistance and opposition are *dispersed* through a web of relations amongst a wide social cast, and are understood in terms of the repositioning of [the] individual […] in relationship to the community'.[33] Internal colonialism separates Ella from herself and from her diasporic web of relations in a violent schizophrenic splitting. In order to heal she must renounce internalized racist and classist views and acknowledge the creolized Grove Town community as her own.

Ella's phenotypic features enable her to pass as white and thereby move within different social spheres. Mrs. Brassington, wife of the local Methodist parson, takes her on as a ward. She removes Ella from the bush shanty that she shares with her mother and ushers her into the Brassington home in the gentrified town of Morant Bay. Mrs. Brassington offers to send Ella to America as the companion of her friend Mrs. Burns, a wealthy white woman, so that she can get away from Grove Town completely and among high society. However, Ella's movements are circumscribed due to her position as a mixed-race subject in America. The upper echelons of white society that surround her exert a recolonizing influence which restricts her bodily movements to the point where she resembles an automaton. Brodber describes Ella as 'Mrs. Burns' sidekick, her little dolly baby and she dressed her in warm finery. So it was only on the odd occasion that she got a fleeting sensation of something lost – the yellow fire of the sun in [...] Jamaica'.[34] The longer that she is in America, Ella's sense of affinity with her homeland grows increasingly dim while her zombification intensifies. Soon after her arrival, Ella marries the bourgeois Irish-American Selwyn Langley, who takes over the role of puppeteer from Mrs. Burns. He regards Ella as 'a doll', 'a marvellously sculpted work waiting for the animator'.[35] Here and elsewhere throughout the text Brodber emphasizes that colonized identity is a zombified performance. Selwyn uses Ella as inspiration and native informant for a 'coon show' that he develops called *Caribbean Days and Nights* and he exhibits 'a neocolonial interest in her stories'.[36] She tells Selwyn about her encounter with Ole African, the local obeahman in Grove Town, and discloses that when Mrs. Brassington asks whether Ella knows him, she denies it. In doing so, Ella not only disavows her fellow Afro-Caribbean people, but also their spiritual beliefs. Correspondingly, Brodber writes that 'Ella had not told the half. She did not know it'.[37] Selwyn's exploitative neocolonial influence separates Ella from herself even more incisively. As a result, she observes passively that 'Her story seemed to her now to have some part missing but she dismissed the thought and pressed on'.[38] In order to assimilate in America and thereby please her new husband, Ella must disavow her Afro-Caribbean heritage while they are in public and claim only the Irish half. Ella ponders, 'if he wanted her to be full Irish girl, well what of it?'[39] However, her 'one teeny little lie' festers within her and becomes calcified in the form of a tumour that leeches onto her body.[40]

Ultimately, Ella must escape her disastrous marriage and return to Grove Town in order to reclaim her diasporic community so that they may heal her. Brodber recounts, 'They all knew that no matter what their age or state that to get that grey mass out of that rigid, staring, silent female would take seven days and that she should be there until the end of the cure.'[41] The creolized population of Grove Town congregates in a community-wide effort to cure Ella. They achieve this through a myal dance ceremony, which is 'organized around rituals designed to prevent duppies from doing harm, helping people recover their lost shadows [...], and generally to propitiate the world of spirits'.[42] The recovery of lost shadows entails reversing acts of 'spirit thievery' – in other words, curing zombification.[43]

The communal dance also draws Ella and the natural environment into its powerful rhythm:

> The shaking did not cease but became a mighty hissing electric storm as she infected each little body with her tremors and each transmitted the infection to the other. Shook, shimmy and shake in the whole colony [...] as they electrified the sap in the base of the mango tree so that its branches reared their heads and kicked their feet like so many wild jennies with no stockings on their can-can.[44]

Myalism is a spiritual 'group practice' which extends here to 'the whole colony' – including the Jamaican landscape itself – in a double movement of interanimation and interillumination that galvanizes its participants into spiritual action and clarity.[45] The inclusion of the mango tree suggests that myalism is a naturalized phenomenon and that such animistic practice is *rooted* within Jamaican soil. Once freed by the naturalized performance of the myal dance, Ella comprehends that she no longer has to perform a (re)colonized identity for Selwyn and his American audience. Nor does she have to perform the role of compliant British subject, and at the novel's end she resolves to become a teacher in order to subvert the colonial education system from the inside.

Conclusion

Kincaid, Pineau and Brodber scrutinize early-to mid-twentieth-century Caribbean colonial relations from the contemporary perspective of the neocolonial subject. They enact a textualization of diasporic resistance via their respective portrayals of obeah, quimbois and myalism. The discursive reification of obeah within colonial and contemporary administrative documents as a 'superstition' or a 'crime' is a process in which diasporic identity and autonomy become elided – because they are legal documents, these written colonial accounts become the 'official', thus authoritative, accounts of obeah and its practitioners. Nonetheless, this delegitimization of obeah through the written (colonial) sign can also be vitiated through decolonial writing practices. Kincaid, Pineau and Brodber accomplish this through their womanist writing, which restores cultural legitimacy to obeah and its derivatives as valid epistemologies. They disrupt the recolonizing forces which impinge upon the black female body and mind by abrogating Western discursive constructions of obeah and reinstating its cultural validity.

Rather than placing their faith in the (neo)imperial state's universalizing, secular discourses of identity and community, these writers give primacy to diasporic epistemologies. Kincaid, Pineau and Brodber mobilize the bildungsroman as a tool of cultural decolonization via the process of resignification. Their womanist narratives depict obeah, quimbois and myalism as discursive forms which not only accommodate black female subjectivity but which also foster creolized Caribbean spiritual communities. This diasporic web of relations crisscrosses the Caribbean and transcends state boundaries, moving beyond the constrictive networks of the British Commonwealth and the French DOMs. They highlight the inextricable links that exist between obeah and Caribbean culture, which serve to strengthen not only familial ties but also more macroscopic affiliative networks, especially between multiple generations of the creolized diasporic community. These authors portray obeah as a vital element of the collective archipelagic unconscious that undergirds communal relationships and acts as an important structuring force within Caribbean society across social, linguistic and geographic lines. They demonstrate that obeah is a form of lived resistance by which the lived Caribbean body recovers its autonomy in order to restore the health of the (neo)colonial *body politic*.

Notes

1. Alice Walker defines womanist as 'a black feminist or a feminist of color', or a woman 'committed to [the] survival and wholeness of entire people, male *and* female. Not a separatist' (*In Search of Our Mothers' Gardens: Womanist Prose* (San Diego: Harcourt Brace Jovanovich, 1983), xi). A womanist writerly perspective is one of inclusiveness, but which centres on the lived experiences of women of colour.
2. I use 'obeah' alternately to denote this particular practice in its strictest sense and as a comprehensive term that includes derivatives of obeah such as quimbois and myalism.
3. Jamaica Kincaid, *Annie John* (New York: Farrar, Straus and Giroux, 1983).
4. Gisèle Pineau, *L'Exil selon Julia* (Paris: Éditions Stock, 1996). Pineau, *Exile According to Julia*, Trans. Betty Wilson (Charlottesville: University of Virginia Press, 2003).
5. Erna Brodber, *Myal* (London: New Beacon Books, 1988).

6   DOM is an acronym for *Départements d'Outre Mer*, or 'Overseas Departments'.
7   'Combined and uneven development' is a Marxist concept that theorizes capitalist modes of production as uneven processes whereby the capitalist state expands and accumulates wealth while the exploited territory experiences impoverishment and underdevelopment.
8   Kincaid has a firsthand connection to the world of obeah in that her mother practised obeah rituals and healing treatments at home and also consulted an obeahwoman regularly.
9   Margarite Fernández-Olmos and Lizabeth Paravisini-Gebert, *Creole Religions of the Caribbean: An Introduction from Vodou and Santería to Obeah and Espiritismo* (New York: New York University Press, 2011), 179.
10 Fernández-Olmos and Paravisini-Gebert, *Creole Religions*, 171.
11 Selwyn J. Cudjoe and Jamaica Kincaid, 'Jamaica Kincaid and the Modernist Project: An Interview', *Callaloo* 39 (Spring 1989), 406.
12 Kincaid, *Annie John*, 108.
13 The Caribs are indigenous Americans who inhabit parts of the continental and archipelagic Caribbean.
14 Kincaid, *Annie John*, 110.
15 Ibid., 123.
16 Ibid.
17 Ibid., 125–26.
18 Ibid.
19 Nicolas J. Saunders, *The Peoples of the Caribbean: An Encyclopedia of Archaeology and Traditional Culture* (Santa Barbara: ABC-CLIO, 2005), 250.
20 Kincaid, *Annie John*, 117.
21 Ibid.
22 Pineau, *Exile*, 173.
23 Marie, the name of the narrator, is also Pineau's middle name.
24 Pineau, *L'Exil*, 129.
25 Pineau, *Exile*, 44, 45. Man Ya cannot speak French and only knows Guadeloupean Creole French; she has difficulty understanding when her family members speak Creole, as they pronounce the rhotic 'r' sound rather than the typical non-rhotic Creole pronunciation, more like a 'w' sound.
26 Pineau, *Exile*, 44, 45.
27 Ibid., 12.
28 Ibid., 8.
29 Ibid., 104.
30 Ibid., 124.
31 Brodber, *Myal*, 35.

32 Ibid., 1.
33 Shalini Puri, *The Caribbean Postcolonial: Social Equality, Post-Nationalism, and Cultural Hybridity* (New York: Palgrave, 2004), 146.
34 Brodber, *Myal*, 46.
35 Ibid., 46, 47.
36 Ibid., 80; Puri, 'Marvelous Realism', 156.
37 Brodber, *Myal*, 56.
38 Ibid.
39 Ibid., 43.
40 Ibid.
41 Ibid., 1.
42 Fernandez-Olmos and Paravisini-Gebert, *Creole Religions*, 174. 'Duppy' is Jamaican Creole for 'ghost' or 'spirit'.
43 Brodber, *Myal*, 98.
44 Ibid., 2.
45 Fernandez-Olmos and Paravisini-Gebert, *Creole Religions*, 173; Brodber, *Myal*, 2.

19

Secularism in India: Principles and Policies

Manav Ratti

What are the ways in which religion, nationalism and the state intersect with one another – with both successes and challenges – within postcolonial nations? This chapter explores this question by focusing on India, and in particular on India's state policy of secularism. Indian secularism is a policy that aims to have equal respect for all religions and religious groups for the sake of democracy, minority rights, equality of citizenship and for building a sense of nationhood. This chapter presents the distinctive features of secularism in India, the criticisms this secularism has faced and events in India that have posed a challenge to secularism. India offers a fascinating case for this study, for it is the world's largest democracy, it is the second most populated country in the world and it has a high percentage of religious believers. Peoples following every major world religion – from Christianity to Judaism to Islam – are found in India, with several of these religions having been founded, and continuing to flourish, in the country. India has been the birthplace of Buddhism, Hinduism, Jainism and Sikhism, and contains the world's largest populations of the last three religions, with Hindusim as the majority religion, followed by approximately 80 per cent of Indians. India has also been colonized for centuries by Western nations – including the UK, France and Portugal – and has therefore experienced, and continues to experience, the successes and perils of building a sense of nationhood. India's period of postcolonial independence, achieved from British rule in 1947, is relatively short when compared with the several centuries of colonization it has endured. Given the above history and influence of religion and politics, how has India addressed, or not addressed, the relations between religion and the state?

What is Indian secularism?

There are many varieties of secularism, relating to diverse fields such as philosophy, physics, religion, theology and politics. In this chapter, I will be focusing on the political form of secularism, but would first like to offer definitions of the common understandings of secularism, those in relation to religion. In a religious sense, the word 'secular' is defined by the *Oxford English Dictionary* (*OED*) as follows: 'of or belonging to the present or visible world as distinguished from the eternal or spiritual world; temporal, worldly'. Similar to this definition is the following sense of the 'secular' from the *OED*: 'belonging to the world and its affairs as distinguished from the church and religion; civil, lay, temporal. Chiefly used as a negative term, with the meaning non-ecclesiastical, non-religious, or non-sacred'. From these two senses, the OED offers the following philosophical definition of *secularism*: 'The doctrine that morality should be based solely on regard to the well-being of mankind in the present life, to the exclusion of all considerations drawn from belief in God or in a future state'. What broadly emerges from these definitions is an opposition between the secular and secularism as against religion and spirituality, that is, an opposition between the observable, material world and any spiritual, transcendental worlds or ideas. This opposition between the sacred and the secular develops within a Christian framework, informing the development and success of secularism as a form of politics in the West.[1] In India, with the majority of its religious systems, traditions and contexts different from the West, the development and adoption of secularism as a politics has had to adapt to these specific contextual features of Indian societies. The philosophical distinction between secularism and religion is relevant for the idea of secularism within politics because the special responsibilities and powers of political secularism are manifest in its relations with religion and religious groups.

In India, the political variety of secularism can be known as state secularism, constitutional secularism or simply secularism (or Indian secularism). For the purposes of this chapter, I will use secularism and Indian secularism. In the Indian context, therefore, *secularism* concerns itself with the laws and practices of the state. From the domain of politics, the *state* is: 'a legally formalized entity having accepted jurisdiction over a territory and a population and the capacity, within that territory, to make rules binding on the whole population and to enforce those rules through generally accepted legal procedures and applications of force'.[2] The state thus emerges as a political organization that has a centralized government, one which acts through enforcements such as laws, the police and the military.

Indian secularism has been influenced by the long history of European colonization in India, and thus Western influence on India, for state secularism was first developed in Western nations. From British colonization to political independence in 1947, India was influenced by Western ideas of the nation as a secular institution, an idea inaugurated by the French Revolution. To understand India's relation with political secularism, it is therefore important to consider colonization, the forms of anticolonial struggle, and finally postcolonial nationalism in India. The East India Company was granted royal charter by Queen Elizabeth I in 1600, and in 1608 the first British ships reached India. The Company would have increasing political and military rule in India, known as Company Rule, which was formalized in 1757 and lasted until 1858. In 1857, Indians launched a mass-scale military resistance, the Mutiny of 1857, but in which the British ultimately prevailed. However, such a large military effort by the Indians led the British to strengthen their presence in India. 1858 thus saw the dissolution of the East India Trading Company and the British government taking direct rule of India, signalling the start of what is known as the British Raj, Direct Rule or Crown Rule. This period lasted until 1947, when India achieved political independence.

The relation between British colonialism and Hinduism as the religion of the majority bears some description, for it gives insight into some of the politics of state secularism in contemporary India. The British, encountering the diversities of beliefs and practices within Hinduism, sought to organize these beliefs and practices into the concept of 'religion', for the purposes of governance and reform. The British colonial enterprise thus sought governance for the purpose of regulation, and intended reform as part of a modernizing, enlightening project based on Christianity as the model of religion.[3] This construction of Hinduism as 'religion' served to emphasize difference, and even opposition, between Hinduism and Islam, in the process legitimizing British rule. But it was this same consolidated and oppositional 'Hinduism' that would go on to spur a Hinduism that was anticolonial and nationalistic. As Ashis Nandy has argued,

Over the last 80 years, most ideologues of Hindu nationalism have neither come from orthodox Hinduism nor have they flaunted their orthodoxy the way Gandhi did, by proclaiming himself a Sanatani Hindu. They have proudly affirmed their links with the 19th-century Hindu reform movements, which they see as analogues of a masculine Protestantism, cleaning up a degraded, distorted faith to make it fit the needs of a national state.[4]

It was this amplified notion of 'Hinduism' (and its antagonized religious 'others', especially Islam) that in part fuelled the Partition of India is 1947. The premise of Partition is the Two-Nation theory, that different religious groups require physically separate national spaces. Partition, however, is one of the largest forced displacements of peoples in history. It resulted in approximately a million deaths and the displacement of approximately twelve million peoples.[5] This violence was fuelled in part by a British policy of divide and rule, by antagonism between Hindus and Muslims, as well as antagonism between other religious groups, such as between Hindus and Sikhs, and Sikhs and Muslims. Partition continues to have devastating consequences for India and Pakistan. Since 1947, the two countries have gone to war four times and have had numerous border disputes and military standoffs. The cultural memories of Partition continue in part to fuel tensions among some Hindus, Muslims and Sikhs in India and Pakistan.

The idea of secularism was especially advocated by India's first prime minister after independence, Jawaharlal Nehru (1889–1964). Nehru was a non-believer whose commitment to secularism was shaped by his studies in the UK at Cambridge University, where he had studied natural sciences. He was so closely identified with secularism that it even came to be addressed as Nehruvian secularism. In 1945, he asserted that 'the future government of India must be secular in the sense that government will not associate itself with any religious faith but will give freedom to all religious functions'.[6] Another leader committed to secularism was Mohandas Karamchand Gandhi, who insisted on a sense of 'Indianness' that should exist independently of any religious identities, and which should inspire ordinary people to identify with that Indianness, as an antidote to sectarianism, particularly between Hindus and Muslims, especially in the wake of Partition. Gandhi stated that 'nationalism is greater than sectarianism [...]. In that sense we are Indians first and Hindus, Mussalmans, Parsis, Christians after'.[7]

Although India at independence in 1947 adopted the ideals and practices of state secularism, the word 'secularism' officially appeared in the Indian constitution in 1976, as part of the 42nd Amendment to the constitution.

This amendment changed the Preamble from describing India as a 'sovereign democratic republic' to a 'sovereign socialist secular democratic republic'. What emerges from the above narrative is that as a way to build a cohesive and strong sense of nationhood for India, the nation was founded as a secular nation, meaning that the state would not identify with any religion, would consider all religions to be equal, and in the process would affirm the values of liberalism (freedom of belief) and equality (of all religions and all peoples), including equality of citizenship (the peoples becoming 'citizens' of the 'nation'). Thus secularism in India has had a close relationship with nationalism, so that the values and ideals of secularism – liberalism and equality – linked nationalism with the ideals of democracy, even to the degree that democracy can be argued to *be* nationalism for India.[8]

The ideals of liberalism and equality also shape features of India's state secularism that make it unique and different from state secularism in Western nations. In Western nations such as France and the United States, state secularism is premised on a *mutual exclusion* or separation model (also called the *wall of separation* model), that the state and religion should be kept separate, that one should not influence or interfere with the other. Western state secularism upholds the equality of all religions, as well as the principle of *nonestablishment*, that is, not establishing any religion as the official state religion. Indian state secularism was modelled on the constitutions of France and the United States, and is similar to these constitutions in having no official state religion and in its affirmation of the equality of all religions.

There are key differences between Western and Indian state secularism, and to appreciate these differences it is necessary to understand everyday culture and religion in India. Rajeev Bhargava accounts for four main features of the cultural contexts that shape Indian state secularism.[9] First, there is an enormous diversity of religious beliefs and practices (to say nothing of the large overall population), which can produce not only exemplary coexistence but also conflict within and between religious groups. Second, there is a special emphasis on communities, since religious identity across Indian religions, especially Hinduism, is defined and expressed through social practice. Third, given a state that values liberalism and equality, there is a need to reform some oppressive religious practices that create inequality and deny freedoms. Finally, and specifically for Hinduism, there is the need for the state to introduce reforms that promote equality and freedom because Hinduism has no central organized institution, and thus peoples cannot rely only on reforms from within the religion.

As a result of the above cultural factors, Indian secularism has developed several distinctive features, each overlapping with one another. The first is the recognition of group rights for religious communities.[10] This includes the Indian constitution's allowing different laws called 'personal laws' to prevail for different religious communities, including for Muslims, Parsis, Christians and Hindus (the Hindu Marriage Act of 1955 also applies to Buddhists, Sikhs and Jains, and those who are not Muslims, Christians, Parsis or Jews). These personal laws apply to the domain of family life, such as marriage, adoption, maintenance and inheritance. The state envisages personal laws as being a secular concession, in that the state gives each religious community the freedom to follow their own religious laws. This concept of group rights informs the value of liberalism, so that liberalism does not only mean individual rights based on individual freedom of belief and practice, but freedom as well at the level of group rights, namely, the rights of religious groups. Secondly, group-specific or community-specific rights for religious minorities allows for group-differentiated citizenship (i.e. citizenship based on identification with a particular religious group), which does not necessarily contravene the value of equality of citizenship for all citizens.[11] Finally, part of what Rajeev Bhargava defines as the distinctiveness of Indian secularism is the state's having a *principled distance* from all religions. This does not mean that the state does not view all religions as equal. Instead, it means that the state can intervene to different degrees with different religions in order to create an overall sense of harmony and equality necessary for ensuring democracy and nationhood. Bhargava defines the strategy of 'principled distance' as follows:

> whether or not the state intervenes or refrains from actions depends on what really strengthens religious liberty and equality of citizenship for all. If this is so, the state may not relate to every religion in exactly the same way, intervene to the same degree, or in the same manner. All it must ensure is that the relation between religious and political institutions be guided by non-sectarian principles that remain consistent with a set of values constitutive of a life of equal dignity for all.[12]

Examples of the Indian state excluding religion from state policies include the refusal, based on religion, of separate electorates, reserved constituencies, reservations for jobs and the organization of states.[13] Examples of where the state has intervened in religious affairs are the reforms it has undertaken of Hinduism. Within the domain of Hindu temples, the state has reformed temple administration, recognized the rights of Dalits (the group considered outside and beneath the Hindu caste system) to enter temples and has regulated criminals posing as holy men.[14] Within the domain of marriage, the state has made polygamy illegal, has introduced the right to divorce, has abolished child marriage and has given legal recognition to inter-caste marriage.[15] In sum, *principled distance* means that the state must maintain a principled distance from all religious institutions – whether public or private, and whether individual-oriented or community-oriented – for the sake of upholding the values of prosperity, dignity, liberty and equality (including equality of citizenship), at both individual and group levels.[16]

Indian secularism is not simply a legal and political structure that manages the relation between religions and the state, but is about the relationships between different values, with an activist commitment that seeks to manage and propagate those values, including as part of a nation-building project committed to equality for religious groups and equality of citizenship for all peoples, both of which entail defending minority rights. Indian secularism demonstrates a secularism outside of Europe, so that secularism in India is not so much the opposite of 'religion', but as a check against *communalism*. In India, communalism denotes an antagonizing ideology based on exclusively identifying with a particular religion, sect or caste. Communalism is thus commonly used in India to designate violence ('communal violence') between groups – most often religious groups – predicated on ideologies of difference. Indian secularism therefore historically emerged through the intersections of nationalism, communalism and liberal democracy.[17]

Criticisms of secularism

Partha Chatterjee identifies what he views as two contradictions of Indian secularism. The first is that, since independence, the state has involved itself with various religious institutions in the form of regulating them, funding them and even administrating them.[18] For Chatterjee, this was premised on the modernizing aim of reforming Hinduism, work that was undertaken by the state because it has the power and legitimacy to do so, given that Hinduism itself lacks an appropriate institution for reforms. Chatterjee argues, however, that the line is not always clear between reforming Hinduism for the liberal-secular values of equality and dignity, and compromising freedom of religion.[19] This criticism highlights what is both distinctive and problematic about Indian secularism. Unlike the proclaimed ideals of Western secularism, Indian secularism does intervene with religious affairs, as guided by a set of values.

The second contradiction that Chatterjee identifies concerns the personal laws for religious groups, which includes the right to establish their own educational institutions. Chatterjee argues that no objective and accountable procedure exists to determine who from those minority communities would represent them to the state.[20] His solution for how reforms are undertaken in religious communities lies in upholding the values of democracy and for rethinking how toleration operates between the state (including the general body of citizens) and a particular minority religious group. For Chatterjee, the state should accept that a group can elect its own representatives for the process of reforming and regulating that group's practices, and the group can thus have collective rights and self-representation against any of the state's assimilating ideas of universal citizenship. In turn, that group should have democratic political process within the group to ensure that its public institutions and practices are representative of that group.[21] In sum, what Chatterjee calls a 'strategic politics of toleration' would see the religious group 'resist homogenization from the outside, and push for democratization inside'.[22]

Faisal Devji has argued that Indian secularism can be traced to the year after the Mutiny of 1857, namely, the Queen's Proclamation of 1858, which stated that the British colonial government in India would not interfere with Indian religions.[23] This Proclamation, however, did not necessarily mean state neutrality. Instead, the British were in fact guided by values, namely, what to them appeared as a civilizing mission, so that they could not claim to be impartial towards religious groups in India. This partiality was especially evident in the events leading to Partition, when the colonial state was not seen as being a neutral third party, but as having vested political interests, with both the major political parties – the Indian National Congress and the Muslim League – claiming the state favoured the other party.[24] For Devji, postcolonial Indian secularism can be placed within this historical lineage, so that it too is not seen as neutral, especially given its activist values. Moreover, Devji argues, this intervention is the most pernicious aspect of Indian secularism, for it can constitute state partiality and, when linked with activist values, does not permit juridical neutrality, whether that activism has positive or negative consequences.[25]

Like Partha Chatterjee and Faisal Devji, Akeel Bilgrami's criticism of secularism focuses on the relation between the state and different religious communities. Bilgrami argues the state's policy of secularism was simply assumed by leaders rather than *emerging* through substantive negotiation with different religious communities.[26] State secularism would thus be more substantive and less theoretical had it been informed by negotiations and creative dialogue between different religious communities. Bilgrami, however, does not mean that the state should uncritically accept the views offered by different religious groups (which might promote, for example, the subordination of women). This returns us again to secularism's activist values such as democracy and equality. Bilgrami argues that secularists can substantively and persuasively influence different religious groups to adopt secular principles by 'facing up to other substantive doctrinal and political commitments of the communities' and 'democratizing these communities and thereby giving them the confidence to embrace, from elements within their own evaluative framework and point of view, arguments in favour of these principles'.[27]

In their criticisms of secularism, T. N. Madan and Ashis Nandy have turned to the long history of pluralistic religions in India, and the special challenges faced by secularism as it strives to politically address and negotiate India's diverse religions. Madan argues that the development and adoption of political secularism in Western nations has been informed by Christianity and its distinction between the sacred and the secular.[28] For secularism to succeed in India, Madan argues that the task for intellectuals is to make secularism 'context-sensitive', by which he means they should clarify it by drawing upon traditions of religious pluralism in India.[29] Otherwise, the policy will appear to function in a top-down direction, as something imposed by the state, perhaps suggesting that philosophical secularism is somehow 'morally superior' to religious beliefs and practices.[30] Ironically, what this emphasis on secularism can lead to is religious reactionism, even a strengthening of Hindu revivalism and Muslim and Sikh fundamentalism.[31] For Madan, it is not that the major religions in India – Hinduism, Buddhism, Islam and Sikhism – lack elements of the secular, but that those religions *encompass* ideas of the secular rather than *separating* themselves from the secular.[32] For these believers, separating the religious and the secular might not translate well into their beliefs and politics. Madan argues that for secularism to succeed would require people 'to take both religion and secularism seriously and not reject the former as superstition and reduce the latter to a mask for communalism or mere expediency'.[33]

Ashis Nandy argues that a policy of secularism overlooks the long traditions and histories of interreligious tolerance in India, particularly among the peasant classes, as informed by ideas of tolerance that are within the religions themselves. According to Nandy, secularism comes to 'hegemonize the idea of tolerance, so that anyone who is not secular becomes definitionally intolerant'.[34] Nandy's criticism demonstrates secularism's rigid concept of tolerance: that tolerance is worthwhile, and that secularism is the only route towards tolerance. Making a distinction between *religion-as-ideology* (as a public identity, one that the state can identify and categorize) and *religion-as-faith* (as personal belief), Nandy argues that while secularism absorbs the concept of religion-as-ideology, it also interferes with religion-as-faith. He states that secularism 'is hardly appealing to the faithful, to whom religion is an overall theory of life, including public life, and life does not seem worth living without a theory, however imperfect, of transcendence'.[35] The problem with religious ideas containing a theory of public life is that they can be manipulated by individuals and groups, such as those of the conservative Hindu nationalist movement (called *Hindutva*, or 'Hinduness'), who attack the secular state as 'pseudosecular' while arguing that their Hinduism is the 'true' secularism.

In contrast to Nandy's notion of tolerance, Rajeswari Sunder Rajan argues that because Hinduism is the majority religion in India, and because it identifies itself as a tolerant religion, can lead some Hindus to proclaim secularism as an exercise of Hindu tolerance, that tolerance as an act of the religion's benevolence towards minority religions. Hindu tolerance in turn informs the rhetoric of tolerance built into secular nationalism, with Hindus thus privileging themselves as the source of secular nationalism.[36] Sunder Rajan notes, however, that the Hindu violence against other religious groups, especially Muslims, since Independence has not prompted self-reflection on the part of Hinduism, or even to be seen as a crisis for Hinduism. Instead, such violence is seen – through a distancing strategy – as a crisis of secularism. She gives the evidence that in the wake of Hindu violence since Independence, few Hindu religious leaders have condemned such violence.[37] Sunder Rajan argues that secularism 'as the constitutional right to freedom of religion should have freed minorities from the burden of a reciprocal accommodation (even gratitude), but it has always had to yield to the implicit construction of secularism as Hindu tolerance'.[38] It is especially in relation to minority religious groups, and particularly in the relation between Hindus and Muslims, that secularism has faced some of its most grave and critical challenges.

Challenges to secularism

Secularism in India has had it successes, but it has also faced several historical events and challenges since Independence. In this section I highlight some key historical moments that have shown the limitations, vulnerabilities and even failures of secularism. Between 1975 and 1977, during the period known as the Emergency, the ruling prime minister, Indira Gandhi, effectively led a dictatorship, imprisoning any opponents, curtailing civil liberties and censoring the press. She deployed the concept of the 'nation' by claiming to institute economic reforms, but in fact eroded the people's faith in democracy, the very democracy that was central to the idea of state secularism: representation of and equal treatment of all peoples.

In 1984, following the assassination of Indira Gandhi by her Sikh bodyguards, there were massacres of Sikhs in New Delhi and other parts of India, with evidence suggesting involvement of politicians from the ruling Congress party.[39] 1985 saw an elderly Muslim woman, Shah Bano, successfully petition the Supreme Court for alimony. The judgement outraged conservative Muslim leaders, who felt the state should not be meddling in personal divorce laws already established by and for religious communities. The prime minister at the time, Rajiv Gandhi, reversed the Supreme Court decision. This decision was widely perceived as pandering to Muslim voters. It was also condemned as not just privileging a particular religious community, but doing so at the cost of women's rights. Another sign of secularism's failure occurred a few years later, in 1989. The Mandal Commission had recommended a significant increase in quotas in governmental jobs and educational institutions for members of tribes and lower castes. The decision was heavily criticized by upper-caste Hindus, and remains a contentious issue in India. Also in 1989, an armed insurgency began in Kashmir, India's only Muslim-majority state, with insurgents seeking independence for Kashmir. Where the Indian state could have used diplomacy, its response in the 1990s was brutal, effectively converting Kashmir into a conflict zone under the pretence of 'protecting' secular nationalism. Human rights violations have proliferated in the state, including custodial disappearances, civilian killings and sexual violence against women.

Perhaps the most internationally visible example of secularism's failure to address religious violence occurred on December 6, 1992, when hundreds of thousands of members of the Hindu nationalist party destroyed the Babri mosque in Ayodhya, claiming it had been built on top of the birthplace of the Hindu god Ram. The structure fell to the ground within hours. The Hindu Right tried using the Babri mosque crisis to argue that Muslims as a religious minority are a threat to the nation, and thus must be removed from India.[40] The belief here is that India can only be a cohesive nation if it is a Hindu nation.

The war on terrorism started by the United States following the attacks of September 11, 2001, has influenced India in the form of new laws for detention without trial and elaborate methods of surveillance. For Partha Chatterjee, these laws threaten secularism. In Chatterjee's words, 'the results of long years of struggle against by the civil liberties and democratic rights movement were nullified at one stroke'.[41] The war on terrorism also has impacted attitudes within India towards Muslims and presents a challenge to secularism's constitutional guarantee of rights for minority religious groups. As a sign of the connotations and political interests that can now surround the label 'terrorist', at a press conference in 2002, Madhav Govinda Vaidya, a spokesman for the Rashtriya Swayamsevak Sangh (commonly known as the RSS, an organization based on the ideology of Hindu nationalism), stated that 'All Muslims may not be terrorists, but most terrorists are Muslims.'[42]

In 2002, a mob of Muslims burned a train in the eastern state of Gujarat containing Hindu pilgrims returning from Ayodhya. In retaliation, that same year Hindu mobs in Gujarat killed thousands of Muslims and left even more homeless under the watch of the political leader of the state, Narendra Modi, and his Hindu nationalist party, the Bharatiya Janata Party (BJP). The Shankaracharya of Goverdhanpuri, Jagadguru Aadhokshjanand Teerth, condemned the Gujarat violence as 'state terrorism' and called for the arrest of the perpetrators, invoking the National Security Act 'for the sake of unity and communal harmony and to save the Hindu religion from further degeneration'.[43]

In a landslide victory, Narendra Modi was elected Prime Minister of India in 2014. Since then, interreligious provocations and tensions continue in India, with the Hindu right becoming increasingly assertive. In 2014, a politician from the Hindu nationalist party Shiv Sena attempted to force-feed a Muslim who was fasting for the Muslim holy period of *Ramadan*. Also in 2014, members of the Bajrang Dal, a wing of the Hindu nationalist organization Vishva Hindu Parishad (VHP) converted fifty-seven Muslim families to Hinduism, under the guise of giving them BPL (Below Poverty Line) cards, used to identify those in need of government aid. The Bajrang Dal called the ceremony a 'Home Coming' (*Ghar Wapsi*) exercise. In January 2015, on the 66th anniversary of Republic Day, the Indian Ministry of Information and Broadcasting ran an advertisement featuring the Preamble to the Indian constitution, but which omitted the words 'socialist' and 'secular' from the Preamble. With this presence of Hindu nationalism in India, this gives us pause to consider the potential futures of Indian secularism.

Futures of secularism

Secularism in India presents special potentials but also special challenges. Scholars outside India have praised Indian secularism for its resilience towards religious diversity in India, and that the ethos of pluralism in India – which includes tremendous cultural, ethnic, linguistic and religious diversity – augurs well for continued resilience for both secularism and the nation.[44] The distinctiveness of democracy in India is that India is the world's largest democracy, and has a secularism that has an activist and principled distance from religious groups. To maintain this distinctiveness, and in response to the challenges secularism has faced, scholars have called for secularism to have the combined values of respecting democracy, being sensitive to minorities, and taking religion seriously, and even becoming more spiritualized and humanistic itself.[45] [46] Reflecting the enormous pluralism and diversity in India, scholarly work on Indian secularism is itself pluralistic and diverse, emerging within a range of disciplines, including political science, sociology and literary studies.[47] It is from such an interdisciplinary, even holistic, milieu that viable, equitable and representative relations can exist between the state and religious life in India. This diversity of cultural life and intellectual work indicates the necessarily multiple dimensions in which any democratically and nationally committed state policy in India will have to be successful. A representative and effective secularism in India must address a range of identities – including religion, caste, ethnicity, language and gender – across minority and majority groups.

Notes

1. T. N. Madan, 'Secularism in Its Place', in *Secularism and Its Critics*, ed. Rajeev Bhargava (New Delhi: Oxford University Press, 1998), 319.
2. John C. Donovan, Richard E. Morgan and Christian P. Potholm, *People, Power, and Politics: An Introduction to Political Science*, 3rd edn. (Lanham: Rowman & Littlefield, 1993), 19.
3. Rajeswari Sunder Rajan, 'The Politics of Hindu "Tolerance"', *Boundary 2* 38, no. 3 (2011): 77.
4. Ashis Nandy, 'A Disowned Father of the Nation in India: Vinayak Damodar Savarkar and the Demonic and the Seductive in Indian Nationalism', *Inter-Asia Cultural Studies* 15, no. 1 (2014): 104.
5. Urvashi Butalia, *The Other Side of Silence: Voices from the Partition of India* (Durham: Duke University Press, 2000), 3.
6. Stanley Tambiah, 'The Crisis of Secularism in India', in *Secularism and Its Critics*, ed. Rajeev Bhargava (New Delhi: Oxford University Press, 1998), 422.
7. Gyan Pandey, *The Construction of Communalism in Colonial North India* (New Delhi: Oxford University Press, 1990), 238.
8. Rajeev Bhargava, *The Promise of India's Secular Democracy* (New Delhi: Oxford University Press, 2010), 28–33.
9. Ibid., 25, 26.
10. Ibid., 27.
11. Ibid., 27, 92.
12. Ibid., 27.
13. Ibid.
14. Ibid., 28.
15. Ibid.
16. Ibid., 226.
17. Shabnum Tejani, *Indian Secularism: A Social and Intellectual History, 1890–1950* (New Delhi: Permanent Black, 2007), 265.
18. Partha Chatterjee, 'The Contradictions of Secularism', in *The Crisis of Secularism in India*, eds. Anuradha Dingwaney Needham and Rajeswari Sunder Rajan (New Delhi: Permanent Black, 2007), 143.
19. Partha Chatterjee, 'Secularism and Tolerance', in *Secularism and Its Critics*, ed. Rajeev Bhargava (New Delhi: Oxford University Press, 1998), 360.
20. Chatterjee, 'The Contradictions of Secularism', 143.

21 Chatterjee, 'Secularism and Tolerance', 376.
22 Ibid., 378.
23 Faisal Devji, 'Comments on 'The Distinctiveness of Indian Secularism', in *The Future of Secularism*, ed. T. N. Srinivasan (New Delhi: Oxford University Press, 2007), 55, 56.
24 Ibid., 56.
25 Ibid., 57.
26 Akeel Bilgrami, 'Secularism, Nationalism, and Modernity', in *Secularism and Its Critics*, ed. Rajeev Bhargava (New Delhi: Oxford University Press, 1998), 394, 395.
27 Ibid., 400.
28 Madan, 'Secularism in Its Place', 319.
29 Ibid.
30 Ibid., 318.
31 Ibid., 313.
32 Ibid., 319.
33 Ibid., 314.
34 Ashis Nandy, *The Romance of the State: And the Fate of Dissent in the Tropics* (New Delhi: Oxford University Press, 2002), 60.
35 Ashis Nandy, 'The Politics of Secularism and the Recovery of Religious Tolerance', in *Secularism and Its Critics*, ed. Rajeev Bhargava (New Delhi: Oxford University Press, 1998), 333.
36 Rajan, 'The Politics of Hindu "Tolerance"', 82.
37 Ibid., 69.
38 Ibid., 82.
39 Stanley Tambiah, *Leveling Crowds: Ethnonationalist Conflicts and Collective Violence in South Asia* (Berkeley, London and Los Angeles: University of California Press, 1996), 128–31.
40 Mira Debs, 'Using Cultural Trauma: Gandhi's Assassination, Partition and Secular Nationalism in Post-Independence India', *Nations and Nationalisms* 19, no. 4 (2013): 648.
41 Chatterjee, 'The Contradictions of Secularism', 142.
42 Ibid.
43 Rajan, 'The Politics of Hindu "Tolerance"', 69.
44 Lamin Sanneh, 'The Future of Secularism and the Promise of Diversity in India: A Historical Perspective', in *The Future of Secularism*, ed. T. N. Srinivasan (New Delhi: Oxford University Press, 2007), 122.
45 Sonia Sikka, 'The Perils of Indian Secularism', *Constellations* 19, no. 2 (2012): 289.
46 Rajeev Bhargava, 'Religious and Secular Identities', in *Crisis and Change in Contemporary India*, eds. Upendra Baxi and Bhikhu Parekh (New Delhi: Sage, 1995), 341.

47 See Pardeep Kumar, 'Religious Universalism: Swami Vivekananda's Vision', *Philosophy of Religion* 45 (2008): 171–76; Arvind-Pal S. Mandair, *Religion and the Specter of the West* (New York: Columbia University Press, 2009); Manav Ratti, *The Postsecular Imagination: Postcolonialism* (New York: Routledge, 2013); Shabnum Tejani, *Indian Secularism: A Social and Intellectual History, 1890–1950* (Bloomington: Indiana University Press, 2007).

Glossary of Key Terms and Concepts
Dawn Miranda Sherratt-Bado

Creolization: This term denotes sets of processes that occur in linguistic, cultural or creative contexts whereby assimilation or hybridization takes place upon contact between different forms. Linguistic creolization transpires when languages, dialects or pidgins convert into a creole, which tends to occur through acquisition by native speakers. Historically, cultural creolization came about through naturalization into society in territories that were colonized by Europeans, such as was the case throughout the colonial Americas. In its current usage, cultural creolization is applied more generally to postcolonial societies with ethnically mixed populations which are a product of European colonization. Recently a number of postcolonial thinkers, many of whom are of Caribbean origin such as Édouard Glissant, have theorized creative creolization as a methodological approach to artistic production. In this sense, creolization is a form of discourse which does not constitute a fixed unit but rather remains in constant flux. Glissant, a major proponent of this discursive mode, highlights creolization as a paradigm for connectivity and relation across cultural and national borders. For more on the Glissantian theory of creolization, see *Poetics of Relation* (1997).

Decoloniality: Walter D. Mignolo outlines this theoretical paradigm in his treatise *The Darker Side of Western Modernity: Global Futures, Decolonial Options* (2011) and develops it further in his co-edited text with Arturo Escobar, *Globalization and the Decolonial Option* (2013). Mignolo explains that 'decolonial' thought is a theoretical approach that delinks from the colonizing power of hegemonic Western epistemes. Correspondingly, he defines decoloniality as a form of 'epistemic decolonization' that involves 'a rethinking of the epistemic matrix of Western modernity and coloniality' from the position of marginality (2011: 9, 2013: 19). Rather than adopt homologous Eurocentric epistemic structures, Mignolo argues for the reconstruction of non-Western epistemes with attention to localized contingencies and practical applications. The decolonial analytical approach has emerged as a major Latin American movement that engages with local ethnic and indigenous social projects. It also projects outward, across diverse former colonies and cultural contexts. For instance, decolonialists cite thinkers such as Mahatma Gandhi, W.E.B. DuBois, Aimé Césaire and Frantz Fanon as included within the genealogy of this movement. Proponents of decoloniality stress that it contrasts with postcolonialism which, they contend, is 'a project of scholarly transformation within the academy' (Mignolo: 2007: 452). They also emphasize that decoloniality is not analogous to decolonization as it is an epistemological rather than a politico-historical process.

Decolonization: This is a polyvalent term within postcolonial studies that can be applied within numerous contexts. The three main frameworks for discourses of decolonization are politico-economic, historical and cultural. In the first instance, decolonization can refer to either the withdrawal from its formerly colonized territories by a colonial power, or to the acquisition of political or economic independence by former colonies. Secondly, decolonization can denote the historical phase that occurred post-Second World War, during which the world witnessed the dismantling of major imperial powers and the emergence of national liberation movements. Lastly, cultural decolonization designates the need to mitigate the entrenched effects of colonialism within the cultural traditions of former colonies. In *Culture and Imperialism* (1993) Edward Said argues that colonialism was enacted through the enforcement of Western cultural practices. Consequently, he defines cultural decolonization as the next stage of resistance to colonial authority which of necessity must follow political decolonization. For the formerly colonized populations, it is a process which involves extricating their culture from the stronghold of imperialism, which includes countervailing the influence of Eurocentric paradigms and practices.

Diaspora: This term is derived from the ancient Greek word for 'dispersion' and it has come to have a number of contemporary denotations. Initially 'diaspora' was applied exclusively to the population of Jews living in exile from the land of Israel. Its definition subsequently expanded to refer to the historical movements of various peoples scattered from their homeland. In particular, scholars now distinguish between different kinds of diaspora to denote groups who have spread beyond their homelands either voluntarily or involuntarily, as well as to denote the specific cause of their mass dispersion. Diaspora indicates movement within, across and between different geographical and national terrains. Furthermore, it has also become a theoretical concept within postcolonial scholarship as a tool to present diasporic worldviews – ways of presenting the world or ways of thinking about how the world is shaped by diasporic events and traversals. Influential theoretical texts on diaspora are Avtar Brah's *Cartographies of Diaspora: Contesting Identities* (1996), Paul Gilroy's *The Black Atlantic* (1993) and Stuart Hall's 'Cultural Identity and Diaspora' (1990).

Exoticization/Auto-exoticization: Exoticization pertains to the act of rendering an object of a particular discourse exotic, and this has attendant implications either of glamorization, romanticization, stereotyping or condescension. It is a mode of treating or portraying this object as unusual, and can also be a method of consumption. Graham Huggan examines the consumerist effect on representations of postcoloniality in *The Postcolonial Exotic: Marketing the Margins* (2001). He discusses the ways in which the label 'postcolonial' is mediated and manipulated by various exoticizing discourses which stem from European imperialist accounts of the Other. Correspondingly, auto-exoticism is a concept developed by Joep Leerssen in *Remembrance and Imagination: Patterns in the Historical and Literary Representation of Ireland in the Nineteenth Century* (1997). He defines auto-exoticism as 'an interiorized form of exoticism,' 'a mode of seeing, presenting and representing oneself in one's otherness' (66, 37). This can be a negative psychological effect which occurs due to an internalization of imperialist discourse, or it can be a strategic form of appropriating exoticizing discourse as a means of self-empowerment.

Hybridity: A term that originated in biology and was subsequently employed in linguistic and racial theorizations before emerging in postcolonial academic discourse in the 1990s. Hybridity is most frequently associated with Homi K. Bhabha and his work *The Location of Culture* (1994). Bhabha initiates its usage as a paradigm for the liminal position of colonial identity, describing hybridity as a difference 'within' a subject who inhabits 'an in-between reality' (2012: 9). He cites the colonial signifier as 'an act of ambivalent signification' as it represents 'neither one nor other,' instead splitting 'the difference between the binary oppositions or polarities through which we understand cultural difference' (182). Bhabha's deconstructive approach to colonial subjectivity detects a breakdown in 'the symmetry and duality of self/other, inside/outside' which is experienced by both the colonizer and colonized (165). He has received substantial criticism for contending that colonial discourse diverges from other exercises of authority in that it does not discriminate between a self and an Other, but between a self and its doubles. Hybridity is linked to Bhabha's notion of mimicry in that it is a repetition with a difference – the hybrid repeats what is ostensibly disavowed by the colonizing power. While some postcolonial theorists disapprove of Bhabha's conceptualization, arguing that it downplays the violence of colonialism, others such as Paul Gilroy, Stuart Hall and Gayatri Chakravorty Spivak engage with similar theories of hybridity as an antidote to essentialist discourses.

Interculturalism: A theoretical paradigm that emerged in response to criticism of multiculturalist government policies within former imperial states during the post-independence period which deploy assimilationist integration tactics under slogans promoting 'racial harmony'. Interculturalists reject multiculturalism and its terminology as euphemistic and patronizing. Salman Rushdie argues in 'The New Empire within Britain' (1992) that these factors have contributed to 'new imperialist' attitudes within former imperial seats such as Britain that have experienced interracial conflict surrounding the influx of migrants from their former colonies (137). This residual imperialism projects an image of a unified, multiculturalist nation that masks its continued suppression of other cultural groups. Interculturalism therefore represents a rhetorical shift that rejects homogenizing multiculturalist identity politics in favour of cross-cultural dialogue and interactivity as effective methods of community-building. For more on this debate, see Ted Cantle's *Interculturalism: The New Era of Cohesion and Diversity* (2012) and John Nagle's *Multiculturalism's Double-Bind: Creating Inclusivity, Cosmopolitanism and Difference* (2009).

Intersectionality/Intersectionalism: Theoretical axiom posited by Kimberlé Crenshaw in her article 'Demarginalizing the Intersection of Race and Sex' (1989) and developed further throughout her subsequent body of work. Intersectionality is the study of the matrix of systems of oppression that affect female experience, with particular attention to the complex ways in which these oppressive forms interact. Originally applied within the context of black feminist studies, Crenshaw's model is now frequently used by critics to apply to all women. Intersectionalist analyses trace the multiple structures and processes that position female experience in order to show the ways that they are interlinked, rather than considering them discretely. Avtar Brah and Ann Phoenix align intersectionalism with postcolonialism in their joint essay 'Ain't I a Woman? Revisiting Intersectionality' (2004), arguing that 'intersectionality fits with the disruption of modernist thinking produced by postcolonial and poststructuralist theoretical ideas' (82). For more, see Kimberlé Crenshaw, 'The Structural and Political Dimensions of Intersectional Oppression' (2014) and *On Intersectionality: The Essential Writings of Kimberlé Crenshaw* (2015).

Mimicry: Homi K. Bhabha delineates his theory of colonial mimicry in *The Location of Culture* (1994), devoting a chapter to a discussion of 'the ambivalence of colonial discourse' (2012: 121). He examines the ways in which colonial identity performs a (mis)copying of the normative Western example. As Bhabha explains, mimicry is a process by which the colonized subject is (re)produced as 'almost the same, but not quite' (122). He locates a fissure in this act of transaction or translation within 'that conflictual economy of colonial discourse' and argues that such semantic slippage opens ground for disobedience and even mockery (122). Bhabha maintains that mimicry can be a powerful form of subversion as it allows for parodic potential. Therein lies the weakness of colonial authority, which is automatically displaced by its reliance on the necessary deformation of the colonized subject, who must become like the colonizer but always remain different. Here Bhabha builds upon Freudian notions of psychic identification which are theorized in the colonial context by Frantz Fanon in *Black Skin, White Masks* (1952) and fictionalized by V.S. Naipaul in *The Mimic Men* (1967).

Neocolonialism: A term meaning 'new colonialism' that refers to the post-independence exercise of economic, political, cultural or other forms of control over another country by a hegemonic power – especially a former imperial state or a multinational corporation. As a consequence, the neocolony is subject to an extension of various geopolitical structures of dependency and exteriorization. The term 'neocolonialism' was coined by Kwame Nkrumah, former president of Ghana, who analyses this phenomenon in *Neo-Colonialism: The Last Stage of Imperialism* (1965). Nkrumah traces the links between imperialism, globalization and neocolonial relations, which have become enmeshed in networks of indirect influence. He argues that these networks are increasingly difficult to detect and are therefore more insidious than the direct control of colonialism. The title of his text noticeably echoes Vladimir Lenin's *Imperialism: The Highest Stage of Capitalism* (1917), and suggests that although countries like Ghana ostensibly achieved political independence, former imperial powers and emerging superpowers continue to play a decisive role in their interests. As Gayatri Chakravorty Spivak points out in *The Post-Colonial Critic* (1990), the existence of neocolonialism complicates the notion of the 'postcolonial' in that 'We live in a post-colonial neocolonized world' (166). Accordingly, much of postcolonial literature and theory engages with the ways that neocolonialism also operates at the cultural level, which problematizes issues of ideology and representation.

Postcolonialism: A term which can denote either the state of having been a former colony, the cultural condition of a postcolonial society or the epistemological field which investigates these contexts. While the designation 'postcolonial' was originally used by historians and political scientists as a chronological signifier for the post-independence period, it has since acquired a broader usage among critics to address the discursive and material effects of colonization. There is also an ongoing debate regarding whether to use a hyphen in 'post-colonialism'. Some critics maintain that the hyphen indicates a specific form of intellectual discourse surrounding the historical fact of colonialism, and that the unhyphenated word represents an indiscriminate decontextualization of experience. Moreover, the prefix 'post' itself is also problematic since, as many critics contend, it can be seen as meaning simply 'after' colonialism. Several prominent critics deem the 'post' to be a discursive misapprehension due to the entrenchment of various structures of colonialism within contemporary societies. For more on this discussion, see Bill Ashcroft's 'On the Hyphen in Post-Colonial' (1996); Aijaz Ahmad's 'The

Politics of Literary Postcoloniality' (1995); Steven Slemon's 'The Scramble for Post-Colonialism' (1994).

Postnationalism: This concept is attributed to Edward Said, who utilises the term in *Culture and Imperialism* (1993) in his dialogical engagement with Frantz Fanon's decolonization theories. In particular, Said addresses Fanon's chapter in *The Wretched of the Earth* (1961) on 'the pitfalls of national consciousness' (148). Said explains that after the contestatory culture of anticolonial nationalism, 'an entirely new post-nationalist theoretical culture is required' (323). According to Said, the postnational moment follows that of anticolonial nationalism within the decolonization process. Strategic nationalist identity is an 'insufficient and crucial' first step that lays the groundwork for postnationalism, a more 'pluralistic vision of the world' which, he argues, enables true liberation (271, 277). From Said's perspective, postnationalism moves away from essentialisms towards an acknowledgement of the transculturating effects of colonialism. In a more contemporary, generalized sense, postnationalism describes the process whereby national identities lose precedence relative to supranational or global entities.

Strategic essentialism: A term coined by Gayatri Chakravorty Spivak in her article 'Can the subaltern speak?' (1994) in order to denote the mobilization of identitarian essentialism as a way of contesting a politics of oppression. This is a deconstructionist move which facilitates the dismantling of universalist discourses that are enacted through Eurocentric imagery. It is a displacement of Enlightenment humanism by poststructuralist conceptualizations of subjectivity, which Spivak maintains are necessary to postcolonial studies. She describes strategic essentialism as a temporary subjective repositioning which permits opposition to essentializing discourse from within, by redeploying it as a counter-discourse. Spivak cites the Subaltern Studies historiographic project (see 'Subaltern' entry) as a key example, and argues that by resituating the concept of an essential subject, the subalternist historian is able to confront the monolithic representations of the Other that are inscribed via one-sided official colonial accounts. In this way, Spivak asserts, the recovery of a previously silenced subaltern consciousness becomes possible.

Subaltern: Originally a term meaning 'of inferior rank', 'subaltern' was adapted by Marxist theorist Antonio Gramsci to define a person who is socially, politically and geographically outside the hegemonic power structure of the colony and of the metropole. Gramsci's work examines the historiography of the subaltern classes and their lack of control over their representation. Gayatri Chakravorty Spivak subsequently reworked the Gramscian notion of the subaltern in order to denote all that inhabits 'a space of difference' – that is, 'everything that has little or no access to the cultural imperialism' (1992: 45). The field of Subaltern Studies is dedicated to analysing the specificities of subaltern themes in South Asian Studies. For more on Gramsci's theorizations of subaltern culture and consciousness, see *Antonio Gramsci: Selected Cultural Writings* (1991). For Spivak's use of the term, see her essay 'Can the Subaltern Speak?' in *Colonial Discourse and Post-Colonial Theory: A Reader* (1994), as well as 'Interview with Gayatri Chakravorty Spivak: New Nation Writers Conference in South Africa' by Spivak and Leon de Kock (1992).

Transnationalism: A theoretical concept used across various disciplines to denote the phenomenon of transborder social, economic and cultural relationships between individuals, groups, institutions, firms and states. These relations can be patterns of exchange, affiliation or social formation. It is important to note that transnationalism is part of, but not synonymous with, globalization, as globalization is inherently an economic phenomenon which occasions international financial disequilibria. As a genre of writing, 'transnational literature' operates beyond national parameters and as such it is inequivalent to 'postcolonial literature', which entails specific cultural contexts. Transnational literature also differentiates from 'world literature', which tends to have bourgeois connotations in Goethean and Marxist critical theories. For more on transnationalism with relation to postcolonial studies, see Laura Chrisman, *Postcolonial Contraventions: Cultural Readings of Race, Imperialism, and Transnationalism* (2003).

Bibliography
Compiled by Conna Ray

Abraham, Itty. 'The Contradictory Spaces of Postcolonial Techno-Science'. *Economic and Political Weekly* 41, no. 3 (2006): 210–17.

Adelson, Leslie A. *The Turkish Turn in Contemporary German Literature: Towards a New Grammar of Migration*. London: Palgrave, 2005.

Adesocan, Akin. 'New African Writing and the Question of Audience'. *Research in African Literatures* 43, no. 3 (2012): 1–20.

Agamben, Giorgio. *Homo Sacer: Sovereign Power and Bare Life*. Translated by Daniel Heller-Roazen. Stanford: Stanford University Press, 1998.

Agamben, Giorgio. *State of Exception*. Translated by Kevin Attell. Chicago: University of Chicago Press, 2005.

Agamben, Giorgio. 'We Refugees'. Translated by Michael Rocke, http://www.egs.edu/faculty/agamben-we-refugees.html (accessed 8 April 2009).

Ahmad, Aijaz. *In Theory: Nations, Classes, Literature*. London: Verso, 1992.

Ahmad, Aijaz. 'Postcolonial Theory and the "Post-" Condition'. *Socialist Register* 33 (1997): 353–81.

Ahmed, Sara. *Strange Encounters: Embodied Others in Post-Coloniality*. London: Routledge, 2000.

Al-Ali, Nadje and Khalid Koser. *New Approaches to Migration? Transnational Communities and the Transformation of Home*. London: Routledge, 2002.

Aldrich, Robert. *Colonialism and Homosexuality*. London: Routledge, 2002.

Ali, Syed Mustafa. 'Towards a Decolonial Computing'. *Open Research Online*, http://oro.open.ac.uk/41372/ (accessed 13 September 2015).

Allen, Robert C. 'Engels' Pause: A Pessimist's Guide to the British Industrial Revolution'. Oxford University, Department of Economics Discussion Papers, April 2007.

Al-Qady, Towfiq. *Nothing But Nothing*. In *Staging Asylum: Contemporary Australian Plays about Refugees*, edited by Emma Cox, 185–202. Sydney: Currency Press, 2013.

Anderson, Linda. *Autobiography*. London: Routledge, 2011.

Anderson, Warwick. 'Postcolonial Technoscience'. *Social Studies of Science* 32, no. 5–6 (2002): 643–58.

Annan, Noel. 'Kipling's Place in the History of Ideas'. *Victorian Studies* 3, no. 4 (1960): 323-48.

Anzaldúa, Gloria. *Borderlands/La Frontera: The New Mestiza*. San Francisco: Aunt Lute Books, 1987 (2nd edn. 1999).

Appadurai, Arjun. 'Disjuncture and Difference in the Global Economy'. *Theory Culture Society* 7, no. 2 (1990): 295-310.

Appadurai, Arjun and Carol Breckenridge. 'Public Modernities in India'. In *Consuming Modernity: Public Culture in a South Asian World*, edited by Carol A. Breckenridge, 1-19. Minneapolis: University of Minnesota Press, 1995.

Appadurai, Arjun and Carol Breckenridge. 'Why Public Culture?'. *Public Culture* 1, no. 1 (1988): 5-9.

Appiah, Kwame Anthony. *Cosmopolitanism: Ethics in a World of Strangers*. London: Penguin, 2007.

Arac, Jonathan. 'Edward W. Said: The Worldliness of World Literature'. In *The Routledge Companion to World Literature*, edited by Theo D'haen, David Damrosch and Djelal Kadir, 117-25. London: Routledge, 2011.

Arango, Joaquin, Graeme Hugo, Ali Kouaouci, Douglas S. Massey, Adela Pellegrino and J. Edward Taylor. 'Theories of International Migration'. *Population and Development Review* 19, no. 3 (1993): 431-66.

Arendt, Hannah. *Origins of Totalitarianism*. Cleveland: Meridian Books, 1958.

Arondekar, Anjali. *For the Record: On Sexuality and the Colonial Archive in India*. Durham: Duke University Press, 2009.

Ashcroft, Bill. *Post-Colonial Transformation*. London: Routledge, 2001.

Ashcroft, Bill. 'When the Artwork Takes the Pictures'. *Law Text Culture* 10 (2006): 239-58.

Ashcroft, Bill, Gareth Griffiths and Helen Tiffin. *Key Concepts in Post-Colonial Studies*. London: Routledge, 1998.

Ashcroft, Bill, Gareth Griffiths and Helen Tiffin. *The Postcolonial Studies Reader*. London: Routledge, 1995.

Ashcroft, Bill, Ranjini Mendis and Julie McGonegal. *Literature for Our Times: Postcolonial Studies for the Twenty-First Century*. Amsterdam: Rodopi, 2012.

Ashcroft, Bill, Helen Tiffin and Gareth Griffiths, eds. *The Empire Writes Back: Theory and Practice in Postcolonial Literatures*. 2nd edn. London: Routledge, 2002.

Axel, Brian Keith. *The Nation's Tortured Body: Violence, Representation and the Formation of a Sikh Diaspora*. Durham: Duke University Press, 2001.

Bahri, Deepika. *Native Intelligence: Aesthetics, Politics, and Postcolonial Literature*. Minneapolis: University of Minnesota Press, 2003.

Bahri, Deepika. 'Women and the Trauma of Partition in Sidhwa's *Cracking India*'. *Interventions: An International Journal of Postcolonial Studies* 1, no. 2 (1999): 217-34.

Bakhtin, Mikhail. 'Discourse on the Novel'. In *The Dialogic Imagination: Four Essays*, edited by Michael Holquist, 259–422. Translated by Caryl Emerson and Michael Holquist. Austin and London: Texas University Press, 1981.

Balibar, Etienne. *We, The People of Europe? Reflections on Transnational Community*. Princeton: Princeton University Press, 2004.

Ballantyne, Tony. *Webs of Empire: Locating New Zealand's Colonial Past*. Vancouver: University of British Columbia Press, 2014.

Banerjee, Sukanya, Aims McGuinness and Steven McCay, eds. *New Routes for Diaspora Studies*. Bloomington: Indiana University Press, 2012.

Bannerji, Himani. 'Returning the Gaze: An Introduction'. In *Returning the Gaze: Essays on Racism, Feminism and Politics*, edited by Himani Bannerji, ix–xxiv. Toronto: Sister Vision Press, 1993.

Benhabib, Seyla. *Another Cosmopolitanism*. London: Oxford University Press, 2006.

Benson, Jackson J. *John Steinbeck, Writer: A Biography*. New York: Penguin, 1984.

Berger, Stefan and Bill Niven. 'Writing the History of National Memory'. In *Writing the History of Memory*, edited by Stefan Breger and Bill Niven, 146–51. London: Bloomsbury, 2014.

Bhabha, Homi. 'DissemiNation: Time, Narrative, and the Margins of the Modern Nation'. In *Nation and Narration*, edited by Homi Bhabha, 291–322. London: Routledge, 1990.

Bhabha, Homi. *The Location of Culture*. London: Routledge, 2006.

Bhabha, Homi. 'Signs Taken for Wonders: Questions of Ambivalence and Authority under a Tree Outside Delhi, May 1987'. *Critical Inquiry* 12, no. 1 (1985): 144–65.

Bhargava, Rajeev. *The Promise of India's Secular Democracy*. New Delhi: Oxford University Press, 2010.

Bhargava, Rajeev. 'Religious and Secular Identities'. In *Crisis and Change in Contemporary India*, edited by Upendra Baxi and Bhikhu Parekh, 317–49. New Delhi: Sage, 1995.

Bhatia, B. M. *Famines in India: A Study in Some Aspects of the Economic History of India*. London: Asia, 1967.

Bilgrami, Akeel. 'Secularism, Nationalism, and Modernity'. In *Secularism and Its Critics*, edited by Rajeev Bhargava, 380–417. New Delhi: Oxford University Press, 1998.

Blair, Charles. *Indian Famines: Their Historical, Financial and Other Aspects*. Edinburgh: William Blackwood, 1874.

Boas, Taylor C. and Jordan Gans-Morse. 'Neoliberalism: From New Liberal Philosophy to Anti-Liberal Slogan'. *Studies in Comparative International Development* 44 (2009): 137–61.

Boehmer, Elleke. *Colonial and Postcolonial Literature: Migrant Metaphors*. 2nd edn. Oxford: Oxford University Press, 2005.

Boehmer, Elleke. *Empire Writing: An Anthology of Colonial Literature 1870–1918*. Oxford: Oxford University Press, 1998.

Boehmer, Elleke. *Stories of Women: Gender and Narrative in the Postcolonial Nation*. Manchester: Manchester University Press, 2005.

Boehmer, Elleke and Alex Tickell, 'The 1990s: An Increasingly Postcolonial Decade'. *Journal of Commonwealth Literature* 50, no. 3 (2015): 315–52.

Boellstorff, Tom. *The Gay Archipelago: Sexuality and Nation in Indonesia*. Princeton: Princeton University Press, 2005.

Boone, Joseph A. 'Vacation Cruises: Or, the Homoerotics of Orientalism'. *PMLA* 110, no. 1 (1995): 89–107.

Bottoms, Stephen J. 'Putting the Document into Documentary: An Unwelcome Corrective?'. *The Drama Review* 50, no. 3 (2006): 56–68.

Bouson, J. Brooks. *Jamaica Kincaid Writing Memory, Writing Back to the Mother*. Albany: State University of New York, 2006.

Brah, Avtar. *Cartographies of Diaspora: Contesting Identities*. London: Routledge, 1997.

Brager, Jenna. 'Bodies of Water'. *The New Inquiry*, thenewinquiry.com/essays/bodies-of-water/ (accessed 12 May 2015).

Brand, Dionne. *A Map to the Door of No Return: Notes to Belonging*. Toronto: Random House, 2005.

Braziel, Jana Evans. *Artists, Performers, and Black Masculinity in the Haitian Diaspora*. Bloomington: Indiana University Press, 2008.

Braziel, Jana Evans. *Caribbean Genesis: Jamaica Kincaid and the Writing of New Worlds*. Albany: State University of New York Press, 2009.

Braziel, Jana Evans and Anita Mannur. *Theorizing Diaspora*. Oxford: Blackwell, 2003.

Brennan, Timothy. 'From Development to Globalization: Postcolonial Studies and Globalization theory'. In *Global Literary Theory: An Anthology*, edited by Richard J. Lane, 876–87. London: Routledge, 2013.

Brennan, Timothy. 'The National Longing for Form'. In *Nation and Narration*, edited by Homi Bhabha, 44–70. London: Routledge, 1990.

Brouillette, Sarah. *Literature and the Creative Economy*. Stanford: Stanford University Press, 2014.

Brouillette, Sarah. *Postcolonial Writers and the Global Literary Marketplace*. New York: Palgrave, 2007.

Brouillette, Sarah and David Finkelstein. 'Postcolonial Print Cultures'. *The Journal of Commonwealth Literature* 48, no. 1 (2013): 3–7.

Brown, Lisa R. 'Caribbean Life-Writing and Performative Liberation'. In *The Routledge Companion to Anglophone Caribbean Literature*, edited by Michael Bucknor and Alison Donnell, 276–84. London: Routledge, 2011.

Brydon, Diana. 'Cracking Imaginaries: Studying the Global from Canadian Space'. In *Rerouting the Postcolonial: New Directions for the New Millennium*, edited by Janet Wilson, Cristina Sandru and Sarah Lawson Welsh, 105–17. Abingdon and New York: Routledge, 2010.

Burton, Olivia and Mahi Grand. *L'Algérie C'est Beau Comme l'Amérique*. Paris: Steinkis Editions, 2015.

Butalia, Urvashi. *The Other Side of Silence: Voices from the Partition*. Durham: Duke University Press, 2000.

Butler, Judith. *Undoing Gender*. London: Routledge, 2004.

Butt, John and Kathleen Tillotson. *Dickens at Work*. 1957. Reprinted. London: Routledge, 2009.

Casanova, Pascale. *The World Republic of Letters*. Cambridge: Harvard University Press, 2007.

Casteel, Sarah Phillips. 'Autobiography as Rewriting; Derek Walcott's *Another Life* and *Omeros*'. *Journal of Commonwealth Literature* 34, no. 2 (1999): 9–32.

Castells, Manuel. *End of Millennium*. Oxford: Blackwell, 1998.

Castells, Manuel. *The Power of Identity*. Oxford: Blackwell, 1997.

Castells, Manuel. *The Rise of the Network Society*. Oxford: Blackwell, 1996.

Castells, Manuel, Ramon Flecha, Paulo Freire, Henry A. Giroux, Donaldo Macedo and Paul Willis. *Critical Education in the New Information Age*. Lanham: Rowman and Littlefield, 1999.

Castles, Stephen. 'Understanding Global Migration: A Social Transformation Perspective'. *Journal of Ethnic and Migration Studies* 36, no. 10 (2010): 1647–63.

Chakrabarty, Dipesh. 'History and the Politics of Representation'. In *Manifestoes for History*, edited by Keith Jenkins, Sue Morgan and Alan Munslow, 77–87. London: Routledge, 2007.

Chakrabarty, Dipesh. *Provincializing Europe: Postcolonial thought and Historical Difference*. Princeton and Oxford: Princeton University Press, 2000.

Chamoiseau, Patrick. *Childhood*. Lincoln: University of Nebraska Press, 1999.

Chatterjee, Partha. 'The Contradictions of Secularism'. In *The Crisis of Secularism in India*, edited by Anuradha Dingwaney Needham and Rajeswari Sunder Rajan, 141–56. New Delhi: Permanent Black, 2007.

Chatterjee, Partha. 'Secularism and Tolerance'. In *Secularism and Its Critics*, edited by Rajeev Bhargava, 345–79. New Delhi: Oxford University Press, 1998.

Chaudhuri, Amit. 'Huge Baggy Monster: Mimetic Theories of the Indian Novel after Rushdie'. In *Clearing a Space: Reflections on India, Literature and Culture*, edited by Amit Chaudhuri, 113–121. Oxford: Peter Lang, 2008.

Cheah, Pheng. 'What Is a World? On World Literature as World-Making Activity'. *Daedalus* 137, no. 3 Special Issue: 'On Cosmopolitanism' (2008): 26–38.

Cheah, Pheng. 'World against Globe: Towards a Normative Conception of World Literature'. *New Literary History* 45, no. 3 (2014): 303–29.
Cheng, François. *L'écriture poétique chinoise, suivi d'une anthologie des poèmes des Tang*. Paris: Seuil, 2006.
Chomsky, Noam. *Hopes and Prospects*. Chicago: Haymarket, 2010.
Chun, Wendy. 'Scenes of Empowerment: Virtual Racial Diversity and Digital Divides'. *New Formations* 45 (2001): 169–88.
Chute, Hilary and Marjorie Dekoven. 'Comic Books and Graphic Novels'. In *The Cambridge Introduction to Popular Culture*, edited by David Glover and Scott McCracken, 187–94. Cambridge: Cambridge University Press, 2012.
Cleary, Joseph. *Literature, Partition and the Nation State*. Cambridge: Cambridge University Press, 2002.
Clifford, James. *The Predicament of Culture: Twentieth-Century Ethnography, Literature and Art*. Cambridge: Harvard University Press, 1988.
Cohen, Robin. *Global Diasporas*. New York: Routledge, 2008.
Collins, Felicity and Therese Davis. *Australian Cinema after Mabo*. Cambridge: Cambridge University Press, 2004.
Cox, Emma. *Performing Noncitizenship: Asylum Seekers in Australian Theatre, Film and Activism*. London: Anthem, 2015.
Cox, Emma 'Sovereign Ontologies in Australia and Aotearoa–New Zealand: Indigenous Responses to Asylum Seekers, Refugees and Overstayers'. In *Knowing Differently: The Cognitive Challenge of the Indigenous*, edited by G. N. Devy, Geoffrey V. Davis and K. K. Chakravart, 139–57. London: Routledge, 2013.
Cox, Emma., ed. *Staging Asylum: Contemporary Australian Plays about Refugees*. Sydney: Currency Press, 2013.
Cox, Emma. *Theatre & Migration*. Basingstoke: Palgrave, 2014.
Craps, Stef. *Postcolonial Witnessing: Trauma Out of Bounds*. Basingstoke: Palgrave, 2013.
Cruz-Malavé, Arnaldo and Martin F. Manalansan, eds *Queer Globalizations: Citizenship and the Afterlife of Colonialism*. New York: New York University Press, 2002.
Dalleo, Raphael. *Caribbean Literature and the Public Sphere: From Plantation to the Postcolonial*. Charlottesville and London: University of Virginia Press, 2011.
Damrosch, David. *What Is World Literature?* Princeton and Oxford: Princeton University Press, 2003.
Danticat, Edwidge. *Create Dangerously: The Immigrant Artist at Work*. Princeton: Princeton University Press, 2010.
Daoud, K. *Meursault, Contre-enquête*. Alger: Éditions barzakh, 2013.
Da Silva, Denise Ferreira. 'Toward a Critique of the Socio-Logos of Justice: The Analytics of Raciality and the Production of Universality.' *Social Identities* 7, no. 3 (2000).

Davenport, Kiana. *Shark Dialogues*. New York: Plume, 1995.

Davis, Emily. 'The Intimacies of Globalization: Bodies and Borders On-Screen'. *Camera Obscura* 21, no. 2 (2006): 32–73.

Davis, Mike. *Late Victorian Holocausts: El Nino Famines and the Making of the Third World*. London: Verso, 2001.

Debs, Mira. 'Using Cultural Trauma: Gandhi's Assassination, Partition and Secular Nationalism in Post-Independence India'. *Nations and Nationalisms* 19, no. 4 (2013): 635–53.

Derrida, Jacques. *Archive Fever*. Translated by E. Prenowitz. Chicago: University of Chicago Press, 1988.

Derrida, Jacques. *Specters of Marx: The State of the Debt, the Work of Mourning, and the New International*. Translated by Peggy Kamuf. London: Routledge, 1994.

Desai, Guarav and Supirya Nair. *Postcolonialisms: An Anthology of Cultural Theory and Criticism*. New Brunswick: Rutgers University Press, 2005.

De Souza, Eunice. *A Necklace of Skulls: Collected Poems*. New Delhi: Penguin, 2009.

Devi, Mahasweta. 'Pterodactyl, Puran Sahay, and Pirtha'. In *Imaginary Maps*. Translated by Gayatri Chakravorty Spivak. London: Routledge, 1995.

Devji, Faisal. 'Comments on "The Distinctiveness of Indian Secularism"'. In *The Future of Secularism*, edited by T. N. Srinivasan, 54–59. New Delhi: Oxford University Press, 2007.

Didur, Jill. *Unsettling Partition: Literature, Gender, Memory*. Toronto: University of Toronto Press, 2006.

Digby, William. *The Famine Campaign in Southern India*. London: Longman, Green & Co, 1878.

Digby, William. *'Prosperous British India': A Revelation from Office Records*. London: T. Fisher Unwin, 1901.

Dirlik, Arif. 'Literature/Identity: Transnationalism, Narrative and Representation'. *The Review of Education, Pedagogy, and Cultural Studies* 24, no. 3 (2002): 209–34.

Donato, Katerine M. and Donna Gabaccia. *Gender and International Migration: From the Slavery Era to the Global Age*. New York: Russell Sage, 2015.

Donnell, Alison. *Twentieth-Century Caribbean Literature: Critical Moments in Anglophone Literary History*. London: Routledge, 2006.

Donovan, John C., Richard E. Morgan and Christian P. Potholm. *People, Power, and Politics: An Introduction to Political Science*. 3rd edn. Lanham: Rowman & Littlefield, 1993.

Dray, Susan, Russel Beale, Andy Dearden, Alan Jackson, Matt Jones, Matt Kam, Jose Abelnour Nocera and Niall Winters. 'Human-Computer Interaction for Development: Changing Human-Computer Interaction to Change the World'. In *Human Computer Interaction Handbook*, edited by Andrew Sears and Julie A. Jacko, 1375–99. Boca Raton: CRC Press, 2009.

Dreze, Jean. *Famine Prevention in India*. London: London School of Economics, 1988.
Duggan, Lisa. *The Twilight of Equality: Neoliberalism, Cultural Politics, and the Attack on Democracy*. Boston: Beacon Press, 2004.
Earhart, Amy. 'Can Information Be Unfettered? Race and the New Digital Humanities Canon'. In *Debates in the Digital Humanities*, edited by Matthew K. Gold, 309–18. Minneapolis: University of Minnesota Press, 2012.
Edkins, Jenny and Véronique Pin-Fat. 'Through the Wire: Relations of Power and Relations of Violence'. *Millennium: Journal of International Studies* 34, no. 1 (2005): 1–24.
Ekine, Sokari and Hakima Abbas, eds. *Queer African Reader* Oxford: Pambazuka Press 2013
Emerman, Marsha. *On the Banks of the Tigris: The Hidden Story of Iraqi Music*. Melbourne: Fruitful Films, 2015.
Eng, David L. *The Feeling of Kinship: Queer Liberalism and the Liberalization of Intimacy*. Durham: Duke University Press, 2010.
Everett, Anna. *Digital Diaspora: A Race for Cyberspace*. Albany: State University of New York Press, 2009.
Everett, Anna. 'The Revolution Will Be Digitized: Afrocentricity and the Digital Public Sphere'. *Social Text* 20, no. 2 (2002): 125–46.
Everett, Anna, Alexander Champlin and John Vanderhoef. 'Race, Space, and Digital Games: An Interview with Anna Everett'. *Media Fields Journal* 8 (2014): 1–11.
Fanon, Frantz. *Black Skin, White Masks*. Translated by C. L. Markmann. London: Pluto Press, 1986.
Fanon, Frantz. *The Wretched of the Earth*. New York: Grove Press, 1994.
Farrier, David. *Postcolonial Asylum: Seeking Sanctuary before the Law*. Liverpool: Liverpool University Press, 2011.
Farrier, David and Patricia Tuitt. 'Beyond Biopolitics: Agamben, Asylum, and Postcolonial Critique'. In *Oxford Handbook of Postcolonial Studies*, edited by Graham Huggan, 253–70. Oxford: Oxford University Press, 2013.
Fausto-Sterling, Anne. 'Gender, Race, and Nation: The Comparative Anatomy of "Hottentot" Women in Europe, 1815–1817'. In *Deviant Bodies: Critical Perspectives on Difference in Science and Popular Culture*, edited by Jennifer Terry and Jacqueline Urla, 19–48. Bloomington: Indiana University Press, 1995.
Fazila-Yacoobali Zamindar, Vazira. *The Long Partition and the Making of Modern South Asia: Refugees, Boundaries, Histories*. New York: Columbia University Press, 2007.
Felski, Rita. *Uses of Literature*. Malden and Oxford: Blackwell, 2008.

Ferguson, Moira. *East Caribbean: Gender and Colonial Relations from Mary Wollstonecraft to Jamaica Kincaid*. New York: Columbia University, 1993.

Fernández, María. 'Postcolonial Media Theory'. *Art Journal* 58, no. 3 (1999): 58–73.

Fine, Ben. 'Locating Financialisation'. *Historical Materialism* 18, no. 2 (2010): 97–116.

Flanders, Julia. 'The Literary, the Humanistic, the Digital: Toward a Research Agenda for Digital Literary Studies'. *Literary Studies in the Digital Age: An Evolving Anthology*, https://dlsanthology.commons.mla.org/the-literary-the-humanistic-the-digital/ (accessed 12 September 2015).

Foucault, Michel. *The Archeology of Knowledge*. Translated by A. N. Sheridan Smith. London, Routledge, 1977.

Foucault, Michel. *The Birth of Biopolitics: Lectures at the College de France 1978–79*. Translated by Graham Burchell. Basingstoke: Palgrave, 2008.

Foucault, Michel. *The Birth of the Clinic: An Archaeology of Medical Perception*. 1963. Reprinted. New York: Pantheon, 1973.

Foucault, Michel. *The History of Sexuality: The Will to Knowledge*. London: Penguin, 1998.

Foucault, Michel. *Society Must Be Defended: Lectures at the Collège de France 1975–76*. Translated by David Macey. London: Allen Lane, 2003.

Franco Aas, Katja. '"Crimmigrant" Bodies and Bona Fide Travelers: Surveillance, Citizenship and Global Governance'. *Theoretical Criminology* 15, no. 3 (2011): 331–46.

Fukuyama, Francis. *The End of History and the Last Man*. London: Penguin, 1992.

Fulani, Ifeoma. 'Caribbean Women Writers and the Politics of Style: A Case for Literary Anancyism'. *Small Axe* 17, no. 9 (2005): 64–79.

Gabilliet, Jean Paul. *Of Comics and Men: A Cultural History of American Comic Books*. Translated by Bart Beaty and Nick Nguyen. Jackson: University Press of Mississippi, 2005.

Gairola, Rahul. 'Burning with Shame: Desire and South Asian Patriarchy, from Gayatri Spivak's "Can the Subaltern Speak?" to Deepa Mehta's *Fire*'. *Comparative Literature* 54, no. 4 (2002): 307–24.

Gajjala, Radhika. *Cyberculture and the Subaltern*. Lanham: Lexington Books, 2012.

Gandhi, Leela. *Postcolonial Theory: A Critical Introduction*. New South Wales: Allen and Unwin, 1988.

Gates, H. L. *Figures in Black: Words, Signs, and the 'Racial' Self*. New York: Oxford University Press, 1989.

Gates, H. L. *The Signifying Monkey: A Theory of Afro-American Literary Criticism*. New York: Oxford University Press, 1988.

Ghosh, Durba. *Sex and the Family in Colonial India: The Making of Empire*. Cambridge: Cambridge University Press, 2006.

Ghosh, Vishwajyoti, ed. *This Side That Side: Restorying Partition. An Anthology of Graphic Narratives from Pakistan India and Bangladesh*. New Delhi: Yoda Press, 2013.

Gikandi, Simon. 'The Postcolonial Wizard: A Review of Ngũgĩ wa Thiong'o's *Wizard of the Crow* (2006)'. *Transition* 98, no. 1 (2008): 156–69.

Gikandi, Simon. In Patricia Yaeger. 'Editor's Column: The End of Postcolonial Theory?'. *PMLA* 122, no. 3 (2007): 633–51.

Gilbert, Jeremy. 'What Kind of Thing Is "Neoliberalism"'. *New Formations* 80/81 (2013): 7–22.

Gilmore, Leigh. 'Boom|lash: Fact-Checking, Suicide, and the Lifespan of a Genre'. *a/b: Autobiography Studies* 29, no. 2 (2014): 211–24.

Gilmore, Leigh. *The Limits of Autobiography: Trauma and Testimony*. Ithaca: Cornell University Press, 2001.

Gilroy, Paul. *The Black Atlantic: Modernity and Double Consciousness*. Cambridge, MA: Harvard University Press, 1993.

Gilroy, Paul. 'Cultural Studies and Ethnic Absolutism'. In *Cultural Studies*, edited by L. Grossberg, C. Nelson and P. Treichler, 187–198. New York: Routledge, 1992.

Gilroy, Paul. 'Route Work: The Black Atlantic and the Politics of Exile'. In *The Post-Colonial Question: Common Skies, Divided Horizons*, edited by I. Chambers and L. Curti, 17–29. New York: Routledge, 1996.

Gilroy, Paul. *Small Acts: Thoughts on the Politics of Black Culture*. New York: Serpent's Tail, 1993.

Girdlestone, C. E. R. *Report on the Past Famines in the North-Western Province*. Allahabad: Government Press North-Western Provinces, 1868.

Giroux, Henry. 'Beyond Neoliberal Common Sense: Cultural Politics and Public Pedagogy in Dark Times'. *JAC: A Journal of Rhetoric, Culture, & Politics* 27, no. 1–2 (2007): 11–61.

Glave, Thomas, ed. *Our Caribbean: A Gathering of Gay and Lesbian Writing from the Antilles*. Durham: Duke University Press, 2008.

Glissant, Edouard. *Poetics of Relation*. Translated by Betsy Wing. Ann Arbor: The University of Michigan Press, 1997.

Glover, David. *Literature, Immigration, and Diaspora in Fin-de-Siècle England: A Cultural History of the 1905 Aliens Act*. Cambridge: Cambridge University Press, 2012.

Gobodo-Madikizela, Pumla. *A Human Being Died That Night: A South African Story of Forgiveness*. New York: Mariner, 2004.

Goebel, Walter and Saskia Schabio, eds. *Locating Postcolonial Narrative Genres*. London: Routledge, 2013.

Goethe, Johann Wolfgang von. 'On World Literature'. In *World Literature: A Reader*, edited by Theo d' Haen, César Domínguez and Mads Rosendahl Thomsen, 9–15. London: Routledge, 2012.

Goodison, Lorna. *From Harvey River: A Memoir of My Mother and Her Island*. New York: Amistad, 2007.

Gopinath, Gayatri. *Impossible Desires: Queer Diasporas in South Asian Public Cultures*. Durham: Duke University Press, 2005.

Graham, James, Michael Niblett and Sharae Deckard. 'Postcolonial Studies and World Literature'. *Journal of Postcolonial Writing* 48, no. 5 (2012): 465–71.

Griswold, Wendy. *Bearing Witness: Readers, Writers, and the Novel in Nigeria*. Princeton: Princeton University Press, 2000.

Gruesser, J. *Black on Black: Twentieth-Century African American Writing about Africa*. Lexington: University Press of Kentucky, 2000.

Gupta, Abhijit. 'Popular Writing in India'. In *The Cambridge History of Postcolonial Literature*, Vol. 2, edited by Ato Quayson, 1023–38. Cambridge: Cambridge University Press, 2011.

Hai, Ambreen. 'Border Work, Border Trouble: Postcolonial Feminism and the Ayah in Bapsi Sidhwa's *Cracking India*'. *Modern Fiction Studies* 46, no. 2 (2000): 379–426.

Hall, Alice. *Literature and Disability*. London: Routledge, 2015.

Hall, Stuart. 'Popular Culture and the State'. In *Popular Culture and Social Relations*, edited by Tony Bennett, Colin Mercer and Janet Woollacott, 22–50. Milton Keynes: Open University Press, 1986.

Hamner, Robert D. *Epic of the Dispossessed: Derek Walcott's* Omeros. Columbia and London: University of Missouri, 1997.

Harding, Sandra. *Is Science Multicultural?: Postcolonialisms, Feminisms, and Epistemologies*. Bloomington: Indiana University Press, 1998.

Harding, Sandra. *Sciences from Below: Feminisms, Postcolonialisms, and Modernities*. Durham: Duke University Press, 2008.

Hardwick, Louise. *Childhood, Autobiography and the Francophone Caribbean*. Liverpool: Liverpool University Press, 2013.

Haritaworn, Jin. *Queer Lovers and Hateful Others: Regenerating Violent Times and Places*. London: Pluto Press, 2015.

Harrison, Nicholas. *Postcolonial Criticism: History, Theory, and the Work of Fiction*. Cambridge: Polity Press, 2003.

Harvey, David. *A Brief History of Neoliberalism*. Oxford: Oxford University Press, 2005.

Harvey, David. *The Condition of Postmodernity: An Enquiry into the Origins of Cultural Change*. Oxford: Blackwell, 1990.

Harvey, David. *Seventeen Contradictions and the End of Capitalism*. London: Profile, 2015.

Hastings, Gerard. *The Marketing Matrix: How the Corporation Gets Its Power – And How We Can Reclaim It*. London: Routledge, 2013.

Hawley, John C. 'Agencies for Resistance, Prospect for Evolution'. In *The Postcolonial and the Global*, edited by Revathi Krishnaswamy and John C. Hawley, 22–32. Minneapolis and London: University of Minnesota Press, 2008.

Hawley, John C. *Post-Colonial, Queer: Theoretical Intersections*. New York: State University of New York Press, 2001.

Hayes, Jarrod, Margaret R. Higonnet and William J. Spurlin, eds. *Comparatively Queer: Interrogating Identities across Time and Cultures*. Basingstoke: Palgrave, 2010.

Haynes, Jonathan. 'African Cinema and Nollywood: Contradictions'. *Situations: Project of the Radical Imagination* 4, no. 1 (2011): 67–90.

Hazou, Rand. 'Refugitive and the Theatre of Dys-Appearance'. *RIDE: Research in Drama Education* 13, no. 2 (2008): 181–86.

Hennesy, Rosemary. *Profit and Pleasure: Sexual Identities in Late Capitalism*. London: Routledge, 2000.

Hirsch, Marianne. *Narrative Frames: Photography, Narrative and Postmemory*. Cambridge, MA: Harvard University Press, 1997.

Hitchcock, Peter. 'The Genre of Postcoloniality'. *New Literary History* 34, no. 2 (2003): 299–330.

Hoad, Neville. 'Arrested Development or the Queerness of Savages: Resisting Evolutionary Narratives of Difference'. *Postcolonial Studies* 3, no. 2 (2000): 133–58.

Holden, Philip. *Autobiography and Decolonization: Modernity, Masculinity, and the Nation-State*. Madison: University of Wisconsin Press, 2008.

Holden, Philip. 'Postcolonial Auto/Biography'. In *The Cambridge History of Postcolonial Literature*, Vol. 1, edited by A. Quayson, 107–36. Cambridge: Cambridge University Press, 2011.

Holden, Philip and Richard J. Ruppel, eds. *Imperial Desire: Dissident Sexuality and Colonial Literature*. Minneapolis: University of Minnesota Press, 2003.

Hoskote, Ranjit. 'Introduction'. In *Reasons for Belonging: Fourteen Contemporary Indian Poets*, edited by Ranjit Hoskote, xiii–xv. New Delhi: Viking, 2002.

Huber, Christoph. 'Mythos, Müll und Marginalia: José Mohica Marins, Prophet von Brasiliens Neuem Kino'. In *Spuren eines Dritten Kinos: Zu Ästhetik, Politik und Ökonomie des World Cinema*, edited by Lukas Foerster and Kordula Rockenhaus, 235–41. Bielefeld: Transcript, 2013.

Huddart, David. *Postcolonial Theory and Autobiography*. London: Routledge, 2008.

Huddart, David. 'Postcolonialism'. In *Encyclopedia of Life Writing: Autobiographical and Biographical Forms*, edited by M. Jolly, 253–54. London: Routledge, 2001.

Huggan, Graham. *The Postcolonial Exotic: Marketing the Margins*. London: Routledge, 2001.

Hughes, L. 'The Twenties: Harlem and Its Negritude'. *Langston Hughes Review* 4 (1985): 29–36.

Hyam, Ronald. *Empire and Sexuality: The British Experience*. Manchester: Manchester University Press, 1990.

Isaacman, Allen, Premesh Lalu and Thomas Nygren. 'Digitization, History, and the Making of Postcolonial Archive of Southern African Liberation Struggles: The Aluka Project'. *Africa Today* 52, no. 2 (2005): 55–77.

Jaivin, Linda. *Halal-el-Mashakel*. In *Staging Asylum: Contemporary Australian Plays about Refugees*, edited by Emma Cox, 113–33. Sydney: Currency Press, 2013.

James, C. L. R. *Beyond a Boundary*. Durham: Duke University Press, 2013.

Jameson, Fredric. *A Singular Modernity: Essays on the Ontology of the Present*. London: Verso, 2013.

Jameson, Fredric. 'Third World Literature in an Era of Multinational Capitalism'. *Social Text* 15 (1986): 65–88.

Jay, Martin. 'In the Empire of the Gaze: Foucault and the Denigration of Vision in Twentieth-Century French Thought'. In *Michel Foucault: Critical Assessments*, Vol. 1, edited by Barry Smart, 201–23. London: Routledge, 1994.

Jeffers, Alison. 'Hospitable Stages and Civil Listening: Being an Audience for Participatory Refugee Theatre'. In *Refugee Performance: Practical Encounters*, edited by Michael Balfour, 297–310. Chicago: Intellect, 2013.

Jeffers, Alison. *Refugees, Theatre and Crisis: Performing Global Identities*. Houndmills, Basingstoke: Palgrave Macmillan, 2012.

Johansen, Emily and Alissa G. Karl. 'Introduction: Reading and Writing the Economic Present'. *Textual Practice* 29, no. 2 (2015): 201–14.

Kaplan, Caren. 'Resisting Autobiography: Out-Law Genres and Transnational Feminist Studies'. In *De/Colonizing the Subject: The Politics of Gender in Women's Autobiography*, edited by Sidonie Smith and Julia Watson, 115–38. Minneapolis: University of Minnesota Press, 1992.

Kaplan, E. Ann. *Looking for the Other: Feminism, Film, and the Imperial Gaze*. London: Routledge, 1997.

Kapur, Manju. *A Married Woman*. London: Faber and Faber, 2003.

Karpinski, Eva C. *Borrowed Tongues: Life Writing, Migration, and Translation*. Waterloo: Wilfred Laurier Press, 2012.

Khanna, Ranjana. 'Indignity'. *Positions: East Asia Cultures Critique* 16, no. 1 (Spring 2008): 39–77.

King, Bruce. *Modern Indian Poetry in English*. 2nd edn. New Delhi: Oxford University Press, 2001.

King, C. R. *Postcolonial America*. Urbana: University of Illinois Press. 2000.

Kotz, David M. 'Financialization and Neoliberalism'. In *Relations of Global Power: Neoliberal Order and Disorder*, edited by Gary Teeple and Stephen McBride, 1–18. Toronto: University of Toronto Press, 2011.

Krishnan, Sanjay. 'Formative Dislocations in V. S. Naipaul's *The Enigma of Arrival*'. *MFS: Modern Fiction Studies* 59, no. 3 (2013): 610–27.

Krishnaswamy, Revathi. 'Toward World Literary Knowledges: Theory in the Age of Globalization'. *Comparative Literature* 62, no. 4 (2010): 399–419.

Kristeva, Julia. 'Word, Dialogue and Novel'. *Desire in Language: A Semiotic Approach to Literature and Art*. New York: Columbia University Press, 1980.

Kumar, Akshaya. *Poetry, Politics and Culture: Essays on Indian Texts and Contexts*. New Delhi and Abingdon: Routledge, 2009.

Kumar, Amitava. *World Bank Literature*. Minneapolis: University of Minnesota Press, 2003.

Kumar, Priya. *Limiting Secularism: The Ethics of Coexistence in Indian Literature and Film*. Minneapolis: University of Minnesota Press, 2008.

Kuntsman, Adi and Esperanze Miyake, eds. *Out of Place: Interrogating Silences in Queerness/Raciality*. York: Raw Nerve Press, 2008.

Kurtz, Matthew. 'A Postcolonial Archive? On the Paradox of Practice in a Northwest Alaska Project'. *Archivaria: The Journal of the Association of Canadian Archivists* 60 (2007): 63–90.

Lane, Christopher. *The Ruling Passion: British Colonial Allegory and the Paradox of Homosexual Desire*. Durham.: Duke University Press, 1995.

Lazarus, Neil. *The Postcolonial Unconscious*. Cambridge: Cambridge University Press, 2011.

Lazarus, Neil. 'What Postcolonial Theory Doesn't Say'. *Race & Class* 53, no. 1 (2011): 3–27.

Lejeune, Philip. *On Autobiography*, edited by P. J. Eakin. Translated by Katherine Leary. Minneapolis: University of Minnesota Press, 1989.

Lentin, Ronit. 'Femina Sacra: Gendered Memory and Political Violence'. *Women's Studies International Forum* 29, no. 5 (2006): 463–73.

Levine, Philippa. 'Sexuality and Empire'. In *At Home with the Empire: Metropolitan Culture and the Imperial World*, edited by Catherine Hall and Sonya O. Rose, 122–42. Cambridge: Cambridge University Press, 2006.

Lionnet, Françoise. 'New World Exiles and Ironists from Évariste Parny to Ananda Devi'. In *Postcolonial Poetics: Genre and Form*, edited by Patrick Crowley and Jane Hiddleston, 14–34. Liverpool: Liverpool University Press, 2011.

Liu, Alan. 'Where Is Cultural Criticism in Digital Humanities'. In *Debates in the Digital Humanities*, edited by Matthew K. Gold, 490–510. Minneapolis: University of Minnesota Press, 2012.

Long, Maebh. 'Precarity, the Humanities and Slow Death'. *Australian Humanities Review* 58 (2015): 93–99.

Loomba, Ania, Suvir Kaul, Matti Bunzl, Antoinette Burton and Jed Esty, eds. *Postcolonial Studies and Beyond*. London: Duke University Press, 2005.

Madan, T. N. 'Secularism in Its Place'. In *Secularism and Its Critics*, edited by Rajeev Bhargava, 297–320. New Delhi: Oxford University Press, 1998.

Madsen, D. *Post-Colonial Literatures: Expanding the Canon*. London: Pluto, 1999.

Mahase, Anna. *My Mother's Daughter: The Autobiography of Anna Mahase Snr. 1899–1978*. Trinidad: Royards Publishing Co, 1992.

Majeed, Javed. *Autobiography, Travel, and Postcolonial Identity: Ghandi, Nehuru and Iqbal*. Basingstoke: Palgrave, 2007.

Majumdar, Rochona. *Writing Postcolonial History*. London: Bloomsbury, 2010.

Malin, Jo. *The Voice of the Mother: Embedded Maternal Narratives in Twentieth-Century Women's Autobiographies*. Edwardsville: Southern Illinois University Press, 2000.

Mamdani, Mahmood. *When Victims Become Killers: Colonialism, Nativism and Genocide in Rwanda*. Princeton: Princeton University Press, 2001.

Manalansan, Martin F. *Global Divas: Filipino Gay Men in the Diaspora*. Durham: Duke U.P., 2003.

Manalansan, Martin F. 'In the Shadows of Stonewall: Examining Gay Transnational Politics and the Diasporic Dilemma'. *GLQ* 2 (1995): 425–38.

Mandair, Arvind Pal. *Religion and the Spectre of the West: Sikhism, India, Postcoloniality, and the Politics of Translation*. New York: Columbia University Press, 2009.

Marsh, Pauline. 'The Primitive, the Sacred and the Stoned in Richard J. Frankland's *Stone Bros*'. *Studies in Australasian Cinema* 6, no. 1 (2012): 29–43.

Martinez-San Miguel, Yolanda. 'Postcolonialism'. *Social Text* 27, no. 3 (2009): 188–93.

Marx, John. *Geopolitics and the Anglophone Novel, 1890–2011*. Cambridge: Cambridge University Press, 2012.

Marx, Karl. *Capital*, Vol. 1. In *Karl Marx, Friedrich Engels, Collected Works*, Vol. 35. London: Lawrence & Wishart, 1996.

Massad, Joseph A. *Desiring Arabs*. Chicago: University of Chicago Press, 2007.

Masters, Cristina. 'Femina Sacra: The "War on/of Terror", Women and the Feminine'. *Security Dialogue* 40 (2009): 29–49.

Mbembe, Achille. 'Necropolitics'. In *Biopolitics: A Reader*. Translated by Libby Meintjes, edited by Timothy Campbell and Adam Sitze, 161–92. Durham and London: Duke University Press, 2013.

Mbembe, Achille. 'Necropolitics'. *Public Culture* 15, no. 1 (2003): 11–40.

McClintock, Anne. *Imperial Leather: Race, Gender, and Sexuality in the Colonial Contest*. London: Routledge, 1995.

McCormack, Donna. *Queer Postcolonial Narratives and the Ethics of Witnessing*. London: Bloomsbury, 2014.

McKay, Nellie. 'The Narrative Self: Race, Politics, and Culture in Black American Women's Autobiography'. In *Women, Autobiography, Theory: A Reader*, edited by Sidonie Smith and Julia Watson, 96–107. Madison: University of Wisconsin Press, 1998.

McKinney, Mark. *Redrawing French Empire in Comics*. Columbus: The Ohio State University Press, 2013.

McLeod, J. *Beginning Postcolonialism*. Manchester: Manchester University Press, 2000.

McNally, David. *Global Slump: The Economics and Politics of Crisis and Resistance*. Oakland: PM Press, 2011.

McPherson, Tara. 'Why Are the Digital Humanities So White? or Thinking the Histories of Race and Computation'. In *Debates in the Digital Humanities*, edited by Matthew K. Gold, 139–60. Minneapolis: University of Minnesota Press, 2012.

Mehrotra, Arvind Krishna, ed. *A History of Indian Literature in English*. London: Hurst and Company, 2003.

Mehta, Binita and Pia Mukherji. 'Introduction'. In *Postcolonial Comics: Texts, Events, Identities*, edited by Binita Mehta and Pia Mukherji, 1–26. London: Routledge, 2015.

Menon, Ritu and Kamla Bhasin, eds. *Borders and Boundaries: Women in India's Partition*. New Brunswick: Rutgers University Press, 1998.

Mercer, Kobena and Isaac Julien. 'Race, Sexual Politics and Black Masculinity: A Dossier'. In *Male Order: Unwrapping Masculinity*, edited by Rowena Chapman and Jonathan Rutherford, 97–164. London: Lawrence & Wishart, 1988.

Mignolo, Walter. 'DELINKING: The Rhetoric of Modernity, the Logic of Coloniality and the Grammar of De-Coloniality'. *Cultural Studies* 21, no. 2 (2007): 449–514.

Mignolo, Walter. 'I Am Where I Think: Remapping the Order of Knowing'. In *The Creolization of Theory*, edited by Françoise Lionnet and Shu-mei Shi, 159–92. Durham and London: Duke University Press, 2011.

Miller, Ann. *Reading 'Bande Dessinée': Critical Approaches to French-Language Comic Strip*. Bristol: Intellect Ltd, 2007.

Mills, Charles Wade. *The Racial Contract*. Ithaca: Cornell University Press, 1997.

Mills, Sara. *Gender and Colonial Space*. Manchester: Manchester University Press, 2005.

Mishra, V. and Hodge, B. 'What Is Post(-)colonialism?' In *Colonial Discourse and Post- Colonial Theory*, edited by P. Williams and L. Chrisman, 276–90. New York: Columbia University Press, 1994.

Misrahi-Barak, Judith and Joshil K. Abraham, eds. *Dalit Literatures in India*. Hoboken: Taylor and Francis, 2015.

Montag, Warren. 'Necro-Economics, Adam Smith and Death in the Life of the Universal'. *Radical Philosophy* 134 (Nov.–Dec. 2005): 7–17.

Moore, Jason. 'Capitalism as World-Ecology: Braudel and Marx on Environmental History'. *Organization and Environment* 16, no. 4 (2003): 431–58.

Moore-Gilbert, Bart. *Postcolonial Life-Writing: Culture, Politics, and Self-Representation*. London: Routledge, 2009.

Mootoo, Shani. *Cereus Blooms at Night*. London: Granta, 1998.

Moraes, Dom. *Selected Poems*, edited by Ranjit Hoskote. New Delhi: Penguin Books, 2012.

Moretti, Franco. *Distant Reading*. New York: Verso, 2013.

Morrison, Toni. *Playing in the Dark: Whiteness and the Literary Imagination*. New York: Vintage, 1993.

Morrison, Toni. 'Unspeakable Things Unspoken: The Afro-American Presence in American Literature'. In *Toni Morrison: Modern Critical Views*, edited by H. Bloom, 201–30. New York: Chelsea House, 1990.

Morton, Stephen. *States of Emergency: Colonialism, Literature and Law*. Liverpool: Liverpool University Press, 2013.

Mufti, Aamir. 'Auerbach in Istanbul: Edward Said, Secular Criticism, and the Question of Minority Culture'. *Critical Inquiry* 25 (1998): 95–125.

Mullins, Greg. *Colonial Affairs: Bowles, Burroughs, and Chester Write Tangier*. Madison: University of Wisconsin Press, 2002.

Muñoz, José Esteban. *Disidentifications*. Durham: Duke University Press, 1999.

Nail, Thomas. *The Figure of the Migrant*. Stanford: Stanford University Press, 2015.

Nair, Neeti. *Changing Homelands: Hindu Politics and the Partition of India*. Cambridge, MA: Harvard University Press, 2011.

Nakamura, Lisa. *Cybertypes: Race, Ethnicity, and Identity on the Internet*. New York: Routledge, 2002.

Nand, Brahma, ed. *Famines in Colonial India: Some Unofficial Historical Narratives*. New Delhi: Kanishka, 2007.

Nandy, Ashis. 'A Disowned Father of the Nation in India: Vinayak Damodar Savarkar and the Demonic and the Seductive in Indian Nationalism'. *Inter-Asia Cultural Studies* 15, no. 1 (2014): 91–112.

Nandy, Ashis. 'The Politics of Secularism and the Recovery of Religious Tolerance'. In *Secularism and Its Critics*, edited by Rajeev Bhargava, 321–44. New Delhi: Oxford University Press, 1998.

Nandy, Ashis. *The Romance of the State: And the Fate of Dissent in the Tropics*. New Delhi: Oxford University Press, 2002.

Nash, Vaughan. *The Great Famine and Its Causes*. London: Longmans, Green, 1900.

Nayar, Pramod K. 'The Digital Dalit: Subalternity and Cyberspace'. *The Sri Lanka Journal of the Humanities* 37, no. 1–2 (2011): 69–74.

Needham, Anuradha Dingwaney and Rajeswari Sunder Rajan, eds. *The Crisis of Secularism in India*. New Delhi: Permanent Black, 2007.

Nield, Sophie. 'The Proteus Cabinet, or "We are Here but not Here"'. *RIDE: Research in Drama Education* 13, no. 2 (2008): 137–45.

Nixon, Rob. 'Neoliberalism, Slow Violence, and the Environmental Picaresque'. *MFS: Modern Fiction Studies* 55, no. 3 (2009): 443–67.

Nkrumah, K. *Ghana: The Autobiography of Kwame Nkrumah*. New York: International Publishers, 1979.

O'Callaghan, Evelyn. *Women Writing the West Indies, 1804–1939: 'A Hot Place Belonging to Us'*. London: Routledge, 2004.

Olney, James. *Memory and Narrative: The Weave of Life Writing*. Chicago: University of Chicago Press, 1998.

Ong, Aihwa. *Neoliberalism as Exception: Mutations in Citizenship and Sovereignty*. Durham: Duke University Press, 2006.

Opubor, Alfred E. and O. Oreh, eds. 'The Status, Role and Future of the Film Industry in Nigeria'. In *The Development and Growth of the Film Industry in Nigeria*, edited by Alfred E. Opubor and Onura E. Nwuneli, 1–24. Lagos: Third Press International, 1979.

Pandey, Gyanendra. *The Construction of Communalism in Colonial North India*. 1990. Reprinted. New Delhi: Oxford University Press, 2012.

Parati, Graziella. *Migration Italy: The Art of Talking Back in a Destination Culture*. University of Toronto Press, 2005.

Parry, Benita. *Delusions and Discoveries: India in the British Imagination 1880–1930*. London: Allen Lane, 1972.

Parry, Benita. *Postcolonial Studies: A Materialist Critique*. London: Routledge, 2004.

Patke, Rajeev S. *Postcolonial Poetry in English*. Oxford: Oxford University Press, 2006.

Paquet, Sandra Pouchet. *Caribbean Autobiography: Cultural Identity and Self-Representation*. Madison: University of Wisconsin Press, 2002.

Peck, Jamie. *Constructions of Neoliberal Reason*. Oxford: Oxford University Press, 2010.

Philip, Kavita, Lilly Irani and Paul Dourish. 'Postcolonial Computing: A Tactical Survey'. *Science, Technology, Human Values* 40 (2015): 799–824.

Piketty, Thomas. *Capital in the Twenty-First Century*. Translated by Arthur Goldhammer. Cambridge, MA and London: Belknap, 2014.

Porter, Bernard. *The Lion's Share: A History of British Imperialism 1850 to the Present*. 1975. Reprinted. 5th edn. London: Routledge, 2005.

Povinelli, Elizabeth. *Economies of Abandonment*. Durham: Duke University Press, 2011.

Povinelli, Elizabeth. 'The Woman on the Other Side of the Wall: Archiving the Otherwise in Postcolonial Digital Archives'. *Differences* 22, no. 1 (2011): 146–71.

Prakash, Gyan. 'Postcolonial Criticism and Indian Historiography'. *Social Text* 31/32 (1992): 8–19.

Prasad, Amit. *Imperial Technoscience: Transnational Histories of MRI in the United States, Britain, and India*. Cambridge: MIT Press, 2014.

Primorac, Ranka. 'Reasons for Reading in Postcolonial Zambia'. *Journal of Postcolonial Writing* 48, no. 5 (2012): 497–511.

Pritam, Amrita. *The Skeleton and That Man*. London: Oriental University Press, 1987.

Quayson, Ato and Girish Daswani. *A Wiley Companion to Diaspora and Transnationalism*. Hoboken: Wiley Blackwell, 2013.

Radhakrishnan, R. 'Postcoloniality and the Boundaries of Identity'. *Callaloo* 16, no. 4 (1993): 750–71.

Rak, Julie. *Boom!: Manufacturing Memoir for the Popular Market*. Waterloo: Wilfrid Laurier University Press, 2013.

Ramanujan, A. K. *Collected Poems*. New Delhi: Oxford University Press, 1995.

Ramazani, Jahan. *The Hybrid Muse: Postcolonial Poetry in English*. Chicago: Chicago University Press, 2001.

Ramazani, Jahan. 'Poetry and Postcolonialism'. In *The Cambridge Companion to Postcolonial Literatures*, edited by Ato Quayson, 938–81. Cambridge: Cambridge University Press, 2012.

Ramazani, Jahan. *A Transnational Poetics*. Chicago: University of Chicago Press, 2009.

Rancière, Jacques. *The Politics of Literature*. Translated by Julie Rose. Cambridge: Polity Press, 2011.

Rao, Rahul. 'Global Homocapitalism'. *Radical Philosophy* 194 (2015): 38–49.

Rao, Rahul. 'Queer Questions'. *International Feminist Journal of Politics* 16, no. 2 (2014): 199–217.

Ratti, Manav. *The Postsecular Imagination: Postcolonialism, Religion, and Literature*. New York and London: Routledge, 2013.

Ray, Sangeeta. *Engendering India: Women and Nation in Colonial and Postcolonial Narratives*. Durham: Duke University Press, 2000.

Richards, Thomas. *The Imperial Archive: Knowledge and the Fantasy of Empire*. London: Verso, 1993.

Rigoni, Isabella. 'Intersectionality and Mediated Cultural Production in a Globalized Post-Colonial World'. *Ethnic and Racial Studies* 35, no. 5 (2002): 834–39.

Robertson, Roland. *Globalization*. London: Sage, 1992.

Rosenberg, Leah. 'Anglophone Caribbean Literature and the Canon'. In *The Routledge Companion to Anglophone Caribbean Literature*, edited by Michael Bucknor and Alison Donnell, 347–55. London: Routledge, 2011.

Rosendahl Thomsen, Mads. *Mapping World Literature: International Canonization and Transnational Literatures*. London: Continuum, 2008.

Sáez, Elena Machado. *Market Aesthetics: The Purchase of the Past in Caribbean Diasporic Fiction*. Charlottesville: University of Virginia Press, 2015.
Said, Edward. *Covering Islam: How the Media and the Experts Determine How We See the Rest of the World*. London: Vintage, 1997.
Said, Edward. *Culture and Imperialism*. New York: Vintage, 1993.
Said, Edward. *Orientalism*. New York: Vintage, 1979.
Said, Edward. *Out of Place: A Memoir*. New York: Vintage, 2000.
Said, Edward. *The World, the Text and the Critic*. Cambridge: Harvard University Press, 1983.
Sakar, Bhaskar. *Mourning the Nation: Indian Cinema in the Wake of Partition*. Durham: Duke University Press, 2009.
Salverson, Julie. 'Change on Whose Terms? Testimony and an Erotics of Injury'. *Theater* 31, no. 3 (2001): 119–25.
Sankara, Edgard. *Postcolonial Francophone Autobiographies: From Africa to the Antilles*. Charlottesville: University of Virginia Press, 2011.
Sanneh, Lamin. 'The Future of Secularism and the Promise of Diversity in India: A Historical Perspective'. In *The Future of Secularism*, edited by T. N. Srinivasan, 114–23. New Delhi: Oxford University Press, 2007.
Sassen, Saskia. *The Global City*. Princeton: Princeton University Press, 1991.
Sassen, Saskia. *The Mobility of Labour and Capital. A Study in International Investment and Labour Flow*. Cambridge: Cambridge University Press, 1988.
Sayed, Asma. *Writing Diaspora: Transnational Memories, Identities and Cultures*. London: Inter-Disciplinary Press, 2014.
Scarry, Elaine. *The Body in Pain: The Making and Unmaking of the World*. Oxford: Oxford University Press, 1985.
Sedgewick, Eve. *Epistemology of the Closet*. Berkeley: University of California Press, 1990.
Sedgewick, Eve. *Tendencies*. Durham: Duke University Press, 1993.
Sen, Amartya. *Development as Freedom*. Oxford: Oxford University Press, 1999.
Senghor, L. 'Negritude: A Humanism for the Twentieth Century'. In *Colonial Discourse and Post-Colonial Theory*, edited by P. Williams and L. Chrisman, 27–35. New York: Columbia University Press, 1994.
Sharp, Joanne P. *Geographies of Postcolonialism*. London: Sage, 2008.
Shepard, Todd. *The Invention of Decolonization: The Algerian War and the Remaking of France*. Ithaca and London: Cornell University Press, 2006.
Shepard, Todd. 'Pieds-Noirs, Bêtes Noires: Anti-"European of Algeria" Racism and the Close of the French Empire'. In *Algeria & France 1800–2000: Identity, Memory, Nostalgia*, edited by Patricia M. E. Lorcin, 150–63. Syracuse: Syracuse University Press, 2006.

Siebers, Tobin. *Disability Aesthetics. Corporealities: Discourses of Disability.* Ann Arbor: University of Michigan Press, 2010.

Sikka, Sonia. 'The Perils of Indian Secularism'. *Constellations* 19, no. 2 (2012): 288–304.

Simmonds, Catherine. *Journey of Asylum – Waiting.* In *Staging Asylum: Contemporary Australian Plays about Refugees*, edited by Emma Cox, 135–84. Sydney: Currency Press, 2013.

Sinclair, Stéfan and Geoffrey Rockwell. 'Teaching Computer Assisted Text Analysis: Approaches to Learning New Methodologies'. In *Digital Humanities Pedagogy: Practices, Principles, and Politics*, edited by Brett D. Hirsch, 241–54. Cambridge: Open Book Publishers, 2012.

Singh, A. and P. Schmidt. *Postcolonial Theory and the United States.* Jackson: University of Mississippi Press, 2000.

Siskind, Mariano. *Cosmopolitan Desires: Global Modernity and World Literature in Latin America.* Evanston: Northwestern University Press, 2014.

Slemon, Stephen. 'The Scramble for Postcolonialism'. In *De-Scribing Empire: Post-Colonialism and Textuality*, edited by Chris Tiffin and Alan Lawson, 15–30. London: Routledge, 1994.

Smith, Martha Nell. 'Frozen Social Relations and Time for a Thaw: Visibilities, Exclusions, and Considerations for Postcolonial Digital Archives'. *Journal of Victorian Culture* 19, no. 3 (2014): 403–10.

Smith, Sidonie and Julia Watson. *Reading Autobiography: A Guide for Interpreting Life Narratives.* 2nd edn. Minneapolis: University of Minnesota Press, 2010.

Smith, Sidonie and Julia Watson. 'Witness or False Witness: Metrics of Authenticity, Collective I-Formations, and the Ethic of Verification in First-Person Testimony'. *Biography* 35, no. 4 (2012): 590–626.

Sommerville. Siobhan B. 'Scientific Racism and the Emergence of the Homosexual Body'. *Journal of the History of Sexuality* 5, no. 2 (1994): 243–66.

Spencer, Robert. *Cosmopolitan Criticism and Postcolonial Literature.* London: Palgrave Macmillan, 2011.

Spivak, Gayatri. *Death of Discipline.* New York: Columbia University Press, 2003.

Spivak, Gayatri. 'Three Women's Texts and Circumfession'. In *Postcolonialism & Autobiography: Michelle Cliff, David Dabydeen, Opal Palmer Adisa*, edited by Alfred Horung and Ernstpeter Ruhe, 7–22. Amsterdam: Rodopoi, 1998.

Spivak, Gayatri. 'Three Women's Texts and a Critique of Imperialism'. *Critical Inquiry* 12, no. 1 (1985): 243–61.

Spurlin, William J. *Imperialism within the Margins: Queer Representation and the Politics of Culture in Southern Africa.* Basingstoke: Palgrave Macmillan, 2006.

Stitt, Jocelyn. 'Gendered Legacies of Romantic Nationalism in the Works of Michelle Cliff'. *Small Axe*, 24 (2007): 52–72.

Stoler, Ann Laura. *Race and the Education of Desire: Foucault's History of Sexuality and the Colonial Order of Things*. Durham: Duke University Press, 1995.

Stora, Benjamin. *La Gangrène et l'oubli: La Memoire de la Guerre d'Algérie*. Paris: Éditions La Découverte & Syros, 1998.

Sunder Rajan, Rajeswari. 'The Politics of Hindu "Tolerance"'. *boundary 2* 38, no. 3 (2011): 67–86.

Tambiah, Stanley. 'The Crisis of Secularism in India'. In *Secularism and Its Critics*, edited by Rajeev Bhargava, 418–54. New Delhi: Oxford University Press, 1998.

Tambiah, Stanley. *Leveling Crowds: Ethnonationalist Conflicts and Collective Violence in South Asia*. Los Angeles: University of California Press, 1996.

Taussig, Michael T. *The Devil and Commodity Fetishism in South America*. Chapel Hill: The University of North Carolina Press, 1980.

Tejani, Shabnum. *Indian Secularism: A Social and Intellectual History, 1890–1950*. New Delhi: Permanent Black, 2007.

Ten Kortenaar, Neil. *Postcolonial Literature and the Impact of Literacy: Reading and Writing in African and Caribbean Writing*. Cambridge: Cambridge University Press, 2011.

Terras, Melissa. 'Infographic: Quantifying Digital Humanities'. *UCL Centre for Digital Humanities*, http://blogs.ucl.ac.uk/dh/2012/01/20/infographic-quantifying-digital-humanities/ (accessed 11 September 2015).

Thomas, Sue. *Telling West Indian Lives: Life Narrative and the Reform of Plantation Slavery Cultures 1804–1834*. New York: Palgrave, 2014.

Tiffin, H. 'Post-Colonial Literatures and Counter-Discourse'. In *The Post-Colonial Studies Reader*, edited by B. Ashcroft, G. Griffiths and H. Tiffin, 95–98. New York: Routledge, 1995.

Tölölyan, Kachig. 'The Contemporary Discourse of Diaspora Studies'. *Comparative Studies of South Asia, Africa and the Middle East* 9, no. 1 (2007): 107–36.

Tsika, Noah A. *Nollywood Stars: Media and Migration in West Africa and the Diaspora*. Bloomington: Indiana University Press, 2015.

Vanita, Ruth, ed. *Queering India: Same-Sex Love and Eroticism in Indian Culture and Society*. London: Routledge, 2002.

wa Thiong'o, Ngũgĩ. *Globalectics Theory and the Politics of Knowing*. New York: Columbia University Press, 2012.

wa Thiong'o, Ngũgĩ. *Penpoints, Gunpoints, and Dreams*. Oxford: Oxford University Press, 1998.

Wainaina, Binyavanga. *One Day I Will Write about This Place*. Minneapolis: Graywolf Press, 2011.

Wake, Caroline. 'Caveat Spectator: Juridical, Political and Ontological False Witnessing in *CMI (A Certain Maritime Incident)*'. *Law Text Culture* 14, no. 1 (2010): 160–87.

Wake, Caroline. 'To Witness Mimesis: The Politics, Ethics and Aesthetics of Testimonial Theatre in *Through the Wire*'. *Modern Drama* 56, no. 1 (2013): 102–25.

Warwick Research Collective. *Combined and Uneven Development: Towards a New Theory of World-Literature*. Postcolonialism across the Discipline 17 Series. Edited by Graham Huggan and Andrew Thompson. Liverpool: Liverpool University Press, 2015.

Weber, Devra. *Dark Sweat, White Gold: California Farm Workers, Cotton, and the New Deal*. Berkeley and Los Angeles: California University Press, 1994.

Wedderburn, R. *The Horrors of Slavery and Other Writings by Robert Wedderburn*, edited by I. McCalman. New York: Marcus Wiener Publishing, 1991.

Whitlock, Gillian. *The Intimate Empire: Reading Women's Autobiography*. London: Cassell, 2000.

Whitlock, Gillian. *Postcolonial Life Narratives: Testimonial Transactions*. Oxford: Oxford University Press, 2015.

Wilkenson, Linden and Michael Anderson. 'A Resurgence of Verbatim Theatre: Authenticity, Empathy and Transformation'. *Australasian Drama Studies* 50 (2007): 153–69.

Wilkinson, Richard and Kate Pickett. *The Spirit Level: Why Equality Is Better for Everyone*. London: Penguin, 2010.

Williams, Patrick and Laura Chrisman. *Colonial Discourse and Post-Colonial Theory: A Reader*. New York: Columbia University Press, 1994.

Xavier, Subha. 'Entre féminisme et voyeurisme: L'éros migrant chez Calixthe Beyala'. *Revue Zizanie* 1, no. 1 (2015): https://www.academia.edu/28056503/_Entre_f%C3%A9minisme_et_voyeurisme_l_%C3%A9ros_migrant_chez_Calixthe_Beyala_

Xavier, Subha. *The Migrant Text: Making and Marketing a Global French Literature*. Montreal: McGill-Queen's University Press, 2016.

Yeager, Patricia. 'Editor's Column: The End of Postcolonial Theory?'. *PMLA* 122, no. 3 (2007): 633–51.

Yoo-Hyeok Lee, Ezra. 'Globalization, Pedagogical Imagination, and Transnational Literacy'. *CLCWeb: Comparative Literature and Culture* 13, no.1 (2011): http://dx.doi.org/10.7771/1481-4374.1705.

Young, Paul. 'Political Economy'. In *Charles Dickens in Context*, edited by Sally Ledger and Holly Furneaux, 243–51. Cambridge: Cambridge University Press, 2011.

Young, Robert J. C. *Colonial Desire: Hybridity in Theory, Culture and Race*. London: Routledge, 1995.
Young, Robert J. C. 'The Postcolonial Comparative'. *PMLA* 128, no. 39 (2013): 683–89.
Young-ah Gottlieb, Susannah. *Regions of Sorrow: Anxiety and Messianism in Hannah Arendt and W.H. Auden*. Stanford: Stanford University Press, 2003.
Zecchini, Laetitia. *Arun Kolatkar and Literary Modernism in India*. London: Bloomsbury, 2014.
Ziarek, Ewa Plonowska. 'Bare Life'. In *Impasses of the Post-Global: Theory in the Era of Climate Change*, Vol. 2, edited by Henry Sussman, 194–211. Ann Arbor: Open Humanities Press, 2012.
Žižek, Slavoj. *First as Tragedy, Then as Farce*. London: Verso, 2009.
Zlotnik, Hania. 'The Global Dimensions of Female Migration'. *Migration Information Source*. Migration Policy Institute, 3 March 2003. Web.

Index

Abraham, Joshil 3
Adebayo-Begun, Jide 71, 80
Adichie, Chimamanda Ngozi 71, 80
    'Jumping Monkey Hill' 81–4
African American literature 273–87
Agamben, Giorgio 44–7, 48, 152, 172,
    216–19, 220, 221, 222, 225, 226
Ahmed, Sara 242
Algeria 159–66, 215
anthropocene 20
anthropology 255, 257, 259
apartheid 181
Arendt, Hannah 44, 216, 219–20, 221,
    223–4, 225–6, 232
Ashcroft, Bill 193
asylum 7, 14, 15, 141–4, 146, 148–9,
    150–5, 215, 219, 232, 233
Australia 141–57, 198–200, 232–3
    aboriginal Australia 141–57, 198–200
autobiography 180

Barker, Clare 2
Benjamin, Walter 224, 275
Bhabha, Homi 1, 6, 14, 85, 169, 192,
    274–5, 325, 326–7
Bhopal disaster 39–41, 43, 47
bildungsroman 178, 181, 291, 292, 294,
    304
Brazil 195–8
Brennan, Timothy 1–2
Brodber, Erna, *Myal* 300–3
Brouillette, Sarah 19, 71–4, 126, 184
Brueck, Laura 4
Burmese war 60–1
Burton, Olivia 163–6
Butalia, Urvashi 168

Canada 193–5
Caribbean 14, 15, 72, 76, 78, 127, 178,
    184–8, 201, 237, 291–304
Casanova, Pascale 11, 19
Chamoiseau, Patrick 181
Cheah, Pheng 12, 26–7
choreography 143
Coetzee, J. M. 73
cosmopolitanism 12, 13, 14, 17, 20, 21,
    41, 84, 132, 145, 258, 263, 326
Craps, Stef 14
creolization 14–16, 179–80, 277, 291,
    293–4, 297–8, 301, 302, 304, 323
creolized. *See* creolization

Dalit literary studies 2, 3–4, 109, 313
Dalit Panthers 4
Damrosch, David 11
Danticat, Edwidge 16, 17–18, 184–6, 263
Davenport, Kiana, *Shark Dialogues* 58–9,
    63–6
Deckard, Sharae 5, 19
decolonization 1, 16, 20, 55, 59, 89, 108,
    125, 128, 129, 134, 168, 169, 170,
    171, 179, 191, 192–3, 200, 203,
    303–4, 323, 324
Derrida, Jacques 274, 275
    Spectres of Marx 37, 38
diaspora 15, 76, 78, 130, 133, 167, 177,
    186, 201, 222, 223, 238, 253–70,
    260–1, 262–3, 324
diasporic. *See* diaspora
Dickens, Charles 53, 54, 55
digital humanities 105–19
Douglass, Frederick 21
drama. *See* theatre

environment 2, 5, 17, 20, 40, 41, 46, 90, 92, 93, 97, 98, 101, 181, 303
  animals 20

faith 291–304
Fanon, Frantz 6, 77, 179, 184, 185, 187, 239, 323
Farrier, David 14, 233
film 191–203
film festivals 191
first/third world 56, 110, 112, 115
Foucault, Michel 34, 58, 169, 192, 216–20, 275, 276
Francophone postcolonialism 162–3, 256, 264
Frears, Stephen, *Dirty Pretty Things* 233–4
Fukuyama, Francis 35

Gajarawala, Toral Jatin 4
games/gaming 205–212
Ghosh, Vishyajyoti 168–73
Gilmore, Leigh 187
Gilroy, Paul 76, 78, 261, 275, 285–7, 324, 325
globalectics 22, 24
globalization 1, 2, 6–7, 12, 13, 16, 18–19, 21–2, 24, 27, 34, 36, 41, 43, 56, 57, 59, 89, 109, 110, 111, 134, 145, 154, 167, 168, 205, 234, 238, 240, 243, 256, 257–8, 262–3, 323, 327, 329
Global South. *See* first/third world
Goethe, Johann Wolfgang von 11, 12, 13–14, 17
Goodison, Lorna 181
Gordimer, Nadine 74–5
Graham, James 5, 19
graphic texts 159–60, 159–73

Haiti 17
Hall, Alice 3
Hall, Stuart 286–7
Harvey, David 34, 58

Hawaii 58–9, 63–6
Hawley, John C. 12
Huggan, Graham 71, 84
hybridity 14, 85, 126, 180, 238, 243, 245, 248, 249, 277, 278, 286, 287, 323, 325

India 3–4, 38, 59–62, 90–101, 109, 111, 116–18, 125–36, 166–71, 224–30, 232–3, 237, 243–4, 248, 307–20. *See also* Partition of South Asia
interculturalism 325
interdisciplinarity 12, 255, 257, 259, 294, 319
intersectionality 326
Israel 224

James, C. L. R. 182, 184
Jameson, Fredric 231
justice (injustice) 11–12, 14, 23, 24, 25, 27, 39, 40, 41, 43, 54, 56, 60, 61, 179, 181, 225

Kanafani, Ghassan 222–3
Kincaid, Jamaica 185, 186, 291–3, 294–8, 300

Laferriere, Dany 264, 267–9
Lamming, George 184, 185
LGBT rights 240

Marx and Engels, *The Communist Manifesto* 18
Mbembe, Achille 220
migration 16, 143, 255–70, 256–8
mimicry 192, 325, 326
Misrahi-Barak, Judith 3
Moretti, Franco 5
Mufti, Aamir 224
Mullins, Greg 239–40

Naipaul, V. S. 180, 185
Negritude 279

neocolonial(-ism) 2, 7, 15, 44, 57, 58, 62, 66, 76, 83, 108, 109, 110, 114, 116, 119, 127, 191, 192–3, 205–12, 233, 279, 291–3, 302, 303, 327
Ngugi wa Thiong'o, *Wizard of the Crow* 22
Niblett, Michael 5, 19
Nigeria 74, 79, 200–3, 233

obeah 293

Pacific islands 233
Pakistan 224
Palestine 224
partition of South Asia 166–73, 225–7
Pineau, Gisela, *Exile According to Julia* 298–300
planetary 12, 15–17, 22, 24, 27, 41, 47
plays. *See* theatre
postcolonialism 276–9, 327
postcolonial life-writing 177–87
postcolonial literary marketplace 72–5, 78–84
postcolonial medical humanities 2
postnationalism 328
Primorac, Ranka 82
Puar, Jasbir 240–1

radical 5, 7, 11–16, 19, 25–7
Ramazani, Jahan 14
refugees 143, 148, 233–4
resistance 4, 5, 7, 12, 14, 16, 17, 38, 57, 58, 77, 81, 83, 84, 125, 126, 154, 155, 179, 184, 189 n.17, 195, 216, 239, 249, 291, 293, 297, 301, 303, 324
rhizomes 2, 297
Roy, Arundhati 37
  The God of Small Things 21
Rwanda 228–9

Sa, Shan 264, 265–6, 269
Said, Edward 182, 238–9, 276
St Lucia 14–15
Satrapi, Marjane, *Persepolis* 180
Satyal, Rakesh, *Blue Boy* 248–9
secularism 291–304, 307–20
Sen, Amartya 12
sexuality 237–48, 248–9
Sidhwa, Bapsi, *Cracking India* 225–6, 229–31, 232
signifyin(g) 281–5
Sinha, Indra, *Animal's People* 5, 38–48
Siskind, Mariano 14
Spivak, Gayatri 112, 276
Steinbeck, John 53, 54, 55
strategic essentialism 328
Subaltern Studies 57, 328

Taliban 233
theatre 141–57
Thiara, Nicole 4
transcultural 13–14, 201, 328
translation 4, 12, 39, 132–4, 266, 326
transnational(ism) 14, 20, 329

verbatim theatre 147–57

Walcott, Derek, *Omeros* 15
Whitlock, Gillian 180–1, 186
World Bank Literature 21, 22
world literature 5, 11–19, 23–4, 25
world-systems, world literary systems 18–20, 215–16

Zambia 74
Zimbabwe 82
Žižek, Slavoj 37–8

www.ingramcontent.com/pod-product-compliance
Lightning Source LLC
Chambersburg PA
CBHW050134240426
43673CB00043B/1665